HomeBaking

HomeBaking

THE ARTFUL MIX OF FLOUR AND TRADITION AROUND THE WORLD

Jeffrey Alford and Naomi Duguid

Location photographs by Jeffrey Alford and Naomi Duguid

Studio photographs by Richard Jung

RANDOM HOUSE CANADA

National Library of Canada Cataloguing in Publication

Alford, Jeffrey

  HomeBaking : the artful mix of flour and tradition around the world / Jeffrey Alford and Naomi Duguid.

Includes index.

ISBN 0-679-31274-9

  1. Baking. 2. Cookery, International. I. Duguid, Naomi II. Title. III. Title: Home baking.

TX763.A244 2003   641.8′15   C2003-904074-7

Printed in China

10 9 8 7 6 5 4 3 2 1

Book design by Level

A Note About Home Baking

Home baking is different from professional baking, just as cooking at home is different from cooking in a restaurant. Ovens are different, ingredients can be different, and, most of all, our motivations and expectations are different.

In many parts of North America, home baking has taken a back seat to professional baking over the last few decades, and it's too bad. On the positive side, we probably can buy better bread (at farmers' markets, bakeries, natural foods stores, and supermarkets) than at any other time in history, and we have commercially made cakes and pastries that are unimaginably good. But with the rise of professional baking, home baking has suffered. Here in the city, we don't know of a single household where someone bakes on a regular basis. People are busy. Both parents generally work, and anyway, baked goods can be easily purchased.

In this book, and in these recipes, we raise the flag of home baking because we believe that if home baking traditions wither, then as a culture, and as home cooks, we lose a great deal. Not only do we lose these foods for future generations to enjoy, and all of the tastes, smells, and textures that they embody, but we lose the traditions themselves. Going relaxedly into the kitchen to make bread or a batch of cookies, knowing that you can and that it's an easy, rewarding thing to do, is as important as the food itself.

So in the recipes we try to put a more casual approach back into baking. Not everything has to be exact or perfect, whether it is a bread, a flatbread, a cake, a cookie, or a pie. Part of a yeasted dough can be put away for later, used perhaps to make a simple fruit cake or tart or a savory flatbread. It may seem silly to take a dough and see how many different shapes of rolls you can make, but maybe silly is good, and so are whimsy and fun.

The point of it all, it seems to us, is to have fun baking, and to make good food for yourself and for the people you love.

QUICK SWEDISH RYE *(page 158)*

Home Baking for Every Occasion

Bread rusks with olives, Crete, Greece

WE BURY OUR HANDS IN A BIG BOWL OF FLOUR, add water and salt, perhaps butter and sugar. We make a batter or a dough, then maybe let it ferment. We shape the dough or pour the batter. We bake it, and it becomes food! This is one of life's great transformations, from grain to flour to food. It embodies generations of creativity and artfulness, of care and human effort, all around the world.

HomeBaking is all about this process, this art, this daily rhythm of turning flour into food. We write about Naomi's grandmother's treacle tarts, about a rye bread from Gotland Island in Sweden, about a Thai tuile, and about a flatbread in faraway Turkmenistan, but what powers the engine, our engine, is that incredible magic of working with flour, simple flour, to make food we love.

We are home bakers, and it is home baking that this book is most specifically about. Home baking is an enormous subject; it's also a subject too personal to fit tidily into straightforward descriptions of techniques and results. A home baker makes a pie in a particular way "because that's the way my grandmother made it." The breads, pies, and cakes that we grew up with are foods filled with personal history, foods that resonate with meaning. We hold on to them because they embody a part of who we are, a part of where we come from. Kneading a bread dough, or baking a cake on someone's birthday, or having homemade cookies or crackers to put out when friends stop by, these are things that feel good, like riding a bicycle, or quilting a quilt, or walking in the woods.

In the course of working on this book, we bought a rundown old farm two hours northwest of where we live in downtown Toronto. Soon after we bought it, we began fixing up the farmhouse, an eight-hundred-square-foot wood-framed saltbox. We peeled off what seemed like a hundred years' worth of wallpaper and took down all the lathe and plaster, and we put in new windows, new wiring, and new insulation. We'd never renovated a house before, so by the end of each day, we were exhausted, our hands swollen, our bodies stiff and aching. We bought a cast-iron cookstove and put in a chimney, and winter came. We then returned to the city, happy to be back with the comforts of our city home, happy to be baking in a well-equipped kitchen where everything was easy.

Throughout the fall and winter, to learn more about baking, Naomi went on trips to Portugal, Germany, and Hungary, and Jeffrey traveled to Ireland and Nepal. We visited bakeries and stayed on farms and in people's homes. When we'd come back from a trip, sometimes on a weekend we'd drive north to the farm, clearing the lane if there were large drifts of snow, and chopping wood for the stove to keep the house warm. We began feeling more at home at the farm. It reminded us of the places where we'd been. The smoke from the juniper in the cookstove smelled like Nepal; the wind that lashed against the house felt like a winter gale on the coast of Ireland. We liked the feeling of connection to farms and villages around the world,

and we liked, if only for a weekend at a time, having our daily rhythms patterned by simple necessities.

When spring arrived, we were outside working one day when we saw a Mennonite family traveling by horse and buggy to Sunday services. The buggy wasn't going fast, it wasn't going slow, just purposefully making its way down the road. But we stood there wondering how the world looked from the buggy. How big do the barns look, and how tall the trees? What is the size of a hundred-acre farm when you're traveling by buggy, and what's the *real* distance to town?

It was buggy speed, it occurred to us at that moment, that cleared the land, that built these barns, that made the farms. It was buggy speed that cultivated the soil and harvested the grain and brought family and friends together. And it was buggy speed that first gave life to the wonderful world of home baking.

Our decision to buy the farm had nothing at all to do with baking, but over time the farm has come to influence how we bake and how we think about baking.

We realize that many of the recipes we are including here came originally from farmhouse kitchens not unlike our own. They're several generations old, from a time when most people in North America and Europe lived on farms (in 1870, 85 percent of North Americans lived on farms; now only 3 percent do). People cooked in cookstoves fired with wood, and there was no electricity.

Because of the farm, we're more relaxed bakers. Our expectations have changed. In the city, we have floors that are level and walls that meet at right angles, but at the farm everything is less than precise, including, sometimes, what we bake. We had never used a wood-fired cast-iron cookstove before. When we'd try to stabilize our oven temperature, we couldn't always do it. And if we were an ingredient short, we'd think twice about going five miles into town. Perhaps we could do without. And, of course, sometimes things didn't turn out perfectly, but then they still tasted good.

The farm has been a constant reminder of how skills and expectations are relative. We have friends nearby who bake only with whole wheat flour. They grow their own hard red wheat and mill it, and that's what they bake with. When they make an apple pie, it's with whole wheat flour, and the pie bakes in the same stove that heats the house. Their whole wheat apple pies might not taste right to a baker who would never use whole wheat flour in a pie, but then that baker's pie, made with bleached white pastry flour, probably wouldn't taste very good to our friends.

We like white flour, and we like whole wheat. We like the clean lines of our home in the city, and we like the wonderful irregular lines of the plank-wood walls at the farm. There are times to be precise, and times to deliberately work against the impulse to be precise. Flavor and taste are relative.

Last spring, a neighbor asked if he could plant our forty-acre field with organic hard red spring wheat. The field had been left to meadow for more than twenty years, so his tractor moved slowly up and down the field, turning the soil, plowing in the tall grasses and wild flowers. Stones popped up, and dark rich soil. It seemed so easy compared to all the human effort that it must have taken a century ago to clear the land without machinery, to cut the trees, to extract the roots, to toss aside the rocks.

When the wheat began to sprout and grow, we felt like royalty. All around the farmhouse, 360 degrees, wheat grew! Rain fell and watered the field. Weeds grew, but the wheat grew faster. And when it reached knee-high, it began to sway with the ever-present wind blowing from Lake Huron.

Our neighbor came to harvest the grain in September with a space-age combine, a tractor that looked like a moon vehicle. He went up and down the field, filling the air with straw dust, the wheat berries collecting in the combine, a digital monitor in his cab measuring the berries by the ton. And then he was done, and all was quiet.

It's our turn, we thought, sitting there looking out across the field; it's time to turn all that wheat into flour, and all that flour into food.

We have divided the book into four sections: Pastry, Bread, Smaller Breads, and Cakes and Cookies. An introduction to each section sets out information on techniques and equipment and terminology. Within each section, there are two or three chapters, each covering one aspect of the world of home baking. But home baking doesn't always easily divide itself into categories, which is part of its appeal. With the same dough you can make a loaf of bread, some rolls, or flatbread or a sweet cake or tart. So you'll find that recipes occasionally cross categories.

When you read through a recipe, if there is a particular ingredient, technique, or piece of equipment that is unfamiliar, go to the Glossary of Ingredients and Techniques (Glossary) in the back of the book. There you will find descriptions of the ingredients and equipment used in the book, plus explanations, for example, of all-purpose flour, stand mixers, kamut or spelt flour, malt syrup, and dough scrapers.

The recipes included in *HomeBaking* have their roots in home and family baking traditions from North America and around the world. In selecting recipes to include, we gravitated toward older-style recipes, cakes, for example, that tend not to be as sweet or as rich as many are now, but cakes you can eat several slices of without feeling you've overdone it. While a big part of our research involved travel, an equally important part involved reading through old cookbooks (traveling, as we imagined it, through time). Those original sources are listed in the Bibliography.

Loaves in couches, *Della Fattoria bakery, Petaluma, California*

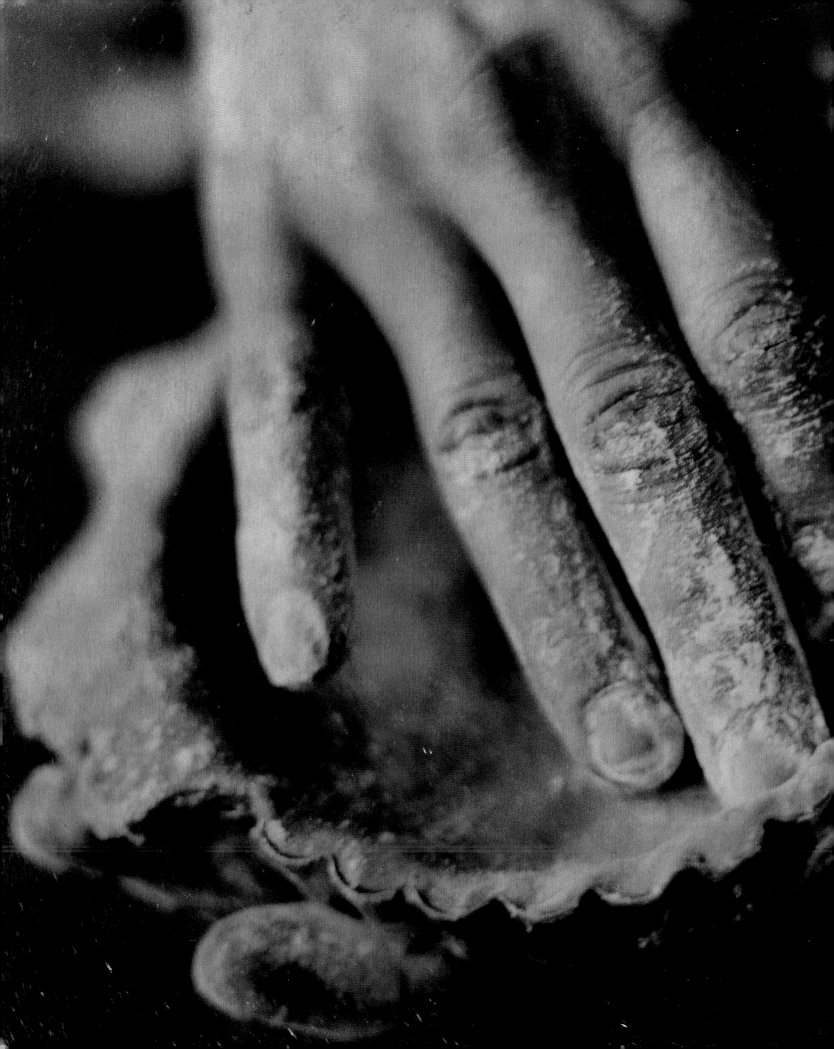

ONE | PASTRY

Sweet Pies, Tarts, and Pastries
Savory Tarts and Pies

Simplest Apple Pie *(page 18)*

PIES, TARTS, AND PASTRIES ARE AS DIVERSE, as wildly different one from another, as French food is from Thai or Mexican, but they all have two important things in common: They rely on creativity and imagination, and they are just plain fun to make. Roll out a dough, use it to hold a mound of fresh fruit, or some slow-cooked onions, and suddenly you have a meal, a special occasion, something that's much more than the sum of its parts.

If you're inclined to be intimidated by the idea of pastry, don't be. There's nothing scary about it once you embark. Rolling out pastry is a quick, fun thing to do. Enjoying the process, rather than worrying about the result, is the way to make good pastry, for pastry's happiest being handled little and lightly, without the heavy hand that anxiety often produces. That's the zen of pastry: cool hands and surfaces, a quick light touch, and a feeling of pleasure.

Our pastry section ranges widely. It includes almost every kind of dough found elsewhere in the book, an introductory course in baking. There's flour and water kneaded into a simple dough for wrapping. There's risen bread dough flattened as a base for sweet fruit or wrapped around a savory filling (for more about bread doughs, see page 110). And then there are all the members of the butter- or lard-enriched pastry dough family of European and North American tradition, from phyllo dough and puff pastry to flaky pastry and pâte sablée. They make delectable bases or wrappers for both sweet and savory tarts. Most of them can be made and baked impromptu; many can be made ahead and stored in the freezer, then taken out at the last minute, shaped, filled, and baked.

Language and Technique

You don't need to know any of this to make the recipes in this book, for each recipe is self-explanatory. But if you've ever wondered about terminology, or about what makes one kind of pastry different from the next, you may find this section interesting.

As we've explored the world of pastry, we've learned about our own pastry preferences and prejudices, as well as other people's. Here are some of the words used to describe pastry and what they mean, followed by a description of the basic categories of pastry dough used in this book.

First, there's **flaky,** used to describe the best classic American piecrusts. Flakiness is the texture of pastry that separates as you bite into it, with fine indistinguishable layerings, and that seems to melt in your mouth, disolving rather than needing to be chewed. Flakiness is achieved when the fat—butter, lard, or shortening—is blended with the flour into large crumbs or flakes. As the pastry cooks, the fats melt and steam-cook the little individual bundles of flour, keeping them separated in fine-textured layerings.

Then there's **tender**. Tender describes an easy-to-bite-into texture, soft, not chewy. Tenderness can come from using soft (low-gluten) flours such as cake or pastry flour, and also from using more fats—butter, egg yolk, high-fat milk products—in the dough.

The opposite of tender is **tough**. Tough comes if you use all-purpose or bread flour moistened with water to make plain pastry (see below) and mix or knead it too much, for then gluten strands, tough elastic strands of protein, form and develop.

(They're what you need to hold up loaf breads, but they make pastry tough-textured.)

On the other hand, tough also means **strong**. The dough that makes strudel or phyllo sheets, for example, is strong; it's made with all-purpose or bread flour and kneaded well to develop its strength so that it can be rolled out very thinly and stretched without breaking. The only reason it doesn't seem tough is that it's rolled very thin and it's coated with butter before being layered or rolled up and baked.

The word **rich** often comes into descriptions of piecrusts as well as of cookies. It describes a lush quality that comes from plenty of butter or oil or lard, and/or from egg yolks. Fats absorb flavor. When the fats melt in your mouth as you eat, they moisten the whole mouthful and blend flavors agreeably.

People's tastes differ, especially their tastes in pastry. Generally, in North American tradition, pie pastry should be flaky and tender, the crust indistinguishable from the filling, melting in the mouth. In home-baked European tarts and galettes, there's usually an egg included in the pastry, or some heavy cream, making it tender, richer, and less flaky, what's known as short crust pastry (see page 14). In European sweet crust tarts, the crust is more like a cookie, almost crisp, and distinctly separate from the filling. There's no flakiness, just richness and a firm bite.

BASIC PASTRY The basic piecrust in this book isn't even rolled out, it is just mixed, chilled, pressed into the pan to make a bottom crust, and the rest sprinkled on top of the filling to make a nubbled top crust (see Simplest Apple Pie, the photograph opposite and page 18).

PLAIN PASTRY American-style piecrust pastry (often called flan pastry in England) is made with flour, butter or lard or shortening, and a little cold water. Ideally, it is flaky and tender, an unobtrusive backdrop for fillings of all kinds (see Quick Pastry, page 20).

There are several tricks to getting tender, flaky plain pastry: If you work with pastry flour rather than with all-purpose, you'll have a more tender dough because there's less gluten in the pastry flour. It's easier to get a flaky pastry with shortening or lard than with butter, because shortening and lard are soft, even when cool, so they blend more evenly into the flour. And the lard or shortening coats the flour well, thus helping prevent the formation of tough gluten strands when the water is added, which makes for extra tenderness too. (Julia Child's trick is to use a blend of butter for its flavor, and shortening for flakiness and tenderness.)

You may be like us when you make a last-minute batch of quick pastry—more likely to have all-purpose than pastry flour on hand, and hardheaded enough to want to work with butter only. Just follow the recipe, and use as little water as possible, making sure it's ice cold (to discourage the formation of gluten).

CREAM CHEESE PASTRY is a variant of plain pastry, less flaky than the classic version, a kind of "never fail" crust for those whose priority is tenderness. It is strong and smooth, ideal for pies with runny or moist fillings. Like the best home-cooking recipes, the proportions are easy to remember (see Rugelach, page 36, and Martha's Mother's Cookies, page 392): equal weights of butter, soft cream cheese, and flour. Cream cheese pastry can be made in a food processor, but it shouldn't be kneaded or handled a lot or it may toughen. The pastry is strong, so if it is stretched it may "snap back" (shrink during baking). Just roll it out as far as it is happy to go and then drape it into a pie plate or over a filling; never stretch it to fit.

SHORT CRUST PASTRY (*pâte brisée* or "broken pastry" in French) is the standard English and European plain pastry. It's less flaky than American piecrust pastry and often richer. Most often an egg is used to moisten the flour (see Pissaladière, page 72), which results in a rich tender pastry. Similarly, when cream or sour cream is

used to moisten the flour rather than ice water, the dough is more tender and also generally less flaky (see Leekie Pie, page 102).

SWEET CRUST PASTRY, a distinctive and delicious version of short crust pastry, is used for open-faced tarts, large and small, and it can also be used for galettes or crostata (see Free-form Fruit Galette, page 21). There's a fair amount of sugar in the dough, as well as egg yolks. It makes a firm flavorful shell or crust that contrasts well with a soft moist filling such as custard or fruit (see Sweet Tart Pastry, page 27). It's often called **pâte sablée** because of the slightly granular, even texture of the cooked crust (*sablé* means "sandy" in French), but it's also called **pâte sucrée,** or sweet pastry. The dough can be used to make fine-textured butter cookies known as sablés (page 382).

Sweet crust pastry is easy to make using all-purpose or pastry flour. The flour, butter, and sugar are bound together by egg yolks, no water. The egg is worked into the dough by hand, in an easy rubbing technique known in French as *fraisage*. The dough can be handled without fear of toughness because it is so fine-textured and rich. The pastry browns very quickly because of all the sugar in the dough. It is often baked "blind"— that is, the pastry shell is pricked, weighted with rice or beans on a sheet of foil, wax paper, or parchment, then prebaked until just touched with color. The fillings then go into the shell before the tart is put back in the oven to finish baking.

PUFF PASTRY is made of flour and water dough that is folded many times around a thin layer of butter. This results in pastry that is actually made up of hundreds of thin layers of strong dough separated by butter. During baking, the water in the butter turns to steam and the layers puff up, unless they're weighted down by a topping, in which case they bake to a rich flakiness. Unlike plain pastry, puff pastry must be made with strong flour, either all-purpose or, in Europe, bread flour.

We use "rough puff," a practical home cook version of puff pastry that is straightforward to make and very easy to use (see page 46). It makes a tender, flaky, and flavorful bottom crust for both sweet tartlets (see Portuguese Egg Tarts, page 52) and savory tarts (see Alsation Onion Tart, page 104).

When making puff pastry, keep the pastry and butter cool, and chill the dough between foldings. Store the pastry flat (no extra folds or wrinkles) in the refrigerator or freezer. When rolling it out, roll out from the center and don't roll the rolling pin over the edges (if you do, you risk gluing the layers together). For an even rise, trim the edges with a sharp knife just before using.

STRUDEL DOUGH/PASTRY is used for another version of thin layers of dough with butter in between, but with strudel the layers are made by rolling up thinly stretched dough. Strudel dough is made of all-purpose or bread flour and water and kneaded until very smooth. It's left to soften in a warm place for an hour or so, then stretched very, very thin to a large sheet. The dough is brushed with butter and rolled up around sweet or savory fillings to make a long tube that is sliced after baking (see Cherry Strudel, page 62).

Remember with strudel dough, unlike other pastry dough, to keep the dough warm and protect it from the air. Be patient as you stretch it, and have fun.

PHYLLO DOUGH (also spelled **filo**) is dough that is stretched until very thin, like strudel dough, then cut into sheets. The sheets are brushed with melted butter, stacked, and used to enclose sweet or savory fillings (see Mediterranean Phyllo-Semolina Pie, page 64). The dough bakes into thin parchmentlike layers, golden brown and brittle, often softened by the addition, right after baking, of a sugar syrup (or, in savory baking, of more melted butter).

You can make phyllo using the recipe for strudel dough (page 63) or do as we do and buy frozen phyllo. Store it in the freezer and thaw it in the refrigerator.

Useful Tools to Have on Hand

You don't need a kitchen full of special equipment to make good pastry. You'll want a smooth **rolling pin** (we like using a tapered wooden pin, but use whatever you feel most comfortable with) and a smooth work surface for rolling out. We use our **dough scraper** for every kind of dough. It's a metal blade about 4 inches long and 3 inches wide with a handle along one side. The blade is useful for keeping your work surface clean of stray bits of dough (see photograph on page 71). It's also handy for helping to detach doughs that stick a little as you roll them out.

Pastry doughs often need to be refrigerated or placed in the freezer to chill. Seal them in **plastic wrap** beforehand so they don't pick up any odors.

For baking, you'll want pie plates, several tart rings, and a baking sheet, as well as muffin tins or tartlet pans. (Whether you have older cookware or modern nonstick pans, they all should be lightly greased to prevent sticking, unless your pastry is very buttery.)

Pie plates come in various sizes. We use an 8-inch diameter **metal pie plate** (measured across the top, not including any rim), and we also bake yeasted-dough pies in a heavy 9-inch **cast-iron skillet**. For French sweet crust tarts, we use a **fluted tart pan** with a removable bottom. It's useful to have both a 9-inch and a 10-inch pan. For baking tartlets, we use **muffin tins**; you can also use **tartlet pans**. Standard muffin tins have 6 or 12 cups that are about 3 inches across the top, 2 inches across on the bottom, and 1¼ inches deep. We also bake some tarts in a 13-by-9-inch shallow **baking pan** or **cake pan**.

For baking pastry blind, you'll need **parchment paper** or foil, and dried beans, rice, or pastry weights to place on the empty shell before you prebake it.

SWEET PIES, TARTS, AND PASTRIES

simplest apple pie

Makes one 8-inch square apple pie, topped with crumbled, rich sweet pastry

PHOTOGRAPH ON PAGE 12 *We love this apple pie. Not only is it the simplest version of apple pie we know, just one step from a crumble, but every time we make it, it is exactly what we most want to be eating—for breakfast, for dessert, anytime. It is of Eastern European Jewish origin, and we were first taught how to make it by our friend Dina, who'd long ago learned it from her mother.*

The pastry is rich with egg yolks and sour cream. It needs no rolling out, no special handling: Some is pressed into the pan to make the bottom crust, and the rest is just crumbled over the top of the filling. The little edges of the topping turn golden brown as the pie bakes. The filling starts as a huge mound of grated apples, then melts and shrinks during baking into a succulent sweet mass. Use McIntosh apples (soft tired ones are fine) so that the grated apples will melt as they cook. Serve in generous rectangular slices, from the pan.

2 cups all-purpose flour

½ cup sugar, plus optional extra for apples

12 tablespoons (1½ sticks) unsalted butter,
cut into small cubes, softened

2 large egg yolks, at room temperature

3 tablespoons sour cream

Scant 1 teaspoon minced lemon zest (optional)

Up to 2 tablespoons cold water, if needed

About 3 tablespoons fine fresh bread crumbs (see page 333)

8 medium-to-large McIntosh apples (nearly 4 pounds)
(see headnote)

2 tablespoons fresh lemon juice

Mix the flour and ½ cup sugar in a medium bowl. In another medium bowl, break the butter up into bits with a fork or your fingertips. Add the egg yolks and sour cream and beat with a wooden spoon. Add to the flour mixture and stir. Add the lemon zest, if using. Use your fingers to break up lumps so the mixture has a coarse cornmeal texture. Add water a little at a time if needed to make the dough come together, blending it in, then pull the dough together into a mass. Place in a heavy plastic bag and refrigerate while you prepare the apples.

Position a rack in the upper third of the oven and preheat the oven to 350°F. Grease an 8-inch square baking pan and sprinkle the bottom generously with the bread crumbs.

Peel the apples. Using a coarse grater, grate the apples; you should have about 8 cups. Place the apples in a bowl, add the lemon juice and a little sugar if you wish, and toss well.

Remove the dough from the refrigerator, cut it in half, and set one half aside. Place the other half in the cake pan and press it evenly to cover the bottom; it will be less than ¼ inch thick. Pile on the grated apples, mounding them up in the middle; the pile will look high, but it will shrink during baking. Crumble the reserved dough over the apples to cover.

Bake for 1 hour, or until the top of the pie is touched with golden brown. Serve hot or at room temperature.

treacle tart

Makes one 8-inch tart, lightly filled with sweet golden syrup, with an optional pastry lattice top

My English grandmum, who lived for fifty years in a log cabin in northern British Columbia (see Grandmum, page 406), used to make this as a last-minute dessert. She'd bake it just before the meal, then take it out of the woodstove oven and put it on the counter to cool and set while we ate. It's a simple plain pastry shell topped with a little golden syrup—delicious, sweet, direct, with no other flavorings to complicate things. It's served in thin, fine slices, very sweet but not overwhelming, more in the style of a European tart than a North American pie.

Golden syrup is a by-product of sugar refining (like molasses), with a clean sweet taste. It was developed in England in the nineteenth century and is available in specialty stores and some supermarkets in the United States. In Great Britain and Canada, it is a standard grocery store item (see Glossary).

Make up the quick pastry and chill it while the oven preheats, then fit it into the pan, spoon in the syrup, and bake for just twenty minutes. Don't be dismayed when you take it out to see the syrup bubbling away and looking messy: The tart must cool before it is served so the syrup has a chance to firm up. Then it's wonderful.

½ recipe Quick Pastry (page 20)

1 to 2 tablespoons finely grated fresh bread crumbs (see page 333)

About ¼ cup Lyle's golden syrup, or substitute maple syrup

Place a baking stone or unglazed quarry tiles, if you have them, on a rack in the center of your oven. Preheat the oven to 350°F.

On a lightly floured surface, roll the pastry out into an 11-inch round. Drape it over an 8-inch pie plate. Use your knuckles to ease the pastry down into the edges of the pan. With a sharp knife, trim off the ragged bits of pastry to make an even edge. If you have time, place in the refrigerator, preferably inside a plastic bag, to chill for 10 minutes. If you have enough dough trimmings to make a lattice, chill them too, wrapped in plastic.

When ready to bake, to make a lattice, gather the dough trimmings together and roll out on a lightly floured surface. Cut into narrow strips, about ½ inch wide.

Take the tart shell from the refrigerator and sprinkle the bread crumbs over the bottom. Spoon on the syrup 1 tablespoon at a time, drizzling it evenly over the bottom; don't worry if there are small gaps—they'll get filled in as the syrup flows during baking. Arrange the pastry strips, if using, in a lattice over the syrup, laying them on in a criss-cross pattern (see Note).

Place the pan on the stone or tiles, or on a baking sheet, and bake for 25 to 30 minutes, until the pastry is touched with gold. Set on a rack to cool for at least 20 to 30 minutes before serving. Serve thin slices, accompanied, if you wish, by a tart sorbet or black coffee.

NOTE The simple lattice my grandmother put on her treacle tart was a casual decoration, made very quickly. She'd take a strip of leftover pastry trimming, twist it several times, and lay it across the center of the tart, pinching it against the sides at each end. She'd lay the second at a right angle across the first. The remaining strips went on the same way. Sometimes she had very little pastry to work with and there would be only three strips in each direction; other times there'd be more.

PUFF PASTRY SYRUP TART You can also use about ½ pound puff pastry, homemade (page 46) or all-butter store-bought, to make this tart. Bake at 375°F for 20 to 25 minutes, or until puffed at the edges and lightly touched with gold.

quick pastry

Makes about 1 pound pastry, enough for two 8-inch pies or tart shells

It's easiest to get tender pastry if you use pastry or cake flour rather than all-purpose, and if you use shortening or lard instead of butter. Whatever ingredients you use, the pastry should be handled as little as possible.

We like the taste of pastry made with butter and we don't like using shortening, however practical it is. And, like many people, we always have butter and all-purpose flour handy. So if we want a quick pastry at the last minute, this is it.

Then the question is, how to get the butter evenly distributed in the flour. This is the easiest and most effective method we know: grating frozen butter on a box grater. It takes just a moment, and the flakes of butter are easy to blend with the flour. It's a method we learned from Jane Grigson's comprehensive Fruit cookbook, and it cured us forever of pastry anxieties. Grigson was a wonderfully clear and practical English food writer who wrote a newspaper column for years, as well as a number of gracefully written and very informative cookbooks.

1½ cups all-purpose flour, sifted, or 1¾ cups cake or
   pastry flour, sifted

Scant 1 teaspoon salt

12 tablespoons (1½ sticks) frozen or very cold
   unsalted butter

2 tablespoons fresh lemon juice

Cold water as needed

Place the flour and salt in a bowl. Grate the butter on the coarse side of a box grater, then cut it into the dry ingredients with two knives, a pastry cutter, or your fingertips. Add the lemon juice and mix, tossing with your fingers or with a fork. Add cold water, 2 tablespoons at a time, until the pastry just comes together: You will need from 4 to 7 tablespoons water, depending on your flour. Pull the dough together and place in a heavy plastic bag. Flatten (from outside the bag) into a disk. Then remove from the bag and cut in two. Put each piece in a heavy plastic bag, and flatten into a disk. Seal well and refrigerate for at least 30 minutes, or up to 2 days; or freeze for up to a month.

free-form fruit galette

Makes 1 open-faced fruit-filled pastry; serves 6

PHOTOGRAPH ON PAGE 22 *Here galette means a kind of free-form fruit tart made of quickly rolled out pastry, folded up over a filling and baked on a baking sheet, not in a pie plate or tart pan. The more general meaning of galette in French is something flat and baked, from a low cake (galette des rois, the Epiphany cake, for example) to a large crisp cookie.*

Free-form galettes such as this have become better known in North America in the past twenty years, as cooks and chefs have mined French rural cooking traditions for good ideas. (The Italian version is known as a crostata.) They're attractively irregular in shape and have proportionately more crust and less fruit than a pie plate—baked pie. Galettes are a home baker's improvised pie, perhaps as a quick response to a last-minute need for something sweet to serve at the end of a meal. This recipe is a more orderly version of the rather haphazard galette described in End-of-Summer Galette, page 30. Make it with whatever fruit is in season, as long as it isn't terribly juicy.

½ recipe **Quick Pastry (page 20)** or **Sweet Tart Pastry (page 27)**, made with all-purpose flour

About 3 tablespoons finely chopped **walnuts or almonds, lightly toasted**, or toasted **fresh bread crumbs** (see page 333)

¼ to ½ cup **sugar**, or more if using tart fruit, plus extra for sprinkling

About 1½ cups coarsely chopped **plums or apricots or whole berries**, or a mixture

Position a rack in the center of the oven and preheat oven to 350°F.

On a lightly floured work surface, roll out the pastry to a rough oval about 9 by 12 inches. Place on a baking sheet. Sprinkle the nuts over the center, leaving a generous 3-inch border all around, then sprinkle on about 2 tablespoons sugar. Mound the chopped fruit on top. Sprinkle on 2 or so more tablespoons sugar. Fold the edges of the pastry over the filling, leaving a central opening about 2 to 3 inches across. Sprinkle a little sugar on the crust.

Bake for about 35 minutes, or until the crust is really golden. (The sweet tart pastry will turn a deeper gold because of the sugar in the dough.) Let cool on a rack for at least 20 minutes before serving.

NOTE If you like the taste and texture of nuts with fruit, you can sprinkle more chopped nuts on the fruit before folding up the sides of the pastry.

FOLLOWING PAGES: FREE-FORM FRUIT GALETTE *made with sweet pastry. Rolling pin collection.*

Assembly-line pies Many of the treasures of the baker's kitchen originated in rural

communities where there were many mouths to feed and where people needed to eat a lot because

they did physical labor every day. Whenever cooks made pastry, they would make a lot, then use it to

make a whole lot of pies. The pies would go quickly; after all, there were many people eating.

These days we may not be baking for large numbers of people, and we can walk or drive to the grocery

store and buy what we might be short of. But the large-batch approach to baking is often still practical,

because so much can go in the freezer. And for the same effort, why not make more? Extras can always

be given to friends.

Home-baked pie for sale, Amish and Mennonite schools auction, Bruce County, Ontario, Canada

Our friend Mary, who grew up in Saskatchewan, described what baking was like when she was a child. "We'd make fifteen pies at one time. We'd set up an assembly line. It was easy. We'd never make just one pie."

"Pie was dessert," she continued. "There was no other dessert; dessert meant pie. And now, it's so strange, but none of my kids eat pie. Three kids and not one will eat pie. They say that cooked fruit seems weird, that they like their fruit fresh!"

"Mary," we said, "we like cooked fruit. You can always bring pies here."

fruit custard tart

Makes one 9- or 10-inch custard tart with a firm, sweet tart crust, filled with creamy custard and colored with berries or dotted with prunes

Sweet tart pastry is especially good for a custard tart. The slightly crisp crust is a great textural contrast to the creamy filling. The pastry shell is prebaked, then filled with custard, topped with fruit, and baked again. The pastry stays firm, and if you use fresh berries, there's also a nice contrast between the hint of tartness in the fruit and the smooth sweet custard and sweet crust.

These tarts are dazzling with fresh berries in the summer, blueberries or raspberries. In winter, when summer's fresh fruit bounty feels remote, prunes soaked in tea or rum make a beautiful seasonal alternative, the dark fruit gleaming in the pale custard.

If you make a 9-inch tart, you will probably have enough pastry trimmings and custard to make three or four tartlets as well. Instructions for shaping and baking the tartlets follow.

1 recipe Sweet Tart Pastry (page 27)

1 cup heavy (whipping) cream

2 large eggs

¼ cup vanilla sugar (see Glossary) or sugar

Pinch of salt

Scant ¼ cup ground blanched almonds

1½ to 2 cups blueberries or raspberries, or 25 small pitted prunes or 12 large prunes, halved, soaked for at least 2 hours in tea, Armagnac, or rum and drained

Place a baking stone or unglazed quarry tiles, if you have them, on a rack in the center of the oven and preheat the oven to 375°F.

On a lightly floured surface, or between two sheets of wax paper, roll the pastry out into a large round about ⅛ inch thick. Place a 9- or 10-inch fluted tart pan with a removable bottom on a baking sheet. Drape the dough over the pan and gently ease it into the bottom edges. Roll your rolling pin across the top to cut off the excess against the sharp edges of the tart pan. If you wish, use excess pastry to line several 2- to 3-inch tartlet pans or muffin cups.

Prick the pastry shell(s) all over. Line the pastry shell(s) with parchment or wax paper and place pie weights or dried beans on top to weigh the pastry down. Bake for 15 to 18 minutes (10 for tartlets), or until the pastry is touched with light brown at the edges.

Remove from the oven and remove the paper and pie weights. Set aside to cool for 20 minutes.

Whisk together the cream, eggs, sugar, salt, and almonds in a bowl. Pour into the baked crust, filling it about three-quarters full (use any extra to fill the tartlets, if making). Add the berries by the handful, or dot the soaked prunes in the custard (use one per tartlet).

Bake for 20 minutes. Remove the tartlets, if you made them. Lower the heat to 350°F and bake for another 5 to 10 minutes. The custard should be setting around the edges but still wobbly in the center, and the crust should be browned. Transfer to a rack to cool and set for an hour before serving. Or cool, cover, and refrigerate. The tart is very good chilled or at room temperature.

PEAR OR APRICOT CUSTARD TART This same approach works well with fresh pear halves or lightly poached apricot halves. If making tartlets, chop the pears into chunks and use several chunks in each tartlet; or use 1 apricot half per tartlet.

sweet tart pastry

Makes nearly 1 pound pastry, enough for one 9- or 10-inch tart

Sweet tart pastry is ideal for filled tarts and fruit tarts, because it has a firm, slightly sandy texture that is strong enough to hold moist fillings and provides a great contrast in texture. In French, this pastry is called pâte sablée *or* pâte sucrée. *The pastry can also be used to make plain cookies, known as* sablés *(see page 382). The goal here is a firm pastry rather than a melting texture. The dough can be mixed and blended without any worry about making it tough by overworking it.*

With all-purpose flour, the crust is crisper; with pastry flour (which is closer to French flour), the baked pastry is more tender.

1¼ cups all-purpose flour, or 1⅔ cups pastry flour, sifted

⅓ cup sugar

Pinch of salt (optional)

8 tablespoons (1 stick) cool unsalted butter,
   cut into small pieces

3 large egg yolks

This pastry is traditionally made on a cold work surface (preferably marble), but we find it easier to work in a large ceramic bowl. Sift the flour into a bowl or onto a work surface. Add the sugar and salt, then add the butter and blend together with your fingertips. Make a well in the center and add the egg yolks. Use your fingers to gradually incorporate the yolks into the flour mixture; it will feel a little messy until the yolks have started to mix well with the flour.

Once the yolks and flour are somewhat mixed, if using a bowl, turn the dough out onto a cool work surface. Pull a bit of moistened dough away from the mass, and rub it firmly along the counter under the heel of your hand to smooth it. Lift it off the work surface with a dough scraper and move it to the side, then repeat with another section of the dough. This process of blending the dough is called *fraisage,* and it can feel very liberating if you are more accustomed to handling pastry doughs with restraint and a very light touch. Gradually the dough will be smooth and quite stiff. When all the dough has been blended, pull the pastry together into a mass. Place in a heavy plastic bag, flatten into a disk, and seal the bag well.

Refrigerate for at least 30 minutes and for as long as 24 hours before rolling it out. Alternatively, you can freeze the pastry for up to 1 month. Bring it back to refrigerator temperature before using.

Because this pastry tends to stick to surfaces, it's easiest to roll it out between two sheets of wax paper.

butter tarts

Makes 12 substantial, 2½-inch-wide, open-faced tarts, filled with a rich brown-sugar-flavored filling

Everyone who grew up in Ontario, as I did, takes butter tarts for granted. Only when we travel farther afield do we discover they're a regional specialty. They're a standard item at country fairs and farmers' markets in Ontario, and now factory-baked versions are sold individually packaged in large groceries and local convenience stores.

I have always found butter tarts irresistible. They're simple tarts in the sugar pie tradition, with a rich crust and a sweet filling made of farmhouse staples: brown sugar, butter, and eggs. Nowadays they're often made with raisins and with a high thick crust, so the crust outweighs the filling. We prefer ours with less crust, so crust and filling balance each other, and without the raisins, so the taste and texture are smooth.

½ recipe (1½ pounds) Classic Farmhouse Pastry (page 29)

1½ cups packed light brown sugar

Pinch of salt

2 large eggs

1 tablespoon white or rice vinegar

½ teaspoon pure vanilla extract

4 tablespoons unsalted butter, melted

Scant 2 tablespoons Lyle's golden syrup, or substitute
   corn syrup

Place a baking stone or unglazed quarry tiles, if you have them, on a rack in the center of the oven. Preheat the oven to 375°F.

Place one 12-cup muffin tin or two 6-cup muffin tins near your work surface. If your tins are not non-stick, lightly butter them.

Lightly dust the work surface with flour. Cut the pastry in half and set one half aside, loosely covered. Roll out the other half to a rectangle about 16 inches long and 6 inches wide. Use a cookie cutter or a glass to cut out six 3½-inch rounds, staggering them down the length of the dough (set the scraps aside to be rolled out later to make cookies; see below). Place a round in one of the depressions in the muffin tin, fitting it gently into the cup; the pastry will come only partway up the sides of the cup. Place the remaining pastry rounds in the tin, then roll out and cut the remaining dough, to make 12 tart shells in all. Cover with plastic wrap

and refrigerate for 10 minutes or more, while you make the filling.

Combine the sugar, salt, eggs, vinegar, and vanilla in a bowl and stir to mix well. Pour in the melted butter and stir. Add the syrup and stir until blended.

Spoon about 1 tablespoon of the filling into each tart shell (you may have a little extra filling).

Place the tin(s) on the baking stone or tiles, or on a baking sheet, and bake for 20 minutes, or until the crusts are lightly golden in spots. The filling will bubble up and rise into a mound as it bakes; once the tarts are out of the oven, it will subside to make a level top surface. Use a large spoon to lift the tarts out of the muffin tins and transfer to a rack. Let stand for 10 minutes or more to cool and firm up before serving. Serve warm or at room temperature.

BUTTER TARTS WITH RAISINS If you want to try the "with raisins" option, soak about ½ cup raisins in hot tea for 30 minutes; drain. Place 4 raisins in each tart shell before spooning in the filling.

PASTRY COOKIES Pastry scraps can have a second career as cookies, rolled out fairly thin, cut into squares or rounds, plain or sprinkled with a little cinnamon sugar. Bake as you would Sablés (page 382), in the middle of the oven. The thinner they are, the more quickly they'll bake.

classic farmhouse pastry

Makes just over 3 pounds pastry, enough for two double-crusted 8-inch pies or 24 tartlets

Madame Benoit started writing about food before the Second World War. She became the best-known food writer and cooking teacher in Canada, both in French and in English, and was the first person I ever saw teaching cooking on television. She had an unmistakable high-pitched voice and a reassuring lack of anxiety; somehow she projected reliability and good sense. Her practical approach to food was distinctive, and reminiscent of that of Edouard de Pomiane, with whom she studied at the Sorbonne in the 1920s before returning home to Montreal.

This recipe is adapted from Madame Benoit Cooks at Home, *published in 1978. The pastry is strong enough to hold juicy fillings but still tender. Use it for apple pies and other fruit pies, either open-faced or double-crusted.*

5 cups all-purpose flour

¼ cup packed light brown sugar

1 teaspoon salt

½ teaspoon baking powder

2 cups lard or vegetable shortening

2 large eggs

2 tablespoons white wine vinegar

¼ to ½ cup cold water

Combine all the dry ingredients in a bowl and stir to mix well, breaking up any lumps in the sugar. Cut in the lard or shortening to make an evenly moistened mixture that resembles coarse crumbs. Mix the eggs and vinegar and add ¼ cup cold water and mix. This may be enough to moisten the dough so that it can be pulled together, but if not, add a little more cold water. When the dough just comes together, pull it into a mass.

Turn the dough out onto a work surface and cut it into 2 pieces. Place each piece in a heavy plastic bag, flatten out to a disk, and seal well. Refrigerate for at least 30 minutes; the dough can be refrigerated for up to 3 days or frozen, well wrapped, for up to 1 month.

End-of-summer galette The last days of summer arrived, with their shorter days and cooler nights. The wheat had been harvested from our fields and now we lit the woodstove both morning and evening to take the chill off and warm us all. It was time to try baking in the stove for the first time. There was a plain pastry dough in the freezer, and in our pantry was a four-quart basket of dark, purply-blue damson plums from the local farmers' market. What more did we need?

We stoked the fire and pushed in the damper so the fire's heat would flow around the oven. I chopped about two cups of plums, then realized we were out of sugar, so I added some melted honey to them. The thermometer we'd placed in the oven read 375°F when I started to roll out the pastry. I put it on a baking

AUTUMN'S COLORS: *Cherry trees in Provence, Mont Ventoux, France. Wheat harvest in Grey County, Ontario, Canada.*

sheet, then spread some of the melted honey in the center. Lacking any almonds or other nuts to chop finely, I sprinkled on some granola, then mounded on the sweetened chopped plums. I drizzled some of their juices over the mound, roughly folded over the sides of the pastry, and put the galette into the oven.

An hour after it went in, the galette was done, touched with light brown. One flap of the pastry had unfolded, so some of the juice had leaked out onto the pan, giving a kind of caramelized finish. The oven temperature had varied from 350° to 275°F during baking, but the galette seemed none the worse. It was delicious, sweet and tart, as damsons are, a wonderful way to celebrate the harvest.

country apple pie in a potato crust

Makes 1 double-crusted 8-inch apple pie with a thick, tender crust; serves 6 to 8

This country pie (often called a "pasty" in England), made with a potato-based dough wrapped around a filling of chopped apples, has the quintessential taste of its origins in rural England. It's sparked with a little dried ginger, an unusual touch. The pie must have originally been made as a free-standing pastry baked on an iron plate (known in some parts of the British Isles as a "girdle") set out over an open fire, but we bake ours in a pie plate in the oven. Eat it fresh and hot right as it comes out of the oven. Leftovers are delicious the next day, at room temperature or reheated.

CRUST

1 pound potatoes, preferably floury (baking) potatoes, peeled and cut into chunks

About 2 tablespoons unsalted butter

¼ teaspoon salt

¼ teaspoon powdered ginger

1 tablespoon sugar

About 1 cup all-purpose flour

FILLING

2 large or 3 medium crisp apples, such as Empire, McIntosh, or Northern Spy, peeled and thinly sliced

About 3 tablespoons chilled unsalted butter, cut into 4 thin pieces

Scant ½ cup sugar

Place a rack in the center of the oven and preheat the oven to 400°F. Lightly butter an 8-inch pie plate.

Put the potatoes in a saucepan, add water to cover, and bring to a boil. Cook until tender. Drain, then return the potatoes to the pan, add the butter, and mash while still hot, adding the salt, ginger, and sugar. When the potatoes are smooth, add ½ cup flour and stir. Add another scant ½ cup flour and stir and knead it in, then turn the dough out onto a lightly floured surface and knead until smooth, several minutes.

Cut the dough in half. Roll each half out to a round 9 to 10 inches in diameter.

Line the greased pie plate with one round of dough. Add the chopped apples, mounding them in the middle. Drape the other pastry sheet over the apples and press the edges together firmly to seal. Make an X-shaped cut, each arm of which should be about 2 inches long, in the center of the pie crust.

Bake for about 45 minutes. The pie should be touched with golden brown. Lift the pie from the oven and quickly slip one slice of the cold butter under each flap of the cut top of the pie. Sprinkle about 2 tablespoons sugar onto each slice of butter. Place the pie back in the oven and bake for another 5 minutes, or until golden brown all over.

Let stand for 5 minutes and serve hot, or let cool slightly and serve warm.

ricotta pie topped with streusel

Makes 1 streusel-topped 10-inch cheesecake; serves 8

This couldn't be simpler: A quick yeasted dough is flattened to make a bottom crust and then covered with lightly sweetened ricotta or cream cheese. The filling is topped with streusel—sweetened rich crumbs of flavor. Like other yeasted pies and cakes, this has a great texture. There are two short waits, as the batter and the dough ferment and gain flavor, then into the oven it goes.

CRUST

3 tablespoons sugar

¾ cup milk

2 teaspoons active dry yeast

About 1¾ cups pastry or cake flour, sifted

Pinch of salt

STREUSEL

11½ tablespoons cold unsalted butter, cut into small chunks

⅓ cup sugar

1 cup all-purpose flour

FILLING

Scant 1½ cups ricotta, or slightly less than 12 ounces cream cheese

2 large eggs

1 teaspoon pure vanilla extract

¼ cup sugar

¼ teaspoon cinnamon

Pinch of salt

In a medium bowl, stir the sugar into the milk, then stir in the yeast to dissolve. Stir in 1 cup of the flour to make a smooth batter. Cover and set aside to rest for an hour.

Sprinkle the salt and ½ cup more flour over the batter and stir to mix. Turn out onto a well-floured surface and knead until smooth. The dough will be quite soft. Cover with plastic wrap and set aside to rise for 1 hour.

Place a rack in the center of the oven and preheat the oven to 350°F. Butter a 9- or 10-inch cast-iron or other ovenproof skillet.

To prepare the streusel, combine all the ingredients in a bowl and work them together, rubbing the lumps of butter between your thumb and fingers until you have large coarse crumbs. Set aside in a cool place.

To prepare the filling, place the ingredients in a bowl and beat together, by hand or with a mixer, until smooth.

Press the dough into the bottom of the skillet with your fingertips. Let it rest if necessary, then press it out to the edges all around. Spread the filling on the dough, leaving a narrow rim all around. Sprinkle on the streusel.

Bake for 35 minutes, or until the filling is just set and the dough is touched with gold. Let cool for 30 minutes before serving. Serve from the skillet, or transfer to a large flat plate. Serve warm or at room temperature.

bread baker's fruit tart

Makes 1 fruit-topped open tart with a bottom crust of sweetened, buttery bread dough

Until the Second World War, in many parts of Europe bread baking at home was a regular thing, and cakes and tarts were often made by taking a small loaf's worth of risen bread dough and enriching it with butter, sugar, and sometimes eggs. From the Ukraine to France to Scotland, the old recipes persist, and so does a taste for a sweetened yeasted dough.

This cross between a tart and a cake is rich and sweet enough to taste like a special treat, yet simple enough to eat as a casual snack. Make it when you're making any of the white breads in the Family Breads chapter, or Almond Milk Bread (page 132) or Snowshoe Breads (page 300). Or use a white dough that you've frozen—let it come to room temperature before making the tart. You'll be pleased by how simple the recipe is, and it's foolproof.

This recipe, inspired by one the great food writer and cook Edouard de Pomiane created, is a simple open-faced cherry tart using a yeasted dough enriched with butter. The dough, tender and rich, is topped with slightly sweetened fruit. We suggest using apples, pears, or rhubarb because their seasons are longer, but also see the variation for a cherry version.

3 pears or 2 apples, peeled, cored, and thinly sliced,
     or 1½ cups sliced (¼-inch lengths) rhubarb
2 tablespoons fresh lemon juice (if using apples or pears)
About ¼ cup sugar
About ¾ pound plain white bread dough (see headnote)
     or Standby Dough (page 367), risen and at room
     temperature
About 8 tablespoons (1 stick) unsalted butter,
     softened
About 2 tablespoons cold unsalted butter,
     cut into small chunks

If using pears or apples, place the fruit in a bowl with the lemon juice and about 2 tablespoons sugar, and toss gently to mix.

If using rhubarb, place it in a bowl and pour over boiling water. Swirl it around, then drain in a colander and refresh under cold water. Repeat twice, then return the drained fruit to the bowl. Add ¼ cup sugar and toss to mix well. Set the fruit aside, loosely covered.

Place a rack in the upper third of the oven and preheat the oven to 450°F. Butter a 9- or 10-inch cast-iron skillet or fluted tart pan with a removable bottom.

Turn the dough out onto a lightly floured work surface. Flatten it out gently to a round or square about 9 inches across. Scoop up small pieces of the softened butter and distribute them over the dough. Roll the dough up, pinch the edges to seal, and then fold it in half. Dust your work surface again with flour, then flatten the dough and knead gently to distribute the butter evenly. If you have the time, place the dough in a bowl, cover, and let rest for 10 minutes.

Flatten the dough out to a round. Place it in the prepared pan, pressing and dimpling it with your fingertips to encourage it to stretch to the edges. Prick all over with a knife tip or a fork. Distribute the fruit over the dough, leaving a ½-inch rim around the edge. If using pears or rhubarb, sprinkle on the chunks of cold butter, as well as a little more sugar. Bake the tart for 20 to 25 minutes in the upper third of the oven until the edges are starting to brown and crisp.

Remove from the oven and let stand for at least 20 minutes before serving. Serve warm or at room temperature. The tart is delicious the next day. Refrigerate if keeping any longer than 1 day.

NOTE We also like to use a cooked apple topping: Cook chopped apples in about 2 tablespoons melted butter oven medium heat, adding sugar to taste (and cinnamon, if you wish) partway through cooking, until softened, about 10 minutes. Let cool to room temperature before placing on the dough. Do not add cold butter.

SIMPLEST CHERRY TART If you have 2 to 3 cups good ripe cherries available, pit them, and then, without sugaring them, arrange them on the pricked dough in two layers. Sprinkle on ¼ cup sugar, or to taste, and bake as instructed, omitting the cold butter chunks. The cherries will look a little blackened and mushy when done, but the tart tastes heavenly. As usual, let cool for 20 minutes or more before serving.

Men with ripe pears, Tbilisi, Georgia

rugelach

Makes 32 small triangular pastries with a sweet prune or dried apricot or jam filling

In Polish culinary tradition, rugala *means a rolled-up curved bun, like a simple croissant. A related word,* rugelach, *is the name of another rolled-up baked good, a quite different one, that comes from the culinary traditions of the Jewish communities of Poland. Rugelach are wedge-shaped pieces of pastry rolled up around sweet flavors such as sweet prune paste or apricot jam.*

This is our version of rugelach, with two pastry doughs to choose from; both are tender and rich. One is a simple cream cheese pastry; it's the one most people are familiar with these days. The other, made with a blend of sour cream and egg yolk, we think is probably the older version. Whichever one you make, chill the dough for at least two hours, or overnight, before shaping, filling, and baking.

CREAM CHEESE DOUGH

8 ounces (1 cup) cream cheese, softened

½ pound (2 sticks) unsalted butter, softened

2 cups all-purpose flour

¼ teaspoon salt

OR

SOUR CREAM DOUGH

½ pound (2 sticks) plus 2 tablespoons unsalted butter,
   at room temperature

¼ cup sour cream (full-fat)

2 tablespoons sugar

2 large egg yolks

2 cups all-purpose flour

¼ teaspoon salt

FILLING

About ¾ cup Prune Paste (page 37), Dried Apricot Compote
   (page 40), or thick jam

To make the cream cheese dough, using a mixer, cream together the cream cheese and butter. Add the flour and salt and mix just until combined. Transfer to a plastic bag and chill for at least 2 hours, or overnight. Or, *to make the sour cream dough,* using a mixer or a wooden spoon, beat together the butter, sour cream, and sugar in a bowl until smooth. Add the egg yolks and beat in. Add the flour and salt and mix just until combined. Place in a plastic bag and chill for at least 2 hours, or overnight.

Line two baking sheets with parchment paper or wax paper. Remove the dough from the refrigerator and cut into 4 equal pieces. Place 2 pieces back in the plastic bag and refrigerate while you work with the other 2.

One at a time, working on a lightly floured surface, flatten each piece with the palm of your hand, then roll out to a 6- to 7-inch round, rolling from the center outward and rotating the dough to help get an even round. Cut the round into 8 wedges (like slicing up a pie).

If using prune paste, place a blob in the center of each wedge. *If using dried apricot compote,* place a piece of apricot in the center of each one. Starting at the point, roll up each wedge (the fruit will show on the sides) and transfer to one of the baking sheets. *If using jam,* thinly spread jam all over each wedge, then roll the wedge up loosely and transfer to a baking sheet. Repeat with the remaining dough and filling.

Refrigerate, loosely covered, for 20 minutes.

Preheat the oven to 375°F. Bake the rugelach for about 12 minutes. They should be just beginning to turn golden. Let cool briefly on the sheets to firm up before transferring to a rack to cool completely.

prune paste

Makes about 2 cups thick sweet prune paste

Prunes, like dried apples and dried apricots, are a centuries-old way of storing the warmth of summer during long, cold, winter months. No wonder then that cooked prune fillings appear so frequently in home-style cakes and cookies from northern and eastern Europe. This is a simple recipe: The prunes are soaked in strong tea, then simmered in orange juice until broken down and thickened to a paste.

1 pound pitted prunes, coarsely chopped

About 2 cups boiling water

2 tea bags Earl Grey or other aromatic black tea

About 2 cups good orange juice

Place the prunes in a medium bowl and pour over enough boiling water to cover them completely. Add the tea bags and steep until the prunes are very plump and most, if not all, of the liquid has been absorbed, about 3 hours. Drain off any extra liquid and discard the tea bags.

Put the moistened prunes in a pot, add enough orange juice to cover, and cook over medium heat for 10 to 15 minutes, until the prunes are broken up and thickened.

Let cool to room temperature, then transfer to a well-sealed container and refrigerate or freeze until ready to use.

danish log

Makes 1 filled pastry about 15 inches long and 4 inches wide, filled with sweet apricot compote, apple compote, or prune paste; serves about 12

There's lots of butter in Denmark, and no shortage of it in Danish pastry. Every time we bite into a slice of Danish log, we're reminded of the lush rain-fed pastures we traveled through in southern Denmark, the dairy cows happily grazing, and the tall modern metal windmills turning in the ever-present winds from the sea.

In Denmark, slices or individual pastries made with a yeasted dough layered with butter and filled with soft sweet fillings are known as Viennese. Their essence is the layering of the butter into the dough. It's not a difficult process. You just need a cool dough and butter at the same temperature. Make the dough some evening when you've got other tasks to do at home, then refrigerate or freeze it for later use.

Bakers and pastry makers produce all sorts of elaborately shaped individual Danishes, but this recipe is for the easiest and most forgiving one we know. The pastry is rolled out, then wrapped around a simple filling to make one long pastry. It's served cut into "Danish"-sized slices. Kids like to cut wide slices, while cautious eaters can take narrower portions.

Danish pastries are best eaten the day they're baked. Start shaping the log anywhere from an hour and a half to six hours before you plan to serve it. This recipe makes just over two pounds of dough, enough for two logs, so you can use half the dough and freeze the rest for another time. Defrost overnight in the refrigerator.

DOUGH (FOR 2 LOGS)

1 cup cold milk

1 tablespoon active dry yeast

¼ cup sugar

2¾ cups all-purpose flour

½ teaspoon salt

1 large egg

½ pound (2 sticks) cold unsalted butter

FILLING (FOR 1 LOG)

About ¼ cup Almond Paste (page 55) (optional)

Scant ½ cup Dried Apricot Compote (page 40), Dried Apple
   Compote (page 40), or Prune Paste (page 37)

1 large egg or egg white, beaten, for egg wash

About 2 tablespoons pearl sugar or granulated sugar

Start making the dough 5 hours or more before you wish to serve the Danish log.

Measure the milk into a small bowl, sprinkle on the yeast and 1 tablespoon of the sugar, and whisk to blend and dissolve the yeast. Set aside.

In a food processor or the bowl of a stand mixer fitted with the paddle attachment, combine the flour, the remaining 3 tablespoons sugar, and the salt and pulse or mix briefly to blend. Add the egg and mix well. Take 1 stick of the butter from the refrigerator and cut off half of it; return the remaining ½ stick to the refrigerator. Chop the butter into chunks, add to the flour mixture, and process or mix briefly. Give the milk-yeast mixture another good stir and, with the processor going or with the mixer on low, add it to the flour.

Using a processor: Process for 20 seconds after a dough ball forms, then turn the dough out onto a lightly floured surface, using a rubber spatula to scrape all of the dough out of the bowl. Knead for about 4 minutes, until smooth, incorporating flour as necessary. *Using a stand mixer:* Mix for 30 seconds, then switch to the dough hook and knead at medium speed for 3 minutes. Turn the dough out onto a lightly floured surface.

Flatten the dough and place it in a plastic bag. Refrigerate for 30 minutes to an hour.

When ready to proceed, take the remaining butter out of the refrigerator and thinly slice it onto a plate. The slices will quickly soften a little, so they'll be the ideal texture, softened but not greasy. Lightly flour your work surface and turn the dough out. Using floured cool hands and then a floured rolling pin, flatten the dough into a rectangle about 18 inches by 12 inches. Lay the slices of butter over half the dough, overlapping the slices if necessary. Fold the bare half of the dough over the buttered half and pinch the edges to seal.

Lightly tap the top of the dough package all over with your rolling pin to flatten it and to push the butter out to the edges, then roll from the center outward to make a rectangle about 16 inches by 10 inches. Fold the dough into thirds, like a business letter, then fold it crosswise in half. Place it back in the plastic bag and refrigerate for 20 minutes or so.

Reflour your work surface lightly and turn out the dough. Using floured cool hands and then a lightly floured rolling pin, flatten it into a rectangle about 16 inches by 8 inches. Fold it in thirds like a business letter, then flatten it a little and fold crosswise in half. Place it back in the plastic bag, seal well, and refrigerate for an hour.

The dough is now ready to be used to make logs. Cut it in half and flatten each half into a thick rectangle.

Unless you are making 2 logs right away, place 1 piece in a well-sealed plastic bag and store in the refrigerator for up to 2 days, or in the freezer for up to a month. If you are not ready to use the other piece, place it in a plastic bag, and refrigerate immediately.

When ready to assemble the Danish log, make sure your filling is at room temperature and your dough is chilled. *If using the apricot compote* (or another filling that is lumpy), puree it in the food processor. Line a baking sheet with parchment paper or wax paper.

On a lightly floured surface, using a lightly floured rolling pin, roll the dough outward from the center in both directions to make a rectangle about 16 inches long and 6 to 7 inches wide. Transfer to the prepared baking sheet.

If using almond paste, spread a thin layer in a 3-inch band down the center of the dough, leaving a ¼-inch border at each end, and top with filling. *If not,* spread the filling in a 3-inch-wide band down the center of the dough, leaving a ¼-inch border at each end.

Pull the sides up over the center and pinch closed, making a raised seam down the length of the log. Pinch the ends of the dough closed so the filling doesn't seep out. Cover with plastic wrap and let rest for 30 minutes. The dough will become a little puffy but will not really rise.

Meanwhile, place a rack in the center of the oven and preheat the oven to 400°F.

Just before baking, brush the egg wash lightly over the dough. Sprinkle on the sugar. Using kitchen scissors, snip across the seam at ¾-inch intervals to make a series of parallel slashes about 1½ inches long down the length of the log.

Bake for 20 minutes, or until the log is golden and the edges of the top seam are touched with darker gold. Transfer to a platter or board and let rest for 30 minutes or so, then cut into slices to serve.

dried apple compote

Makes almost 1½ cups compote

Dried apple compote, as prepared in the recipe below, is an age-old way of making use of the apple crop through the winter, and it is always a welcome filling for a freshly made pie or pastry.

2 ounces (about 2 cups) dried apples, store-bought
  or home-dried
3 cups water
Pinch of salt
½ cup golden raisins (sultanas)
Two 1½-inch strips lemon zest
½ cup wildflower or clover honey, or any mild honey

Place the apples and water in a pot and bring to a boil. Stir thoroughly, then remove from the heat and let stand for 30 minutes.

Add the remaining ingredients to the pot and bring to a boil. Reduce the heat to low and simmer, uncovered, for an hour, or until most of the liquid has evaporated. Transfer to a bowl to cool.

Store in the refrigerator for up to 2 weeks or in the freezer for several months, until ready to use.

dried apricot compote

Makes about 1¼ cups dense compote

This beautiful golden orange–colored compote gives intense flavor to pastries. We love it.

1 cup dried unsulfured apricots, coarsely chopped
A 1-inch strip of lemon zest
2 cups water
1 cup sugar

Place the apricots, lemon zest, and water in a nonreactive pot and bring to a boil. Add the sugar and stir until dissolved, then lower the heat and simmer very gently for 1½ hours. Remove from the heat.

You can leave the compote with large chunks of apricot or mash lightly into smaller chunks, depending on your preference and on what you will be using it for. (We tend to prefer the large chunks.) Or process to a smooth thick puree for Danish Log (page 38) or Kazakh Dried Fruit Pastries (page 42). Stored well covered in the refrigerator or freezer, this keeps well for several months.

Tibetan herder, near Xiahe, Gansu, China

kazakh dried fruit pastries

Makes 16 round fried and steam-cooked pastries, filled with dried fruit compote

We've never been to Kazakhstan (an independent central Asian republic that used to be part of the Soviet Union), but we hope to go someday. We have been to the neighboring republics of Uzbekistan, Tajikistan, and Turkmenistan, and also to China's Xinjiang Province, just to the south across the mountainous border. In all these places we've eaten incredible local breads, savory pies, and pastries of many kinds. And from what people tell us, Kazakh home baking is at least equal to that of its neighbors, if not better.

Alma-Ata, the capital of Kazakhstan, is famous throughout the region for its apples. They grow on the northern slopes of the Tian Shan Mountains that frame the city, and they make their way into a great number of baked goods. Here, in this uniquely prepared pastry, a compote of dried fruits (apples or apricots) is the treasure hidden inside.

1 cup all-purpose flour

2 tablespoons sugar, plus sugar for sprinkling

½ teaspoon baking powder

Pinch of salt

4 tablespoons unsalted butter, melted, or ¼ cup vegetable oil

Scant ½ cup lukewarm water

About ¼ cup chopped almonds

About 1½ cups Dried Apple Compote (page 40) or

Dried Apricot Compote (page 40), pureed

Vegetable oil for shallow frying

Combine the flour, sugar, baking powder, and salt in a bowl or a food processor. Stir or process as you add the butter or oil and then just enough water to form a dough. Turn the dough out onto a lightly floured surface and knead until smooth or process in a food processor until a ball of dough forms, then process for another 20 seconds.

Wrap the dough well in plastic and let rest for 30 minutes to 1 hour (the longer rest makes the dough easier to roll out).

Place a small bowl of water by your work surface. Lightly flour a large baking sheet.

Cut the dough into 4 pieces. Work with 1 piece at a time, keeping the others covered. On a lightly floured surface, roll the dough out as thin as possible, to about 16 inches square. Cut into 4 pieces. The dough pieces do not have to be tidy squares, as you will be folding them up around the filling.

Place about ½ teaspoon chopped almonds on the center of one square and top it with a generous tablespoon of the compote. Wet your fingertips with water and use them to moisten the edges of the dough, then lift the edges of the dough up over the filling, pleating it in large folds and leaving a small opening in the center (the water will help the dough stick to itself), making a round pastry. Set aside on the floured baking sheet, and prepare the remaining pastries. Cover the pastries with plastic to prevent them from drying out.

In a large heavy skillet, heat 3 tablespoons oil over medium heat. When it is hot, add only as many pastries as will fit without crowding open side down, and fry until dark golden brown, about 5 minutes. Use a spatula to turn them over and fry on the other side to the same color, about 4 minutes. While they are cooking, place a cupful of hot water and a lid for the skillet by the stove.

If cooking on an electric stove top, turn another element on to high about 2 minutes before the pies are browned; then, when the pastries are cooked, transfer the skillet to the hot element. Alternatively, if cooking with gas, once the pies have browned, raise the heat to high. Immediately pour in just enough hot water to cover the bottom of the skillet, then put on the lid, and let steam for 20 to 30 seconds. Remove the lid, transfer the pies to a plate, and sprinkle with sugar. Repeat with the remaining pies, adding oil as necessary before frying each batch.

Serve the pastries warm or at room temperature, with hot tea.

NOTE The pastries can be frozen, uncooked or cooked. Defrost before cooking or reheating. To reheat cooked pies, brush with a little melted butter and place on a baking sheet in a 350°F oven for 10 minutes, or until warmed through.

Log cabins, quilts, and the aesthetics of baking If it's Friday night, there's only one place I want to be, and that's at Laverne Baker's Auction Centre in Hanover, Ontario. The auction begins at five-thirty and ends well after midnight. I like to go around ten o'clock, because that's when Laverne usually auctions the tools, and tools are my favorite thing to buy, especially old ones—augers and adzes, jack planes, froes, and drawknives.

Often I don't even know what kind of tool I'm bidding on, but if it looks old and interesting, and if the price is right, I try to buy it. The first few times I went to the auction, I let some pretty good tools get away because I was shy about bidding, having never spent much time at auctions. But now I jump right in, waving my hand, giving a nod. I think Mr. Baker even recognizes me, maybe not, but when there is a box of old tools, he'll sometimes look my way, expecting a bid. Nothing like almost being a regular.

Late at night, after the auction is over, I drive back home and bring all my purchases into the house. I pour myself a beer, and check out each tool under a bright light. I steel-wool a broadaxe, maybe sharpen the cutting edge of an adze, taking possession of them.

I have this ambition about building a log cabin, and I figure that if I buy enough tools, somehow the cabin will get built. I'm sure this is just an excuse for my buying habit, but I don't care. A while ago I found two excellent books—*Building and Restoring the Hewn Log House* and *Building with Stone,* both by Charles McRaven. He builds and restores old log houses using all the same kind of old tools I've bought. He's also a fanatic recycler of wood, as I am. It's dusty, frustrating work, but anyone who likes old tools probably recycles wood; it's the same sort of thing. I also like repairing old patchwork quilts. It has to do with somehow working alongside the people who—a hundred, hundred-fifty years ago—first used the tools, who built the barns, who sewed and quilted the quilts.

Working with wood is just like baking. With baking, we prefer the crude, the imperfect—the galette that's irregular in shape, the cake that's clearly homemade. They have their own proportions, the proportions of asymmetry, of imperfection—so much more appealing to our eyes, more original and hand-crafted—just like the lines of the weathered logs of an old log cabin or the faded colors, never intended, in a late-nineteenth-century patchwork quilt.

If we work against the temptation to make every cookie uniform, every pie with a perfect crust, every bread a smooth, even loaf, then we give back to the recipe its individuality. Each cookie, each bread, can have its own character, so I, who like dry textures, can have a thinner cookie that cooked a little brown and crisp at the edges, and my kids, who like soft and moist, will look for the fatter cookie that is softer to the bite.

And next time I go to the auction, maybe I'll find a ratchet hoist or a "comealong." That's what I really need to begin the cabin.

Carpenter's workshop in a rural museum, Gotland, Sweden

rough puff

Makes 1½ pounds pastry for sweet or savory tarts and tartlets

Before we tried our hand at it, puff pastry was one of those mysteries that intimidated us. But, like other areas of baking, it soon generously yielded its secrets.

We make the simplified version of puff pastry often called rough puff. In traditional puff pastry, a strong dough is folded over layers of butter, then folded and rolled out six times. This results in hundreds of fine layers of dough, separated by the thinnest of layers of butter. In the oven's heat, the steam given off as the butter melts makes the layers separate and the dough puff up. The result is a light, airy, flaky pastry.

In rough puff, we start with a richer basic dough and make fewer folds. The resulting pastry is flaky and puffed, but not as high. Rough puff is great for simple tarts, both sweet and savory. It's lush to bite into and airy in the mouth and it's a very useful and practical item to have in the freezer.

2 cups all-purpose flour

1 teaspoon salt

½ pound (2 sticks) frozen unsalted butter

1 tablespoon fresh lemon juice

6 tablespoons ice water, or as needed

By hand: Place the flour and salt in a bowl and mix well. Coarsely grate half the butter, then add to the flour with a pastry cutter or two knives and cut in to blend. Add the lemon juice, then add ¼ cup ice water. Mix gently with your hands, then try to pull the dough together. If the dough is still dry and will not come together into a mass, add a little more water as needed.

Using a food processor: Coarsely chop half the butter. Place the flour and salt in the bowl of the processor, add the chopped butter, and process briefly to the texture of coarse meal. Add the lemon juice and ¼ cup ice water and process briefly. If the dough is still dry and will not come together into a kneadable mass, add more water as necessary.

Turn the dough out onto a lightly floured surface and knead briefly, until evenly moist and smooth. Place in a plastic bag, flatten to a disk, and seal well. Chill in the refrigerator for at least 30 minutes. (This basic dough can be refrigerated for up to 3 days.)

When ready to proceed, place the dough on a lightly floured surface. You want to flatten it out to a rectangle about 16 inches long and 10 inches wide. (After being chilled, the dough will be a little moist; lightly dust any sticky places with flour and keep surfaces lightly dusted.) First use a lightly floured rolling pin to flatten the dough, then roll it out, rolling from the center outward. Use a dough scraper as necessary to unstick it from your work surface. Set aside, lightly covered.

Use a sharp knife to cut the remaining ¼ pound frozen butter into thin slices. Put it in a food processor and process until the butter stops making banging noises against the sides (about 30 seconds). Stop and feel the texture of the butter: There will probably still be small lumps. Process for another 30 seconds and test again. The butter should be a smooth paste still quite stiff with cold, just spreadable, like a thick cream cheese. Pulse and test again if necessary until you get the right texture (up to 2 minutes total).

Place the dough with a short end facing you. Use a long metal spatula to spread half the butter onto the bottom two-thirds of the dough rectangle, leaving a 1-inch margin at the bottom and sides. Fold the top third over, toward the center, then, like folding a letter, fold the bottom third over that. Dust very lightly with flour and rotate 90 degrees, so that once more a short end is facing you. Roll out, rolling from the center outward, until once again the rectangle measures about 16 inches long and 8 to 10 inches wide. Spread the remaining butter evenly over the bottom two-thirds of the rectangle, leaving a margin as before, and again fold over first the top third and then the bottom third.

Lightly dust the dough with flour, rotate it 90 degrees, and roll out to the same-sized rectangle. You need to do two more foldings (known as "turns"), not to enclose any more butter, but just to create more layers. Fold the top third of the dough over the center, then fold the bottom third over that. If the dough is starting to get springy and to resist, you may want to let it rest for 5 minutes; cover and refrigerate it any time you let it rest. Rotate and then roll out and fold the dough for the fourth time. Chill for at least 30 minutes before using. You can refrigerate the dough for up to 3 days, or freeze, well sealed in plastic, for up to a month (make sure that the dough lies flat and that the edges do not get bent over). To thaw, place frozen pastry in the refrigerator.

To use the dough, dust the work surface with a little flour, because the dough will be a little moist. Use a lightly floured rolling pin to flatten the dough, then roll it out, rolling just to the edges, not over them.

Just before baking, trim each edge with a sharp knife to create a clean edge so the pastry can puff as it should. Save the trimmings: Assemble side by side to make a patchwork of dough, or dust the trimmings with sugar and bake on a baking sheet for 5 to 7 minutes at 425°F to make a delicious snack.

FOLLOWING PAGES: *Farm woman outside the central market in Mulhouse, Alsace, France.*
TERESA'S COCONUT CUSTARD TARTS *(page 53).*

Himalayan story A while back, thanks to a writing assignment from *Gourmet* magazine, I had the chance to travel midwinter to Nepal, to a small mountain village in the Himalayas called Marpha. The village is in the valley of the Kali River, which is situated between the Annapurna and Daulagiri massifs, so there are high mountains on all sides. Marpha, along with a few other villages in the valley, is home to the Thakalis, a trans-Himalayan group of whom there are only eight to ten thousand people altogether. The valley is on an old salt route between Tibet and Nepal, and the Thakalis have thrived here for generations, acting as middlemen and innkeepers.

My job was easy. I just had to hang out in the restaurant of the lodge where I was staying, talking to anyone who would talk to me and otherwise watching village life pass by. I'd walk up to the small flour mill

OPPOSITE: *Sliced apples drying, Marpha, Nepal.* ABOVE: *The Annapurna massif from above Marpha.*

on the edge of the village and watch as people put their grain through the heavy millstones that were powered by the cold mountain stream passing swiftly under the mill. And I'd watch people working in the fields, sometimes in blowing snow (it was February), readying the soil for spring.

One day, several friends and relatives in the lodge assembled and everyone sliced apples from morning till night—hundreds of locally grown apples that had been stored for several months in a stone shed. The slices were put onto long poles, and the poles loaded with apples were then hung up to dry. It was a beautiful sight, all the apple slices and the long lengths of pole. And it was a reminder that dried apples, and other dried fruits, are staple foods in many parts of the world.

portuguese egg tarts

Makes 12 substantial puff pastry tartlets, filled with a rich egg custard

We know egg tarts from Hong Kong and Macao, and from Hong Kong bakeries in North America. They're one of the positive legacies of Portuguese colonial rule. What a treat it was to go to Portugal and sample the originals, in all their lush simplicity. Teresa, a pastry baker from the Minho, in northern Portugal, invited me to come back into the bakery one day to watch how she made egg tarts and coconut tarts (see page 53). She was making the tarts in large quantity for her bakery in the village of Soajo, beginning with seventy egg yolks and adding everything else to scale.

This is a home baker's version of those egg tarts. And like Teresa's, they're made with puff pastry shells that have been frozen. They're smooth and delicious, sweet but not cloying, and yellow with egg yolk (especially if you use good free-range eggs). Teresa baked hers near the top of a very hot oven, and her tarts had large black splotches on top. We suggest you bake them in a hot oven, then finish them briefly under the broiler.

½ recipe (¾ pound) Rough Puff (page 46), or
   ¾ pound store-bought all-butter puff pastry
Scant 1 cup sugar
Scant ½ cup all-purpose flour
Pinch of salt
1¾ cups whole or reduced-fat milk
2 drops pure vanilla extract (optional)
6 large or extra-large egg yolks, preferably free-range

Set out one 12-cup or two 6-cup muffin tins. Cut the pastry into 3 equal pieces. Work with 1 piece at a time, keeping the remaining pastry loosely covered with plastic in the refrigerator. On a lightly floured surface, roll the dough out to a very thin square about 10 inches across. Using a plate or a pot lid as a guide, with a very sharp knife, cut out four 5-inch circles. Place each circle over a muffin cup and then gently press down to slide it into place. Repeat with the remaining dough. Wrap the muffin tin(s) in plastic and put in the freezer while you prepare the filling.

Place a rack in the upper third of the oven and place a baking stone or unglazed quarry tiles, if you have them, on the rack. Preheat the oven to 475°F.

Mix together the sugar, flour, and salt in a bowl; set aside.

Heat the milk and optional vanilla almost to a boil in a heavy saucepan. Sift the flour mixture over the milk and use a wooden spoon to stir it in. Cook over medium-low heat for about 5 minutes, stirring constantly to prevent sticking, until the mixture thickens and coats the spoon. Remove from the heat and set aside.

Place the egg yolks in a bowl and whisk until smooth. Stir in a little (about ½ cup) of the hot milk mixture, then gradually add the egg mixture to the saucepan, whisking to keep it smooth. Transfer to a jug or large measuring cup with a spout.

Remove the pastry shells from the freezer. Pour the filling into the shells, filling them nearly to the top, and immediately place on the baking stone or tiles, (or on a baking sheet) on the oven rack. Bake for 7 minutes. Turn the oven to broil and cook for another 2 to 4 minutes, until the filling is well touched with dark brown patches. Wearing oven mitts, tip the tartlets out onto a rack and let cool.

These are best eaten warm or at room temperature, within 24 hours. If keeping for longer than 6 hours, refrigerate, covered.

teresa's coconut custard tarts

Makes 12 puff pastry tartlets, filled with egg custard, topped with a fine crisp coconut crust

PHOTOGRAPH ON PAGE 49 *I first saw these delicate-looking tartlets in Soajo, Portugal, in Teresa's shop (see page 52). The shells were made of puff pastry and, on top of the dense, deliciously eggy custard filling, there was a thin, pale brown, crisp crust. How was it done? I wondered. It took watching Teresa after-hours in the bakery for me to discover her secret. Unlike the egg tart filling, this filling isn't cooked ahead, but just sets as the tarts bake in the oven.*

½ recipe (¾ pound) Rough Puff (page 46), or
   ¾ pound store-bought all-butter puff pastry
4 large eggs
1 cup sugar
2 tablespoons all-purpose flour
Pinch of salt
3 tablespoons finely ground dried shredded coconut
   (see Note)
Confectioners' sugar for dusting

Set out one 12-cup or two 6-cup muffin tins.

Cut the chilled puff pastry into 3 equal pieces. Work with 1 piece at a time, keeping the remaining pastry loosely covered with plastic in the refrigerator.

On a lightly floured work surface, flatten the pastry with a well-floured rolling pin. Then roll it out as thin as possible to about a 10-inch square. (The dough may resist or spring back; if it does, begin working on another piece and let the first one rest for several minutes.)

Using a plate or a pot lid as a guide, with a very sharp knife, cut out four 5-inch circles of pastry. Place each over a muffin cup and press down lightly so the pastry slides into place; it may not come completely to the top of the cup. Repeat with the remaining puff pastry. Wrap the muffin tin(s) in plastic and place in the freezer until just before using.

Place a baking stone or unglazed quarry tiles, if you have them, on a rack in the lower third of the oven and preheat the oven to 425°F.

To prepare the filling, place the eggs in the bowl of a mixer, or another large bowl, and beat at medium speed for about a minute. Gradually add the sugar, then beat at medium-high speed for 4 minutes. Add the flour and salt and beat for 30 seconds. Add the coconut and beat briefly, about 20 seconds.

Pour the filling mixture into the frozen tart shells, filling them about two-thirds full. Sprinkle generously with confectioners' sugar, and let stand for 15 minutes undisturbed.

Once the oven has preheated, place a baking sheet on the rack. Wait another 10 minutes before placing the tarts in the oven on the baking sheet. Bake for 12 to 15 minutes, or until the tops are a light golden brown. Wearing oven mitts, carefully tip the tarts out onto a rack to cool to lukewarm or room temperature.

The tarts remain delicious for 2 to 3 days. If keeping for longer than 12 hours, seal in plastic and keep in a cool place or in the refrigerator.

NOTE If you really love coconut, once the tarts have cooled, sprinkle a little soft grated coconut on top.

down-under fruit pastries

Makes eight 4-inch square puff pastries, topped with almond paste and plum halves

At the edge of Sydney's Waterloo district, there's a small, comfortable café called Strangers with Candy. The coffee is good, the sandwiches generous, and the pastries are all made on the premises by Veronica, alias Ronnie, one of a trio of owners. Ronnie makes her wonderful fruit pastries using puff pastry. She tops the dough with a little almond paste, and then on the almond paste go plum or apricot halves. The pastries are easy to shape, a pleasure to eat, and almost better the day after baking. Great with coffee or tea at any time. Here's our interpretation of those Down-Under pastries.

8 soft ripe plums

Scant 1/2 cup sugar, or more to taste

1/2 recipe (3/4 pound) Rough Puff (page 46), or

   3/4 pound store-bought all-butter puff pastry

About 3 tablespoons Almond Paste (page 55)

Confectioners' sugar for dusting (optional)

Place a rack in the center of the oven and preheat the oven to 350°F.

Cut the plums in half and discard the pits. If the plums are large, the halves will be too big to fit on the pastries: Cut a narrow slice off each half plum to make the hemispheres smaller. Place the fruit in a bowl, sprinkle on several tablespoons of the sugar (if your plums are very tart, sugar both fruit and pastry more generously), and toss well. Set aside.

Cut the pastry in half and place half in the refrigerator, covered with plastic. Sprinkle your work surface with 2 to 3 tablespoons sugar, spreading it out in an area about 9 inches square. Place the pastry on the sugar and dust the top of it with a very little flour. Roll out the pastry on the sugared surface to a square about 9 inches across, rolling from the center outward. Use a sharp knife to trim the edges, then cut into 4 squares. Reserve the trimmings.

Turn the squares over sugared side up. Thinly spread about 1 teaspoon almond paste in a diagonal band about an inch wide from one corner to an opposite corner on one square, starting and stopping just short of the corners. Place 2 plum halves cut side down, side by side, on the almond paste. Sprinkle on a little sugar. Place the pastry on a large ungreased baking sheet. Repeat with the remaining 3 squares, leaving 1 inch between pastries on the baking sheet, then resugar your work surface and repeat with the other piece of pastry. Place the sugary pastry trimmings on the sheet to bake alongside; they make nice treats.

Bake for about 35 minutes: The fruit will have softened and the pastry at the open corners will have puffed and turned golden at the edges. Use a broad spatula to transfer the pastries (and "trimmings cookies") to a wire rack to cool for at least 30 minutes.

Just before serving, sift on a dusting of confectioners' sugar, if you wish.

APRICOT PASTRIES You can use apricots instead of plums, but they should be lightly poached first (or use poached and preserved apricot halves). Combine 2 cups water with the sugar in a large saucepan or skillet and bring to a boil, stirring to dissolve the sugar. Add 8 apricots, halved and pitted. Simmer briefly until slightly softened and golden, about 5 minutes, then set aside to cool in the syrup. Refrigerate until ready to use. Lift the apricots out of the syrup and dry them before placing them on the almond paste; do not toss them with sugar. Bake as directed above.

almond paste

Makes about ¾ cup dense, smooth paste

This paste is very quick to mix together, and a thin layer of it is a great way to shield pastry from the moistness of fruit, as in the Down-Under Fruit Pastries. Or, if you wish, spread some under the fruit fillings in the Danish Log (page 38) for another layer of flavor. It keeps well in the freezer for several months.

1 cup ground almonds

⅓ cup confectioners' sugar

2 tablespoons unsalted butter, softened

1 extra-large egg white, briefly whisked

½ teaspoon pure almond or pure vanilla extract (optional)

Place the almonds in a food processor and pulse briefly. Add the sugar, butter, egg white, and extract, if using, and process until smooth. Refrigerate in a well-sealed container, or store in the freezer if not using within 2 days. Let the frozen paste stand at room temperature for about an hour to soften before using.

jamaican coconut pie

Makes 1 open-faced 8-inch short-crust pie, filled with sweetened coconut–brown sugar paste

There is a Jamaican bakery in Kensington Market in downtown Toronto, not far from where we live. We stop in there nearly every time we pass by. We have no choice but to stop: The smells that come out of the bakery are like warm welcome arms that reach out and pull us in, and once we're in, we are in! There are breads lined up on shelves against the wall, and behind a long glass display case below the counter there are rows of irresistible sweet baked goodies. There is coconut-this, coconut-that, palm-sugar-this, and brown-sugar-that, everything equally enticing.

This pie, known as gizada in Jamaica, is often made and sold as individual tarts, but we like to bake ours in a pie plate and top it with a skinny lattice crust. It's one of the easiest pies we know, and like everything sweet and baked from Jamaica, it's super yummy. The slices are beautiful, with a sweet rich brown-sugar-and-coconut filling.

DOUGH

1 cup all-purpose flour

8 tablespoons (1 stick) cold unsalted butter,
   coarsely chopped

1 tablespoon sugar

¼ teaspoon salt

1 large egg yolk

1 to 2 tablespoons ice water, or as needed

FILLING

Scant 1¼ cups dried unsweetened shredded coconut
   or sweetened shredded coconut

½ cup boiling water (if using dried coconut)

1 cup packed light or dark brown sugar

¼ cup cornstarch

2 to 3 tablespoons unsalted butter, shortening, or lard

Place the flour and butter in a food processor and process to the consistency of a fine meal. Add the sugar, salt, and egg yolk, and pulse briefly to combine. Add 1 to 2 tablespoons ice water and pulse. Try to pull the mixture together into a dough; if it's still dry and crumbly, add a little more water.

Transfer the dough to a heavy plastic bag and press it from the outside into a disk. Refrigerate for 1 hour, or until ready to use.

Meanwhile, prepare the filling: If using dried coconut, place 1 cup of it in a bowl and pour over the boiling water. Let stand for 10 to 15 minutes.

In a small bowl, mix together the sugar and cornstarch, then stir into the coconut mixture. Or mix the sugar and cornstarch in a medium bowl and stir in 1 cup of the sweetened shredded coconut.

LEFT TO RIGHT: *Coconuts at a market, Salvador, Brazil; coconut palms, southern Thailand.*

Melt the butter in a small pot over medium-low heat. Add the coconut-sugar mixture and cook for about 2 minutes, stirring occasionally to prevent burning or sticking, until the mixture thickens.

Transfer to a bowl to cool to room temperature, then, if not using immediately, refrigerate, covered. (You should have about 1½ cups filling.) Thirty minutes before using it, take the filling out of the refrigerator. It hardens once cooled, but it can be stirred and softened with a wooden spoon.

Stir the remaining ¼ cup coconut into the filling and set aside.

Place a rack in the upper third of the oven and preheat the oven to 375°F.

Roll out the pastry on a lightly floured surface to a round 10 to 11 inches in diameter. Drape it over an 8-inch pie plate and gently ease it into the round. Trim off the edges just wider than the edge of the pie plate; reserve the trimmings.

Spread the filling in the pie shell, mounding it in the center and then spreading it outward. Use the trimmed pastry edges to make lattice strips if you wish (see the Note on page 19), and place on top of the filling. (Alternatively, you could dust them with sugar or cinnamon sugar, see Glossary, and bake them as cookies on a baking sheet until they start to turn golden, 7 to 10 minutes, depending on thickness.)

Bake the pie until lightly touched with brown, about 35 minutes. Let stand for at least 10 minutes to firm up and serve warm or at room temperature, with a scoop of mango or lemon sorbet for contrast, if you wish.

mince tarts

Makes 16 double-crusted tarts or about 30 shallow open tarts, made with rich short crust pastry and filled with fruity mincemeat

You can make mince pies, but we like individual mince tarts. We make them either in muffin tins, open-faced with just a pastry decoration on top, or as small free-standing closed tarts, baked on a baking sheet. (The amount of mincemeat you'll need depends on the type of tart you make; with double-crusted tarts, you'll use proportionately less filling.) Open or covered, each tart is substantial—three or four mouthfuls of intense flavor in a rich and tender short crust.

PASTRY

2 cups all-purpose flour

Pinch of salt

½ pound (2 sticks) half-frozen unsalted butter

1 large egg

About 2 tablespoons light cream

FILLING

1¼ to 2 cups homemade Mincemeat (page 59) or store-bought

1 large egg, beaten, for egg wash

Sugar for sprinkling

Make the pastry at least 1 hour before assembling the tarts.

By hand: Combine the flour and salt in a bowl. Using the coarse side of a box grater, grate the butter into the bowl. Cut the butter in with a knife, then toss with your fingers, rubbing the bits of butter, until the mixture has the texture of coarse meal. Add the egg and mix briefly. Gradually stir in the cream until the dough just comes together.

Using a food processor: Chop the butter. Combine the flour and salt in the processor bowl, add the butter, and pulse until the mixture has the texture of coarse meal. Add the egg and pulse briefly to mix. Gradually add the cream, pulsing just until the dough comes together.

Transfer the dough to a heavy plastic bag and flatten into an 8-inch square. Refrigerate for at least 30 minutes.

Place a rack in the center of the oven; preheat to 375°F.

Cut the pastry in half. Return half to the refrigerator, covered. On a lightly floured surface, roll out the dough to a 12- to 14-inch square.

To make small double-crusted tarts: Using a 3-inch round cutter, cut out an even number of rounds. Put a generous tablespoon of mincemeat in the center of one round and brush the pastry border with the egg wash. Lay another round on top, brush it with egg wash, and crimp the edges together by pinching them between your fingers and thumb. Cut one slit or several decorative slashes in the top. Sprinkle generously with sugar. Place on an ungreased baking sheet and repeat with the remaining pastry rounds. Then roll out the remaining dough and repeat.

To make open-faced tarts: Using a round cutter, or using a plate or pan lid as a guide, cut out 3¼- to 4-inch rounds of dough. Drop into muffin cups: There will be some rippling of the dough, and it won't come up to the top edge; don't worry. Spoon about 1 tablespoon filling into each one. Cut out small stars, circles, or strips from the pastry scraps, rerolling if necessary, to decorate the tops. Alternatively, cut out small rounds to place like "hats" on the center of the filling, leaving a border of filling. Brush tops with egg wash. (Depending on how many muffin pans you have, you may need to shape and bake in two batches.)

Bake until pale gold, about 20 minutes. Transfer to a rack to cool; serve warm or at room temperature.

NOTES The pastry makes enough for one double-crusted 8-inch pie or two 8-inch pie or tart shells.

These tarts freeze very well: Let cool completely, then seal in plastic bags and freeze. Let thaw overnight in the refrigerator, then bring back to room temperature, or heat on a baking sheet in a 300°F oven for about 10 minutes if you want to serve them warm.

mincemeat

Makes about 8 cups dark, richly flavored, fruit-based
mincemeat

*Mincemeat, a traditional English filling for Christmas
pastries, is really a confit of dried fruits and candied
citrus peel and, in this recipe, apple. (*Confit *is the
French word for a method of slow-cooking meat or other
perishable food in fat to preserve it for long keeping.)
The fruit is chopped small, then tossed with sugar and
spices and minced suet (beef fat). This mincemeat is
bound with suet but, unlike traditional mincemeats of
Victorian times, contains no other meat. The whole
mixture is baked for three hours in a low oven, to melt
the suet and soften all the peel and dried fruits. When the
mixture is cooled, each small element has a fine coating
of suet and will keep almost indefinitely. The flavor—
tart citrus and sweet dried fruit blended with spices and
sugar—is complex and intense.*

*Mincemeat is one of those ingredients that is tempting
to buy rather than make yourself, but there are two
reasons for bothering: It's actually easy to make and to
make in quantity so you have extra for the next time;
and you can be sure of the quality of the ingredients. If
possible, use organic fruits and unsulfured dried fruit;
buy your suet from a shop that sells naturally raised or
organic meat.*

**About 1 pound firm apples (3 to 4 medium),
    cored but not peeled, chopped into ¼-inch cubes**
½ pound suet (beef fat), finely chopped (see Notes)
2¼ cups dark raisins
2 cups currants
1¾ cups golden raisins (sultanas)
**About 1½ cups finely chopped mixed Candied Citrus Peel,
    homemade (page 60) or store-bought (see Notes)**
2¼ cups packed light brown sugar
Grated zest of 2 oranges
Grated zest of 2 lemons
½ cup freshly squeezed orange juice (from 2 to 3 oranges)

¼ cup freshly squeezed lemon juice (from 2 lemons)
1 teaspoon freshly ground black pepper
1½ teaspoons grated nutmeg (almost a whole nutmeg)
1½ teaspoons cinnamon
1 teaspoon ground cloves
1 teaspoon powdered ginger
¼ to ½ cup cognac or other brandy

Mix all the ingredients except the cognac together in a
large bowl and toss well. Cover and set aside in a cool
place for 8 to 12 hours, or overnight.

Preheat the oven to 225°F.

Place the mincemeat mixture in a casserole or roast-
ing pan, cover loosely with a lid or foil, and bake for
about 3 hours, stirring the mixture several times.

Remove from the oven and stir the cognac into the
hot mixture. Taste a small spoonful: It will be delicious.
Transfer to hot sterilized jars and seal with sterilized lids
(see page 173). Unless you're really in a rush, let stand
for 1 week before using to allow the flavors to blend.

NOTES To prepare the suet, use a large sharp knife to
cut the suet from the tough outer skin layer, holding the
knife at an angle to cut and scrape it off in strips. Cut the
strips crosswise to make small pieces. Discard any hard
or sinewy bits, or any with meat attached. A ½ pound of
suet produces just over 1 cup of very densely packed
finely chopped suet.

Measuring the amount of candied peel to start with
is necessarily approximate. If it's dried out and too
tough to chop easily, place in a little warm water and
microwave for 1 minute; repeat if the peel is still too
tough. (Once it's easy to chop, don't worry if it still
seems somewhat hard; the long slow bake of the minced
mixture will soften it well.)

You can also store the mincemeat in the freezer,
once it has stood for several weeks gaining flavor. When
Christmas is over, if we still have mincemeat left, we
transfer it to a plastic container and freeze it until the
following autumn.

candied citrus peel

Strips or segments of tart-sweet peel coated in sugar

Candied citrus peel is a useful ingredient to have around, especially in the winter, to brighten holiday cakes and desserts, or perhaps just to snack on as a sunny-tasting treat. We use the peel (including the pith) of lemons, oranges, and/or grapefruit (or citrons, if we can get them). It's boiled until soft, drained, and simmered in a sugary syrup until impregnated with sugar. After the pieces sit out on trays to dry for a few days, they can be tossed with sugar to coat, or dipped in chocolate for a candied treat. They're very beautiful and keep for a long time well wrapped.

Begin with organic (unwaxed and untreated) fruit. That's really the only requirement—that and a sharp paring knife for peeling. You might want to make a medley of different fruits—say, three oranges, four lemons, and two grapefruits (the peel of pink grapefruit is particularly beautiful)—or just one kind of fruit (using, say, twelve lemons)—or several kinds but unmixed. Suit yourself.

6 to 12 assorted fruits: organic lemons, grapefruits, oranges, and/or citrons (see headnote and Note)

SYRUP
2 cups sugar
1 cup water
Sugar for coating (optional)

Wash and dry the fruit. Peel the fruit in segments: This is easiest if you cut off the stem end, slice down through the peel in 4 or more places with a sharp knife, and then peel. Reserve the fruit for another use. (We store the fruits in tightly sealed plastic bags to prevent them from drying out until we want to squeeze them for juice.)

Trim off any discolored areas from the peels. Scrape off any membranes clinging to the pith, but leave the white pith on the inside of the peels intact. Place the peels in a large pot and add about 8 cups water, or enough to cover by 2 to 3 inches. Bring to a boil. Use a wooden spoon to stir and push the peels under the water, and boil over medium-high heat until the peels are soft (usually about an hour, but less for peels from thin-skinned oranges such as Valencia). Drain, then refill the pot with water, bring to a boil, and boil for another 15 to 20 minutes.

Once you've put the peels on for their second boil, prepare the syrup: In a heavy pot, dissolve the sugar in the water and bring to a boil. Lower heat and simmer until the peels are ready. (If you are making a large quantity—say, more than the peels from 6 grapefruit or 12 lemons—you may need to increase the amount of syrup; just increase in proportion so that the ratio of sugar to water is always 2 to 1.)

Drain the peels and immediately add to the simmering sugar syrup. Again use a wooden spoon to ensure that all peels are covered with liquid, pressing carefully with the back of the spoon. Simmer over medium-low heat, uncovered, for 1 to 1½ hours, stirring every once in a while so all the peels are evenly exposed to the syrup—the liquid will gradually reduce. Watch to make sure the peels don't stick or burn.

Line two baking sheets or large trays with wax paper. Lift the peels out of the syrup with a slotted spoon, pausing to let the syrup drain off them, and transfer to the baking sheets—lay them flat, without touching. (This is our favorite part of the process, as the peels are very beautiful, the orange and grapefruit peels a deep gold to orange and the lemon a paler yellow. They look like pieces of stained glass, especially when they are peel side up.) Leave out for 1 to 3 days to dry (timing will vary

Berber man at a rural market, Anti Atlas mountains, Morocco

depending on the climate and/or how dry your house is), turning them occasionally.

If you're not going to coat the peels with chocolate (see the variation below), coat them with granulated sugar before storing them. Place about ½ cup sugar in a paper bag, add a small batch of peels, and toss to coat, then transfer to a sealed container. Repeat with the remaining peels.

CHOCOLATE-DIPPED PEEL If you wish, you can melt dark chocolate and then dip each piece of candied peel in it to coat, either partially or completely. Use peel segments, or cut into thinner strips and dip those. Lay on a wax paper–lined tray to cool and set. Serve with ice cream or a soft-textured dessert, or as a sweet treat.

NOTE If you wish to finely chop the peels for use in baking, do so after the first boiling, using scissors or a sharp knife to cut them into dice. You can also cut them into thinner ½-inch-wide strips, or do as we do and leave them in large curving segments. (They're so attractive that way.) Boiling the peels helps wash out bitterness.

The remaining syrup will be sweet-tart and heavily citrus flavored. It's wonderful over ice cream or as a glaze for a fruit tart. We store it in the freezer.

cherry strudel

Makes 1 strudel, about 15 inches long, with a moist filling of cherries on a flavored soft pillow of bread crumbs; serves 8 to 10

PHOTOGRAPH ON PAGE 67 *The small bed-and-breakfast I stayed in when I first arrived in Hungary was in Abda, a village just up the Danube from the beautiful town of Győr. It was early June, and fields of lush green grass and flowering poppies lined the small country roads. In the garden of the bed-and-breakfast, the cherry tree was loaded with ripe fruit. On the morning I left, there was a special treat with my breakfast, a wide slice of rétes (pronounced "raytesh")—strudel fresh from the oven, filled with cherries from the garden and plenty of bread crumbs to soak up their juice and good flavor. When she saw how much I liked the strudel, my hostess wrapped another two generous slices in brown paper to sustain me during my drive down the Danube valley toward Budapest. Cherry season in Hungary.*

Strudel is made in home kitchens all through the region that used to be the Austro-Hungarian Empire. There are many versions, using fillings both sweet and savory. This dough is like a strong elastic unleavened flatbread dough, stretched by hand until very thin, then rolled up around the filling. Don't worry if you get the odd hole or tear as you stretch it; the dough gets rolled up on itself, so small flaws don't matter. What you do need is a little patience and a sense of excitement as you take a small ball of dough and extend it to make a large fine sheet.

This recipe makes about half a pound of dough, enough for one strudel, which will stretch to a rectangle almost two feet square. The filling is very simple. Since cherry season is short, for most of the year this strudel is made with bottled sour cherries. Usually imported from Hungary, they come already pitted and are excellent. Use freshly ground or grated bread crumbs from a white or mostly white loaf with all the crusts trimmed off (see page 333).

DOUGH

Scant 1 cup unbleached all-purpose flour

Generous pinch of salt

½ large egg, beaten (see Note)

2 tablespoons unsalted butter, melted

¼ cup plus 1 tablespoon warm water

FILLING

About 8 tablespoons (1 stick) unsalted butter, melted

3 to 4 tablespoons finely ground almonds (optional)

1 to 1½ cups packed fresh bread crumbs (see headnote)

1½ cups pitted sour cherries, fresh or bottled

   (drained if bottled, syrup reserved; see headnote)

¼ cup sugar, or to taste

Place the flour and salt in a food processor and process to mix. Add the egg and melted butter and process to mix. With the machine running, pour in the water and process until the dough comes together in a ball, then continue for another 10 to 15 seconds.

Turn the dough out onto a lightly floured surface and knead briefly. It should be soft, smooth, and quite moist, not stiff. If it feels stiff, wet your hands as you knead to moisten the dough a little more. Place the dough under an upside-down bowl to keep it warm and moist, and let rest for 30 minutes to 1 hour.

Place a rack in the center of the oven and preheat the oven to 350°F. Line a baking sheet with parchment or wax paper.

Set out the melted butter and the ground almonds, if using. Place the crumbs, cherries, and sugar in a bowl and toss to mix. If using bottled cherries, add 2 or 3 tablespoons of the reserved fruit syrup and toss to blend. Set aside.

Place a cotton cloth (a heavy tablecloth works well) on a small work surface: A freestanding table, or the end of a counter that you can reach from three sides, is ideal. Traditionally, much larger sheets of strudel were stretched around large work tables or dining room tables and the task was much more difficult. Rub all-purpose flour into the cloth and then dust it with a little more flour.

On a lightly floured work surface, use a rolling pin to roll the dough out to a circle, rolling from the center outward and getting it as thin as you can. Cover with plastic wrap and let rest for about 1 minute; this gives the gluten time to relax before you start stretching it more.

Slide your rolling pin under the dough and carry it on the pin over to the floured cloth. Lay it on the cloth so that the dough hangs over the edge. You're going to use gravity and the backs of your hands to stretch the dough. Lift an edge of the dough up and drape it over the backs of your hands and forearms. Pull your hands apart gently to stretch the dough. Drop it back down, letting it hang over the edge, then rotate dough and cloth so another portion hangs down, and repeat stretching. Work your way around the edge of the dough, stretching a section at a time. You'll notice a thick rough edge all the way around—don't worry, it will get trimmed off, and meanwhile its weight helps stretch the dough.

Soon you'll have a sheet more than 24 inches by 20 inches. Use a sharp knife to trim off the thick rim all around and discard, leaving you with a piece of dough about 24 inches by 18 inches.

Center the dough on the cloth, with a short edge facing you. Trim the short edge farthest from you to a straight line. Brush melted butter all over the dough, leaving a bare strip about 1 inch wide along the trimmed edge. Sprinkle the almond powder, if using, all over the butter. Mound the cherry-crumb mixture across the dough, about 4 inches from the near edge, leaving 1 inch clear on either side; it should be high and about 4 inches wide. Use the cloth to help you roll the front edge of the dough up over the filling. Turn the sides of the dough over, up onto the mound, then continue to roll the strudel away from you. Wet the straight-cut far flap with a little water to help it seal, then place the strudel seam side down on the paper-lined baking sheet. Brush with melted butter. Bake the strudel for 35 to 40 minutes, until well touched with brown; brush it several times with butter during baking. When it comes out of the oven, brush again with butter and sprinkle with several tablespoons of sugar, then transfer to a platter to sit for 15 minutes or more. Serve in slices.

HOMEMADE PHYLLO SHEETS You can also cut the stretched dough into six 8-by-10-inch rectangles for phyllo (it won't be as thin as commercial phyllo.) Stretch each of the rectangles a little thinner, dust lightly with flour, stack, and freeze flat in a well-sealed plastic bag. Defrost in the refrigerator when ready to use for Mediterranean Semolina-Phyllo Pie (page 64) or other recipes. (Makes 6 phyllo sheets.)

NOTE To measure ½ egg, beat the egg with a fork in a small measuring cup until the yolk and white are blended, then pour out half.

mediterranean phyllo-semolina pie

Makes one 13-by-9-inch pie with a sweetened, creamy semolina filling, enclosed in layers of flaky pastry
and drenched with honey syrup

PHOTOGRAPH ON PAGE 66 *In the West we've come to refer to all the sweet pastries made with phyllo as* baklava,
*a word of Turkic origin. They're usually made of a filling of chopped nuts encased in layers of phyllo dough, baked, and
then infused with syrup. The result is chewy and intensely sweet. This "pie" from Lebanon is a variation on the baklava
tradition: Instead of nuts, the layers of buttered phyllo enclose a creamy filling made of cooked sweetened semolina.
The taste and the texture are wonderful, and, like all baklava, it tastes even better after it has rested for twelve hours.
The pie can be made either with phyllo sheets or with the fine strands of phyllo known as* kataif *or* kanefe *(see Crunchy
Phyllo Pie below).*

*Phyllo pastry can be made by hand, but the easiest approach is to buy a package of frozen phyllo. The best phyllo is
handmade, so if you find a source for it, buy plenty. Defrost frozen phyllo overnight in the refrigerator.*

FILLING

2 cups milk

½ cup coarse semolina (not semolina flour)

½ cup sugar

2 large eggs

1 tablespoon cornstarch

2 tablespoons unsalted butter

1 teaspoon pure vanilla extract

SYRUP

½ cup honey

½ cup sugar

¼ cup water

8 tablespoons (1 stick) unsalted butter, melted
About ½ pound homemade phyllo sheets (page 63) or
defrosted frozen store-bought

Combine the milk, semolina, and ¼ cup of the sugar in
a heavy pot. Cook over medium heat, stirring frequently, until the mixture thickens. Remove from the
heat and let cool to room temperature.

In a bowl, whisk together the eggs, cornstarch, and
the remaining ¼ cup sugar. Add to the semolina mixture and stir in. Heat gently over medium heat, stirring,
until it becomes very thick and coats the spoon; don't
let it boil. Remove from the heat and stir in the butter
and vanilla. Set the filling aside to cool to room
temperature.

Meanwhile, make the syrup: In a small saucepan,
combine the honey, sugar, and water and stir to dissolve
the sugar. Bring to a boil. Set aside to cool to room
temperature.

Preheat the oven to 375°F. Butter a 13-by-9-inch
baking pan. Place the melted butter and a pastry brush
by your work surface. Half the phyllo sheets will go
under the filling, half on top: The number of sheets will

vary with the brand you buy (we've found we use 8 to 10 top and bottom).

Lay 1 phyllo sheet over the bottom of the pan, and brush it with butter. Lay on more sheets, brushing each with butter, until you have used half the sheets. Spread on the semolina filling. Top with remaining sheets of phyllo, brushing each with butter. Brush the top with butter. Using a sharp knife, score a pattern through the top few sheets—a diagonal crisscross is traditional—to mark out servings.

Bake for 30 minutes, or until golden brown.

Immediately after taking the pie out of the oven, pour the cooled syrup all over the top. Let stand for at least 2 hours. The pie tastes even better after 12 hours; the filling sets and flavors have time to blend.

NOTE: Most cooks in Syria and Lebanon use ghee rather than melted butter for making baklava and related phyllo dishes. Ghee is butter that has been clarified of all milk solids, so that it keeps well. We like the browning that happens when we use whole butter for these pastries, and with refrigeration, there's no need to worry about the keeping qualities of the butter.

CRUNCHY PHYLLO PIE Made with store-bought frozen phyllo strands, called *kataif* or *kanefe,* this is a very attractive pie and has a good crunch as you bite into it. You will need the same weight of phyllo, defrosted. Melt about 8 tablespoons (1 stick) unsalted butter and let it cool a little, then toss the strands in the butter. Lay half the strands in the bottom of your pan, spreading them and pulling them out so they lie somewhat flat. Spread on the filling evenly, then top with the remaining half of the phyllo strands, stretching them to lie flat also. Bake for about 30 minutes, or until golden. Pour the room temperature syrup over, as above, then let stand for at least 2 hours

FOLLOWING PAGES: MEDITERRANEAN PHYLLO-SEMOLINA PIE. CHERRY STRUDEL *(page 62).*

The fields of the Dingle peninsula, Ireland

irish curd pie

Makes 1 round or square pie, filled with sweetened cheese and topped with a golden egg-and-sugar crust

I can't remember there being a single restaurant in town, let alone a coffee shop, or a bakery with sweet treats, when I lived one winter, close to thirty years ago, outside the town of Dingle, in County Kerry, in the southwestern corner of Ireland. There were fifty-two pubs (some of the pubs had food), but not a single restaurant.

Nowadays everything is different. There are many fine restaurants to choose from in Dingle, there are coffee shops and bakeries, and there is even an organic market. What's more, along with a revival in Gaelic language and literature, there is a revival of old culinary treasures, like this curd pie, which I tasted for the first time in a Gaelic bookstore-cum-coffee shop-cum-music store. The pie tasted of long ago, but the shop was definitely of a new era!

The pie is a form of cheesecake. Its simple crust is strong enough to hold in the moist rich filling. We use pressed cottage cheese because it's easier to find here than the pot cheese that was used in the original.

PASTRY

1¼ cups all-purpose flour

1 tablespoon sugar

½ teaspoon salt

6 tablespoons cold unsalted butter, cut into small chunks

About ¼ cup cold water

FILLING

2 cups (about ¾ pound) pressed cottage cheese

¼ cup vanilla sugar (see Sugars in the Glossary)
  or granulated sugar

2 tablespoons unsalted butter, softened

¼ teaspoon salt (if cheese is unsalted)

½ teaspoon minced lemon zest (optional)

3 large eggs, separated

TOPPING

1 large egg, beaten

1 tablespoon unsalted butter, melted

1 tablespoon sugar

2 tablespoons all-purpose flour

In a medium bowl, mix together the flour, sugar, and salt. Cut in the butter with two knives, or with a pastry cutter, or with your fingertips. Make a well in the center and pour in 3 tablespoons cold water. Stir to moisten (you may need to add more water). Turn out onto a lightly floured surface and knead very briefly until supple. Place in a plastic bag, shape into a disk, seal, and refrigerate for 1 hour (or up to 2 days).

Place a rack in the center of the oven and preheat the oven to 350°F. Lightly grease a 9-inch pie plate or an 8-inch square cake pan.

On a lightly floured surface, roll out the pastry to a 10-inch round or a 10-inch square, then lay it in the pan. Cover with plastic wrap and refrigerate while you prepare the filling and topping.

In a large bowl, beat together the cottage cheese, sugar, butter, salt, and zest, if using. Beat the egg yolks, and stir them in. Beat the egg whites until fairly stiff. Fold into the mixture and set aside.

Brush the pastry shell with a little of the beaten egg. Mix the rest of the beaten egg with the remaining topping ingredients.

Transfer the filling to the crust, mounding it a little in the middle. Pour over the topping, starting at the center and moving in a circle outward. The topping will flow out to the edges, so don't worry if it doesn't reach the sides of the pan when you first pour it on.

Bake the pie for 35 to 40 minutes, or until the crust is golden. Serve the pie hot or at room temperature. Accompany with fresh or preserved fruit if you wish.

SAVORY TARTS AND PIES

pissaladière

Makes one 13-by-9-inch open-faced savory pastry, topped with slow-cooked onions and dotted with black olives and anchovy strips; serves 4 to 6

PHOTOGRAPH ON PAGE 76 *Madame Jouanneau used to make this for lunch, occasionally, during the winter long ago when I stayed at her pension in Tours. I was seventeen, and Madame and her husband took me under their collective wing. Madame had large blue eyes, a wide, open face with high cheekbones, a loud voice, and a generous spirit. She turned out wonderful food for her boarders every lunch and supper, year-round. She was from the Midi and her husband from Lyons, and they laid an extraordinarily generous table. On gray winter days in the Loire Valley, this tart from the South of France was a much-needed taste of the Mediterranean.*

Pissaladière is sometimes made using a bread dough, and then it looks more like pizza. But this pastry-based version is the one I know, topped with slow-cooked onions, strips of anchovy, and small black Niçoise olives. In charcuteries and in some bakeries in France, you sometimes see pissaladière with small chunks or slices of tomato as well. It makes a brighter-looking tart; do include tomato, if you like, for a "modern" take on the traditional recipe.

PASTRY

1½ cups all-purpose flour

¼ teaspoon salt

12 tablespoons (1½ sticks) cold unsalted butter

1 large egg

About 2 tablespoons ice water

TOPPING

Scant 2 tablespoons olive oil

2 pounds onions, thinly sliced (about 6 cups)

2 or 3 sprigs thyme

1 bay leaf

¼ teaspoon salt

Pinch of ground cloves

Water

20 to 25 small anchovy fillets (see Note)

About 15 Niçoise or other small black olives

At least 2 hours before you wish to serve the tart, make the pastry: Place the flour and salt in a bowl. Use the coarse side of a box grater to grate the butter into the bowl, then toss with the flour. Use a knife or pastry cutter to cut in the butter so that you have small buttery crumbs. Break the egg into the bowl and mix in lightly with a fork. Add the ice water, starting with 2 tablespoons, tossing and mixing to moisten the flour. If necessary, add more water, just enough so that the dough comes together in a mass when you pull it together.

Transfer to a heavy plastic bag. Press from outside the bag to make a flat disk about 6 inches across. Seal well and refrigerate while you prepare the topping (the dough can be made up to 2 days ahead).

Place a rack in the center of the oven and preheat the oven to 375°F. Lightly oil a shallow 13-by-9-inch baking pan.

To prepare the topping, heat the olive oil in a large heavy skillet. Add the onions, thyme, bay leaf, salt, and cloves and cook over medium heat, turning frequently, until the onions wilt and soften. Lower the heat slightly and continue to cook: After they release their liquid, the onions will soften further, but as the liquid evaporates, the onions may start to stick—add a little water as necessary to prevent sticking (¼ cup, or perhaps a little more). The whole cooking process will take about an hour. When done, the onions will be very soft and sweet-tasting. Remove from the heat, and remove and discard the thyme sprigs and bay leaf. Set aside to cool to lukewarm.

While the onions are cooking, prepare the crust: Lightly flour a work surface and turn out the dough. Flatten the dough by banging on it with a lightly floured rolling pin, then roll it out to a rectangle a little larger than the baking pan, rolling from the center outward.

Transfer the dough to the baking pan and gently ease it into the corners. Trim off extra dough with a sharp knife (see the variation). If necessary, use scraps of trimmings to patch any holes, pressing down on the edges of the patch to seal well. Prick the dough all over, about ten times, with a fork to prevent puffing, then line it with foil or parchment paper. Weight the foil with dried beans or rice or pastry weights.

Bake the crust for about 10 minutes, until the edges are firm and just touched with color. Remove from the oven and remove the foil and weights.

Spread the cooked onions all over the bottom of the crust. Make a pattern with the anchovies, as you please. Arrange the olives to make a pattern or randomly, as you please.

Place the tart back in the oven and bake for about 15 minutes, until the edges are touched with brown and pulling away from the sides of the pan. Let cool for at least 10 minutes and serve warm or at room temperature.

NOTE We use anchovy fillets packed in oil. If instead you have salted anchovy fillets, soak them in water to rinse off the extra salt, then pat dry. Toss them in a little olive oil to coat before using on the tart.

SMALL APPLE TREAT Each time we make this, we have a little pastry left over. We like it best as a wrapper for chopped apple: Roll the pastry out to a fairly thin round, place some chopped apple in the center, and sprinkle generously with sugar. Pull the edges of the pastry up over the apples, to make a small round pastry, and pinch the pleats to seal all round. Prick the top several times with a fork. Bake at 375°F on a baking sheet until just touched with gold, about 15 minutes. (Makes 1 small sweet pastry.)

onion pletzel and potato pletzel

Makes 4 savory flatbread rounds, each about 10 inches in diameter, topped with chopped onion or with tender slices of potato

The classic pletzel of Polish- and Russian-Jewish tradition is homey and welcoming, a flatbread topped with onions that steam-cook and soften as the bread bakes. As we worked with onion pletzel, figuring out a recipe, we decided to try making a potato version too. It's a knockout, and one of the best ways we know to use up leftover boiled potatoes.

The dough is an easy yeasted one, lightly enriched with fat or oil or butter. Make four pletzels (in Yiddish, the plural is pletzelech) the same, or two onion and two potato, or whatever pleases you. Serve as you would pizza, for lunch or a casual supper. Accompany with salad, or cooked greens, or a light soup.

DOUGH (FOR 4 PLETZELS)

1 teaspoon active dry yeast

1 cup lukewarm water

2 cups all-purpose flour

1 teaspoon salt

2 tablespoons melted chicken fat (see Fat in the Glossary)
  or unsalted butter, melted

Coarse cornmeal for dusting

About 2 tablespoons melted unsalted butter, olive oil,
  or melted chicken fat for brushing

ONION TOPPING (FOR 1 PLETZEL)

1 teaspoon poppy seeds

¼ cup minced onion

About ¼ teaspoon coarse salt

POTATO TOPPING (FOR 1 PLETZEL)

1 medium waxy (boiling) potato, boiled and thinly sliced

About ¼ teaspoon coarse salt

1 teaspoon minced scallion or chives (optional)

About 1 tablespoon finely chopped cracklings
  (see Fat in the Glossary) (optional)

In a large bowl, blend the yeast into the water to dissolve it thoroughly, then stir in 1 cup of the flour to make a smooth batter. Sprinkle on the salt and stir in the fat or butter. Add the remaining 1 cup flour and turn and fold to form a dough.

Turn the dough out onto a lightly floured surface and knead for 5 minutes, or until smooth and supple. Place in a clean bowl, cover with plastic wrap, and let rise in a draft-free place for 2 to 2½ hours, until doubled in volume.

Turn the dough out onto a lightly floured surface and cut into 4 equal pieces (each will weigh about 7 ounces). Flatten each into a round and then let rest, loosely covered, for 10 to 15 minutes.

Meanwhile, place a baking stone or unglazed quarry tiles, if you have them, on a rack in the upper third of the oven. Preheat the oven to 475°F.

Sprinkle coarse cornmeal on your work surface. Flatten each dough round into an 8-inch circle, using your palms or a rolling pin. Then use your fingertips to dimple the surface of the rounds and relax them, so that they stretch out farther. Cover and let proof for 15 minutes.

Market scene, Tbilisi, Georgia

Prepare one round at a time. First brush it all over with butter, olive oil, or chicken fat. *For each onion pletzel,* sprinkle on the poppy seeds, onion, and coarse salt, leaving a narrow rim clear of topping all around. *For each potato pletzel,* arrange thin overlapping slices of the cooked potato on the dough round, leaving a narrow rim clear of topping. Sprinkle the potato with coarse salt, and with the chopped scallion and cracklings, if using. Brush with butter, oil, or chicken fat.

As each round is ready, slide it onto a cornmeal-dusted peel (see page 114) or the back of a baking sheet, and transfer to the hot baking stone or tiles. You will probably have room to bake only 2 pletzels at a time; do not prepare the second 2 until you have room to bake them. Bake for 10 to 12 minutes, until the edges are risen and light brown and, on the onion pletzel, until the onions are very soft.

OPPOSITE: PISSALADIÈRE (page 72). ABOVE: Old town, Colmar, Alsace, France.

central asian lamb pies

Makes 16 small, golden, succulent lamb-filled pies; allow 3 or 4 per person

When we travel in our mind's eye, we get hungry, and perhaps no remembered travel makes us more hungry than trips to central Asia. The food that we eat there, whether from a stall in a local market or at a small neighborhood restaurant, is almost always direct, relatively simple, and very good. Tomatoes taste like tomatoes, melons like melons, bread like bread, and lamb like lamb. We don't know why the food tastes so good. Maybe it's the dry desert air, or perhaps it's because agribusiness hasn't interfered and food still tastes the way it should. But whatever the explanation, eating in central Asia is a great pleasure.

These juicy little morsels, four mouthfuls each, come from Kazakhstan, where they are known as belyashi. *They closely resemble the lamb pies called* somsa *that are served in neighboring Uzbekistan. The major difference between the two is that these are cooked in oil and then steamed, whereas* somsa *are baked in a tandoor oven.*

Belyashi are a great late-afternoon snack or appetizer. Serve them with sliced tomatoes or radishes sprinkled with a little salt, or a salad of winter greens, and follow with a large cup of black tea, central Asian style.

DOUGH

1 cup all-purpose flour

½ teaspoon salt

½ teaspoon baking powder

¼ cup rendered lamb fat (see Fat in the Glossary), unsalted butter, softened, or vegetable shortening

About ⅓ cup lukewarm water

FILLING

2 tablespoons finely chopped lamb fat or unsalted butter

3 small onions (about 6 ounces total), finely chopped

½ pound lamb, chopped or ground

1 teaspoon salt

¾ to 1 teaspoon freshly ground black pepper

About 1 tablespoon lamb cracklings (see Fat in the Glossary) (optional)

Peanut or vegetable oil for shallow frying

Make the dough at least an hour before you wish to serve the pies.

By hand: Combine the dry ingredients in a bowl. Stir in the softened fat and just enough water to form a dough. Turn out and knead on a lightly floured surface until smooth.

Using a food processor: Place the dry ingredients in the processor bowl, add the softened fat, and process to blend them well. With the blade whirling, add the water through the feed tube until a ball of dough forms. Process for another 20 seconds.

Wrap the dough well in plastic and let rest for 30 minutes to 1 hour (a longer rest makes the dough easier to roll out).

Meanwhile, make the filling: In a large heavy skillet, heat the fat or butter over medium heat. Sauté the onions until well softened and caramelized to golden brown, about 15 minutes.

Transfer to a bowl, add the lamb, salt, and pepper, and mix well. Mix in the cracklings, if using.

Place the bowl by your work surface, together with a small bowl of water. Lightly flour a large baking sheet.

Cut the dough into 4 pieces. Work with 1 piece at a time, keeping the others covered. Roll the dough out as thin as possible, to about 16 inches square. Cut into 4 pieces; the pieces do not have to be tidy squares, as you will be folding them up around the meat. Place a scant 2 tablespoons lamb filling in the center of a square. Wet your fingertips with water and use them to moisten the edges of the dough, then pleat the dough up in large folds over the meat to make a round pastry, leaving a small opening in the center (the water will help the dough stick to itself). Flatten the pie lightly with your palm: It should be ½ to ¾ inch high. Place on the lightly floured baking sheet. Prepare the remaining pies, keeping the shaped ones covered with plastic to prevent them from drying out.

In a large heavy skillet, heat about 3 tablespoons oil over medium heat until hot. Put in as many meat pies as will fit without crowding, filling side down, and fry gently until dark golden brown, about 5 minutes. Use a spatula to turn them over and fry on the other side to the same color, about 4 minutes. While they are cooking, place a cup of hot water and a lid for the skillet by the stove.

If cooking on an electric stove top, turn another element on to high about 2 minutes before the pies are browned; when the pastries are cooked, transfer the skillet to the hot element. Alternatively, *if cooking with gas,* once the pies have browned, raise the heat to high. Immediately pour in just enough hot water to cover the bottom of the skillet, then put on the lid and let steam for 20 to 30 seconds. Remove the lid and transfer the pies to a warm plate. To cook the remaining pastries, place the skillet back over medium heat, add more oil to the pan as necessary and repeat. Serve the pies hot, or cover to keep warm while you cook the remaining pies.

Turkoman couple at the sheep market, Ashkhabad, southern Turkmenistan. FOLLOWING PAGES: *Tibetan nomad and his flock, Changtang region. Evening light near Burang, western Tibet.*

farmhouse meat pie

Makes 1 succulent, meat-filled double-crusted pie; serves 4 to 6

This winter classic from French Canada is known as tourtière, *and is traditionally served at* réveillon, *the late-night (originally after midnight mass) party and celebration on Christmas Eve. It's made with ground pork lightly flavored with aromatics and onion and baked in a rich piecrust until golden brown. (Many people make their tourtière with a blend of veal and pork.) The trick to making a moist tourtière is to add bread crumbs to the filling to absorb extra juices from the pork.*

You might consider making a double recipe while you're at it, then freeze one tourtière after it's baked, to have on hand for a cold snowy day. Serve hot or warm, with salad or wintry pickley things or bitter greens.

Farmhouse and barn, Grey County, Ontario, Canada

DOUGH

2½ cups all-purpose flour

½ teaspoon salt

¼ teaspoon baking powder

½ pound (1 cup) lard, or 1 cup vegetable shortening

1 large egg

1 tablespoon white vinegar

2 to 3 tablespoons cold water as needed

FILLING

1 pound (2 cups) ground pork

1 medium onion, chopped (about ½ cup)

1 garlic clove, minced

½ teaspoon salt

½ teaspoon soy sauce

¼ teaspoon dried oregano

1 bay leaf

¼ teaspoon freshly ground black pepper

Scant ¼ teaspoon ground cloves

½ cup water

¼ to ½ cup dried bread crumbs

Make the dough at least an hour before you wish to start baking.

Place all the dry ingredients in a bowl and stir to mix well. Cut in the lard or shortening to make evenly moistened crumbs. Mix together the egg and vinegar and stir in. Try pulling the dough together. If it is still crumbly, add 2 tablespoons cold water and mix; if this is not enough to moisten the dough thoroughly, add a little more cold water. When the dough just comes together, pull it into a mass.

Cut the dough into 2 not quite equal pieces. Place each piece in a heavy plastic bag, flatten it out to a disk, and seal well. Refrigerate until 10 minutes before you roll it out. (The pastry keeps for 3 days in the refrigerator or for 1 month, well sealed in plastic, in the freezer. Defrost overnight in the refrigerator before using.)

When you are ready to proceed, place a baking stone or unglazed quarry tiles, if you have them, on a rack in the center of the oven. Preheat the oven to 500°F.

To prepare the filling, place the pork and onion in a heavy saucepan over medium heat. Stir to break up lumps in the meat. Add all the remaining ingredients except the bread crumbs and stir as the mixture comes to a boil. Reduce the heat and simmer for 15 to 20 minutes, stirring to break up any remaining lumps in the meat, until the onions are completely softened and golden.

Remove from the heat and add ¼ cup bread crumbs. Stir, then let stand 10 minutes. If there is still liquid in the mixture, add the remaining bread crumbs and stir well. Let stand for another 10 minutes. The filling should be moist but without much extra liquid. Let cool.

Place the larger piece of pastry on a lightly floured work surface and flatten it with the palm of your hand, then use a rolling pin to roll it out to an 11-inch circle. If the pastry sticks to the surface, use a dough scraper to gently detach it.

Lay the pastry over an 8-inch pie plate and use your knuckles to ease the dough into the plate. Spoon in the cooled filling, mounding it in the center. Roll out the second piece of pastry to a 9-inch round and lay it on top, then crimp the edges together by pinching them between your thumb and forefinger all around, or by pressing down with the back of a fork to seal. Cut 3 or 4 slits in the top of the pie to allow steam to escape.

Bake the pie until well browned on top, about 20 minutes. If after 10 minutes the edge is starting to darken too much, place a strip of foil over the edge to protect it. Serve hot or warm.

NOTES The pie can be stored, once cooled, well sealed in plastic, in the refrigerator for up to 3 days or in the freezer for up to 1 month. Defrost overnight, then reheat thoroughly in a 300°F oven before serving.

The baking soda is unusual in a piecrust, but quite common in recipes from Quebec. The soy sauce gives an extra depth of flavor to the filling.

easy cheese and bean rounds

Makes 12 to 15 tender round breads, about 4 inches in diameter, filled with melted cheese

These rounds are our take on pupusas, *the Nicaraguan and Salvadoran corn breads that are made of fresh masa filled with meat, refried beans, or cheese. Pupusas are slowly cooked on a* comal *(a clay baking surface) or on a metal skillet over a fire. We've never been in either Nicaragua or El Salvador, but we've eaten many pupusas, made by Nicaraguans and Salvadoreans living in North America. Dough made only of masa (processed corn dough) is fragile, so it takes a lot of practice to make traditional pupusas. One day we added cooked beans to the dough rather than putting them in the filling. We found we had a smooth beautiful dough that still tasted of corn but was much easier to handle. We filled it simply with a little cheese. So here they are, nontraditional corn-bean pupusas with a warm taste of corn and melted cheese. Fill them with a quick grated cheese mixture, or with anything else you fancy (see the variation). Serve hot or warm, on their own or with a little salsa or salad as a snack or light meal.*

DOUGH

½ cup drained cooked or canned white beans
    (navy beans or small white beans; see Glossary)

½ cup lukewarm water

1 tablespoon corn oil

1 teaspoon salt

1¼ cups masa harina (see Corn in the Glossary)

FILLING

Scant ½ cup loosely packed coarsely grated cheese,
    such as Oaxacan string cheese (see Glossary),
    Monterey Jack, or even mild or medium Cheddar

1 tablespoon minced chives or scallion greens,
    or more to taste (optional)

Corn oil for cooking and shaping

In a food processor, process the beans, water, and oil to make a puree. Add the salt, then gradually add the masa, processing until a dough forms. Turn out into a bowl and let stand, well covered with plastic, for 30 minutes.

To prepare the filling, combine the cheese and optional chives or scallions in a bowl. Set aside.

Heat a heavy skillet over medium heat. Place a bowl of water and a small saucer of corn oil by your work surface. Grease the skillet with an oiled cloth or paper towel.

Wet your hands well with water, then scoop up a scant 2 tablespoons of dough (about 1 ounce). Place it on one palm and flatten it to a disk about 3 inches across. Place about 1 teaspoon of the cheese mixture in the center and fold the edges of the dough up over the filling all around to cover it, then lightly oil the palm of your free hand and use it to flatten the dough to a flat disk about 4 inches across. If the dough cracks, don't worry—just mend the break by pressing the edges back together or patching with a pinch of extra dough.

Place the pupusa seam side down on the heated skillet to start cooking while you shape the next one. (If you have room for 3 pupusas in your skillet, you can get a dozen to 15 cooked in 15 to 20 minutes.) The pupusas will cook slowly over medium heat, gradually getting lightly flecked with brown. Turn each pupusa over after about 3 minutes and cook on the other side for about 2 minutes, until firm and lightly golden, then transfer to a plate. Repeat with the remaining dough and filling, oiling the skillet as needed.

NOTE Pupusas also make great campfire food.

SPICY BANANA ROUNDS Smear the flattened dough with a little chile oil, then top it with a teaspoon of chopped ripe banana, before sealing and flattening the disk and cooking it, as above. The combo is sweet and hot and very, very good.

new york–style calzones

Makes 6 half-moon-shaped calzones, about 8 inches long, filled with salami and melted cheese

People tell us that if we like calzones, which we do, then we would really like calzone in Italy. And we think that they must be right, but we have a hard time imagining how they could be better than calzones in New York City (see NYC Calzone, page 87) or, even more wonderful, calzones at home! Wrap a simple yeasted dough around mozzarella cheese and a little salami, bake in a 500°F oven, and eat hot and steamy right out of the oven. What could be better? Our son Tashi could eat calzones for dinner every night. Maybe he would get tired of them eventually, maybe not.

DOUGH

1½ cups lukewarm water

1 teaspoon active dry yeast

About 4 cups all-purpose flour

1½ teaspoons salt

Olive oil for coating

FILLING

6 ounces thinly sliced Genoa or other salami

¾ pound mozzarella, coarsely grated

Coarse semolina for dusting (optional)

Place the water in a bowl and stir in the yeast. Add 2 cups of the flour and stir to make a smooth batter. Sprinkle on the salt and stir it in. Add another 1½ cups flour and stir and fold to incorporate. Turn out onto a floured surface and knead until smooth, incorporating more flour as necessary, about 5 minutes.

Oil a clean bowl with about a tablespoon of olive oil, place the dough in the bowl, and turn to coat with oil. Cover and set aside to rise until doubled, 1½ to 2 hours.

Turn the dough out onto a lightly floured surface and cut into 6 equal pieces. Set aside, loosely covered.

Cut the salami slices in half, then mix with the grated cheese. Divide the filling into 6 equal piles and set aside.

On a lightly floured surface, begin rolling out 2 pieces of dough, leaving the others covered. The dough will be elastic and spring back, so alternate between the 2 until each is rolled out to a thin round about 8 inches in diameter and ¼ inch thick. Place a pile of filling in the middle of one half of each round, making sure there's a clean ½-inch rim of dough, then fold the dough over to make a half-moon shape. Pinch the edges of the dough together and then fold the edge back up over the seam and pinch again, to make a secure doubled seam.

Place the calzones on a surface dusted with semolina or flour and cover loosely. Repeat with the remaining pieces of dough and let rise, covered, for 30 minutes.

Place a baking stone or unglazed quarry tiles, if you have them, on a rack in the center of the oven and preheat the oven to 500°F. Depending on the size of your oven, you may have to bake in batches.

Just before baking, if not using a stone or tiles, place a baking sheet on the center oven rack to preheat. Cut 2 or 3 short slashes in the top of each calzone. Use a semolina-dusted peel or large spatula to transfer the calzones to the baking stone or tiles (or baking sheet), and bake for 10 minutes, or until well touched with light brown on top. Transfer to a rack to cool for 5 minutes, then serve, whole or cut in half.

NYC calzone I will always be a kid from Wyoming when I'm in New York City. It makes no difference how many times I visit, how many subway lines I manage to figure out, how many street names I memorize, or how good I am with my east and west, I will always be a wide-eyed, small-town kid, a bit overwhelmed. My neck will always be sore from looking up too much, and I'll never stop bumping into people on the sidewalks, not watching where I'm walking, looking too closely at everything else.

Then there is that matter of where to eat. New York has all the big restaurants, the names I read about in magazines, the chefs I see on television. Le Cirque and Daniel, Gramercy Tavern and Jean-Georges—they're like names of Caribbean islands in a newspaper ad in the middle of the winter. But for me they're not New York. I want a slice of pizza, a street pretzel, coffee in a paper cup. I want to look in the window of one of those long, narrow ground-floor restaurants in Greenwich Village, where a guy is throwing pizza dough and someone else is wrapping calzones and someone else is tending the oven; where there is a ballgame on the television, and people are speaking a little bit loudly. And I want to walk into the restaurant, all steamy and warm, and get a calzone on a paper plate and a Coke, and I want to sprinkle on red pepper flakes and lots of Parmesan cheese.

Yum.

Curbside pretzels, lower Manhattan, New York

middle eastern pizzas with lamb and pine nuts

Makes 10 thin round flatbreads, lightly topped with savory lamb and pine nuts; allow 2 to 3 per person

PHOTOGRAPH ON PAGE 90 *Versions of these yeasted rounds topped with savory lamb are found from Lake Van in eastern Turkey to Aleppo (in Syria) and Jerusalem. Some are small and delicate, others are thick and chewy; some have a thick tomato-based topping, others are barely flavored with a light smear of plain minced lamb. All are called* lachmanjun, *or* lachma bi ajun, *literally meaning "bread with meat" in Arabic.*

This recipe is as close as we can come to reproducing the soft breads lightly topped with aromatic minced lamb and a few pine nuts that we tasted in Aleppo some years ago. They were served rolled up around a sprig of fresh mint—a very portable lunch or savory treat at any time.

For the topping, you can buy ground lamb, but for a more interesting texture, begin with lean boneless lamb and finely chop it by hand with a cleaver (instructions for both are given below). Amounts are small, so the job goes quickly, and it results in a pleasingly uneven texture. The topping is not bound with a sauce, just flavored with a little tamarind and spices. Spread it casually over the center of the breads, and don't worry about bare patches. There's plenty of flavor, and a nice balance between the succulent lamb and the grain taste of the bread.

Serve for lunch with slices of ripe tomato, a bowl of plain yogurt, and a pile of good olives.

DOUGH

1 teaspoon active dry yeast

2 cups warm water

1 cup whole wheat flour

About 3 cups all-purpose flour

1½ teaspoons salt

1 tablespoon olive oil

FILLING

½ pound boneless lamb, trimmed of fat,
    or ½ pound lean ground lamb

1 tablespoon tamarind pulp

About 2 tablespoons hot water

1 to 2 tablespoons olive oil, or a small piece of lamb fat

1 medium yellow onion, finely chopped

4 garlic cloves, minced

¾ teaspoon salt

⅛ teaspoon cinnamon

Generous grinding of black pepper

Olive oil for brushing

2 to 3 tablespoons pine nuts

Sprigs of mint (optional)

In a large bowl, dissolve the yeast in the warm water, then stir in the whole wheat flour and 1 cup of the all-purpose flour. Stir well to make a smooth batter, then cover and let stand for at least 10 minutes, or as long as 3 hours.

Stir the salt and then the olive oil into the batter. Add the remaining flour gradually, stirring and folding it in until the dough becomes too stiff to stir. Turn out onto a lightly floured surface and knead for 6 to 8 minutes, until smooth and elastic.

Place in a lightly oiled bowl, cover, and let rise until at least doubled in bulk, 1½ to 2 hours.

Meanwhile, prepare the filling: If using a chunk of lamb, place it on a secure cutting surface and, with a sharp cleaver, chop finely and repeatedly to the texture of ground meat (this will take 3 to 5 minutes); set aside.

Place the tamarind pulp in a small bowl, add the hot water, and use your fingers to dissolve the tamarind in the water. Once it has softened, press the mixture through a sieve placed over a bowl. Discard the pulp and set the tamarind liquid aside.

Heat a large heavy skillet over high heat, then lower the heat to medium and add the oil or lamb fat. Tilt the skillet (or use a spatula) to spread the oil or melted fat. When the skillet is well oiled, add the onion and garlic and cook, stirring occasionally, until softened and starting to turn golden. Add the lamb, stirring well to break up lumps. Stir in the tamarind liquid and cook, stirring occasionally, for about 5 minutes. Stir in the salt, cinnamon, and pepper and cook for another minute. Drain off any excess liquid and set the filling aside to cool to room temperature. (The filling can be prepared a day ahead and refrigerated, covered.)

Lightly oil one or two 9- or 10-inch cast-iron or other heavy ovenproof skillets or griddles. Place a rack 4 to 6 inches below the broiler element and turn on the broiler.

Turn the dough out onto a lightly floured surface. Cut it into 10 equal pieces. Shape each into a ball. Work with 1 dough ball at a time, leaving the remaining balls covered to prevent drying. On a lightly floured surface, flatten a dough ball with the lightly floured palm of your hand, then roll it out to a thin round 8 to 9 inches in diameter.

Place an oiled skillet over medium heat and heat until hot. Place the bread in the skillet and cook for about 3½ minutes, until the bottom is firm; the top will be soft and uncooked. (Note: If the skillet is too hot, the breads will be stiff and crisp, fine to eat but a little difficult to roll up; lower the heat slightly if necessary.) Brush the top surface lightly with olive oil, then spread a generous tablespoon of the filling over the bread. Sprinkle on about 10 pine nuts, and place the skillet under the preheated broiler. Cook for about 2½ minutes, until starting to turn golden on top. Remove from the broiler. Lift the bread out of the pan and place 3 or 4 mint leaves or a whole sprig on top, if using, then roll up the bread. Wrap in a paper towel and serve hot and fresh.

Repeat with the remaining breads. As you get more comfortable with the process, you will find it easy (and quicker) to work with two skillets, rolling out a second bread once the first has started to cook.

FOLLOWING PAGES: MIDDLE EASTERN PIZZAS WITH LAMB AND PINE NUTS. *Bakery selling* lachmanjun, *Aleppo, Syria.*

hearty white bean pie

Makes one 8-inch square bread, stuffed with a savory bean filling; serves 6 to 8

The next best thing to traveling someplace where the food is great, we think, is having a friend who is a great cook and travels there, then comes home and makes all the local specialties over and over again, trying to get them mastered, and needs us to taste them all.

Our friend Dawnthebaker discovered this tender bean-filled bread, called lobiano, *while traveling in Georgia, in the Caucasus. She first learned how to make it in Raja, a town in the mountains. When she got back from her trip, she worked on it in our kitchen, trying to get it just right. In truth, each version tasted great to us.*

Lobiano is made of baking powder–raised bread dough wrapped around a filling of cooked white beans (lobio means "bean" in Georgian). Lard enriches both the dough and the beans; for a vegetarian version, substitute olive oil or butter. When you cut into the pie, the beans stay in place, so you have a dense moist tidy slice. Lobiano makes a very attractive easy lunch or supper, especially with chopped greens or herbs served alongside.

Oh, and it's also very nice when your friend lets you include her discovery in your cookbook.

DOUGH

2 to 2½ cups all-purpose flour

Generous 1 tablespoon lard or bacon drippings
   (see headnote)

1 cup lukewarm water

1 teaspoon salt

Generous ½ teaspoon baking powder

FILLING

2 cups well-drained cooked or canned navy beans
   (see Glossary)

1 tablespoon lard or bacon drippings (see headnote)

½ teaspoon salt (a little less if using bacon drippings)

½ teaspoon freshly ground black pepper, or more if you wish

Melted butter or olive oil for brushing

Place the flour in a bowl, add the lard or drippings, and cut it in with two knives or a pastry cutter to blend. Add the water, salt, and baking powder and stir to blend. Turn the dough out onto a lightly floured surface and knead until very smooth. Let rest, well covered with plastic to prevent drying out, for 30 minutes to 1 hour.

Meanwhile, stir together the filling ingredients in a bowl and set aside.

Place a rack in the upper third of the oven and preheat the oven to 375°F. Lightly grease a baking sheet.

On a floured surface, roll the dough out to a 16-by-8-inch rectangle. Spread the filling mixture over half the rectangle, leaving a ½-inch rim around the edges. Fold over the dough and seal to make a square. Transfer to the baking sheet. Brush the top of the pie with about 2 teaspoons melted butter or oil.

Bake until pale golden and firm, 20 to 25 minutes. Serve warm or at room temperature, in rectangular slices.

OPPOSITE: *Women at the main market, Tbilisi, Georgia.* FOLLOWING PAGE: *Uighur men chatting over tea and flatbreads, Kashgar oasis, Xinjiang, China.*

About taste "The nose and the mouth are connected," explains scientist Marcia Pelchat of the

Monell Chemical Senses Center in Philadelphia, where she is speaking to a small gathering of chefs and

food writers, "and this concept is critical to understanding the role of smell in flavor."

Ms. Pelchat instructs us to pinch our noses, making sure that our sense of smell is completely cut off.

Next, she gives us three jelly beans, each a different flavor. She tells us to slip them one at a time into our

mouths, chew, then try to detect the flavor of each. I taste nothing—no flavor at all. We're then told to let

go of our noses, and instantly there's a rush of flavor—coconut, strawberry, banana—flavors as big as could

be. "There are only a few tastes—sweet, sour, bitter, salty, and *umami* [the Japanese concept of a fifth taste],"

she continues. "It's odor that makes flavors different."

Then Ms. Pelchat passes a small plastic bottle around the room. When it comes to me, I open it and smell. Nothing. The person sitting next to me opens it and smells. Nothing. The next person opens, smells, and immediately cries out, "Yuck!"

"This is androstenone, a pig pheromone found in boar saliva," Ms. Pelchat explains with some obvious pleasure. "It's also found in truffles. For people who can smell it, it smells like a ripe locker room. For those who can't, there's no odor whatsoever. Many people who have an otherwise normal sense of smell can be profoundly insensitive to androstenone. This is called a specific anosmia and is thought to have a genetic basis."

Ms. Pelchat continues, making it clear that people taste in different ways. I start thinking about the tastes of travel, about the smells, and about the implications of smells genetically coded into different people in different ways. I think about western China, about Kashgar, an oasis town on the edge of the Takla Makan Desert. It's a place where I have intense memories of the food tasting extraordinarily good, especially the bread. In my mind's eye I see stacks of flatbreads topped with black onion seeds (nigella), baked in clay tandoor ovens, then dipped into bowls of hot black tea. I picture the thick, delicious handmade noodles tossed with quickly cooked tomatoes, green chiles, and red onions, and served with grilled strips of lamb seasoned with ground cumin. And I smell the scent of the famous melons of central Asia, the essence of sweet.

Food is so much a part of place, I sit there thinking—part of me in Philadelphia, part of me in Kashgar. The dry desert air surely affected how the food tasted to me in Kashgar. And the snow-covered mountains, the Pamirs, that I could see in the distance when I looked out my window each morning. And the layers of history—the fact that Marco Polo came this way, and the fact that he probably ate the same style of noodles, the same flatbreads, the same grilled lamb.

It's just like when people travel to Paris: "Oh, the food!" they say. But how much of their reaction is about the pleasure of being in Paris, and how much due to the food itself? Who we are, and how and where we eat, has a huge impact on how food tastes to us.

Me? I like Philadelphia, and Ms. Pelchat is great, but I'd sure like to be in Kashgar. I can smell the lamb grilling, the fragrance of the melons, the breads fresh from the oven. . . .

golden mixed-greens pies

Makes 2 large, oval, tender-crusted, golden brown covered pies, filled with cooked greens or greens and sweet potato; each serves 6 to 8

PHOTOGRAPH ON PAGE 98 *This pretty free-form pie is an example of improvising to make something useful out of a mistake. We were trying to make a brioche dough for sticky buns but accidentally added too much flour. There we were with a yeasted dough that we didn't want to throw away. That was the starting point for this pie, a kind of Russian-style pirog. The crust is an egg-rich dough softened with a little butter and slightly sweet; the filling can be mixed greens or greens and sweet potato—we give both options below. Make it ahead, then serve it warm or at room temperature; we (especially Naomi) like eating cold leftovers the next day.*

The dough recipe is a large one, making enough for two big pies. But it freezes well, so we usually use half right away for one pie, and freeze the other for later.

DOUGH (ENOUGH FOR 2 PIES)

2 teaspoons active dry yeast

¼ cup warm milk

1½ to 2 cups all-purpose flour

4 extra-large eggs

¼ cup sugar

1½ teaspoons salt

2 tablespoons unsalted butter, softened

1 cup pastry or cake flour

ONIONY GREENS FILLING (FOR 1 PIE)

½ pound dandelion greens (1 large bunch)
  or other bitter greens, such as endive

1½ pounds spinach (2 large bunches),

1 tablespoon bacon grease, butter, or olive oil

2 garlic cloves, sliced

¼ to ⅓ cup chopped scallions (white and most
  of the green parts of 2 large or 4 small)

About 1½ teaspoons salt

GREENS AND SWEET POTATO FILLING
(FOR 1 PIE)

1 pound sweet potatoes, peeled and cut into 1-inch chunks
  (about 3 cups)

½ pound dandelion greens, or 1 pound spinach

1 tablespoon bacon grease, butter, or olive oil

3 garlic cloves, minced

About 1½ teaspoons salt

Generous grinding of black pepper

About 2 tablespoons unsalted butter, melted, per pie

To make the dough, dissolve the yeast in the lukewarm milk and stir in ¼ cup of the flour.

By hand: Break the eggs into a large bowl and whisk briefly to blend them. Add the yeast mixture and the remaining 1¼ cups all-purpose flour and stir with a wooden spoon until very smooth. Add the sugar, salt, and butter and mix well. Add the pastry flour ½ cup at a time, mixing well. Turn the dough out onto a lightly floured surface and knead for 10 minutes, or until it is smooth and firm, incorporating additional all-purpose flour only as necesssary.

Using a stand mixer: Break the eggs into the bowl of the mixer. Using the whisk attachment, whisk the eggs briefly to blend them. Change to the dough hook. Add the yeast mixture and the remaining 1¼ cups all-purpose flour and mix on low speed until very smooth. Add the sugar, salt, and butter and mix well. Add the pastry flour and knead on low speed for 5 minutes, or until smooth and firm.

Transfer the dough to a clean bowl, cover well with plastic, and let rise in a cool place for 2 hours, or until doubled.

Meanwhile, prepare the filling (or fillings).

For the oniony greens filling: Thoroughly wash the greens and spinach, then chop them into 1-inch lengths, discarding any thick stems; set aside. Heat the bacon grease, butter, or oil in a large heavy skillet or wok over medium heat. Add the garlic and scallions and cook for about 1 minute, until the scallions begin to soften. Raise the heat to high, add the chopped greens and salt, and cook, stirring constantly, until they start to wilt. Cover, lower the heat slightly, and let steam for about 1 minute. Turn out the greens onto a platter to cool to room temperature. Taste for salt, and set aside.

For the greens and sweet potato filling: Place the sweet potatoes in a pot with about 1 inch of cold water and bring to a boil, then cover and simmer over medium-low heat until just tender. Drain and set aside.

Thoroughly wash the greens, then chop them into about 1-inch lengths, discarding any thick stems. Heat the grease, butter, or oil in a large heavy skillet or wok over medium heat. When it is hot, add the garlic and sauté briefly, then toss in the greens and salt, raise the heat, and cook, stirring constantly, until the greens start to wilt. Cover, lower the heat slightly, and steam for about another minute. Transfer to a platter to cool to room temperature, then toss with the sweet potatoes and black pepper. Taste for salt and set aside.

Place a rack in the center of the oven and preheat the oven to 450°F. Lightly grease a baking sheet (or two, if making two pies) with butter or bacon grease.

Turn the dough out onto a lightly floured surface and cut in half. (If not making two pies now, place half the dough in a plastic bag and refrigerate for up to 24 hours before using, or freeze for up to a month. Thaw overnight in the refrigerator and bring back to room temperature before continuing.)

For each pie, cut the dough into 2 slightly unequal pieces: The larger one will be the bottom crust. Press the cut edge of the larger piece in flour, then flatten it on a lightly floured surface into an oval. Use a rolling pin to roll the dough out into an oval about 16 inches long and 10 inches wide. The dough may spring back a little—if it does, start flattening the smaller piece of dough in the same way, moving from one to the other to give the dough time to relax so you can stretch it farther. Roll the smaller piece of dough into an oval about 15 inches long and 8 inches wide.

Place the larger piece of dough on the prepared baking sheet. Mound the filling on it, leaving a generous 1-inch rim all around uncovered. Place the top over the filling, and pull down on the sides if necessary to stretch it over. Fold the edges of the bottom dough up over the edges of the top to seal in the filling, then twist it, making a twisted rolled edge all around to seal. Use a sharp knife to make about 10 slits in the top crust. Brush with the melted butter.

Bake the pie for 8 minutes, then lower the heat to 400°F and bake for another 8 to 10 minutes (if making two pies, bake one at a time). The pie will be a deep, rich golden brown.

Transfer the pie to a wire rack to cool for 20 minutes.

Serve warm or, our preference, at room temperature. Because the pie is an oval, the easiest way to serve it is in slices cut right across the pie.

FOLLOWING PAGES: GOLDEN MIXED-GREENS PIE. HIMALAYAN STEAMED DUMPLINGS *(page 100)*.

himalayan steamed dumplings

Makes 24 beef-filled dumplings; serves 4 to 6

PHOTOGRAPH ON PAGE 99 *These dumplings, called* momos, *are Tibetan in origin, but they're also made by the Thakalis and Sherpas who live on the Nepal side of the Himalayas (see page 50). They resemble the steamed pork-filled dumplings you find in China (jiao-zi). They're generally made with yak meat. If, like us, you don't have easy access to yak, this beef version is just about as good.*

It may not be traditional, but we take the easy, high-tech route for making momos: a food processor for both the filling and the dough.

FILLING

1 pound lean beef, such as round steak,
    cut into 3 or 4 pieces

2 medium onions (½ pound), quartered

2 large garlic cloves, halved

A 1-inch piece of ginger, peeled and roughly sliced

1 teaspoon salt

2 tablespoons soy sauce

WRAPPERS

4 cups unbleached all-purpose flour

About 2 cups warm water

Peanut or vegetable oil for coating

To make the filling, put the beef, onions, garlic, ginger, salt, and soy sauce in a food processor and process to a paste. Transfer the filling to a bowl, cover with plastic wrap, and refrigerate until ready to assemble the dumplings. (The filling can be made up to 24 hours ahead.)

To make the dough, wash and dry the food processor bowl. Place the flour in the processor and put the lid on. With the processor on, gradually add the water until a dough begins to form. Depending upon your flour, the dough may need the full 2 cups of water, or as little as 1¾ cups. Once there is a ball of dough spinning around inside the processor, turn it off.

Turn the dough out onto a lightly floured surface and knead briefly, just to get a feel for the dough. It should be fairly stiff, not too sticky; knead in a little flour if necessary. Set the dough aside, covered with plastic wrap, for at least 30 minutes, or up to 8 hours at room temperature; if longer, the dough should be refrigerated (for up to 2 days, then brought back to room temperature before using).

When ready to assemble the dumplings, prepare the steamer: Use peanut or vegetable oil to lightly oil one large or two smaller bamboo steamer baskets (or use another steaming device that fits over a pot of boiling water).

Cut the dough into 3 equal pieces, then cut each piece into 8 equal pieces. Work with 1 piece at a time, keeping the remaining pieces covered with plastic. On a lightly floured surface, flatten the dough into a disk. With a rolling pin, roll it out until it is approximately 4 inches in diameter. Place 1 level tablespoon of the filling in the middle of the dough, then pick up the edges in several places, gather them together over the filling, and twist and squeeze to seal the top, making a kind of topknot. Place in a steamer basket topknot side up, and continue to form the other dumplings.

Fill a wok or pot with about 3 inches of hot water (or to come just below the steamer basket), place on a burner, and place a steamer basket over the water; the water should not touch the dumplings. Cover the steamer, bring the water to a boil, and steam the dumplings for 10 to 12 minutes, until the filling and wrappers are cooked through. Serve hot.

The dumplings can be served with a small bowl of soy sauce for dipping (or soy sauce mixed with a little rice vinegar), but they are also good simply on their own.

NOTE We've given instructions for rolling out momos as it's traditionally done, one by one. When the crew was baking for the photo shoot, they used a more streamlined approach: After dividing the dough in thirds, they rolled out each sheet and then cut out 4-inch rounds of dough with a pastry cutter, rerolling the scraps to get all 24 rounds.

Reading prayers, near Samye, Tsangpo Valley, Tibet

leekie pie

Makes 1 double-crusted pie with a lush leek filling; serves 6

I will always have fond memories of the cookbooks that I first cooked my way through, front to back. One of those I especially loved was Anna Thomas's Vegetarian Epicure. *There were actually two volumes, and they came at a time in the 1970s when good creative vegetarian cooking was just starting to take off. Several of the dishes I remember best from the book were the kinds of savory baked pies and casseroles that were very popular then. They were great for potlucks, for cold winter days, for dinners where there were old and young people alike. But as foods do, just like so many other things in life, savory pies and casseroles went out of fashion.*

Now it's time to bring them back, and leekie pie is a good place to start. It's filled with cooked chopped leeks flavored with bacon and black pepper, then made rich with the addition of a seasoned custard. It could easily have come from French peasant tradition, perhaps from Normandy, but it is actually an old English recipe. It has a very traditional country taste and holds together beautifully; the pastry is easy to work with and tender. The pie makes a great appetizer or an irresistible centerpiece for a hearty lunch or supper.

DOUGH

2 cups cake or pastry flour, or 1¾ cups all-purpose flour

8 tablespoons (1 stick) unsalted butter, chilled

¼ teaspoon salt (or just a pinch if using salted butter)

About ½ cup light cream, chilled

FILLING

1 to 2 tablespoons unsalted butter

About 5 cups finely chopped leeks, white and pale green
 parts only, well washed (see Note)

1 cup water

Freshly ground black pepper

2 slices bacon, cut into small pieces

1 large egg

Scant ¼ cup milk

¼ teaspoon salt

Pinch of freshly grated nutmeg

Make the pastry 2 hours, or as long as 3 days, before you bake the pie.

By hand: Place the flour in a medium bowl. Using the large holes of a box grater, grate in the chilled butter. Using a pastry cutter or two knives, or your fingertips, blend the butter into the flour. Add the salt. Add the cream and give a brief stir just to ensure all the flour is moistened, then gather the dough together with your hands.

Using a food processor: Coarsely chop the butter. Put the flour, salt, and butter in the processor and process to the consistency of a coarse meal. With the machine running, add the cream, processing just until the dough forms a ball. Turn the dough out and gather it together with your hands.

Place the dough in a heavy plastic bag, press it into a disk about 6 inches across, and refrigerate for at least 30 minutes. (The dough can be refrigerated for up to 3 days.)

An hour and a half or so before you wish to serve the pie, heat a large heavy skillet over medium-high heat. Add the butter; when it begins to sizzle, add the chopped leeks and stir well to coat with butter. Add the water and bring to a boil. Let simmer, uncovered, for about 5 minutes, or until the leeks are softened but not completely cooked. Grind pepper over generously, add the bacon, and set aside to cool to lukewarm.

Meanwhile, place a rack in the lower third of the oven and preheat the oven to 400°F. Lightly butter an 8-inch pie plate, or an 8-inch square baking pan.

Turn the pastry out onto a lightly floured surface, and cut it in two, one piece slightly larger than the other. Roll the larger piece out to a 10-inch round or 9-inch square and line the pie plate or dish with the dough. Place the filling in the pie shell, mounding it a little in the center. Roll out the second piece of dough in the same way, to a slightly smaller round or square, and place it over the leeks; seal the edges well by pinching or crimping, and trim off any excess dough. Cut a 1½-inch square hole in the center of the top.

Bake the pie for 40 to 45 minutes, or until it is browning well. In a medium bowl, whisk together the egg and milk, then stir in the salt and nutmeg. Remove the pie from the oven and pour the egg mixture into the hole. You may have to spoon it in a little at a time and allow a moment for the liquid to seep into the filling before adding more, and it may not all quite fit—stop when you can add no more.

Place the pie back in the oven and bake until the custard is set, 10 to 15 minutes. Let stand on a rack for at least 10 minutes before serving. Serve hot or at room temperature.

NOTE You'll need to start with about 2 pounds (4 to 5 medium-large) of leeks. To trim, cut off the coarsest green leaves as well as the root end.

alsatian onion tart

Makes 1 square, open-faced savory tart with a flaky puffed crust, topped with slow-cooked onions flavored with a little bacon; serves 4 to 6

In the 1880s, my great-grandfather traveled from England to Alsace to work as a designer for Zuber et Fils, a manufacturer of wallpaper. He ended up marrying the boss's daughter, but they divorced before the First World War, somewhat scandalously. Luckily, my mother's third cousin, Paul-René Zuber, who was born around 1900 and lived in Alsace, had a great sense of family, and though we were related only distantly, he kept in touch with us.

The house he and his wife, Christiane, lived in after his retirement was a rambling, magical place in Mulhouse, full of books and creaking corridors and surrounded by a large garden. Paul-René and Christiane lived well into their nineties—intelligent, curious, alert. They were remarkable readers, and very creative people. But their weak point was food—neither one liked to cook or paid much attention to what they ate. Jokel, their wonderful German son-in-law, once said plaintively, "Imagine, I married into the only household in France where people don't care about food."

Jokel cared, and whenever he came to Alsace for a visit, he cooked for a crowd. This delicious onion tart makes me think of those special family meals. Serve it on its own or with fresh tomatoes or a green salad.

½ recipe (¾ pound) Rough Puff (page 46), or
¾ pound store-bought all-butter puff pastry
4 slices (slightly less than ¼ pound) bacon, finely chopped
4 medium-to-large yellow onions, finely chopped (4 cups)
2 tablespoons heavy cream
About ¼ teaspoon salt
Several grindings of black pepper

On a lightly floured surface, roll out the pastry to a square slightly larger than 9 inches across or an 8-by-10-inch rectangle: Take care to roll from the center out and to roll just to the edges of the pastry, not over them. Place the rolled-out pastry on a small nonstick baking sheet, cover loosely with plastic wrap, and refrigerate.

Cook the bacon in a large skillet over medium-low heat until it renders its fat, about 10 minutes. Add the onions and cook over medium heat, stirring frequently, until well softened and lightly golden, 20 to 30 minutes. Remove from the heat and let stand for 5 minutes, then stir in the cream and season to taste. Let cool to room temperature.

Meanwhile, place a baking stone or unglazed quarry tiles, if you have them, on a rack in the lower third of the oven and preheat the oven to 450°F. Once the oven has reached full temperature, if not using a stone or tiles, place a large baking sheet on the rack. Preheat the sheet, or continue to heat the stone or tiles, for 10 minutes.

With a very sharp knife trim the edges of the pastry to make a clean edge (reserve the trimmings for another purpose; see page 47). Prick the dough all over with a fork, leaving a ¼- to ½-inch unpricked margin all around the edges. Spoon the cooled onion mixture onto the pricked area of the pastry, first mounding it in the center, then spreading it toward the sides.

Bake for 5 minutes, then lower the oven temperature to 425°F. Bake for 10 more minutes, or until the pastry rim is golden brown. (As the pastry bakes, the edges will puff up, framing the filling; who needs a tart pan?) Let stand for 5 minutes before serving.

Transfer the tart to a flat plate. Cut into slices and serve warm.

NOTE To reheat, place the tart on a baking sheet in the center of a preheated 300°F oven until it is warmed through, about 8 minutes.

Farm buildings near Malaucène, northern Provence, France

savory mushroom strudel

Makes 1 strudel, about 12 inches long and 5 inches wide, filled with a tarragon-flavored mushroom sauce; serves 6

This yeasted dough made with flour and cooked potato is more fragile and softer than classic strudel dough, and more tender when baked. We like it for savory strudel, wrapped around mushroom duxelles flavored with tarragon or dill and enriched with sour cream—a very eastern European combination.

This recipe is enough for two doughs. You can make two strudels and freeze one, or use the second half of the dough to make a simple fruit tart (see the variation).

DOUGH (FOR 2 STRUDELS)

1 tablespoon active dry yeast

¼ cup lukewarm water

About 1½ cups chopped boiled potatoes,
   at room temperature

About 2¼ cups all-purpose flour

2 tablespoons unsalted butter, softened

½ teaspoon salt

FILLING (FOR 1 STRUDEL)

About 1½ pounds mushrooms, such as portobellos or
   button mushrooms, cleaned and trimmed

2 tablespoons unsalted butter

¼ cup minced shallots

About 2 tablespoons dry red wine

½ teaspoon salt

1 tablespoon all-purpose flour

2 tablespoons sour cream (full-fat)

2 tablespoons minced fresh tarragon or dill

About 8 tablespoons (1 stick) unsalted butter, melted

About 1 cup fresh bread crumbs (see page 333)

In a small cup, dissolve the yeast in the water. Place the potatoes in a food processor and process until smooth. Add the flour, butter, and salt and process to the consistency of a coarse moist meal, pulsing if necessary to process the ingredients evenly. Stir the yeast mixture, then, with the processor running, pour it in and process until a ball forms. Process for about 20 seconds longer, then turn the dough out onto a lightly floured surface and knead for several minutes, until very smooth.

Place the dough in a clean bowl, cover with plastic, and set aside in a warm place to rise for 1 hour, or until nearly doubled.

Meanwhile, prepare the filling: Place one half the mushrooms (about 3 loosely packed cups) in the food processor and pulse just until finely chopped; you do not want a paste. Empty into a bowl and repeat with the remaining mushrooms. Set aside.

Melt the butter in a large heavy skillet over medium heat. Add the shallots and cook until translucent and softened, about 5 minutes. Add the mushrooms and cook, stirring frequently, until they release their liquid, about 5 minutes. Raise the heat and stir vigorously for 30 seconds. Add the wine and salt and cook for another 15 seconds at high heat, then lower the heat to medium.

Sift the flour over the mushrooms, stir in, and cook for 2 minutes. Remove from the heat. Add the sour cream and stir in, then stir in the tarragon or dill. Transfer to a bowl to cool to room temperature; drain off any excess liquid before using.

Place a rack in the center of the oven and preheat the oven to 350°F. Line a baking sheet with parchment paper or lightly grease it with butter.

Turn the dough out onto a lightly floured surface and cut it in half. Wrap one half in plastic and refrigerate for use within 24 hours, or freeze for up to 1 month. (Thaw overnight and bring to room temperature before using.)

Flatten the remaining dough with your hands, then use a rolling pin to roll out to a large circle or oval. Place a tablecloth on your work surface and rub it with flour. Place the dough on the cloth, then pick up one side, lay it over the backs of your hands, and pull your hands apart gently to stretch it. The dough is soft and a little fragile, so it may tear—don't worry if it does, just pinch the edges together to seal. Repeat, stretching all around the dough following the method described on pages 62–63 until you have a rectangle a little larger than 16 inches by 24 inches. Be patient; it *will* stretch.

Use scissors or a sharp knife to trim off the thicker edges all around the dough; discard. Rotate the dough if necessary so one 16-inch side is nearest you. Brush the dough generously with melted butter. Sprinkle the bread crumbs over the dough, leaving about a ½-inch border clear all round.

Mound the mushroom filling in a long log across the dough about 5 inches from the edge closest to you, making a mound about 4 inches wide and leaving a 1-inch strip clear at each end of the log. Fold the bottom edge of the dough up over the filling, then fold over the sides and roll the strudel away from you.

Gently lift the strudel onto the prepared baking sheet seam side down. Brush lightly with butter. Bake for about 30 minutes, brushing again with butter after 10 minutes. The strudel will be pale golden when done.

Transfer the strudel to a platter and let stand for 10 minutes before serving. Serve in thick slices, accompanied by wilted winter greens or braised root vegetables.

QUICK STONE-FRUIT TART We like to use the other half of the strudel dough to make a quick open-faced fruit tart, baking it in the 350°F oven after the strudel comes out. Butter a 7- or 8-inch round or square cake pan. Flatten the dough into it, pressing with your fingertips to flatten the center and leave the edges puffy. Brush all over (including the crust edges) with melted butter. Sprinkle several tablespoons of bread crumbs or finely chopped nuts over the bottom, then sprinkle with several tablespoons sugar. Chop 3 or 4 sweet ripe nectarines or peeled peaches or about 6 apricots and heap onto the center of the tart, along with a handful of blueberries, if you have them. Sprinkle on more sugar, 2 tablespoons or more, and dot with butter. Let stand, loosely covered, for 20 minutes, then bake for about 30 minutes. Just before the tart comes out, brush the edges of the crust with a little melted butter and sprinkle on a little more sugar. When done, the crust will be coming away from the edges and will be touched with light brown.

TWO | BREAD

Festive Breads

Family Breads

Artisan–Style Loaves

BREAD IS A PERSONAL THING, AND SO IS BREAD MAKING. We are more than a little bit bread-obsessed, the two of us, and we probably lost any sense of perspective on the subject a long time ago. We have a very liberal interpretation of what makes bread. It can be flat like a tortilla, fried like a crepe, crusty like a huge hearth loaf, sweet and soft like challah, crisp like a cracker, even baked in the sand (as bread is sometimes in North Africa). Bread can be made with wheat, rye, barley, corn, sorghum, millet, chickpea flour, even bean sprouts. Bread is food we love, the food we bite into day after day, year after year, the food we never get tired of—because it is bread. Bread is one of those special foods: Whenever it's not there, something important is missing.

We've divided the huge world of breads into two sections. In this first one are sweet loaves, pan-baked breads, and artisan-style hearth loaves. In the next section, Smaller Breads, you'll find flatbreads, crackers, and rolls, as well as skillet breads and pancakes.

Here in North America, the bread that we can buy is getting better and better by leaps and bounds. Artisan bakeries, and artisan-style breads (inspired by some of the great time-honored European bread-making traditions) are available as never before. But sometimes people, in commenting about bread in North America, go so far as to say that these are the first good breads ever made in North America ("a region without a true bread tradition"). It's simply not true. We have a rich heritage of bread making, from Native American flatbreads to the home and family bread making of pioneers and farm cooks to a 1970s-inspired focus on whole grain breads and organic flours.

We feel passionately that bread is too big a subject, and too personal, to make "good bread" something narrowly defined. Good bread does not need a professional baker or a professional oven. And the process of bread making can be as rewarding as the bread itself.

This section opens with a chapter of sweet loaves and breads made for special occasions. Many of these

Festive Breads are made with a yeasted dough that is flavored with fruit or nuts and sweetened with sugar. Others are leavened with baking powder—breads to make quickly, without kneading, without rising time.

The second chapter, Family Breads, has recipes for breads that are straightforward to make, breads that our grandmothers might have made in farmhouse kitchens. These are usually baked in bread pans, and are ideal for slicing, toasting, and sandwiches.

The third chapter in this section is a collection of recipes for artisan-style breads. Most come from European peasant traditions, from places where there's a home-baking or community-baking tradition using wood-fired ovens with stone hearths. With some ingenuity, using a modern home oven and a baking stone, we can reproduce most of the characteristics of artisanal breads, their good flavors and their distinctive crusts.

Technique

After years of working with yeasted doughs, of making flatbreads, pan loaves, and hearth breads, we've settled into some basic approaches. First, we like the flavor and texture we get when we make slow-rise breads: That is, we cut back on the amount of yeast, we let the dough rise at cool temperatures, and we give it longer periods of fermentation (rising or resting) than many recipes do. The extra time gives the yeasts and bacteria in the dough time to develop, and it's that development, or fermentation, that gives bread good flavor.

With slow-rise doughs, timing is more flexible, which is always an asset in home baking. Most often we'll let a bread rise overnight; we don't spend time thinking about it as it's doing the work of gaining flavor. Then we come back to it when it's convenient for us. Fit bread around your schedule, not yours around it. And make a big batch of bread and freeze some, because bread freezes extremely well.

One basic rule of thumb: Measure the liquid you are using, then add 1 teaspoon salt for every cup of liquid (water, milk, yogurt, etc.). With experience, you can do the rest by eye. You can play with the proportions of white and whole wheat flours, or add a few raisins or a little of another nonwheat flour such as rye or buckwheat to vary the taste and texture. Bread is flexible. Flour measurements are a little imprecise, both because flours vary and because bread can be made from a wet dough or a stiffer dry dough. It's a matter of preference, habit, taste.

To test if bread has risen enough, use the "poke test": Press a moistened finger briefly into the dough. If the dent stays dented it's ready. This test is especially useful when you're trying to determine if shaped breads or rolls are ready to be put in the oven.

To test if a loaf has baked enough, tap on the bottom of the loaf to see if it sounds hollow, and then use the "pinch test": Pinch the loaf at the corners or at the bottom edge. It should feel firm, not soft. If it still feels soft, place it back in the oven for another five or ten minutes. When baking pan loaves, take them out of the pans to test them. If you need to bake them a little longer and you have a baking stone or unglazed quarry tiles in your oven, bake them straight on the hot surface, rather than putting them back in the pans.

Language

Here's a quick introduction to some terms you'll see in the recipes.

The word **ferment** is sometimes used to describe the process happening in the dough while it is rising for the first time, after being kneaded. During that time, yeasts and bacteria are growing in the dough (hence the term **fermentation**), giving it flavor and life. Generally, if fermentation happens at relatively low temperatures (between 60° and 65°F), the dough will have a better flavor, and it will also take longer to rise. We use the word **proof** when talking about the time the bread dough spends after it's shaped into loaves, and before it is baked. The word comes from an older time, when yeasts were not as reliable

as they are now, and it was necessary to make sure ("prove") the dough had enough leavening to rise well during baking.

Many of these bread recipes begin with some kind of **starter dough,** or batter, that is then incorporated into the bread dough. These do add to the elapsed time—that is, the amount of time from when you first think you'll make a bread until the moment you finally take it out of the oven—but they don't add extra work time. And, most important, they give you better flavor and texture for the same amount of effort.

Here are the terms used for those starter doughs: We often use the **sponge** method of mixing doughs, especially when we have a whole wheat flour dough. It gives the flour time to fully absorb the liquid and the dough a chance to develop some flavor. The sponge method involves starting to make a dough, with yeast and water and some of the flour, then setting it aside for a while before proceeding to add salt and the remaining flour.

To get the good flavor that comes from slow fermentation we often use a **poolish.** The poolish (sometimes translated as "sponge," but actually it is a different thing) has the texture of a batter and is made of equal volumes of water and flour, leavened with just a little yeast. The poolish sits fermenting for twelve hours or longer, then becomes an ingredient in the dough. Like an Italian biga or an old white dough (see page 112), a poolish is used to give extra flavor, but it's a little quicker to make because it's just stirred together rather than kneaded. We like the flexibility it gives and the improved flavor and texture.

A **biga** (the Italian name) is a starter dough made of yeast, water, and flour, mixed and briefly kneaded, then left to ferment for eight to twenty-four hours, or longer if it's more convenient (it can be stored well sealed in plastic in the refrigerator for several days). Then it is cut into pieces and added when you start making the bread dough. The bread recipe will call for yeast, flour, water, salt, and biga; the biga is used mainly to give extra flavor, not for its leavening power.

Beirut, Lebanon

An **old dough**, also called old white dough, is like a biga, used to add flavor. Like a biga, it's a kneaded, lightly yeasted dough that's left to ferment and then used as the basis of a larger batch of dough. The only difference is that the old dough has some salt in it. The old dough method is a holdover from the days when home bakers would hold back some dough from a previous batch of bread to serve as the starter for the next batch. These days, an old dough is added to a yeasted liquid to give flavor and some leavening.

In just one recipe (Smooth Onion Rye, page 208) we use a **rye sour,** another kind of flavor-giving starter dough that is widely used in traditional European rye breads. It's made of rye flour stirred into a batter and left to ferment for a short time. Like the other starter doughs, it's there mostly for flavor, though it also contributes to the leavening of the bread.

All these methods improve the taste and texture of the bread. And they start to feel like shortcuts to good bread: If you have a poolish or biga or old dough that is eight hours old or more (probably stored in your refrigerator), you can use it to produce good bread very quickly, bread that will have the flavor of a slow-rise loaf. But none of these methods requires keeping a starter and feeding it regularly—all of them start from flour and water and a little yeast whenever you want.

That's why we like them, because they require less attention, and you can be more impromptu in your approach to bread making. And that's how we see slow-rise and starter-dough techniques: as an easy way to get good-quality bread in a free-floating, unscheduled home kitchen.

Temperatures

Lukewarm water or milk is about 100°F; it feels just warm to the touch. Most bread recipes that use yeast call for the dry yeast to be sprinkled onto a lukewarm liquid; the temperature must not be so hot (over 115°F) that it kills the yeast, but if it's lukewarm, it will help the yeast become active quickly. **A warm place** for proofing loaves means a temperature between 70° and 75°F, with no cold drafts. This warmth encourages yeast activity and also makes the carbon dioxide in the dough expand (so the bread rises). **A cool place for an overnight rise** will help a yeasted dough ferment slowly. Bread doughs ferment and develop good flavor at relatively low temperatures. Any temperature from 54° to 65°F will produce a long slow rise, so a cool spot near a window, or in a wine cellar, is an ideal place for a bread dough to do an overnight or other long rise. We sometimes put a bread dough in the crisper drawer of the refrigerator to slow its overnight rise. We don't keep our refrigerator very cold, so this works well; the dough rises a little, but it still needs to come to room temperature and finish its rise before it is shaped.

BAKING TEMPERATURES Hearth breads and flatbreads are often baked at higher temperatures than pan loaves, 450° to 550°F. In wood-fired bakers' ovens, the temperatures can reach 750°F. At higher temperatures, bread bakes more quickly, of course, and it has a thinner, crackly crisp crust. Pan loaves are baked at lower temperatures than hearth loaves because the metal pan conducts and holds heat; high temperatures mean the sides and bottom of the loaves might scorch before the center of the loaf is baked. Because rye loaves are often denser in texture than wheat flour loaves, they must be baked at a lower temperature.

Every time the door of a preheated kitchen oven is opened, the oven loses heat. For this reason, if you will be baking a number of loaves at a time, preheat the oven to twenty-five to fifty degrees hotter than you need for baking the bread. Once you've got all the breads in the oven, reduce the temperature to the level you want; you may find the oven has dropped even lower, but probably not by much.

Basic tools

Making bread is most fun when you have a few basic tools you like. You may want to use a **heavy-duty stand mixer** fitted with a **dough hook** for kneading. Even so, you'll still want the equipment you'd need for making a dough by hand:

A large heavy bowl (or two or three bowls), preferably a glazed ceramic bowl that feels good and doesn't lose heat quickly

A large wooden spoon, for stirring wet doughs

A dough scraper (see the photograph on page 71), for keeping the work surface clean (use the dull edge of a long straight knife as a substitute)

Shaping and baking breads requires a few more tools, most of them useful for other kinds of baking too:

A BAKING STONE or **A COLLECTION OF UNGLAZED QUARRY TILES** These are used as a baking surface in your oven. Try to find a large rectangular stone, so that you have as large a baking surface as possible. Or look for unglazed quarry tiles, which are inexpensive, in any tile store. The stone or tiles go on an oven rack in your oven and there must be a 1-inch or wider gap between the sides of the stone or tiles and the oven wall, to allow air to circulate.

Baking stones and tiles serve two purposes: Breads baked directly on them, whether hearth loaves or flatbreads, develop a great bottom crust, like the crust from a baker's oven. And, almost as important, they help hold the oven's heat. Every time you open the oven door, the oven temperature drops, but with a stone or tiles, it stays more even. The stone also protects the bottom of a loaf pan from the direct heat of the oven's bottom heating element, evening it out. We use our baking stone for all our baking, placing cookie sheets or tart or cake pans right on it.

A SHARP FINE KNIFE or **SINGLE-EDGED RAZOR BLADE** Cutting slashes in the top of loaves and rolls gives the bread more room for expansion as it rises in the oven's heat. Hold the knife or blade at a 45-degree angle to the top of the dough when you slash (see the photograph on page 149).

BREAD PANS The most versatile pans for baking standard loaves, as well as some sweet loaves and some rolls, are standard 9-by-5-inch pans. Slightly smaller bread pans, 8 inches by 4 inches, are useful for some of the sweet loaves.

For many of the artisanal breads, you'll also want the following:

A PEEL This traditional baker's tool is used to transfer hearth loaves into a hot oven. A peel looks like a flat wooden tray with a handle (the word comes from the French word *pele,* meaning "shovel"). Peels are available at specialty stores. You can also improvise by using the back of a baking sheet. To use a peel, slide the bread onto the floured peel or flip it over onto the surface, depending on the recipe. Open the oven door, place the peel on the hot stone or unglazed quarry tiles, and then pull it back with a quick jerk, leaving the bread on the stone or tiles. It sounds tricky, but it isn't difficult. If your first try yields a slightly lopsided loaf, it doesn't matter, for the bread will still be good—and you'll have embarked on making hearth breads at home.

ROUND BOWLS OR BASKETS Many of our artisanal breads are shaped into boules (rounds), and proofed using an improvised home version of a bakery technique: Each shaped loaf is placed upside down in a 7- to 9-inch shallow **wooden bowl** lined with a **cotton cloth** (such as a tea towel) that has been well dusted and rubbed with flour. The bowl helps the bread hold its shape while rising, and the flour-dusted cloth keeps it from sticking to the bowl. (The original bakery technique uses flour-dusted *bannetons,* wicker baskets, to hold boules or long loaves as they rise, and flour-dusted *couches,* heavy cotton cloths, to hold baguette-shaped loaves.)

A SMALL WATER SPRAYER This is an easy way of getting moisture onto loaves as they start baking. We often call for spritzing the breads with water several times in the first minutes of baking. The moisture helps create a good crust; before the crust sets, it also helps keep it soft so the bread can expand without cracking.

LEFT TO RIGHT: *Ripening grain, Brittany, France; grain elevator at dusk, Saskatchewan, Canada.*

FESTIVE BREADS

challah

Makes 3 large golden brown, tender, braided loaves or 12 minichallahs, or 18 onion rolls, or a combination

Challah is a bread of celebration. The word challah *comes from the Hebrew word for "portion" used in the commandment in the Bible to give a portion of the dough as an offering to God. (In observant households, a pinch of dough is tossed into the back of the oven with a prayer, to be burned as an offering before the loaves are baked.) Over time, this word for portion, a reminder of religious obligations, became the word for the bread traditionally eaten by the Jews of central and eastern Europe at the Sabbath meal. (The Hebrew word for regular bread is* lechem.*) At some time in the Middle Ages, a Sunday loaf from southern Germany was adopted by the Jewish community as the Sabbath bread. As Jews from Germany moved into Poland, Russia, Hungary, and other parts of Europe, so did challah, and it then was brought to North America by Jewish immigrants from central and eastern Europe.*

Challah is rich with eggs and is made with oil rather than butter, so it is pareve *(it can be served at either a meat or a dairy meal). It is light and airy and makes great toast. Because this is a slow-rise recipe, the bread keeps much better than most store-bought versions; for longer keeping, freeze the bread, then cut off slices for toast directly from the frozen loaf.*

Most challah recipes are very similar. The variations have to do with the amount of oil used and how much the dough is sweetened. This recipe is for a slightly sweet bread. Challah is traditionally shaped as a braided loaf, but the dough also makes wonderful twists, like mini-challah braids, and onion rolls. Instructions for all three are given below.

2 teaspoons active dry yeast

2½ cups lukewarm water

5½ to 7 cups all-purpose flour

3 extra-large eggs

½ cup sugar

1 tablespoon salt

⅓ to ½ cup sunflower or other mild vegetable oil

TOPPING

1 egg, beaten with 1 teaspoon water, for egg wash

About ¼ cup poppy seeds (optional)

In a large bowl, or the bowl of a stand mixer, stir the yeast into the warm water to dissolve it. Stir in 2 cups of the flour to make a smooth batter. Cover and let rest for 2 hours.

When ready to proceed, make the dough.

By hand: Stir the eggs, sugar, salt, and oil into the sponge, then stir in 2½ cups flour, a cup at a time, until smooth. Sprinkle on another ½ cup flour and fold the dough several times, then sprinkle flour generously on your work surface and turn the dough out. Knead, incorporating additional flour as necessary to prevent stickiness, until it is very smooth, about 10 minutes.

Using a stand mixer: Fit the mixer with the dough hook. Add the eggs and oil to the sponge and mix briefly. Sprinkle on the salt, add the sugar and 3½ to 4 cups flour, and mix at low speed for 30 seconds. Increase the speed to medium low and mix for 2½ to 3 minutes, until the dough is smooth and soft and a little sticky.

Turn out onto a lightly floured surface and knead briefly.

Place the dough in a large oiled bowl, cover well with plastic, and let rise until more than doubled in volume, about 6 hours—or overnight if more convenient.

Pull the dough gently together and turn it out onto a lightly floured surface. Cut it into 3 equal pieces (each will weigh about ⅓ pound).

Divide 1 piece of dough into 3. Roll these 3 pieces of dough out under your palms to strands about 20 inches long—try to have the middle section of each strand a little fatter and both ends tapering. Lay the 3 strands so they cross one another at the middle on a slight diagonal; then working from this center point outward, braid the strands loosely and tuck the ends in. Transfer the bread to a baking sheet and cover with plastic wrap. Repeat to make two more loaves (or use one or both of the remaining dough pieces to make rolls or buns—see the variations).

Let the breads rise for 45 minutes to 1 hour.

Position a rack in the lower third of the oven and preheat the oven to 375°F.

Just before baking, brush the egg wash generously over the loaves, then sprinkle on the optional poppy seeds (set the egg wash aside). Bake for 15 minutes. Brush the breads with the egg wash again, then lower the heat to 350°F and bake for another 20 to 25 minutes. The loaves should sound hollow when tapped on the bottom. Let cool on a rack for 30 minutes or more before slicing.

MINICHALLAH TWISTS Cut the dough into 3 pieces as directed above, then divide each piece into 4 equal pieces. Shape each of these into a minichallah: Roll it under your palms into a strand about 15 inches long, then cut it lengthwise almost in thirds, leaving one end attached. Braid the strands, and place on a baking sheet. Place the twists side by side on the baking sheet, leaving a little space between them; use a second sheet if necessary. Cover and let rise for 45 minutes. Preheat the oven to 375°F and follow the instructions for brushing the twists with egg wash before and after sprinkling on the optional poppy seeds, and for baking. (Makes 12 twists.)

ONION ROLLS Cut the dough into 3 pieces as directed above, then flatten each piece into a rectangle about 6 inches by 4 inches. Set aside while you mince 1 small onion. In a small bowl, toss the onion with 2 teaspoons vegetable oil and ¼ teaspoon salt. Cut each rectangle into six 2-inch squares. Place on a baking sheet, nearly touching. Place a little onion mixture on top of each roll, pressing it on to help it stick. Cover and let rise for 45 minutes. Preheat the oven to 375°F. Just before baking, brush the edges of the rolls with the egg wash and sprinkle a few poppy seeds onto the onion on each roll, if you wish (and brush again with egg wash as directed). Bake as directed. (Makes 18 rolls.)

NEW YEAR'S CHALLAH COIL At Rosh Hashanah, the New Year, challah is shaped into loose coil-shaped loaves, rather than braided. To make a challah for Rosh Hashanah, follow the shaping instructions for the Greek Easter Spiral on page 122.

ukrainian christmas bread

Makes 1 beautiful twisted and stacked golden bread, about 9 inches across and 5 to 6 inches tall

I made a close friend in high school named Lianne, and we are good friends still. The first year I knew her, she invited me to her house for her birthday dinner. "It's also Christmas in my house," she warned. "You'll find the food strange." Lianne's birthday falls on January 6, Ukrainian Christmas Eve, and her parents, who had been raised in Ukrainian farm communities in Manitoba, spoke Ukrainian as their first language and maintained the customs they'd grown up with.

Their traditional feast on Christmas Eve consists of twelve courses, all meatless, a form of fasting while celebrating. We started with a ritual soup called kulcha, *made of simmered wheat berries flavored with honey and black poppy seeds, a cross between soup and gruel; I loved it. Then there was borscht, made from beets that Lianne's mother had pickled in the fall, and* pirohe, *delicate dumplings filled with potato or cheese and served with mushroom sauce, and fish served several ways, and soon I lost track. The food was all new to me, and exhilarating, sometimes overwhelming, but not strange. I couldn't wait until her next birthday.*

On the table, along with wineglasses and candles, was a Christmas bread called kolach, *elaborately twisted and braided. It's traditionally presented as three breads stacked one on top of the other and topped by a candle. Kolach may be a holdover from the sun and earth worship of the pre-Christian era, a rich decorated celebratory bread, round and golden like the sun (the word comes from the Ukrainian* kolo, *meaning "circle"), and made to celebrate the solstice (now the Christmas season). The bread is moist and rich with butter and eggs and has a slightly denser-than-brioche texture.*

This recipe makes one very beautiful bread. To make the traditional three breads, see the Note below. This bread keeps well.

2 teaspoons active dry yeast

1 cup lukewarm water

⅓ cup sugar

1 cup milk, heated to lukewarm

8 tablespoons (1 stick) unsalted butter, melted

1 teaspoon salt (½ teaspoon if using salted butter)

2 large eggs, beaten

6 to 7 cups unbleached all-purpose flour

1 egg, beaten, for egg wash

In a small bowl, dissolve the yeast in the warm water, then add 1 teaspoon of the sugar and stir well. Set aside.

In a large bowl, dissolve the remaining sugar in the warm milk. Stir in the melted butter, salt, and eggs, then add 2 cups of the flour and stir until smooth. Add the yeast mixture and stir in well, always stirring in the same direction. Add 4 to 5 cups more flour, 1 cup at a time, stirring and turning to incorporate it; when the dough becomes too difficult to mix, turn it out onto a well-floured surface and knead for 5 minutes or more, adding flour if necessary, until firm (not soft), smooth, and elastic.

Place the dough in a large clean bowl and cover tightly with plastic wrap. Let rise in a fairly warm place (about 70°F) until doubled in volume, about 3 hours.

Pull the dough away from the sides of the bowl and deflate it, then cover and let rise again until doubled, about 1 hour.

Butter or grease a 9-inch round cake pan or cast-iron frying pan (or use a 9- or 10-inch flan ring set on a baking sheet).

Turn the risen dough out onto a lightly floured surface. Cut into 6 equal pieces (first cut the dough in half, then cut each piece into 3). Set 4 pieces aside, lightly covered. Roll the remaining 2 pieces out under your palms into ropes about 33 to 36 inches long. Lay 1 piece diagonally across the other at the center of each, then, working from that center point, twine the ropes around each other, toward each end, to make a long coiled rope. Make a circle of the rope, pressing the ends together, and place it in the buttered pan or ring.

Roll out the remaining 4 pieces of dough into 24-inch lengths and, following the instructions above, use them to make 2 coiled ropes. Then use the same technique to twist the 2 coils around each other to make a double coil. Lay the coil inside the dough in the pan to form a circle, and pinch the ends together, trimming them at an angle as necessary to make a neat joint. There will be a small circular gap in the center of the bread. Cover and let rise until almost doubled in volume, about 45 minutes.

Meanwhile, place a rack in the lower third of the oven. If you have a baking stone or unglazed quarry tiles, place them on the rack. Preheat the oven to 350°F.

Brush the top of the risen dough generously with egg wash. Transfer to the stone, tiles, or a baking sheet and bake for about 1 hour. The bread should have a rich golden crust and sound hollow when tapped on the bottom. (The bread starts to turn golden very early in the baking because of the egg wash. This does not mean the bread has baked, but it may tempt you to take it out too early. *Be sure to use the "hollow tap" test (see page 111) to make sure it has baked through.*) Let the bread stand for at least 1 hour on a wire rack to firm up before slicing.

NOTE To make the traditional three breads, triple the recipe as follows: Increase the yeast to 4 teaspoons and the milk to 5 cups; triple the quantities of sugar, butter, eggs, and flour. Divide the risen dough into three, then shape each loaf separately. You will probably have to bake them in two batches unless your oven is very large, since only two breads will fit on a regular rack. The breads must be completely cool and firm before being stacked—make them a day ahead if possible.

greek easter spiral

Makes 1 large coiled bread, flavored with spices and studded with almonds

One Easter, I spent two weeks in Crete, most of the time hanging around George's bakery (see Last Easter at the Bakery, page 399, and photographs opposite). Every day the warm smell of Easter cookies came streaming from the oven. During Holy Week, it was the turn of the Easter breads, called lambropsomo—*golden mahleb-and-mastic-scented spirals of enriched white bread studded with almonds. Here's one version of those breads; make and enjoy it at any time of year. It keeps well for a good week, and it makes excellent toast.*

Mastic and mahleb find their way into many sweet rolls and breads in the eastern Mediterranean and the Arab world. Mastic is a resin, harvested from the acacia tree, and a little of it gives breads and cakes an aromatic taste that intensifies other flavors. It's sold as small crystals and must be pounded or ground to a powder. The Greek island of Chios, west of Izmir in Turkey, is the world's primary producer. Mahleb is the kernel of a kind of black cherry, and it gives a fragrant scent of peach to baked goods. It's sold as whole kernels (like tiny almonds) or as ground powder. Buy the kernels if you can find them, store them in the freezer to keep fresh, and grind them in a spice grinder just before using (see Notes).

STARTER DOUGH

¼ teaspoon active dry yeast

1 cup milk, heated to lukewarm

2 cups all-purpose flour

BREAD

About 2 tablespoons dried orange peel,

    or 1 tablespoon minced candied orange peel

4 tablespoons unsalted butter, melted,

    plus extra melted butter for brushing

2 large eggs

2 tablespoons sugar

2 teaspoons active dry yeast

1½ to 2½ cups all-purpose flour

2 teaspoons salt

¼ teaspoon mahleb (see Notes)

Pinch of mastic (see Notes), pounded to a powder

TOPPING

10 to 12 blanched whole almonds (see Notes)

1 egg, beaten with 1 tablespoon milk, for egg wash

Make the starter dough 12 to 24 hours before you wish to bake the bread: In a medium bowl, dissolve the yeast in the milk, then stir in the flour. Knead briefly in the bowl or on a lightly floured work surface to make a smooth dough. Set aside, loosely covered with plastic wrap, to ferment overnight, or for as long as 24 hours.

If using dried orange peel, boil it in a saucepan of water for 20 minutes; drain and repeat. Finely chop, measure out about 1 tablespoon, and set aside. *If using candied peel,* rinse with warm water, finely chop, and set aside.

Cut the starter dough into 6 pieces and place in a large bowl, or the bowl of a stand mixer fitted with a dough hook. Add the melted butter, eggs, sugar, and yeast.

By hand: Stir with a wooden spoon to blend the starter dough into the butter-yeast mixture. Add the chopped orange peel and stir in. Add about 1 cup of the flour, the salt, mahleb, and mastic, and stir and turn until combined. Turn out onto a well-floured surface and knead, incorporating flour as necessary, until very smooth, firm, and still a little sticky, about 7 minutes.

Using a stand mixer: Mix with the dough hook until the starter dough has blended into the other ingredients. Add the chopped orange peel, 1½ cups of the flour, the salt, and spices, and knead on low speed for about 5 minutes. The dough should be firm but a little sticky; sprinkle on a little more flour and knead in, if necessary.

Transfer the dough to a clean bowl, cover with plastic wrap, and let rise for 2½ hours. (You will have just under 2 pounds of dough.)

Turn the dough out onto a lightly floured surface. Roll it under your hands into an 18- to 20-inch-long cylinder, tapered at one end. Starting with the fatter end, coil it loosely to make 1½ turns, laying the tapered end up over the center like a loosely coiled snake. Set the bread on a baker's peel (or an upside-down baking sheet) generously dusted with flour or cornmeal. Brush with melted butter and stud with the almonds. Cover loosely with plastic wrap and let rise for 1 hour.

Meanwhile, place a baking stone or unglazed quarry tiles, if you have them, (or a baking sheet) on a rack in the lower third of your oven and preheat the oven to 375°F.

Brush the risen bread with the egg wash, and transfer to the stone or tiles (or baking sheet). Bake for 40 to 45 minutes. The top should be a deep golden brown, and the bread will sound hollow when tapped underneath. Place on a rack to cool before slicing.

SHAPING OPTIONS You can shape this bread into a large ring ("crown"), or a loose knot, or a simple boule (large round loaf), whatever shape pleases you. We like the look of this irregular coiled shape.

EASTER EGG BREAD At Eastertime, dyed-red hard-cooked eggs, ancient symbols of spring and fertility, are baked in these breads. Boil one or several eggs and then dye them (using an edible dye) a strong red. Place on the shaped loaf when you're putting on the almonds: Put a single egg in the middle of the coil, or place several on top of a crown or a boule. The dough will rise around them as it bakes, so they become quite embedded in the bread.

NOTES You can find mastic and mahleb at specialty shops or through mail order.

If your almonds are unblanched (skin on), blanch them in boiling water for 1 minute, then drain and rub off the skins.

Of toast and dunking When I was a child, I'd flee the kitchen whenever anyone was buttering toast or—even worse—scraping a burned edge off toast. The sound was painful to me, like fingernails on a chalkboard. Maybe sound is why I've never liked biting into crisp toast or dried crackers. I've always preferred barely toasted toast, where there is the toasted flavor but no noise. As for the crackers and the crisp cookies that the rest of my family loved, I'd dunk them in whatever I was drinking to soften them. But dunking wasn't acceptable when I was a child, certainly not in polite company. I knew I could do it at home, but not at someone else's house.

Because my taste in toast is narrow, I like making my own instead of leaving it to someone else's judgment. Making it can be a wonderful ritual, a chance to bake your own food, a second baking that changes the texture and the taste, transforms the bread and the eating experience.

As a student in England, I learned to toast bread on an open fire, holding a slice suspended at the end of a long fork at just the right distance from the flame, then turning it to toast the other side. My level of toasted was pale, pale gold, and it was easy to judge and to control. At my grandmother's farm, we'd place slices of homemade bread in a two-sided wire mesh holder and put it on the hot cast-iron wood-fired cookstove. They toasted quickly, then went into a toast rack, English style, where they eventually became wonderfully soft, like fine leather, a good surface for butter and marmalade.

People talk of food discoveries they make when they first travel to France. For me, it was the discovery that dunking was fine—a cultural right, in fact—and that a whole country considered it normal. Dunking not only softens crisp textures, of course. It also blends flavors, bringing the taste of the tea to a dipped sweet cracker, coffee flavor to a dunked crust of bread.

ROBIN'S BREAD *(page 150), toasted, and* DAMSON JAM *(page 175)*

fresh quark stollen

Makes 4 sugar-coated log-shaped loaves, 10 to 12 inches long, 5 inches wide, and about 2 inches tall, with a rich tender crumb studded with raisins and a little peel

PHOTOGRAPH ON PAGE 130 *Stollen is a sweet cake-bread associated with Advent and Christmas, but it's made and sold in many German bakeries throughout the year. Traditional stollen is made with butter and eggs. We don't know when or where a quark version arose, but it's our favorite, hands down. I first came across it several years ago in Ulm, a small town on the upper Danube, east of the Black Forest. I had driven there to look at the town's remarkable bread museum. Even though it was May, nearly all the local bakeries were selling quark stollen, coated with granulated sugar.*

Quark is a fresh cheese made from soured milk, like crème fraîche or the Indian fresh cheese paneer. Like yogurt, it makes baked goods tender and moist. In this recipe, you can use quark or whole-milk yogurt that has been drained through a cloth-lined sieve for an hour.

Because stollen tastes so good if it's been given twenty-four hours to "mature," try making these breads at least two or three days before you wish to serve them. The recipe makes four substantial loaves; extras can be frozen or given away as presents (see Note).

2 teaspoons active dry yeast

½ cup lukewarm water

1 teaspoon sugar

1½ cups whole milk, heated to lukewarm

4 cups all-purpose flour

2 cups (½ pound) quark, or 2 cups drained plain whole-milk
    yogurt (see headnote), at room temperature

1 cup currants

1½ cups golden raisins (sultanas)

1 cup candied lemon or orange peel, homemade (page 60)
    or store-bought, or a mixture, finely chopped, or a mix of
    dried cranberries and chopped dried apricots

1 cup orange juice

1 cup dark rum or strong black tea

2 teaspoons salt

¼ cup sugar

7 or 8 cups all-purpose flour

1 pound cold unsalted butter

TOPPING

About 4 tablespoons unsalted butter (optional)

About ½ cup granulated or confectioners' sugar

The day before you wish to bake, in a large bowl, dissolve the yeast in the lukewarm water and stir in the sugar. Let stand for 5 minutes. Add the milk, then stir in 3 cups of the flour until well mixed. Stir for about 30 seconds longer, always in the same direction. Add the quark or drained yogurt and stir in, then add the remaining 1 cup flour and stir and turn until the dough is smooth. Cover the bowl tightly with plastic wrap and let stand overnight at room temperature.

Meanwhile, mix together the currants, raisins, and candied peel or dried fruit in a bowl. Add the orange juice and rum or tea and mix well. Cover and let stand for 8 hours, turning occasionally.

When ready to proceed, drain the fruit mixture thoroughly in a sieve or strainer set over a bowl, reserving the soaking liquid (you will have about 1 cup liquid and nearly 4 cups plumped fruit). Set the fruit mixture aside (still in the sieve or strainer over the bowl).

Sprinkle the salt over the dough and fold in, then add the reserved soaking liquid and the sugar and fold in. Add about 5 cups flour, 1 cup at a time, first turning and folding to incorporate it, then kneading it into the dough in the bowl.

Cut the butter into chunks and place them in a food processor with 1 cup flour. Process until the texture resembles coarse meal. (Or cut the butter into very small cubes, ¼ inch or less, and toss with the flour, mixing and blending them together with your fingertips.) Add the mixture to the dough and knead in. Let the dough stand, covered with plastic wrap, for about an hour.

Line two baking sheets with parchment paper or wax paper and place near your work surface. Turn the dough out onto a generously floured surface (you'll use another cup or so of flour at this stage). Flatten the dough out to about a 1-inch-thick square or oval. Spread the drained fruit over the lower half of the dough, leaving a wide border, about 2 inches, all around. Fold the sides of the dough over the fruit, then fold the top of the dough over the bottom. Gently knead and roll the dough to help distribute the fruit, incorporating flour as necessary and using a dough scraper to keep your work surface clean. Some of the fruit will break out to the surface as you knead; don't worry, just push it back into the dough.

Cut the dough into 4 equal pieces (each will weigh about 1½ pounds). Working on the floured surface, flatten 1 piece into an oval about 12 inches long and 6 to 8 inches wide. Fold it lengthwise in half to make a mounded oval about 4 inches wide. Brush off any excess flour and transfer the bread to a prepared baking sheet. Repeat with the remaining dough, placing two breads on each sheet. Cover loosely with plastic and let rise for 45 minutes; the breads will be a little puffier but will not double in volume.

Place one rack just above the middle of the oven and another below the middle, making sure there's enough headroom (5 inches clearance) for the breads. Place a baking stone or unglazed quarry tiles, if you have them, on the lower rack. Preheat the oven to 375°F.

Bake the breads for about 1 hour, one baking sheet on each oven rack, switching the sheets around after 20 minutes. When done, the breads will be golden and sound hollow when tapped on the bottom. They'll still be a bit soft, though, so be careful when handling them until they cool.

Just before the breads are done, if you wish to brush them with butter, melt the butter. (The sprinkled sugar will stick to the hot moist loaves with or without the melted butter.)

Transfer the breads onto wire racks set over baking sheets to catch drips and sugar. Brush with the melted butter, if using it. Sprinkle on the sugar generously. Let cool completely, 4 to 6 hours.

Wrap the breads tightly in plastic wrap and let stand at least overnight, or preferably for 24 to 48 hours, before serving: This helps the crumb firm up and improves both texture and flavor. Serve thinly sliced.

NOTE These breads freeze very well. Put out at room temperature overnight to defrost.

provençal quince loaf

Makes 2 round, tender-crumbed, filled breads, each with a whole baked quince inside

We came across this bread—pain au coing in French—at the lively Sunday market in Île-sur-la-Sorgues in Provence. We can't remember the bakery's name or its address; what we do remember is how much we loved the bread.

Here's our version, very close to the original. A good white dough, barely sweetened with honey, is wrapped around a whole quince. The quince bakes inside the bread to a firm-tender texture, like a firm pear, keeping its shape and giving the crumb a seductive perfume. When it's done, cut wedge-shaped slices from the golden-domed bread—and delight in the fruit surprise inside.

Quinces come into season in autumn; look for pale yellow oblong fruits. They're hard even when ripe and have to be baked or simmered to have flavor. When they're cooked, the flesh turns a beautiful pale pink.

OLD WHITE DOUGH

½ teaspoon active dry yeast

1 cup lukewarm water

About 2 cups all-purpose flour

BREAD

½ teaspoon active dry yeast

1 cup lukewarm water

1 tablespoon honey

3 to 4 cups all-purpose flour

2 teaspoons salt

2 medium to large quinces (½ to ¾ pound each),
    washed but not peeled

About 2 tablespoons unsalted butter, melted, for brushing

Make the old white dough 12 to 36 hours before you wish to bake: In a medium bowl, dissolve the yeast in the water. Add 1 cup flour and stir to make a smooth batter. Add about another cup of flour and turn and stir to incorporate, then knead for several minutes, until smooth. Place in a clean bowl, cover with plastic wrap, and let ferment overnight, or for as long as 36 hours.

When ready to proceed, dissolve the ½ teaspoon yeast in the 1 cup water in the bowl of a stand mixer or another large bowl, and stir in the honey. Cut the old dough into 5 or 6 pieces and add.

Using a stand mixer: Fit the mixer with the dough hook. Add 2 cups of the flour and the salt to the bowl and knead at low speed for 4 minutes. Add another cup of flour and knead for another 2 minutes. Turn out onto a lightly floured surface and knead briefly by hand, incorporating more flour if necessary, until the dough is smooth.

By hand: Use your fingers to break up the pieces of old dough in the liquid. Add 2 cups of the flour and the salt and stir to make a smooth batter. Add about 1 more cup flour and stir and turn to combine, then knead, in the bowl or on a lightly floured surface, incorporating more flour as necessary, until the dough is smooth and elastic, about 7 minutes.

Place the dough in a clean bowl, cover well with plastic, and let rise for 4 hours or so. It will have more than doubled in volume and will be puffy.

Turn the dough out onto a lightly floured surface and cut it in half. Let rest, loosely covered, for 5 minutes. Lightly butter a baking sheet.

To shape the breads, flatten 1 piece of dough into an approximate 9-inch round. Place 1 quince on your work surface and drape the dough over the top of it. Pull the dough down around the fruit and turn the package upside down so you can pinch the dough together underneath to enclose it entirely. Place seam side down toward one end of the baking sheet. Shape the other loaf in the same way and place on the baking sheet, leaving at least a 2-inch gap between the breads. Cover the loaves loosely with plastic and let rise for an hour.

Meanwhile, place a rack in the lower third of the oven and preheat the oven to 400°F.

Brush each loaf with about 1 tablespoon melted butter. Place the baking sheet in the oven and bake for 20 minutes, then lower the heat to 325°F and bake for 25 to 30 minutes more. The breads will be pale golden rounds.

Let the breads stand on a rack to cool and firm up for 15 minutes. Slice into wedges, including a wedge of quince with each.

PERFUMED FILLED-QUINCE BREAD To make an even more aromatic treat, cut out the core from 1 or both quinces and fill with a mixture of almonds and sugar, lightly perfumed with rose water. Core the fruit from the top, leaving the bottom intact, to give a "floor" to the opening that will keep the stuffing from falling out. For each quince, stir together 1½ tablespoons sugar, 1 tablespoon chopped toasted almonds, and several drops of rose water. Stuff the filling into the quince, then wrap the quince in dough as described above, and proceed as directed.

almond milk bread

Makes 2 "twin loaves" (each about 1½ pounds), rich with milk, almonds, and butter, or 24 tender dinner rolls

PHOTOGRAPH ON PAGE 131 *Almond milk was a common foodstuff in kitchens of the Middle Ages, especially appreciated on fast days in Christian Europe, when dairy products were forbidden. Traditional almond milk contains no dairy. It is made of ground almonds and boiling hot water, in a proportion of one part almonds to two parts water. They steep for 5 to 10 minutes, the hot water rinsing the fats and flavors from the almonds, then the mixture is strained to remove the granular bits of almond.*

Our "almond milk" is a hybrid, made of ground almonds simmered in cow's milk. It gives these loaves a tenderness, like brioche, but no buttery quality; unlike brioche, they keep very well. They're as delicious on the third day as on the day they're baked, and they make great toast.

1 cup whole, slivered, or sliced almonds

2¼ cups whole milk

1 teaspoon saffron threads (optional)

2 teaspoons active dry yeast

4 tablespoons unsalted butter

4 to 5 cups all-purpose flour

2 large eggs

¼ cup sugar

Scant 1½ teaspoons salt

About 2 tablespoons unsalted butter, melted

Grind the almonds to a powder in a food processor. Place in a heavy pot with 2 cups of the milk and simmer until thickened, about 15 minutes. Transfer to the bowl of a stand mixer or another large bowl and let cool to lukewarm, stirring occasionally to help it cool.

Heat the remaining ¼ cup milk to lukewarm. Place in a small bowl and stir in the optional saffron threads, then dissolve the yeast in the milk. Stir the almond milk to make sure it has cooled to lukewarm, then stir in the saffron milk; set aside.

Cut the butter into small pieces (by hand or in the processor). Place in a bowl, add 1 cup of the flour, and toss to mix well.

Using a stand mixer: Fit the mixer with the dough hook. Add 2 cups flour and the floured butter to the almond milk in the bowl and mix on low speed until smooth. Add the eggs, sugar, salt, and 1¼ to 1½ cups flour and knead for 3 to 4 minutes on low speed, until smooth but still somewhat sticky.

By hand: Add 2 cups flour to the almond milk mixture and stir until smooth. Add the floured butter, the eggs, sugar, and salt and mix in. Add 1 cup flour and stir and turn the dough to incorporate the flour, then turn out onto a generously floured surface and knead for 6 to 7 minutes, incorporating flour as necessary and using a dough scraper to keep the surface smooth. The kneaded dough will be smooth, but still somewhat sticky.

Use lightly floured hands to transfer the dough to a clean dry bowl or a lightly floured surface. Cover with plastic and let proof for 1½ to 2 hours.

PRECEDING PAGES: FRESH QUARK STOLLEN (*page 126*). ALMOND MILK BREAD.

Lightly butter two 8-by-4-inch bread pans. Cut the dough in half and then cut each piece in half again. Set 2 pieces aside, loosely covered, while you work with the other 2. Shape each into a boule, tucking the edges under all round to make a domed round. Set the 2 boules into one of the bread pans seam side down. Repeat with the other 2 pieces of dough to make another "twin loaf." Cover with plastic and set aside to rise for 1½ hours, or until a finger pressed into the dough leaves an indentation.

Meanwhile, place a baking stone or unglazed quarry tiles, if you have them, (or a baking sheet) on a rack in the center of the oven and preheat the oven to 375°F.

Just before baking, brush the tops of the breads with melted butter. Transfer to the stone, tile, or baking sheet and bake for 25 minutes, or until the loaves are touched with gold and sound hollow when tapped on the bottom. Immediately take the loaves out of their pans and place on a rack to cool for at least 30 minutes before slicing.

TENDER ALMOND MILK ROLLS You can also shape wonderful tender rolls with this dough. The full recipe makes 24 medium rolls—or you can make 1 twin loaf and 12 rolls. Like the loaves, the rolls can be brushed with butter before baking, or they can be topped with chopped pistachios. To make rolls, cut the dough in half and repeat two more times; then cut each piece into thirds, to give 24 pieces of dough (each weighing about 1½ ounces). Lightly butter two baking sheets. Roll each dough piece into a round under your cupped palm. To top with nuts, spritz each top with water, then lightly press on some chopped pistachios (about ½ teaspoon). Place the rolls on the baking sheets with a ½-inch space between them; they will expand to touch while rising and baking. Set aside, covered with plastic, to rise for 1¼ to 1½ hours. If not using nuts, brush with melted butter just before baking. Bake (one sheet at a time if necessary) in the center of the preheated oven for 15 minutes, or until pale golden brown. Remove to a rack to cool. (Makes 24 pale golden rolls.)

FRESH FRUIT CAKE We often use one-quarter of this dough (about ¾ pound) to make a simple yeasted cake enriched with a little butter and topped with fruit. Follow the instructions in the Note on page 366.

Ventry, just outside Dingle I first learned to cook, and to bake bread, in Ireland. I lived there in Ventry from October 1974 until April 1975, and it was one of the best times of my life. The house I rented looked out over the ocean; it had four tiny bedrooms, an even smaller kitchen, and a living room with a coal-burning fireplace. The rent was five pounds a week, which was affordable, but I quickly realized that I would need another five pounds a week for coal, and another five pounds for electricity, and that was more than I had saved. So when I met a few travelers, I took them in as boarders for a few days, and when they left I asked them to tell others, hoping that I could continue to share the rent.

Well, time passed and no one arrived, and I thought I would soon have to move on. But after a short trip to Cork—can't remember why I went—I returned to find fourteen strangers in my living room! On the spot, we figured out a system: I would put a pound a day in a jar in the kitchen, and anyone who came to stay would do the same, and all expenses would be paid from what was collected. It worked beautifully. At the end of each week, we always had money left over, so we'd go to the local pub, Quinn's, and buy pints of Guinness with our surplus cash.

In Ventry, in the middle of winter, in a village of twenty-five people, there wasn't a whole lot going on, so we cooked and baked. From the blackberries on the side of the road, we made blackberry jams mixed with sour green cooking apples. We made apple crisps, blackberry crisps, and scones. Each morning Mrs. Long, our landlady and the postmistress, put two pints of milk straight from her cows at our doorstep. We put cream on our crisps and in our scones, and in our tea, and in our Irish coffee.

In Dingle, five miles away, we'd order fifty-pound bags of whole wheat flour and white flour. With the flour, we'd make soda bread, as in every Irish home, and with so many to feed, we'd usually bake twice a day. For variety, we'd add oats or currants or honey to the bread. In January, André from Quebec came through and started making sourdough breads, but none of us changed over. Soda bread remained the bread of choice for the rest of us, but we did like sourdough pancakes.

I gained thirty pounds my winter in Ventry, even though I probably walked five to ten miles a day. Must have been the Guinness.

Cliffs at Slea Head, Ventry, Ireland

new england brown bread

Makes 2 large, cylindrical, steamed breads, moist, fruit-filled, and dark and sweet with molasses

This multigrain soda-raised bread starts as a batter rather than a kneaded dough and is steam-cooked, traditionally in tall cans. Chunks of stale bread go into it, along with buttermilk and molasses and a mixture of rye, wheat, and corn flours. It's a version of what's also called Boston brown bread and is in the time-honored New England tradition of "waste not, want not," a great way to make use of dried-out bread.

The bread is moist, with an intense flavor of molasses, raisins, and grain, almost closer to cake. Let it stand for several hours to cool and firm up before slicing it. The flavor and texture are even better the next day.

1 cup cut-up dried bread

2 cups buttermilk

1 cup light rye flour

1 cup cornmeal

1 cup whole wheat flour

1 cup dark raisins

½ cup molasses

1½ teaspoons salt

2 teaspoons baking soda

Combine the dried bread and buttermilk in a large bowl and set aside to soak for several hours.

Before proceeding, organize a steaming arrangement: Use two coffee cans or tall fruit juice cans, or a large metal mixing bowl (we've used the bowl of our KitchenAid mixer). Butter them well. Fill a pot wide and tall enough to hold the tins with about 4 inches of water. Arrange some sort of platform (a heavy metal rack or even one or two metal lids, inverted, can work well) inside the pot to support the cans or bowl so they're raised off the bottom of the pot. Begin heating the water, so it's at the boil when you're ready to steam your breads.

Stir the soaked bread mixture, then stir in the flours and the raisins. Stir in the molasses and salt. Stir in the baking soda and mix thoroughly.

Pour the batter into the cans or bowl, filling them only two-thirds full. Remove the pot of boiling water from the heat and use oven mitts to protect your hands from the steam; place the cans or bowl on the platform in the pot. Place the pot over high heat and cover tightly with a lid wrapped in a cotton cloth (to make a good seal). Bring back to a strong boil, then lower the heat slightly and steam the breads for 2 hours at a strong simmer. Check the water level occasionally and add more hot water if the pot seems to be boiling dry.

Use a skewer or sharp knife to test the breads for doneness: When inserted into the center, the skewer should come out clean. Let the breads stand for 30 minutes before removing them from the cans or bowl and then another hour or two on a wire rack to firm up before slicing.

NOTE If you wish to freeze one of the loaves, let it cool completely, for at least 8 hours, then wrap tightly in plastic and freeze.

PRECEDING PAGES 136–139: *Souk Sept Ait Abdulla, Anti Atlas mountains, Morocco. Tlacolula market, Oaxaca, Mexico. Normandy, France. Date harvest, Douz oasis, southern Tunisia.*

nigella-date hearth breads

Makes 2 low, round, golden brown hearth loaves (each about 1½ pounds), with a tender crumb, sweetened with dates and gently spiced with nigella seed

We first learned about combining dates and nigella seeds inside a dough from a gifted and thoughtful Algerian baker in Washington, D.C., named Dachman. Nigella seed (see Glossary) has a delightful oniony tang. In this semolina bread, the seeds are baked inside the dough, becoming mellow and blending fabulously with the dates, which soften and sweeten the dough and give it a tender texture.

OLD WHITE DOUGH

1 cup lukewarm water

¼ teaspoon active dry yeast

2 cups all-purpose flour

BREAD

1 teaspoon active dry yeast

1 cup lukewarm water

2½ cups coarse semolina (not fine semolina flour),
plus extra for dusting

2 teaspoons salt

1 cup coarsely chopped pitted dates

2 scant teaspoons nigella seeds

Make the old white dough 12 hours to 2 days before you wish to bake the bread: Place the water in a large bowl, or the bowl of a stand mixer, and stir in the yeast to dissolve it.

By hand: Stir 1 cup flour into the yeast to make a smooth batter, then add the second cup of flour and turn and fold to blend it in. Turn the dough out and knead briefly until smooth; the dough will be soft.

Using a stand mixer: Fit the mixer with the dough hook. Add the 2 cups flour to the yeast mixture and mix at low speed for 3 minutes. Beat at medium for another minute to knead the dough.

Place the kneaded dough in a clean bowl, cover with plastic, and let ferment for 8 hours, or as long as 2 days.

When ready to proceed, dissolve the yeast in the lukewarm water and set aside. Cut the old white dough into 4 to 5 pieces and place in the bowl of a stand mixer

fitted with the dough hook. Add the yeast mixture, the semolina, salt, dates, and nigella and mix on low speed for about 5 minutes. The dates will dissolve into small flecks, coloring the dough. The dough will be smooth and shiny, moist, and stretchy. Transfer the dough to a clean bowl, cover with plastic, and let rise for 3 hours.

Turn the dough out onto a lightly floured surface and cut into 2 equal pieces. Shape each into a boule, tucking the edges under to stretch the top surface to a smooth round dome. Place the shaped loaves on a surface generously sprinkled with semolina, cover loosely with plastic or a damp cloth, and let rest for 30 minutes.

Meanwhile, place a baking stone or unglazed quarry tiles, if you have them, (or a lightly greased baking sheet) on a rack in the middle of the oven. Preheat the oven to 425°F.

Because the dough is soft, the loaves will have spread and flattened as they rested. Don't worry. Slide one onto a wooden peel (or the back of a baking sheet) dusted with semolina. Wet your fingers, then dimple the dough all over lightly with your fingertips. Transfer the loaf onto the hot baking stone or quarry tiles (or baking sheet). Repeat with the other bread (or, if there isn't room for it, leave covered and bake when the first loaf comes out). Lower the heat to 400°F and bake for 25 to 30 minutes. The loaves will be a rich golden brown on top. Tap on the bottom of the loaves to test for doneness; they should sound hollow. Let stand on a rack to cool and firm up.

These loaves can be sliced or torn into chunks. Serve the bread as a snack on its own, with tea or coffee, or with cream cheese or a fresh or aged goat cheese.

fruit and nut powerpack

Makes 2 round, moist, boule-shaped loaves (each just over 2 pounds), flavored with plenty of dried fruit and hazelnuts, or 12 scones

We call this bread "powerpack" because it's so hearty and good and so everything-we-want-to-be-eating when we're eating it. It started out as sconelike rolls, but when we used the dough to make small loaves, we liked them even better. The breads are excellent for slicing and toasting.

Note: *Use unsulfured dried fruit if you can find it.*

2 cups lukewarm water

1¼ teaspoons active dry yeast

2 cups whole wheat flour

½ cup chopped figs

½ cup currants

½ cup coarsely chopped dried apricots

½ cup coarsely chopped pitted prunes

1 cup very hot water

½ cup hazelnuts

3 to 4 cups all-purpose flour

2 teaspoons salt

2 tablespoons honey

½ cup buckwheat flour

Eight to 24 hours before you wish to bake: Place the lukewarm water in a bowl and stir in ¼ teaspoon of the yeast to dissolve it well, then stir in the whole wheat flour, always stirring in the same direction, until a smooth batter forms. Set the sponge aside, covered with plastic wrap, to ferment overnight, or for as long as 24 hours. (If you have to leave it for longer than 24 hours, stir, and then cover again and refrigerate. Don't go longer than 36 hours.)

Meanwhile, place the figs, currants, dried apricots, and prunes in a bowl and pour over the hot water. Stir to mix well, cover, and soak overnight (for at least 5 hours) at room temperature.

Before making the dough, toast the hazelnuts: Place on a baking sheet under the broiler, or toast in a dry heavy skillet over medium heat, until lightly aromatic, less than 5 minutes. Check frequently to make sure the nuts are not burning, shaking the baking sheet or skillet to move the nuts around. Transfer the nuts to a wide shallow bowl or another baking sheet. As soon as they are cool enough to handle, rub them, handful by handful, between your palms or in a towel, to rub off the skins (don't worry about getting off every last bit of skin). Transfer the nuts to a food processor and coarsely chop, or chop by hand. Set aside.

Drain the fruit in a sieve set over a bowl, using a wooden spoon to press on the fruit to push out all the liquid. Reserve the soaking liquid. Place the fruit in a large bowl and stir in the hazelnuts.

Add the reserved soaking liquid to the sponge. Sprinkle on the remaining 1 teaspoon yeast and stir in. Add ½ cup of the all-purpose flour and stir in. Sprinkle on the salt and honey and stir in. Add the buckwheat flour, then add 1½ to 2 cups more all-purpose flour, ½ cup at a time, turning and stirring to mix. Turn the dough out onto a work surface floured with another ½ to 1 cup all-purpose flour and knead well, incorporating more flour as needed, until smooth. Let rest for 20 minutes on the counter, covered with plastic.

Transfer the dough to a clean bowl. Mix ½ cup all-purpose flour into the drained fruit and nuts, then add the whole mixture to the dough. Knead in the bowl (or on your work surface if you prefer) for 5 minutes or more to incorporate the fruit mixture; if the dough is very sticky, add a little more flour. Kneading the fruit in may feel a little messy, but the fruit does get incorporated into the dough fairly soon.

Place in a clean bowl, cover, and let rise for 3 hours, or until almost doubled in volume.

Turn the dough out onto a lightly floured surface and cut it in half. Let stand, loosely covered, while you line two 7- to 9-inch shallow bowls or round baskets with cotton cloth. Dust the cloths generously with all-purpose flour. (If you don't have bowls or baskets, don't worry; the loaves can also rise on the counter.)

Shape a piece of the dough into a boule, tucking the edges under all around to make a smooth mound. Place seam side up in one of the cloth-lined bowls (or on the floured counter). Repeat with the other piece of dough. Cover the loaves with plastic wrap, and let proof for 1½ to 2 hours, until they have nearly doubled and feel airy.

Meanwhile, place a baking stone or unglazed quarry tiles, if you have them, (or a heavy baking sheet) on a rack in the center of the oven. Preheat the oven to 400°F. Fill a sprayer with water.

Transfer the loaves, one at a time, to a flour- or cornmeal-dusted peel (or the back of a floured baking sheet). Slash once right across the center, from side to side, then repeat, to make a cross shape. Transfer to the hot stone or tiles (or baking sheet). Spritz the loaves generously with water. Lower the heat to 375°F and continue to spritz every minute or so for the first 5 minutes of baking. Bake for about 50 minutes. The loaves will sound hollow when tapped on the bottom. Let cool on a rack for at least 30 minutes before slicing them.

DRIED FRUIT SCONES You can also use the dough to make large scone-style rolls; or make scones from half the dough and a loaf from the remainder. Cut the risen dough in half as directed above. Flatten each half (or just one) into an 8- to 9-inch round. Cut out a circle in the center about 2 inches across—use this dough to make a small round roll. Cut the flattened round into 6 wedge-shaped rolls. Place them on a lightly buttered baking sheet in a circle, leaving about ½ inch of space between wedges. Repeat with the remaining dough. Let proof for 45 minutes, loosely covered, then bake at 375°F for about 30 minutes. Bake the round roll(s) alongside. The wedges will rise and bake together and then can be broken apart into individual scones. It's a very attractive presentation. (Makes 12 wedge-shaped scones.)

banana-coconut bread for pam

Makes 2 large loaves, lightly sprinkled with brown sugar

Our friend Pam had just delivered her baby, Ethan. She'd had an anxious pregnancy and was tired, as well as relieved to be home safely with him. We wanted to take her a bread that would keep well and be a bit of a treat. So starting with a method used by Hoppin' John for his Persimmon Bread in his classic cookbook Lowcountry Cooking, *we used pureed banana as the liquid for the dough, then added shredded coconut for texture and interest. It turned out to be a distinctive, easy, moist loaf with a crunch of sugar on top, the best banana bread we know. And more important, Pam loved it too.*

About 8 medium-to-large frozen bananas, defrosted (see Note), or very overripe bananas

4 cups all-purpose flour

1½ teaspoons baking soda

1 teaspoon freshly grated nutmeg

½ pound (2 sticks) unsalted butter, softened

2 cups sugar

¼ teaspoon white or rice vinegar

3 tablespoons dark rum

1 cup dried shredded unsweetened coconut

About 2 tablespoons demerara (see Sugars in the Glossary) or dark brown sugar for topping

Preheat the oven to 350°F. Butter two 9-by-5-inch bread pans.

Puree the bananas (with their juice if using defrosted ones) in a blender. Measure out 3 cups and set aside.

In a medium bowl, combine the flour, baking soda, and nutmeg; set aside.

Using a mixer, beat the butter and sugar until light and fluffy. Add the vinegar and rum and beat briefly. Add the banana puree and the flour mixture alternately, about 1 cup at a time, beginning with the bananas, beating until smooth after each addition. Stir in the coconut.

Spoon the batter into the buttered pans. Sprinkle the top of each loaf with about 1 tablespoon demerara or brown sugar. Bake for 50 to 60 minutes, until golden. Let cool for 20 minutes, then turn out of the pans onto a wire rack to cool completely and firm up.

NOTE To freeze bananas, choose overipe fruit (freezing is an excellent way of storing overripe bananas). Peel them and cut into large chunks. Freeze overnight on a tray or in a container. Once frozen, transfer to a plastic bag, seal, and freeze for up to 1 month. Place in a bowl to defrost at room temperature, and save the juices.

irish raisin and currant loaves

Makes 2 medium-sized sweet loaves, glazed with sugar and laden with raisins and currants

This sweet yeasted loaf, called barm brack, *is lightly spiced with cinnamon and nutmeg.* Barm *means "yeast" or "leaven" in Ireland, and a* brack *is a loaf. Traditionally barm brack is round, probably because it was originally baked in an iron skillet or pot over a fire. Like people in many rural places who figured out how to bake without ovens, Irish cooks used to top the pot with a heavy iron lid on which they'd place hot coals, thus heating from both top and bottom. This recipe calls for oven baking, and the brack is cooked in a loaf pan—we've found it's easier to get the loaf evenly cooked using this shape.*

Brushing the top of the loaves with butter will give them a deeper color; the optional sugar glaze applied at the end of baking adds an attractive sheen. Don't worry if the loaf cracks a little on top during baking; that's normal. The slices have a very pleasing yeast-dough texture and are generously studded with raisins and currants.

1 teaspoon sugar

1½ cups lukewarm milk

1 tablespoon active dry yeast

3½ to 4 cups all-purpose flour

½ teaspoon salt

½ teaspoon cinnamon

¼ teaspoon freshly grated nutmeg

4 tablespoons unsalted butter, softened

1 cup packed light brown sugar

1 extra-large egg or 2 small eggs

1½ cups golden raisins (sultanas) or dark raisins

1 cup currants

1 tablespoon unsalted butter, melted (optional)

GLAZE (OPTIONAL)

1 tablespoon sugar, dissolved in 2 tablespoons hot water

In a small bowl, dissolve the sugar in the lukewarm milk, then stir in the yeast to dissolve. Set aside for 5 minutes.

In a large bowl or the bowl of a stand mixer, mix together 3¼ cups of the flour, the salt, and spices.

By hand: Use a wooden spoon to blend in the butter, then stir in the brown sugar. Pour in the yeast mixture, add the egg, and stir to blend. Beat for 5 or 6 minutes with the wooden spoon, until you have a stiff batter.

Using a mixer: Add the butter and brown sugar to the

bowl and beat together, using the paddle attachment at medium speed. Add the yeast mixture and egg. Beat at low speed for about 4 minutes or until you have a stiff batter.

Fold in the raisins and currants. Cover the dough and let rise for 2 hours: It will increase in volume but will not quite double in size.

Butter two 8-by-4-inch bread pans. Turn the rather sticky, unwieldy dough out onto a generously floured surface and cut it in half; then, with floured hands, shape it into oblong loaves. Transfer to the buttered pans. Cover and let rise for 45 minutes.

Meanwhile, place a rack in the lower third of the oven and preheat the oven to 375°F.

Brush the loaves with melted butter, if desired, and bake for 45 to 50 minutes. The tops of the loaves will be dark brown. Use a skewer to test that they have cooked through: When inserted into the center of each loaf, it should come out clean.

If using the sugar glaze, brush over the tops of the loaves. Turn off the oven and place the loaves back in the oven for 5 minutes.

Remove the loaves from the pans and let cool completely on a rack before slicing. Serve thinly sliced.

NOTE This sweet bread freezes well, tightly sealed in plastic. Leave out overnight to thaw.

vietnamese bread pudding

Makes 1 moist loaf, rich with coconut milk and sweet with bananas and sugar

In Can Tho, a city in Vietnam's Mekong Delta, there's a woman who sells wonderful puddings and cakes in the central market. She's at her small stand most days, starting early in the afternoon. Her banana pudding is one of the best Asian sweets I've ever eaten, a cross between cake and pudding: It is baked or steamed on a large tray, then served in small, firm squares.

This simple bread pudding, called banh choi *in Vietnamese, echoes the flavors and textures of that Can Tho market sweet. The coconut milk, mashed banana, palm sugar, and toasted bread first soak briefly, blending flavors, then bake in a bread pan. Once cooled, it slices beautifully. If you are serving it as a dessert, top the slice of pudding, if you wish, with lemon or mango sorbet.*

1½ cups unsweetened coconut milk (canned or fresh)

¼ teaspoon cinnamon

2 tablespoons palm sugar (see Sugars in the Glossary),
  or 1 tablespoon each maple sugar and light brown sugar

10 to 12 slices fresh or stale Vietnamese Minibaguettes
  (page 226), or 8 to 10 slices white or light whole wheat
  loaf bread, toasted until golden

5 ripe bananas, 4 mashed, 1 sliced crosswise into
  ½-inch medallions (see Note)

2 tablespoons granulated sugar

Place a rack in the center of the oven and preheat the oven to 350°F. Lightly oil or butter an 8-by-4-inch bread pan.

Place the coconut milk in a heavy wide pot and heat until warm. Add the cinnamon and palm sugar and stir to dissolve. Remove from the heat.

Tear the bread or toast into large chunks and add to the coconut milk, stirring to moisten it completely, then add the mashed bananas and stir to mix well. Let stand for 10 minutes.

Pour the mixture into the loaf pan. Top with the banana medallions and sprinkle on the granulated sugar. Bake for about 1 hour, until golden. Let stand for 10 to 20 minutes to firm up before slicing.

NOTE In southern Vietnam, the bananas used for puddings are purple-red and very sweet. If you can find small tropical bananas, well ripened, use them.

FAMILY BREADS

robin's bread

Makes 3 large pan loaves (just over 2 pounds each) with a moist crumb, partly whole wheat, and optionally flavored with sunflower seeds

These loaves are our present-day take on the bread my mother, Robin, used to make. We make Robin's bread regularly, because it makes good sandwiches for the kids' lunch boxes and excellent toast. We like having a spare loaf in the freezer that we can pull out on those evenings we realize there's no bread in the house for the next day's sandwiches (see Bread Rhythms, page 165). The bread is slow-rise and made with a blend of whole wheat and white flours. You can increase the whole wheat to as much as six cups if you wish (for a denser loaf), cutting back the all-purpose proportionately. We suggest letting the dough rise overnight, but you may find it more convenient to make the dough in the morning (about a fifteen-minute job), let it rise during the day, then shape and bake the bread in the evening. The crumb is very moist and tender, and the bread keeps well.

4 cups lukewarm water

2 cups whole or reduced-fat milk

1 teaspoon active dry yeast

3 cups whole wheat flour

2 tablespoons mild honey

8 to 10 cups all-purpose flour

2 tablespoons plus 1 teaspoon salt

2 tablespoons olive oil, vegetable oil,
  or unsalted butter, softened

1 cup hulled unsalted sunflower seeds (see Glossary)
  (optional)

Place the water and milk in a large bowl and stir. Stir in the yeast to dissolve. Add the whole wheat flour and stir to blend in. Stir in the honey. Add about 3 cups of the all-purpose flour and stir, always in the same direction, until you have a smooth batter. Stir in the salt, then add the oil or butter and optional sunflower seeds and stir in. Add 4 to 5 more cups all-purpose flour, 1 cup at a time, turning and folding the dough to incorporate it.

Flour a work surface generously and turn the dough out. Knead for about 10 minutes, incorporating more flour as necessary to prevent sticking (another 1½ to 2 cups), until you have a soft, still moist dough.

Place the dough in a large lightly oiled bowl, cover with plastic, and set aside to rise overnight, or for 8 to 12 hours, whatever is most convenient. The risen dough will be spongy and very moist and sticky.

Flour a work surface generously. Use well-floured hands to pull the dough away from the sides of the bowl and turn it out. Use a dough scraper or sharp knife to cut the dough into 3 equal pieces. Let rest while you butter or oil three 9-by-5-inch bread pans.

Briefly knead 1 piece of dough, incorporating a little flour from the work surface, then flatten to an oval about 10 inches long. Starting from a narrow end, loosely roll up the dough; it will feel soft under your hands. Pinch the seam to seal, and place seam side down in one of the bread pans. Repeat with the remaining pieces of dough. Set aside, loosely covered with plastic, to rise for 40 minutes.

Meanwhile, place a rack in the lower third of the oven and preheat the oven to 400°F. Fill a sprayer with lukewarm water.

Spritz the loaves with water and place them in the oven. After 10 minutes, lower the temperature to 375°F, and bake for about 20 minutes. Rotate the pans and bake for another 20 to 25 minutes.

To test for doneness, take one loaf out of the oven, slide it out of the bread pan, and knock it on the bottom: It should sound hollow. Pinch the bottom corners of the loaf: They should be firm, not yielding. If they are still a little soft, bake the bread for about 10 minutes longer.

When the breads are done, tip them out of the pans and place right side up on a rack to cool and firm up. Do not try to slice them until they have cooled completely.

NOTE To freeze, wrap the cooled loaves separately in plastic bags and seal tightly. Defrost overnight at room temperature, still sealed in plastic.

tender potato bread

Makes 1 large tender-crumbed pan loaf and something more: one 10-by-15-inch crusty yet tender focaccia, 12 soft dinner rolls, or a small pan loaf

Potatoes and potato water give this bread wonderful flavor and texture. The dough is very soft and moist and might feel a little scary if you've never handled soft doughs before. But don't worry: Leaving it on parchment or wax paper to proof and to bake makes it easy to handle.

Once baked, the crumb is tender and airy, with tiny soft pieces of potato in it and a fine flecking of whole wheat. The loaves have a fabulous crisp texture on the outside and a slightly flat-topped shape. They make great toast and tender yet strong sliced bread for sandwiches. The dinner rolls are soft and inviting, and the focaccia is memorable.

4 medium to large floury (baking) potatoes,
    peeled and cut into large chunks
4 cups water (see Note)
1 tablespoon plus 1 teaspoon salt
2 teaspoons active dry yeast
6½ to 8½ cups unbleached all-purpose flour
1 tablespoon unsalted butter, softened
1 cup whole wheat flour

TOPPING

FOR LOAVES AND ROLLS: melted butter (optional)
FOR FOCCACIA: olive oil, coarse salt, and rosemary leaves
    (optional; also see the variation)

Put the potatoes and water in a saucepan and bring to a boil. Add the 1 teaspoon salt and cook, half covered, until the potatoes are very tender. Drain the potatoes, reserving the potato water, and mash well.

Measure out 3 cups of the potato water (add extra water if needed to make 3 cups). Place the water and mashed potatoes in the bowl of a stand mixer fitted with the paddle attachment or in another large bowl. Let cool to lukewarm (stir well before testing the temperature—it should feel just warm to your hand). Mix or stir in the yeast and let stand for 5 minutes.

Using a stand mixer: Add 2 cups of the all-purpose flour and mix for 1 minute. Change to the dough hook. Sprinkle on the remaining 1 tablespoon salt, add the butter and whole wheat flour, and mix briefly. Add 4 more cups unbleached flour, then knead at the lowest speed for 6 minutes. Turn out onto a floured surface and knead briefly. The dough will still be very soft.

By hand: Add 2 cups of the all-purpose flour and stir and turn for 1 minute. Sprinkle on the remaining 1 tablespoon salt, add the butter and whole wheat flour, and stir and turn briefly. Add 2½ to 3 more cups all-purpose flour and stir and turn until all the flour has been incorporated. Turn the dough out onto a generously floured surface and knead for about 10 minutes, incorporating flour as needed to prevent sticking. The dough will be very sticky to begin with, but as it takes up more flour from the kneading surface, it will become easier to handle; use a dough scraper to keep your surface clean. The kneaded dough will still be very soft.

Place the dough in a large clean bowl, cover with plastic wrap, and let rise for about 2 hours. It will have more than doubled in volume.

Turn the dough out onto a well-floured surface and knead gently for several minutes. It will be moist and a little sticky. Divide the dough into 2 unequal pieces in a proportion of one-third and two-thirds (one will be twice as large as the other). Place the smaller piece to one side, loosely covered.

To shape the large loaf: Butter a 9-by-5-inch bread pan. Flatten the larger piece of dough on the floured surface to an approximate 12-by-8-inch oval, then roll it up from a narrow end to form a loaf. Pinch the seam closed and gently place seam side down in the buttered pan. The dough should come about three-quarters of the way up the sides of the pan. Cover with plastic wrap and let rise for 35 to 45 minutes, until puffy and almost doubled in volume.

To make a small loaf with the remainder: Butter an 8-by-4-inch bread pan. Shape and proof the loaf the same way as the large loaf.

To make rolls: Butter a 13-by-9-inch baking pan or a shallow cake pan. Cut the dough into 12 equal pieces. Shape each into a ball under the palm of your floured hand and place on the baking sheet, leaving ½ inch between the balls. Cover with plastic wrap and let rise for 35 minutes, until puffy and almost doubled.

To make focaccia: Flatten out the dough to a rectangle about 10 inches by 15 inches with your palms and fingertips. Tear off a piece of parchment paper or wax paper a little longer than the dough and dust it generously with flour. Transfer the focaccia to the paper. Brush the top of the dough generously with olive oil, sprinkle on a little coarse salt, as well as some rosemary leaves, if you wish, and dimple all over with your fingertips. Cover with plastic and let rise for 20 minutes.

Place a baking stone or unglazed quarry tiles, if you have them, (or a baking sheet) on a rack in the center of the oven and preheat the oven to 450°F. Bake the flatbread before you bake the loaf; bake the rolls at the same time as the loaf.

If making foccacia, just before baking, dimple the bread all over again with your fingertips. Leaving it on the paper, transfer to the hot baking stone, tiles, or sheet. Bake until golden, about 10 minutes. Transfer to a rack (peel off the paper if necessary) and let cool at least 10 minutes before serving.

Dust risen *loaves* and *rolls* with a little all-purpose flour or lightly brush the tops with a little melted butter (the butter will give a browned crust). Slash *loaves* crosswise two or three times with a razor blade or very sharp knife and immediately place on the stone, tiles, or sheet in the oven. Place the *rolls* next to the loaf in the oven.

Bake rolls until golden, about 30 minutes. Bake the small loaf for 40 minutes, the large loaf for 50 minutes. Transfer the rolls to a rack when done to cool. When the loaf or loaves have baked for the specified time, remove from the pans and place back on the stone or tiles (or sheet) for another 5 to 10 minutes. The corners should be firm when pinched and the bread should sound hollow when tapped on the bottom.

Let breads cool on a rack for at least 30 minutes before slicing. Rolls can be served warm or at room temperature.

ANCHOVY-ONION FOCACCIA Instead of the oil, salt, and rosemary, the focaccia can be topped with some slow-cooked onions (see Alsatian Onion Tart, page 104, for guidance; cook onions in olive oil or bacon fat), a scattering of chopped anchovy fillets, and flat-leafed parsley leaves.

FOLLOWING PAGE: *Mountains in eastern Austria*

The baker's wife I went to Hungary and Austria looking for breads. After ten days in Hungary's wide-open spaces, I crossed into Austria on a small winding road and felt I'd entered a different world. In eastern Austria, the hills are steep and thickly wooded. There are piles of firewood outside the tidy houses, and tracks lead off into the forest. In this carefully tended country, villages are neatly set into the landscape, with few straggly edges. Every village has a church or two, and almost every village has a bakery. The bakeries are easy to spot, generally located on the main street and signaled by the traditional pretzel-shaped sign, like those in Germany.

After small-town Hungary, where village bakeries are scarce and there's not much variety in the breads, I feasted on the bakery windows in Austria: loaves thickly coated with sunflower seeds or poppy seeds, rolls studded with green pumpkin seeds, dark rye *vollkornbrot* and domed country-style breads, as well as strudels, Danishes, and other simple sweets. It was astonishing to see such choice and quality so consistently. My only problem was choosing what to buy, what to try.

Most of these village bakeries are still family businesses. Charming, you'll say, and yes, I'd agree. But then I talked to a baker's wife and got another perspective. I'd stopped in a small village framed by steep green hills to have a look at the bakery, then went into the shop to ask a question about one of the breads. Hearing my poor German, the woman behind the counter answered in English. She was in her early thirties, I'd guess, with dark shoulder-length hair and a great smile. She was the baker's wife. Her English was very fluent, so we didn't have to labor with my German. We went out into the courtyard behind the bakery and talked for a long time under the bright sun.

"It's sometimes hard," she said as we watched her young children, two sturdy blond toddlers, play on the grass. "My husband gets up at midnight and works through until eleven in the morning. Then he has a bite to eat, sleeps a little, and wakes up in time to start work again at four. He has dinner with us, sleeps until midnight, then starts his long day again. And his assistant keeps the same hours—next year he'll probably leave us to start his own bakery somewhere. That's how my husband learned his trade, by apprenticing. The assistant is very reliable and capable, but my husband is a perfectionist. He insists on being the last one to leave the bakery so he can make sure that everything has been taken care of as it should be.

"We also sell bread at one of the service centers on the Autobahn to bring in some extra money. Otherwise, we just keep working hard to stay afloat; we don't have any possibility of really changing things or making life easier.

"I shouldn't complain. I have my mother and my mother-in-law in the village, and they love to take care of the children, so I can work in the shop selling. My husband is a very good man. But I wish we had more possibilities, more freedom to change.

"And it's so hard for my husband to take a holiday," she said wistfully. "The people here"—she waved her hand to include the small village in its sheltered valley—"they get very upset when he takes a holiday. They want to be able to walk to the bakery to buy their bread every day. They say they rely on him. We've managed only one trip away. That was six years ago. We went to Morocco, and it was wonderful."

She looked away for a moment to hide her tears.

large-batch whole wheat pan loaves

Makes 4 large whole wheat pan loaves (each weighing more than 2 pounds)

We like whole wheat breads, their good plain taste, their moist texture. We know some unlucky people find them coarse or bitter, just like some people don't like cilantro. For those who do have a taste for whole wheat, these loaves are great family breads.

The poolish is made of all-purpose flour, and there's some all-purpose flour used during kneading, but this is a mostly whole wheat bread, moist and satisfying. Like many breads in this chapter, it's a slow-rise bread, so start to make it two to three days before you want to bake, then fit it into your schedule; the timing is very flexible. It's a large recipe, but the bread freezes very well, so you can eat one loaf right away and have three breads in the freezer for later.

POOLISH

3 cups lukewarm water

Scant ¼ teaspoon active dry yeast

3 cups all-purpose flour

BREAD

6 cups lukewarm water

11 cups whole wheat flour

1 tablespoon mild honey

3 tablespoons salt

2½ to 3½ cups all-purpose flour

About 2 tablespoons unsalted butter or mild vegetable oil for greasing the bread pans

Make the poolish at least 12 hours before using: Place the lukewarm water in a medium bowl. Sprinkle on the yeast and stir to dissolve. Add the flour and stir well until a smooth batter forms. Cover the bowl with plastic wrap or a tight-fitting lid and set aside to ferment for 12 to 36 hours, whatever is most convenient. The batter will develop bubbles and will rise and look lively.

When ready to proceed, place the lukewarm water (just warm to the touch, no hotter) in a large bowl. Add the poolish and stir to dissolve it. Add 2 cups of the whole wheat flour and stir in, always stirring in the same direction. Add another 4 cups whole wheat flour and stir in the same direction until smooth, then stir for 1 minute longer. Now you have a sponge. Cover with plastic wrap and set aside to ferment for 8 to 18 hours.

Stir the honey into the sponge, then sprinkle on the salt. Add the remaining 5 cups whole wheat flour, 1 cup at a time, stirring and turning the dough to combine it completely. The dough will become heavy and difficult to stir. Sprinkle about 1½ cups all-purpose flour over a wide area on your work surface (say, an 18-inch square) and turn the dough out onto it. Use a dough scraper to lift one side of the dough and fold it over, and continue to use the dough scraper to knead by folding the dough over on itself. You will soon need to add another ½ cup flour or more to your work surface, and soon thereafter you will be able to knead using your hands, as the dough gradually gets less sticky and more smooth. Use a dough scraper to keep your work surface clean, and knead for a total of 10 to 12 minutes, until the dough is very smooth but still soft and a little sticky.

Place the dough back in a clean bowl, cover, and let rise for about 4 hours, until at least doubled in volume.

Lightly flour your work surface with all-purpose flour. Turn the dough out and fold it over on itself several times. Use a large knife or a dough scraper to cut the dough into 4 equal pieces (each will weigh nearly 2¼ pounds). Loosely cover the dough, and butter or oil four 9-by-5-inch bread pans.

Gently flatten 1 piece of dough into an oval about 12 inches by 8 inches, then roll it up from a narrow end into a cylinder. Pinch the seam closed and place the bread seam side down in a prepared bread pan. Repeat with the remaining dough.

Cover the loaves with plastic and a cloth and place in a reasonably warm place (68° to 75°F) to rise. After the loaves have been proofing for 1 hour, start preheating your oven: Place a rack in the lower third of the oven and place a baking stone or unglazed quarry tiles, if you have them, (or a baking sheet) on it. Preheat the oven to 425°F. Fill a sprayer with water.

When the loaves have proofed for nearly 2 hours, they will have risen a little but will not have doubled. Slash one loaf two or three times diagonally with a sharp knife, spritz it generously with water, and place in the oven on the stone or tiles (or baking sheet). Repeat with the remaining loaves, then spritz them all generously again. You need to leave only ½ inch space between loaf pans; If they will not all fit in the oven at once, bake in two batches. Close the door and reduce the heat to 400°F. Spritz generously every minute for about 10 minutes, then bake for another 35 minutes. Lower the heat to 375°F and bake for 30 minutes. Remove the loaves from the pans, place on the stone or tiles or oven rack, and bake for a few minutes more, until the corners and edges are very firm when pinched. Let cool completely on a rack before slicing.

NOTE Let the loaves stand for 12 hours before wrapping in plastic to store at room temperature or to freeze. Defrost by leaving them out overnight at room temperature.

quick swedish rye

Makes 2 medium-sized all-rye pan loaves (each about 1¼ pounds), close-textured and tender, aromatic with cumin

PHOTOGRAPH ON PAGE 2 *This all-rye bread, called* matbrod *("food bread") in Sweden, is made of a quickly mixed blend of rye flour, yogurt, and honey, flavored with cumin and leavened with baking soda and baking powder. We were given a sketch of the recipe while we were in Sweden, and it seemed too simple to be true, but in fact it's great, a close-textured, soda-raised all-rye bread. The original instructions called for* fil, *soured milk, for which we've substituted a mix of yogurt and milk. The loaves are compact with a fine, moist crumb texture, good for slicing very thinly. Like all soda breads, these slice and taste even better the second day.*

5 cups light rye flour

2 teaspoons baking soda

1 teaspoon baking powder

1 tablespoon salt

1½ teaspoons cumin seeds

2 cups plain yogurt (full-fat)

½ cup whole or reduced-fat milk

¼ cup mild honey

Place a rack in the center of the oven and preheat the oven to 400°F. Butter two 8-by-4-inch bread pans.

Mix the flour, baking soda, baking powder, salt, and cumin seeds in a large bowl.

In a medium bowl, combine the yogurt, milk, and honey and stir to blend well. (If the honey is stiff, warm it a little to make it more liquid before mixing with the yogurt and milk.) Pour the yogurt mixture into the flour and stir and turn to blend into a well-moistened paste. The dough will be sticky and quite stiff. Continue to beat and stir for several minutes, then spoon into the bread pans. Smooth the tops with a wet spatula.

Place the loaves in the oven. Lower the heat to 385°F and bake for 30 minutes. Lower the heat to 350°F and bake for another 20 minutes, or until the loaves are fairly dark and have pulled away from the sides of the pans. Insert a skewer to make sure the loaves are cooked through; it should come out clean. Turn out of the pans onto a rack to cool for at least 2 hours (and preferably overnight), to give them time to firm up. Serve thinly sliced.

soft white sandwich loaf, american style

Makes 2 large golden pan loaves (each about 1½ pounds), with a tender soft crumb

This is white bread to use in classic North American sandwiches, the ones that go in kids' lunch boxes—with a yielding soft crumb that is also strong enough to hold in a filling and not go soggy. Commercial sandwich bread rarely has much taste; this loaf makes homemade irresistible to kids and adults alike. The flavor comes from the biga that's made ahead. Timing is flexible, and the bread stays delicious and moist for four days (it also freezes well), even though it contains no milk or oil.

BIGA

¼ teaspoon active dry yeast

1 cup lukewarm water

About 2¼ cups all-purpose flour

BREAD

½ teaspoon active dry yeast

2 cups lukewarm water

4 to 5½ cups all-purpose flour

1 tablespoon salt

Make the biga at least 12 hours before you wish to bake the bread: Dissolve the yeast in the lukewarm water, then stir in 2 cups flour. Turn out onto a well floured surface and knead until smooth. Place in a clean bowl, cover with plastic wrap, and let stand for 12 hours to 3 days. Refrigerate if letting stand for more than 24 hours, and bring to room temperature before using.

When ready to make the dough, turn the biga out and cut it into 4 or 5 pieces.

By hand: In a large bowl, dissolve the yeast in the lukewarm water. Let stand for 5 minutes, then add 2 cups of the flour and stir well, always in the same direction. Add the pieces of biga and mix in. Sprinkle on the salt. Add about 2 more cups flour and fold and turn the dough to blend in the flour. Turn the dough out onto a well-floured surface and knead for about 8 minutes, incorporating flour as needed, until smooth and springy.

Using a stand mixer: Place the yeast and water in the mixer bowl and stir to blend. Add 3 cups flour, the salt, and biga. Using the dough hook, mix for 2 minutes at low speed. Add another 1 cup flour and mix another minute at low speed, and then about 2 minutes at the next faster speed. Turn out onto a lightly floured surface and knead briefly, incorporating flour if needed. The dough will be smooth and springy.

Transfer the dough to a large clean bowl, cover it tightly with plastic wrap, and let stand for 1 to 1½ hours, until doubled.

Turn the dough out onto a very lightly floured surface. Cut it in half. Lightly grease or butter two 9-by-5-inch bread pans. Flatten 1 piece of dough gently to a thick oval, then roll up into a smooth log. Pinch the seam closed and place the dough seam side down in one of the pans. Repeat with the other piece of dough. Cover tightly with plastic and let rise about 2 hours, or until doubled in volume.

Place a rack in the center of the oven and preheat the oven to 475°F.

Just before placing the breads in the oven, slash each one down the middle with a razor blade or a sharp knife. Place in the oven, lower the heat to 400°F, and bake for about 45 minutes, or until golden on top. Remove from the oven, take out of the pans, and place in the oven for another 5 minutes or so. The loaves should sound hollow when tapped on the bottom, and the corners should be firm when pinched. Let stand on a rack to cool and firm up for 1½ to 2 hours before slicing.

velvety bean bread

Makes 2 attractive small pan loaves with a rich brown crust and velvet-smooth, fine moist crumb

Cooked pureed white beans are the basis for this nifty bread. Unless you tell people, no one will guess, though they will puzzle over the velvety even texture and the depth of flavor of the bread—and wonder how you achieved them. The bread stays tender and flavorful for a week.

2 teaspoons active dry yeast

1 cup lukewarm water

2 cups drained cooked or canned navy beans (see Glossary),
at room temperature

1 cup whole wheat flour

1 tablespoon olive oil

1 tablespoon salt

2 tablespoons chopped chives (optional)

About 2 cups all-purpose flour

In a small bowl, dissolve the yeast in the lukewarm water.

Process the beans until smooth, and transfer to a large bowl or the bowl of a stand mixer.

By hand: Stir the yeast mixture into the beans. Add the whole wheat flour and stir for 1 minute, always in one direction, to develop the dough. Sprinkle on the oil, salt, and chives, if using, and stir in. Add 1 cup of the all-purpose flour and stir in, then add another ½ cup and turn and stir to incorporate. Turn the dough out onto a surface floured with ½ cup or more all-purpose flour and knead for about 5 minutes, until smooth.

Using a stand mixer: Fit the mixer with the dough hook. Add the yeast mixture and whole wheat flour to the beans and mix for 1 minute at low speed. Sprinkle on the oil, salt, and chives, if using, then add 1 cup of the all-purpose flour. Mix at low speed for 1 minute.

Add another 1 cup flour and mix at medium speed for 2 minutes, then turn out onto a lightly floured surface and knead briefly until smooth.

Place the dough in a clean bowl, cover tightly, and let rise for 3 hours, until almost doubled in volume. (The dough will weigh about 2½ pounds.)

Turn the dough out onto a lightly floured surface and divide it in half. Lightly butter two 8-by-4-inch bread pans. One at a time, flatten each piece of dough, then roll up into a cylinder, tuck the ends in, and pinch the seam to seal. Place seam side down in a loaf pan. Cover and let rise for 2½ hours.

Meanwhile, place a rack in the center of the oven and place a baking stone or unglazed quarry tiles, if you have them, on it. Preheat the oven to 400°F. Fill a sprayer with water.

Slash each loaf lengthwise, place in the oven, and bake for 5 minutes, spritzing the loaves several times with water. Bake for 15 minutes, then reduce the heat to 375°F and bake for 25 minutes, or until the loaves are a rich brown with a matte finish. Turn out of the pans, and test for doneness: The bottoms of the loaves should sound hollow when tapped and the edges feel firm when pinched. Transfer to a rack, and let cool completely before slicing.

pain au son

Makes 1 large, moist, bran-rich and slightly sweet pan loaf

To be called pain au son *("bran bread") in France, a bread must by law contain at least 25 percent bran. We use oat bran, but you can substitute wheat bran, which is lighter and sometimes easier to find. This bread is lightly sweetened and moist—a good keeper.*

2 cups lukewarm water

3 tablespoons light brown sugar or honey

1½ teaspoons active dry yeast

1½ cups oat bran, or 1¾ cups wheat bran,
   plus 2 tablespoons for dusting

3½ to 4½ cups all-purpose flour

2 teaspoons salt

Stir together the water and sugar or honey in a large bowl. Stir in the yeast to dissolve it, then stir in the bran. Set aside to soak for 10 minutes.

Sprinkle 1 cup flour onto the bran mixture and stir in. Sprinkle on the salt and stir, then stir in the flour, 1 cup at a time, until the dough is too difficult to stir. Flour a work surface and turn the dough out. Knead until smooth, incorporating as little additional flour as possible, for about 8 minutes. The dough should be soft and smooth.

Place the dough in a large clean bowl, cover with plastic wrap, and let rise for about 2½ hours, until doubled in volume.

Lightly butter an 9-by-5-inch loaf pan. Turn the dough out onto a lightly floured surface and knead briefly. Let rest for 5 minutes, loosely covered, then flatten gently into an oval about 10 inches long and 8 inches across. Starting at a narrow end, roll up into a cylinder, pinch the seam to seal, and place seam side down in the loaf pan. Cover and let rise for about 1 hour, until nearly doubled in volume.

Meanwhile, place a rack in the center of the oven and preheat the oven to 375°F.

When ready to bake, brush the top of the loaf with water and sprinkle on the remaining bran. Bake for 50 minutes, until golden brown. Turn out of the pan and check for doneness: The bottom of the loaf should sound hollow when tapped and the edges feel firm when pinched. Return to the oven for 10 minutes more if necessary. Let cool completely on a rack before slicing.

FOLLOWING PAGES: *Door in the old city near the main square, Essaouira, Morocco. Affeln-Irhir market, southern Morocco.*

Bread rhythms Every four or five days, my mother would make bread. She bought bread only at Christmas, when she'd pick up a loaf of white—"I'm not going to use my good bread to stuff a turkey," she'd say. Friends exclaimed over her bread; my brother and I took it for granted. She was pretty casual about her bread making. She'd start with warm milk (usually made with milk powder) and water, measured by eye to come up to "about there" in her large bread bowl. The yeast proofed in a glass with a little sugar stirred into the water, then went into the big bowl, all foamy. She usually used a dollop of blackstrap molasses and a little butter or oil. There was always a mix of whole wheat and white flours, and sometimes leftover porridge or leftover boiled potatoes. As time went on, she got into the habit of tossing in some sunflower seeds; they softened during baking and were wonderful little taste nuggets.

She'd show friends who asked for the recipe how she measured by eye, and encourage them by repeating that bread making was flexible and not difficult. But they'd roll their eyes: "You make it look easy," they'd say, "but we can't be as relaxed about it as you are."

Long before it became the thing to do, my mother made slow-rise bread, using relatively little yeast and letting the dough ferment overnight in her cool kitchen. If she couldn't bake next morning, she'd punch the dough down and put it in the fridge to wait until she was ready.

Her loaves were in two shapes—the standard rectangular bread-pan bread and tall cylinders with a dome on top. The cylindrical breads, baked in apple juice cans with one end cut off, made round slices and had soft crusts and a velvety crumb. They were our regular sandwich bread. While other kids had peanut butter and jam sandwiches made with slices of white soft "boughten" bread, we had thicker round sandwiches filled with peanut butter, lettuce, and mayonnaise, or with cheese and lettuce. The firm, moist, even crumb of my mother's bread held its own and never softened into sludge or mush. At the time, we wished we had white bread sandwiches like everyone else. Only later did I realize how lucky we were.

And by the way, the bread also made great toast.

helen's special raisin bread

Makes 2 medium-sized golden loaves (about 1½ pounds each) with a golden crumb dotted with raisins

Whenever we make this bread, we are reminded of Naomi's aunt Helen, who lives out in the country on Vancouver Island. Helen grew up in a German farm community in Saskatchewan, and to this day her kitchen is a place where many happy people get fed, and where everyone likes to be. There is always homemade bread, and when Helen makes pies, there are lots of pies. Her pantry alone could keep a family fed for a very long time.

The reason this bread reminds us of Helen is because of the egg in the dough and the scalded milk, both of which make for a rich, somewhat special raisin bread. In our mental image of Helen making bread in her kitchen, there is always an egg going into the dough. Maybe it's because she always kept chickens, and always had eggs around. Maybe she just likes bread best that way.

2 cups scalded milk, cooled to lukewarm

1 cup warm water

1 teaspoon active dry yeast

1 tablespoon sugar

6½ to 8 cups all-purpose flour

1 large or extra-large egg

**1½ to 2 tablespoons unsalted butter, melted,
    plus extra melted butter for brushing**

1 tablespoon salt

1 cup moist dark raisins (see Note)

Combine the milk and water in a bowl. Sprinkle on the yeast and stir in. Add the sugar and 2 cups of the flour and stir until smooth. Let stand for several minutes.

Add the egg and butter and stir in, then sprinkle on the salt and stir in. Continue to add flour a cup at a time until the dough becomes difficult to stir. Flour a work surface generously and turn out the dough. Knead for about 5 minutes, incorporating more flour as necessary, until the dough is smooth, firm, and elastic.

Place the dough in a clean bowl, cover with plastic wrap, and let rise for 3 to 4 hours, until not quite doubled.

Turn the dough out onto a floured surface and cut it in half. Lightly butter two 8-by-4-inch bread pans.

Flatten one dough piece to a rough rectangle about 8 inches by 10 inches. Sprinkle on half the raisins, leaving a 4-inch-wide band raisin-free at one short edge. Roll up the dough from the opposite edge, pinch the seam to seal, and place seam side down in one of the prepared pans. Repeat with the other piece of dough. Cover with plastic and let rise in a warm place for 1 hour.

Meanwhile, place a rack in the lower third of the oven and place a baking stone or unglazed quarry tiles, if you have them, on it. Preheat the oven to 425°F.

Just before baking, brush the loaves with a little melted butter and slash twice crosswise. Bake until golden, about 30 minutes. Brush the tops of the loaves with a little butter and lower the heat to 375°F; bake for another 5 minutes. Remove from the pans: The loaves should sound hollow when tapped on the bottom. Place on a rack to cool for at least 30 minutes before slicing. Once it's aged a day, this bread makes great toast.

NOTE If your raisins are a bit dry, you can plump them by soaking them in warm water, orange juice, or tea for an hour.

You can, of course, omit the raisins, and then you'll have golden loaves with a close-textured, moist, pale yellow crumb that are great for sandwiches.

irish soda bread

Makes 1 dome-shaped hearth bread loaf, about 8 inches in diameter, with a pale brown roughened crust and moist crumb

Irish soda bread was the first bread I ever made on a regular day-to-day basis. When I was living in Ireland (see page 135), running a kind of impromptu boarding house, I or someone else in the house would make Irish soda bread at least once a day, sometimes twice. It started off as a traditional recipe, but like all recipes, it changed. For one thing, the dough got wetter and wetter as we discovered that it would give the bread more loft.

Sometimes we'd try our hands at sourdough and other yeasted breads, but soda bread was still our favorite. Out of the oven and on day one the bread is delicious but crumbly. The longer it sits, however, the firmer it gets, turning into a very good slicing bread.

Occasionally at night, when people might have the munchies, we'd quickly make up a soda bread batter, add a little extra sweetener, and make sconelike rolls. They too were great.

This recipe is double the standard Irish soda bread recipe, to make one big loaf. It's made with a blend of whole wheat and white flours, with a little oatmeal or rolled oats tossed in. The dough is moister than many and, because it also has some butter in it, the bread keeps very well.

3 cups whole wheat flour

3 cups all-purpose flour

1 tablespoon salt

¼ cup packed light brown sugar

2 teaspoons baking soda

¼ cup oatmeal or rolled oats (see Glossary),
or another ¼ cup whole wheat flour

12 tablespoons (1½ sticks) unsalted butter,
chopped into small pieces

2 cups sour milk, or whole milk soured with
1 tablespoon mild vinegar

Place a baking stone or unglazed quarry tiles, if you have them, (or a baking sheet) on a rack in the center of the oven. Preheat the oven to 375°F.

Mix all the dry ingredients together in a big bowl. Cut in the butter. Pour in the milk and mix well to moisten the flour thoroughly. The batter will be moist and heavy. Use wet hands to pull it together and shape it into a dome about 8 inches in diameter.

Transfer the loaf to a flour-dusted peel or the back of a baking sheet dusted with flour. Cut a ½-inch-deep X across the top of the bread, and transfer the bread to the preheated stone or tiles or baking sheet. Bake for 60 to 70 minutes. The bread will look like an overgrown muffin, with a yellow-brown color. To test for doneness, pinch a bottom edge: It should be firm. Set on a rack to cool. (Like all soda-raised baking, this bread is best left for 12 hours or more before slicing.)

papaya-almond whole wheat bread

Makes 2 large whole wheat loaves (more than 2 pounds each), studded with chunks of dried papaya and whole almonds

We lived on this bread all through the 1980s, and we still love it. It's a good solid whole wheat loaf made with chunks of dried papaya and whole almonds. When you slice it, the papaya is a great surprise, and we never get tired of running across another almond.

5 cups lukewarm water

2 teaspoons active dry yeast

6½ cups whole wheat flour

¼ cup packed light brown sugar

Scant 2 tablespoons salt

2 tablespoons olive oil

3 to 4 cups all-purpose flour

1¼ cups dried papaya, cut into ¼- to ½-inch lengths

1 cup unblanched whole almonds

Place the water in a large bowl and stir in the yeast to dissolve completely. Add 6 cups of the whole wheat flour, 2 cups at a time, and stir to make a smooth batter, always stirring in the same direction. Stir for 1 minute more, then cover and set aside for 2 hours. It will be bubbly and a little risen.

Sprinkle on the brown sugar and salt and stir in, then add the olive oil and stir in. Add the remaining ½ cup whole wheat flour, then add 2½ to 3 cups of the all-purpose flour, about ½ cup at a time, stirring and turning to incorporate.

Generously flour a work surface with all-purpose flour. Turn out the dough and knead for about 10 minutes, incorporating flour from the work surface as necessary to prevent sticking. The dough will be smooth and satiny.

Place the dough in a lightly oiled bowl, cover with plastic wrap, and set aside to rise for 2 hours, or until doubled in volume.

Turn the dough out onto a lightly floured surface. Let the dough rest while you butter two 9-by-5-inch bread pans.

Cut the dough in half. Set one piece aside, loosely covered, and flatten the other piece into a rectangle about 8 inches by 10 inches. Sprinkle on half the chopped papaya and half the almonds. Press them into the dough a bit with the palms of your hands and, starting from a short side, roll up the dough into a loaf. (Don't worry if the odd piece of papaya or almond pops out of the dough; just stick it back in.) Pinch the seam to seal and place the dough seam side down in one of the pans. Repeat with the other piece of dough. Cover with plastic wrap and set in a reasonably warm (70° to 75°F) place to rise for about 30 minutes. A finger pressed gently into the dough should leave a dent; the loaves will rise but not double in volume.

Meanwhile, place a rack in the lower third of the oven and preheat the oven to 400°F.

Use a very sharp knife or a razor blade to make 3 parallel slashes diagonally across the top of each loaf, then immediately place in the oven. Bake for 1 hour, or until golden on top. To test for doneness, lift one loaf out of the pan and tap it on the bottom: It should sound hollow, and the lower corners of the loaf should be firm when pinched. Remove the second loaf from the pan and place the breads on a rack to cool for at least half an hour before slicing.

NOTE This bread freezes very well. Let stand overnight before wrapping in plastic and freezing. Defrost overnight at room temperature.

corn bread with cracklings

Makes 1 low, round, all-cornmeal bread with a moist crumb and a delicious bottom crust

PHOTOGRAPH ON PAGE 171 *We were both raised far from the American South, so we're latecomers to corn bread. As kids we had johnnycake and cornmeal muffins, but we never had true Southern corn bread until we were adults. This quick savory version, baked in a skillet and enriched with cracklings, is moist and full of flavor. Serve it with dinner or snack on wedges of it.*

Scant 1 tablespoon bacon drippings

1 extra-large egg

2 cups buttermilk, or a scant 2 cups milk soured with
  2 tablespoons lemon juice or mild vinegar

1¾ cups plus 2 tablespoons stone-ground white cornmeal

½ teaspoon baking powder

¾ teaspoon baking soda

1 teaspoon salt

1 tablespoon sugar

¼ cup packed pork cracklings (see Note) or
  finely chopped cooked bacon

Place a rack in the center of your oven and preheat the oven to 450°F.

Dollop the bacon grease into a 9- or 10-inch cast-iron skillet and place the skillet in the oven.

In a medium bowl, beat the egg briefly, then stir in the buttermilk or soured milk. Stir in the cornmeal and beat briefly. The batter will be liquid and a little frothy. Let stand for several minutes.

Stir in the baking powder, baking soda, salt, and sugar, then stir in the cracklings. Use an oven mitt to lift the hot greased skillet out of the oven. Pour in the batter (it will sizzle as it hits the skillet) and place the skillet back in the oven. Bake for 18 to 20 minutes. The bread will still be very pale on top but will have a well-browned rim and will have pulled away from the sides of the skillet. Test for doneness with a skewer to ensure that the middle is cooked through: It should come out clean.

Serve directly from the skillet, cut into wedges, or turn out onto a rack and turn right side up. (The crispy dark brown bottom crust will soften if the bread stays in the skillet, but it is an easy and very attractive way of serving it.) Once completely cooled, leftover bread keeps well wrapped in plastic.

NOTE If you are rendering lard (see Fat in the Glossary for instructions), the other product of that easy process is pork cracklings. Store, once cooled, in a plastic bag in the refrigerator or freezer. You can often find cracklings in Latin and Asian grocery stores. Use a cleaver to chop into small bits for this recipe.

FOLLOWING PAGES: (LEFT TO RIGHT) *Salt marsh, Edisto Island, South Carolina; rice-threshing shed, Mansfield Plantation, South Carolina.* CORN BREAD WITH CRACKLINGS.

seville orange marmalade

Makes about 8 cups tart-sweet golden orange marmalade

When I was growing up in Ottawa, Ontario, every year in January or early February, with snow white and thick on the ground and days short and dark, there'd be a strong reminder of southern sun in our house. It was the aroma from my mother's annual marmalade making. The opportunity came only for a brief moment, when bitter Seville oranges were available. These days, so many years later, the oranges still have a short season. (Look for Seville oranges at specialty markets. We've been told that you can freeze them and then use them later for marmalade, but we haven't tried for ourselves.)

This simple and reliable recipe makes a clear, not very sweet marmalade with long thick slices of peel in it. Eat it on buttered toast and taste the enticing mix of sweet and bitter in each intense mouthful. There's little fuss and no tedious peeling in this recipe. While the oranges simmer, the house fills with their bittersweet perfume.

Note on quantities: Seville oranges vary in size from year to year. One year recently the oranges we found at the market were huge. They weighed nearly a half pound each, so there were two oranges to a pound, rather than the nearly three oranges to a pound we were used to (and which this recipe assumes). Weigh your oranges, and work by weight if they weigh on average much more or less than about ⅓ pound (roughly 5 ounces) each. Calculate your water on the basis of weight; allow 2½ cups water per pound of oranges.

The sugar is calculated on the basis of the amount of liquid remaining after boiling and straining, as described in the recipe instructions: Allow 2 cups sugar (or 2¼ cups if you like sweeter marmalade) for each cup of liquid.

6 Seville oranges (2½ to 3 pounds; see headnote), scrubbed

6 to 7 cups water (see headnote)

About 7 cups sugar

Prick each orange several times with a fork. Place in a large heavy pot, add the water, and bring to a boil. Reduce the heat and simmer, covered, for 3 hours or more, until the peel is very soft. Let stand until cool, or for up to 8 hours.

Lift out the oranges; set the pot aside. Cut open the oranges and pull the flesh off the softened peels—don't scrape the peels, just pull off the flesh, leaving the peels with a fuzzy surface. Place them on a plate and set aside.

Put the flesh (and seeds) back into the cooking water, bring to a hard boil, cover, and boil for 10 minutes. (This boiling will help extract the pectin from the seeds.)

Meanwhile, slice the peels into thin or medium slices, whichever you prefer. (You will have 3½ to 4 cups packed chopped peel.) Set aside.

Your jam jars (eight ½-pint jars, or several pint jars and the balance in ½-pint jars) and lids (rings and tops), as well as any equipment you use to handle the jam (such as a funnel, a ladle, a spoon, or chopsticks), must be sterile (see Notes). Put a tray near your stove. Place two or three dry saucers in the freezer to chill.

Place a sieve over a bowl and strain the hot orange liquid through; use a wooden spoon to press the debris against the sieve to extract as much liquid as possible. Measure the liquid; you will have 3½ to 3¾ cups liquid. Calculate the amount of sugar you need (see headnote). Discard the flesh and seeds.

Pour the orange liquid into a wide heavy pot and set it over medium-high heat. As it comes to a boil, use a wooden spoon to stir in the sugar cup by cup until it has all dissolved, then add the chopped peel. Raise the heat and bring to a vigorous foaming boil, stirring occasionally to prevent burning, then keep it at a strong boil: The jam will reach setting point in about 12 to 15 minutes, not more than 20. At the 12-minute mark, do a first test: Take a chilled saucer from the freezer, drop a little marmalade onto it, and give it a moment to cool. Push a finger through it along the plate. If the liquid wrinkles or makes a thick wave ahead of your finger, the jam is at set point. If not, continue to test every 2 to 3 minutes. Remove the pot from the heat while you test, so as not to overcook the jam. Once the jam is ready, let the pot stand for 10 minutes before filling your jars (this helps keep the fruit from rising in the jars).

Place the jam jars on the tray by your stove top. Put your funnel on one jar, and use the ladle to scoop marmalade from the pot, getting a good mix of peel and liquid, and fill the jar, leaving about ⅛ inch headspace. Wipe off any spills or stickiness on the outside with a clean damp cloth. Place a lid on the jar, screw on a ring, and seal tightly. Leave the full jar on the tray while you fill the remaining jars. You should hear the lids pop one by one as they cool.

Once the jars have cooled completely, label them, and store in a cool, dark place. (If the amounts didn't come out evenly and you have one half-full jar, it will need to be refrigerated once it cools.)

NOTE ON EQUIPMENT You will need ½-pint or 1-pint glass jam jars with lids. The lids have two parts, a top and a ring. You will also need tongs for lifting the hot jars, a long-handled wooden spoon for stirring the hot jam, a ladle, a sieve, and a tall heavy stainless-steel pot (of at least 4-quart capacity) for cooking the jam. You will want one or two trays or heavy baking sheets to place the jars on when filling them, and you will find it easiest if you have a wide-mouthed funnel to help when filling the jars with jam. Make sure you have a sterilized plate to place your funnel and ladle on when not using them.

Because the marmalade has long pieces of peel, a normal canning funnel is not very practical for filling the jars. We use a medium-sized plastic yogurt container as a funnel substitute; it helps prevent splashing and frustration. Cut a hole smaller in diameter than your jam jars in the bottom of a yogurt or other plastic container.

NOTE ON STERILIZING EQUIPMENT FOR MAKING JAM All jars and lids (rings and tops) must be sterilized, and so must the ladle and any funnel or other equipment you use that will touch the jam as you transfer it to the jars. Sterilize the equipment, whichever method you use, before putting the jam on to cook. (If equipment isn't sterile, the jam will need to be kept refrigerated even before it's opened.)

The traditional method is to place the jars and lids and equipment in a large pot of water (so everything is immersed), bring to a boil, and boil for 10 minutes; then let stand. Use tongs to remove things from the hot bath just before using.

Another method is to give the equipment a hot wash in the dishwasher, then transfer the jars and rims, and other heatproof equipment, to a heavy baking sheet and place it in a 225°F oven. Any equipment that is plastic (for example, the funnel we use for marmalade, see above), or wooden chopsticks, or the rubber-lined tops can't tolerate the oven's heat for long. Leave in the dishwasher, untouched, until shortly before using, then place in the oven for 5 minutes.

grape harvest jam

Makes about 5 cups thick purple-blue jam with an intense, not very sweet taste of grape

Our grapevines began as a way of creating shade and privacy in the backyard. They're Concord grape vines, hardy and prolific, bearing large purple-blue fruit in September. We compete with the squirrels and the birds for them. This jam is an easy way to carry the taste of that harvest into the winter months—intensely flavored (there's no added water, no pectin), a little tart, a little sweet.

The recipe calls for warm sugar so that when the sugar is added to the simmering fruit, it doesn't cool it.

3 to 3½ pounds ripe Concord grapes

3 cups sugar, or as much as 4 cups if you like your jam sweeter, heated in a 150°F oven until warm

Sterilize five ½-pint jars, lids and rings for them, as well as a ladle and a funnel (see Notes on equipment and sterilization on page 173).

To prepare the grapes, wash them, then sit somewhere comfortable, preferably in autumn sunshine and perhaps with a friend to chat with as you work. One by one (or, if you get good at it, two by two), pick the grapes off their stems and squeeze them out of their skins into a stainless-steel pot; don't worry if a little skin stays stuck to the pulp. Place the skins on a plate; you'll be using them later. (Don't worry about the grape seeds; you'll be straining them out later.) Continue until all the grapes are skinned (it seems long but it gets done fairly fast, in about 15 minutes). Set aside the grape skins.

Place the pot of grape pulp over medium heat, cover, and bring to a gentle boil. Cook for 5 to 6 minutes,

stirring occasionally. When the grapes have broken down into a mush, remove from the heat. Place a large bowl in the sink and set a sieve over it. Pour the grape pulp into the sieve and use a wooden spoon to help push it through the mesh. Discard the seeds.

Add the grape skins to the pulp and bring to a vigorous boil, stirring occasionally. Boil for 1 to 2 minutes (you'll see the mixture quickly turn dark from the color in the grape skins). Gradually add the warm sugar, stirring it in 1 cup at a time. Bring back to a rolling boil and cook, stirring constantly, for another 2 minutes. Remove from the heat and skim off the foam.

Place the hot sterilized jars on a tray or baking sheet on the counter by the stove. Put out the sterilized tops and rings. Use a sterilized ladle to ladle the hot jam into the jars. If you have a little extra left over, ladle it into the skimmed-off foam, for eating immediately.

Place a top and a ring on each jar, then tighten the rings. Let stand while the jam cools and the jars seal; you'll hear them go "pop" gently as the tops seal.

damson jam

Makes about 4½ cups tart dark jam

PHOTOGRAPH ON PAGE 124 *Damson jam, made from tart damson plums, is, like Seville Orange Marmalade (page 172), a taste from my childhood. I loved it then and still my mouth waters at the thought of it. It's thickened but not thick, tart and sweet and a beautiful rich purple in color. The trick is to heat the plums gently so they don't burn or make the mixture cloudy, and to add the sugar slowly so the temperature of the fruit doesn't drop.*

About 3 pounds damson plums, washed and stemmed

1 cup springwater

2½ cups sugar, heated in a 150°F oven until warm

2 tablespoons freshly squeezed lemon juice

Place the plums in a wide heavy pot with the spring-water. Prick each one with a fork. Heat over medium heat to a steady simmer and let simmer for 30 minutes.

Gradually add the sugar, stirring in about ¼ cup at a time, then cook for another 10 minutes at a gentle sim-mer. Stir in the lemon juice, and remove from the heat.

Meanwhile, sterilize four ½-pint jam jars with lids (see the detailed instructions on equipment and steril-izing in the Notes on page 173).

Place a colander or coarse sieve over a bowl and pour in the plum mixture. Pick out the pits as you press the jam through the colander. (Or just pick the pits out of the pot; they'll float to the surface as the plums disinte-grate during cooling, so you will get most of them fairly easily.) Return the jam to the pot and bring back to a simmer. Using a sterile ladle and funnel, pour or spoon the hot jam into the prepared jars, place on the tops and rings, and seal. You will have a little jam left over. Pour into a clean jar and refrigerate. Use this one first, before opening the other jars.

ARTISAN-STYLE LOAVES

dom's large-batch italian boules and focaccia

Makes 4 large hearth-baked boules with an attractively slashed flour-dusted crust, or 3 boules and 2 focaccia, brushed with olive oil

PHOTOGRAPH ON PAGE 181 *Our son Dom is a teenager; in the last year or so he's grown so much that he's now taller than we are. And, because he's growing, he eats a lot, especially a lot of bread, which means our family supply disappears at a rapid rate. So one day we decided to get him to bake, to get him comfortable with making bread. Because this slow-rise Italian bread was one he especially liked, it seemed like a good place to start. Together we figured out a large-batch version, some for eating right away and some for putting in the freezer. In later bakes, we used some of the dough to make farm-style focaccia as well as loaves. Both options are set out below.*

Because of the slow fermentation, this bread has the good full flavor of the best artisanal breads. The crust bakes thin and crisp, then softens over time, as the moisture in the crumb affects it. The breads keep well at room temperature without going stale, and they freeze very well; once they've sat out for twelve hours, we freeze two of them in well-sealed plastic bags. They can be thawed overnight whenever the bread supply is running low.

Note on timing: *This is a slow-rise dough. The timing is very flexible; it can be made over several days, with very little time required at each step. The first time you make it, you might try the following schedule: Stir up the poolish one evening (5 minutes). Add the additional water and flour the next morning or evening, whichever is most convenient (10 minutes). Finish making the dough 6 to 24 hours later (15 minutes). The dough should rise for 4 hours (though you could leave it for 6 if need be). Once you have a risen dough, it will take 3 hours to get all the breads proofed and baked, though most of that is waiting time.*

POOLISH

3 cups springwater

¼ teaspoon active dry yeast

3 cups all-purpose flour

BREAD

6 cups lukewarm water

2 cups whole wheat flour or whole spelt flour

13 to 15 cups all-purpose flour (see Note)

3 tablespoons sea salt

FOR FOCACCIA (OPTIONAL)

2 to 4 tablespoons olive oil

About 2 teaspoons coarse sea salt

About 1 teaspoon rosemary leaves (optional)

Place the springwater in a large bowl and stir in the yeast to dissolve it. Add the flour and stir until a smooth batter forms. Cover and let stand for 8 to 24 hours, whatever is most convenient.

Add the water to the poolish and stir, then add the whole wheat or spelt flour and stir well. Add 4 cups all-purpose flour, 2 cups at a time, stirring always in the same direction, until smooth. Cover and set aside for 4 to 12 hours, as convenient.

Sprinkle the salt onto the sponge and stir it in. Add 7 to 8 cups all-purpose flour, about 2 cups at a time, stirring and folding the dough over to absorb the flour until it's too difficult to stir and fold. Flour a work surface well and turn the dough out. Knead for 5 to 8 minutes, incorporating the flour from the work surface and adding a little extra to the surface if necessary, but try to add as little flour as possible: The dough should be soft, smooth, and almost sticky. Place back in the bowl, cover with plastic, and let rise until doubled, 3½ to 4 hours (or overnight in a cool place).

Turn the dough out onto a well-floured surface and divide into 4 equal pieces. Set aside loosely covered with plastic. Line three 8- to 10-inch round shallow wooden bowls or baskets with cotton cloths (such as tea towels) and flour the cloths well with all-purpose flour, rubbing flour into them. (Prepare four cloth-lined bowls or baskets if not making focaccia.) If you are planning to make focaccia immediately with some of the dough, as soon as the dough has risen, lightly grease two 18-by-12-inch baking sheets with olive oil and sprinkle on semolina, if available.

To shape loaves: On a lightly floured surface, tuck the sides of 1 piece of dough under all around to make a large round boule. Pinch together underneath. Transfer the boule to a bowl or basket seam side up. Repeat with 2 more pieces of dough (or all 3 if not making focaccia). Let rise for 1½ hours, covered loosely with plastic wrap.

Forty-five minutes before you plan to start baking, place a baking stone or unglazed quarry tiles, if you have them, on a rack in the center of the oven. Preheat the oven to 500°F.

To shape focaccia: Divide the remaining dough in half. (If you'd rather make the focaccia later, flatten each half into a disk, seal the 2 pieces in separate plastic bags, and refrigerate for 24 hours or freeze them for up to a month. Bring back to room temperature before using.) Flatten 1 piece on a lightly floured surface. Stretch it over the backs of your hands, then transfer it to a prepared baking sheet and gently press and stretch it out to the size of the sheet. If it's springing back, let it rest for several minutes, then continue to stretch it out, using the pause to begin stretching the other piece of dough. Once both rectangles are stretched, dribble 1 to 2 tablespoons olive oil over each one, then spread it all over with your hands. Dimple the breads all over with your fingertips, then sprinkle on the salt and rosemary, if using. Cover loosely with plastic wrap and let rise for about 45 minutes.

To bake focaccia: Bake on the baking sheets, or transfer the bread directly onto the baking stone or tiles. Bake one at a time, for 12 to 15 minutes, until very browned in patches. Transfer to racks to cool.

To bake loaves: Place a sprayer filled with water near your oven. Dust a peel (or the back of a baking sheet) with semolina, cornmeal, or flour. Flip one boule onto the peel, and lift off the bowl or basket and cloth (see the photograph on page 149). Use a sharp knife or razor blade to slash 3 parallel deep cuts across the top of the loaf, then place it on the far back corner of the hot baking stone or tiles (or on a baking sheet), jerking the peel out from under it. You should have just enough room for another bread. Spritz the loaf vigorously with water and close the oven door. Repeat with one more loaf.

Bake until domed and darkly golden, 25 to 30 minutes; repeat the spritzing three or four times in the first 5 to 10 minutes of baking. To test the bread for doneness, take the loaf out of the oven, tap on the bottom (it should sound hollow), and pinch the bottom edges to see that it's firm. Transfer to a rack to cool. (You'll hear the crust crackling quietly for a while as the bread cools and settles after baking.)

Bake the remaining loaf (or loaves) in the same way. It will have had a 2-hour proof rather than 1½ hours, but the delay won't harm it—in fact, you may prefer the texture of longer-proofed loaves.

NOTE Flour quantities vary with the kind of flour and the weather. In this case, flour amounts also depend on whether you have used whole wheat flour.

Use unbleached all-purpose flour if possible; it gives better flavor and color.

portuguese mountain rye

Makes 2 large wheat-and-rye-flour hearth loaves (each weighing nearly 2 pounds) with an attractive cracked, domed top crust

PHOTOGRAPH ON PAGE 1 *Every few weeks in the village of Sabugueiro in the mountains of central Portugal, a group of village women, including Margarida, in whose house I stayed, fire up the village oven (see At the Village Oven, page 190). Once the oven is hot, they sweep out the coals and test the heat by tossing several small, flattened pieces of dough onto the oven floor. If the breads puff up immediately (like fast-cooking pitas), the oven's a little too hot, so they brush it with a little water. Then in go the loaves, barely shaped. In forty-five minutes to an hour they're done, crusty mounds with attractive cracks created as the moist dough rises in the oven's heat (see the photograph on page 191).*

Here's our version of Margarida's bread, with a complex mixed grain taste and firm yet tender texture very like hers. We make a relatively small batch compared to her dozen loaves: two large loaves, as well as a sourdough starter for the next round of baking. The breads keep beautifully at room temperature.

POOLISH

½ cup lukewarm water

Pinch of active dry yeast

½ cup all-purpose flour, preferably unbleached

RYE STARTER

1 cup lukewarm water

2 cups light rye flour

BREAD

3 cups light rye flour

1 cup whole wheat flour

4 cups lukewarm water

1 tablespoon plus 1 teaspoon fine sea salt

3 to 5 cups all-purpose or bread flour, preferably unbleached

Make the poolish 3 to 4 days before you wish to bake: In a medium bowl, stir together the water and yeast. Stir in the flour to make a smooth batter. Cover and set aside to ferment for 12 to 36 hours, as is convenient.

Make the rye starter: Place the poolish in a medium bowl. Stir in the lukewarm water, then the rye flour. Let stand at room temperature, loosely covered, for 24 hours, then refrigerate for 12 to 24 hours, as is convenient.

The evening before you wish to bake, place the starter in a large bowl and add the rye and whole wheat flours: They should completely cover the starter—*do not stir.* Cover with a tea towel and let stand. Next morning, you'll see the starter bubbling up a little through the flour.

Three hours before you wish to bake, add 3 cups of the lukewarm water to the bowl, along with 1 teaspoon of the salt, and use your hands or a large wooden spoon to stir the whole mixture until smooth. Lift out and reserve 2 cups (about 1½ pounds) of the mixture; this is your starter for the next batch (see the Note on the

PRECEDING PAGES: GALICIAN HEARTH BREAD WITH WHOLE CORN (*page 204*).
DOM'S LARGE-BATCH ITALIAN FOCACCIA (*page 178*) *topped with salt and rosemary.*

Next Generation below). Add the remaining 1 cup lukewarm water to the dough and stir in. Sprinkle on the remaining 1 tablespoon salt, then 2 cups of the unbleached flour, and stir and knead for about 5 minutes, adding extra flour if necessary: The dough should be moist and just a little sticky. Cover well with a cloth and then a layer of plastic and let rise in a slightly warm (70° to 75°F) place for 3 hours. The dough will not quite double.

Meanwhile, place a baking stone or unglazed quarry tiles, if you have them, on a rack in the middle to lower third of the oven and preheat the oven to 500°F.

When you are ready to bake, dust a peel (or upside-down baking sheet) with flour or cornmeal. Place about ¼ cup all-purpose or bread flour in an 8- to 9-inch wooden bowl. Turn the dough out onto a lightly floured surface. Cut the dough in half (it will be sticky). Leave half covered with plastic and, with lightly floured hands, transfer the other piece to the floured bowl. Hold the bowl with both hands and gently toss the dough around in the bowl for nearly a minute: This shapes it into a rough round.

Invert the dough round onto the peel or sheet, so the floured bottom is now on top, and transfer to the preheated baking stone or tiles (or a baking sheet), leaving room for the other bread beside it. Repeat with the other piece of dough (if you don't have room for two loaves, just bake the first bread, then preheat the oven to 500°F again and shape and bake the second). After 15 minutes, lower the heat to 425°F. The breads will take about 45 minutes. When they are done, they should sound hollow when tapped on the bottom. The tops of the breads will be white-floured and very pretty.

Transfer to a rack to cool completely before slicing or wrapping. The bread keeps well for a week or more at room temperature, tightly wrapped in plastic. Or freeze it, once it has cooled completely, in a well-sealed plastic bag. To thaw, leave out overnight to come to room temperature.

NOTE ON THE NEXT GENERATION Store the 2 cups of starter in a well-sealed plastic bag in the refrigerator. It must be refreshed 1 or 2 days before you wish to bake: If you keep it without using it for more than a week, refresh it every 7 days or so. To refresh: Discard half, add 1 cup warm water, and stir in 2 cups rye flour. Take out and let stand at room temperature for 12 to 24 hours before using.

The starter seems to be very forgiving. We took a sad-looking starter that had been forgotten—unrefreshed—in the refrigerator for 3 weeks, refreshed it as directed, and then used it the following day for making the dough. It worked just fine. We're still mystified and amazed by the process.

BACKGROUND NOTE The technique of shaping a very wet dough by tossing it in a well-floured bowl is one I learned in northern Portugal, at Teresa's bakery (see Portuguese Egg Tarts, page 52). Her bakers shaped stacks of mixed grain rye breads like this, tossing them one by one in a floured basket, then flipping them onto a peel and into the hot oven.

country baguettes

Makes six 14-inch-long baguettes with a pale crust and crumb, flecked with amaranth, flaxseeds, and sesame seeds

PHOTOGRAPH ON PAGES 186 AND 187 *These loaves were inspired by the small baguettes, called* pains aux céréales, *that were delivered by a baker each morning to the small rural gîte we stayed in on the Cotentin peninsula of Normandy. Pain aux céréales means multigrain bread. Those breads were flecked with flaxseeds and millet. Because we prefer the taste of amaranth to millet, we use a combination of amaranth, flaxseeds, and sesame seeds in this recipe. The basic dough is like a baguette dough, only with the addition of a little buckwheat flour.*

POOLISH

1 cup lukewarm water

¼ teaspoon active dry yeast

1 cup all-purpose flour, preferably unbleached

BREAD

2 tablespoons amaranth (see Glossary)

1½ cups water

½ cup light buckwheat flour

4½ to 6 cups all-purpose flour, preferably unbleached

2 tablespoons sesame seeds

2 tablespoons flaxseeds

1 tablespoon salt

Coarse semolina or cornmeal for dusting

Make the poolish 24 to 36 hours before you wish to bake: Place the water in a bowl and stir in the yeast so it dissolves well. Stir in the flour until you have a smooth batter. Let stand for at least 6 hours, or as long as overnight, as convenient.

Place the amaranth in a bowl and add lukewarm water to cover. Let soak for 10 minutes, then drain it in a fine sieve and set aside.

Place the 1½ cups water in a large bowl and dissolve the poolish in it. Add the buckwheat flour and stir it in. Add 1 cup of the all-purpose flour and stir to make a smooth batter. Sprinkle on the amaranth, sesame seeds, flaxseeds, and salt and stir in. Add flour, a cup or so at a time, until the dough is too difficult to stir. Turn out onto a lightly floured surface and knead, incorporating more flour only as needed, until the dough is smooth and elastic, about 7 minutes.

Place the dough in a clean bowl, cover with plastic, and set aside to rise for at least 12 hours, or overnight, whatever is convenient.

Flour several cotton or linen cloths, such as large dish towels, with all-purpose flour, rubbing it in, then add a dusting of flour to each.

Turn the dough out onto a lightly floured surface. Cut it into 6 equal pieces. Keeping the rest of the dough loosely covered, shape one loaf: Flatten into a rectangle about 6 inches by 12 inches, then roll up from one long side to make a cylinder about 14 inches long. Place seam side up a few inches from one end of one of the cloths. Make a wrinkle down the length of the cloth on either side of the bread to cradle it. Place a long, straight heavy object, such as a stack of tall books, against the end of the cloth to support the rising dough.

Shape another loaf and place it on the cloth, separated from the first by the wrinkle in the cloth. Repeat, laying the breads side by side in these improvised couches, and supporting the length of the last loaf on each cloth with another long solid object. Let rise, loosely covered with plastic, for 2 hours.

Meanwhile, 45 minutes or so before the breads have finished proofing, place a stone or unglazed quarry tiles, if you have them, (or a baking sheet) on a rack in the upper third of the oven and preheat the oven to 425°F; it should reach the proper temperature at least 20 minutes before you put in the breads. Fill a sprayer with water.

Dust a peel (or the back of a baking sheet) with semolina or cornmeal. Roll a bread onto the peel so it is seam side down. Using a very sharp knife or a razor blade held at an angle to the bread, give it 2 or 3 long diagonal slashes. Spritz with water and place on the hot stone, tiles, or a baking sheet. Repeat with as many breads as will fit; bake in two batches, if necessary.

Bake for 15 to 20 minute, until pale brown spotted with darker brown. (The breads will not have dark edges when done, so be careful not to overbake them.) The crusts will be thin and crisp, and the breads will sound hollow when tapped on the bottoms. Cool on a rack.

Once the breads are completely cool, store them, well sealed in plastic, at room temperature, or in the freezer. Leave out overnight to defrost.

FOLLOWING PAGES: COUNTRY BAQUETTES, *rising and freshly baked.*

pugliese sponge breads

Makes 2 large, low, round hearth breads with a tender crumb and a smooth crust

These unusual breads come from southern Puglia (see Wet Bread, page 202). They're made with a very wet, almost flowing dough and bake quickly into one of the best breads we know.

BIGA

⅛ teaspoon active dry yeast

½ cup lukewarm water

1 cup all-purpose flour, preferably unbleached

BREAD

3 cups lukewarm water

1 teaspoon active dry yeast

5 to 6 cups all-purpose flour, preferably unbleached

1 tablespoon plus ½ teaspoon salt

About 1 cup whole wheat pastry flour or whole wheat flour

Make the biga at least 24 hours before you wish to bake: In a small bowl, dissolve the yeast in the water, then add the flour and stir well to combine. Knead briefly in a bowl to make a soft dough. Cover with plastic wrap and let stand at room temperature for 12 to 24 hours, or refrigerate for up to 3 days, as convenient. Bring back to room temperature before using.

When ready to proceed, place the lukewarm water in a large bowl or the bowl of a stand mixer and stir the yeast in to dissolve it. Cut the biga into 4 or 5 pieces, add it, and stir, breaking up the biga with a spoon or your hand to help it dissolve. Stir in 1 cup of the all-purpose flour. Sprinkle on the salt, and stir in the whole wheat flour. Add 3 more cups all-purpose flour, 1 cup at a time.

By hand: Place a bowl of warm water by your work surface. Wet one hand and forearm with water and begin stirring the dough with your hand; keep your fingers extended and fairly stiff, to make your hand like a paddle, and turn the dough around and round on itself in the same way that a dough hook does. Add another cup of flour, stir it in, and mix for several minutes with your hand. You should begin to see gluten strands clinging to the sides of the bowl as you mix and to feel the strength of the dough as it gets wrapped around your fingers. At the correct consistency, the dough will still be very wet and sloppy but will cling together rather than seeming like a liquid. If the dough still seems too sloppy, add another ½ cup flour or so and continue stirring. Stir for 4 to 5 minutes after the last addition of flour. Clean the sides of the bowl.

Using a stand mixer: Fit the mixer with the dough hook. Add 1 cup flour and mix at low speed for 2 minutes. You can add another ½ cup flour or so if the dough seems more like a liquid than like a sloppy dough with strength, and continue mixing. Mix for a total of 5 minutes at low speed. Transfer to a large bowl.

Cover the bowl with plastic wrap and let the dough stand for at least 3 hours, or as long as overnight if more convenient; it will rise a little but not double in volume.

Meanwhile, place a baking stone or unglazed quarry tiles, if you have them, (or a baking sheet) on a rack in the center or lower third of the oven, and preheat the oven to 500°F. Do not bake until 20 minutes after the oven has reached the correct temperature.

When ready to bake, place a bowl of warm water by your oven, next to the risen dough. If you have a helper, leave the oven door closed and ask your helper to stand by to open it when you're ready; if you're working alone, open the oven door. Immediately wet your hands very well by dipping them into the water, then pick up about half the dough. Moving the dough quickly from hand to hand, try to shape it into a mound—use both hands to shape it, tucking the edges under to tighten the top surface (it will still feel sloppy and oozy)—then drop it onto the preheated stone, tiles, or baking sheet. Or, if you don't want to reach into the oven, drop the dough onto a very wet narrow peel, then tip it sideways off the peel onto the preheated surface and close the oven door. Even if there is room in your oven for both breads to bake at once, the first time around, just bake one at a time to see how it goes.

After 10 minutes, lower the heat to 450°F. Bake for another 20 to 25 minutes, or until the bread is well touched with brown. It should sound hollow when tapped on the bottom. Remove from the oven and let cool for at least 30 minutes before slicing. Raise the oven heat back to 500°F, and shape and bake the second bread.

SMALLER PUGLIESE SPONGE BREADS You can make smaller breads with this dough, and you may find the smaller handfuls of dough a little easier to manage at first. Just pick up about a quarter of the dough each time, and bake in two batches of two loaves each. The baking time will be about 25 minutes for each batch. (Makes 4 loaves.)

FOLLOWING PAGES: *Margarida and neighbors working at the village oven, Sabugueiro, Portugal.*
Their freshly baked breads, hot from the oven.

At the village oven When I reached Sabugueiro, a small village high in the Serra da Estrela in central Portugal, at dusk one evening, I asked the first person I saw, a man repairing a stone wall, if he knew of a room I could rent for a few days. He knocked at a door nearby; a short, strongly built woman with graying hair escaping from her kerchief appeared in the doorway. She paused to listen to his question, then walked over to my car.

"What are you doing traveling all by yourself?" she asked in a strong voice (in Portuguese, of course), and she clearly expected an answer.

In stumbling Portuguese, I tried to tell her that my family was in Canada and that I was there because I was interested in Portuguese bread.

A smile broke across her serious, almost scowling face. "My name is Margarida. I have a room for you. We're baking bread tomorrow."

It turned out that Margarida was one of the women responsible for firing the village oven. In the stable underneath her house, watched by her munching donkey, her sourdough starter was already coming to life, covered with a pile of rye flour. The flour had been milled at the stream-powered mill just below the village.

The next morning, after milking the goats, Margarida carried a pail of warm water down to the stable. I watched and asked questions as she made her dough. The flour and starter were in a loose pile on a traditional kneading trough, a wooden surface that looked like a very large tray, about four feet long and more than two feet wide, with low wooden sides all round. Margarida began by sprinkling a little salt onto the flour, then poured on a lot of warm water. Rolling up her sleeves, she stirred the mixture vigorously with her hands, sloshing it around until the flour and sourdough were well blended in a wet batter. She set some aside as a starter for next time and added more salt and some wheat flour to the batter. Then she started to knead—fold and turn, fold and turn—heaving the large mass of dough around with the ease of long practice. When she was done, it was smooth, and a little sticky to the touch.

With her thumb, she pressed the sign of the cross into the top of the dough, then tenderly covered it with two woolen blankets. After she'd given the waiting donkey its morning hay, we headed down through the village to the baking house, walking at a brisk pace.

Three other women were already there, in thick stockings and leather ankle boots, their long skirts covered by aprons. They had the fire lit and were now feeding it with branches. They swept and tended as I photographed them working, my tripod incongruous and shiny against the baking house's timeworn textures of stone and wood. They asked about my family, laughing patiently at my bad Portuguese, and talked about their grandchildren.

Once they were sure the oven was heating well, it was time to fetch the bread dough. They all headed up the steep cobbled lane, each to her own house. Margarida was last in line. She turned one last time to make sure of me: "Now you'll stay there. You won't leave? And don't let any dogs come in!" I assured her I'd stand guard, and I tried to look reliable. Off she went.

Another half hour and back they came, arriving one by one. The oldest, Teresa, was accompanied by her husband, who was carrying the dough. The others were on their own, the heavy (thirty-five pounds or more) long wooden trays of dough balanced on their heads. Once inside, they helped each other lift the trays onto the wooden table near the oven.

After sweeping out the coals with a long-handled broom, they began placing their hefty lumps of dough into the oven, taking turns wielding a long wooden peel. I watched as Margarida took her turn: One of the other women placed a large flour-dusted loaf on the peel, then Margarida lifted the long handle, raising the flat wooden blade at the far end carrying the dough. She stepped forward, lifting and thrusting the blade deep into the oven, then lowered it onto the oven floor. With a sharp jerk, she pulled the blade out from under the loaf, leaving it near, but not touching, the other loaves. She lifted the peel out, ready for the next loaf, the next lift and jerk and pull. And so it went, loaf after loaf, about sixty in all. It's hard labor, this baking, like much else the village women do, but it was done deftly, almost gracefully, with the occasional good-humored comment.

When it looked as if the oven could hold no more loaves, each woman made a few flatbreads with the last of her dough. The flattened rounds were sprinkled with a little sugar, then into the oven they went and the oven door was wedged shut.

These women, so hardworking, so amused to talk to me, the foreigner, and to watch me photograph them as they worked, now took a break—sort of. They sat on the narrow bench and started to chat, but then one by one, as if they couldn't help themselves, they got up and started sweeping, wiping flour off the table, cleaning their bread trays, organizing the woodpile. As they worked, the specks of flour in the air eddied gently across the shaft of light coming through the window.

As the smell of baking bread drifted from the oven into the village, children began to appear at the baking house door in ones and twos, looking eager and inquiring. Then I understood—the sugared flatbreads! They're done very quickly, these first breads, the children's baking-day treats. One of the women used the peel to lift them out, then immediately closed the oven door to keep the heat in for the long full bake. The children each took a small hot bread from the peel and ran off happily.

In forty-five minutes to an hour the loaves were done. Some were more domed, others were lower mounds; all were crusty disks with a good dusting of white flour on top. They were loaded onto the trays, then each of the women placed her tray of loaves on her head and walked slowly home up the hill.

That evening I had supper with Margarida in her kitchen. We watched a fast-paced sex-and-glamour-laden Brazilian soap opera—so remote from life in a small mountain village—as we spooned up her vegetable soup and ate her good fresh bread. And there was more: a remarkable goat's milk cheese, made in the village. As the flavors of the bread and cheese came together in my mouth so perfectly, I tasted with gratitude the labor and the landscape, the time and the care that had created them.

special spiced rye from gotland

Makes 4 round rye hearth breads (nearly 1¾ pounds each) with a dark brown, soft crust and very smooth crumb

This aromatic bread with a velvety crumb is a form of limpa, *or Swedish hearth bread, slightly sweet and spiced with cumin and tiny pieces of dried orange peel. We learned to make it from Ana, on the island of Gotland in the Baltic off the east coast of Sweden. She's our friend Tina's grandmother, and she makes this* slagbrot—"pulled bread"—*for special occasions. Now she uses an electric oven to bake it; originally it was baked in a wood-fired hearth oven.*

Gotland is an old place, an agricultural island with a beautiful medieval city, Visby, halfway along its west coast. Visby was a member of the Hanseatic League and a very prosperous and cosmopolitan port. We don't know how or when slagbrot *originated, but we do know that we've never seen its like anywhere else. The rye starter for the bread is mixed by "pulling"—rubbed and blended with lots of effort—until it's very smooth. The result is an extremely tender and smooth crumb, like no bread we've ever eaten before.*

Tina's grandmother made her pulled sourdough the afternoon before she baked. She used a trag, *a wide wooden trough (very like the wooden kneading troughs of a hundred years ago or more in North America that you sometimes see for sale at antique markets) to hold the mixture. She inherited it from her grandmother, who was born in the middle of the nineteenth century, so it has generations of sour rye embedded in its smooth wooden sides. She advised us to use vinegar in our sourdough mixture, to substitute for the bacterial flora on the* trag, *and it worked well.*

This recipe makes only a quarter of the traditional recipe, but it is still large. We figure that if you're going to do the work involved, you want to have enough bread from it. You can freeze two or three loaves if you wish.

RYE STARTER

8 cups light rye flour

1½ tablespoons salt

4½ cups very hot water

1 tablespoon white wine vinegar or cider vinegar

BREAD

6 to 7 cups all-purpose flour

Generous ⅓ cup loosely packed dried orange peel (see Glossary)

1 tablespoon active dry yeast

¾ cup lukewarm water

¼ cup sugar, plus a pinch

1 large egg

½ cup honey

¼ cup sunflower oil

1 tablespoon cumin seeds

Cornmeal for dusting

The day before you wish to bake, prepare the starter: Place the rye flour in a wide wooden trough, or a basin or sink, at least 2 feet wide. Dissolve the salt in the hot water and pour onto the flour. Use a strong long-handled wooden spoon or spatula to start stirring the water into the flour, then add the vinegar. Continue to stir and turn to moisten all the flour.

Move the dough to one side of the trough or basin, and brace the trough firmly (or have a friend hold it). Use your spoon or spatula to pull pieces of dough away from the mass and over toward the other side of the trough, smearing it as you pull it across. Keep working away at the dough, gradually moving it bit by bit to the other side. It will probably stick in a mass to your wooden spoon or spatula; use a dough scraper or knife to clean it off. Once you've pulled all the dough across, repeat in the other direction. (It's best if you have a friend to help with the work, to spell you.) Pull the dough a total of six or seven times. It will get increasingly smooth, almost gluey, as you work.

Scrape down the sides of the trough or basin. Cover the starter with 2 cups of the all-purpose flour, then cover with plastic wrap and several layers of cotton cloth. Place in a draft-free place to ferment for 14 to 16 hours.

An hour before proceeding (or the day you make the starter, if it's more convenient), prepare the orange peel: Place the peel in a small pot with about 2 cups of water and bring to a boil. Lower the heat and simmer, half covered, for 30 minutes, checking occasionally to make sure the pot isn't boiling dry; add more water if necessary. When the peel is very tender, drain and chop into approximately ¼-inch pieces. You should have about ¼ cup packed chopped peel. Set aside. (If you make this ahead, place in a well-sealed container and refrigerate.)

When ready to proceed, dissolve the yeast in the luke-warm water and stir in the pinch of sugar. Uncover the starter and add the yeast mixture, the remaining sugar, the egg, honey, oil, and chopped orange peel. Crumble on the cumin. Stir until well blended.

Add 3 cups more all-purpose flour and stir in until completely absorbed: You'll have to fold and stir, and using your hands is easier than using a heavy spoon. Wash your hands and flour the work surface with about 1 cup flour. Turn the dough out and knead until smooth, about 10 minutes. Kneading this dough is like kneading slightly sticky mud pies. You'll find it easiest if you have a dough scraper to help keep the dough from sticking to your hands and to keep the surfaces as clean as possible. Because the dough is sticky, there's a temptation to keep adding flour, but try not to. Just add a little more if you really have to. When ready, the dough will be quite stiff but still sticky.

Cover and let proof for 3 hours. The dough will rise and will be softer, but it will not double in volume. When it is ready, a dent made with a fingertip will stay rather than spring back.

Turn the dough out onto a lightly floured surface and cut it in half. Keep one piece covered with plastic wrap while you shape the first two loaves.

Cut the piece of dough into 2 equal pieces. Working with lightly floured hands, shape 1 into a high mound about 9 inches in diameter, then cup the sides in your hands as you try to tuck down and pull the upper part of the loaf smooth, rolling the dough back and forth between your cupped hands. Place on a large piece of floured wax paper or parchment paper. Repeat with the second loaf and place on another sheet of paper. Let these first 2 loaves proof for 2½ hours, loosely covered with plastic wrap. After an hour, shape the other piece of dough into 2 more loaves and set aside on paper to proof, well covered with plastic wrap.

Meanwhile, put a baking stone or unglazed quarry tiles, if you have them, (or a baking sheet) on a rack in the upper third of the oven and preheat the oven to 425°F.

Lift up one of the proofed loaves from its paper, and gently transfer to a peel dusted with cornmeal. Place on one side of the baking stone, tiles, or sheet, so there is room for another loaf. Place the second loaf beside it. Bake for 45 to 50 minutes until the loaves are a very dark brown with perhaps a few black spots and sound hollow when tapped on the bottom. Pinch the bottom edge to check that it's firm—if not, bake for another 5 to 10 minutes.

Place the breads on a rack and cover with two layers of cotton cloth, to help the crusts soften. Bake the second pair of loaves in the same way.

The loaves should stand, covered, until completely cool before being sliced, preferably for 12 hours or more. Once cooled, the loaves can be frozen, well sealed in plastic. To use, thaw at room temperature for 24 hours, still sealed in plastic.

NOTE ON FLAVOR Ana used some kind of bottled sugar syrup as well as sugar to sweeten the dough. We substituted honey for the syrup, because we found it the closest approximation available here. The only difference we notice is that our loaves are not quite as dark as hers. This recipe has a modest flavoring of orange and cumin, and we like the way all the flavors blend smoothly. If you want the flavors to be more punchy, increase the cumin to 1½ tablespoons and the dried orange peel to ½ cup (to make ⅓ cup soaked and chopped).

salt-raised bread

Makes 1 high round golden dome (about 2½ pounds) with a moist crumb and thin, chewy crust,
plus 1½ pounds unyeasted sourdough starter

*We confess that we don't really understand how this bread works, but we do know that it has good texture and flavor
and is not at all difficult to make.*

*Here's more of what we know: A "salt-raised" bread uses no added yeast. The dough consists of a batter made of
organic flour and springwater with a generous pinch of salt. It ferments on its own in a warm place; then, with the
addition of more flour and salt, it becomes the basis for a very good hearth bread. The only requirements are that you
use springwater, organic flour, and sea salt and that you keep the batter/starter warm for the first twelve hours, as
directed below. The whole process takes less than thirty-six hours—say, from the morning of one day until the early
evening of the next day—but most of that is waiting time that requires very little work.*

*And what is the bread like? Well, it depends on what flour you use. We make a mostly unbleached white flour dough
with a little rye flour for extra moisture and flavor, then shape it into a large round loaf that bakes to a golden brown.
It has a slightly chewy crust and a strong, moist, well-risen crumb. The bread keeps well, but usually gets eaten so quickly
that keeping qualities aren't an issue.*

STARTER

4 cups springwater, heated to lukewarm (about 100°F)

4 cups unbleached bread or all-purpose flour

½ teaspoon fine sea salt

BREAD

5 to 6 cups unbleached all-purpose or bread flour

1 cup rye flour

1 tablespoon plus ½ teaspoon salt

Rinse a large heavy ceramic mixing bowl with hot water
and pour the springwater into it. Add the flour and salt
and stir and beat, stirring always in one direction, until
you have a smooth batter. Continue to stir vigorously
for another 3 or 4 minutes.

Pour several inches of very hot water into a large bowl
or pan (or the sink) and then place the mixing bowl in
it, so the hot water comes more than halfway up the
sides, *but does not come over the top*. Cover the mixing bowl
with a lid and let stand in a draft-free place until the hot
water bath cools.

Take the bowl out of the water bath and give the batter a quick stir. Cover again and let stand in a warm,
draft-free place for 24 to 36 hours, as convenient, stirring it every 6 to 8 hours. Each time you'll see that small
bubbles have risen to the surface, and there will be some
water that has separated from the mixture, which you
need to stir back in.

Stir the batter once more. By now there may be
several bubbles sitting at the surface of the batter, as
well as small holes left by bubbles that have risen to
the surface and burst. Add 2 cups all-purpose or bread
flour, the rye flour, and the salt, and stir and turn
to mix in well. Because the batter will have developed
some structure, you'll have to work a little, always
stirring in the same direction, to encourage it to incorporate the flour. Persist until you have a smooth dough,
then add another 2 cups all-purpose or bread flour and
turn and stir to mix in; you can also knead the dough in
the bowl if it helps incorporate the flour.

Flour your work surface and turn the dough out.
Knead, incorporating flour from the work surface as

necessary, and reflouring the work surface as necessary, to prevent sticking. Because of the rye flour, the dough may feel a little sticky, but try not to incorporate so much flour that it becomes stiff; it should be fairly soft, smooth and elastic.

Place the dough in a clean bowl, cover with plastic wrap, and let rise in a warm, draft-proof place (70° to 75°F) until doubled in volume. This may take as long as 5 hours, depending on the strength of the leaven that has developed. (If you do this phase overnight, the bread may overrise and collapse. Don't worry. Pull the dough together and proceed.)

When ready to proceed, lightly flour your work surface and turn the dough out. Cut off 1½ pounds of the dough (about one-quarter of it) to be used as a starter. Seal in plastic and refrigerate. Line a 9- or 10-inch wooden bowl or round willow basket with a heavy linen or cotton cloth and flour the cloth generously, rubbing flour into it. Set aside.

Briefly knead the dough, then shape it into a round hearth loaf by folding the edges up to the center all around and pressing to hold them in place. Place seam side up in the cloth-lined bowl or basket and cover loosely with plastic wrap. Put in a warm draft-free place to rise for 1½ to 2 hours. When it is ready, the bread will have expanded noticeably and may have several bubbles on the surface, but it probably will not have doubled in volume.

Meanwhile, place a baking stone or unglazed quarry tiles, if you have them, (or a baking sheet) on a rack in the center of the oven and preheat the oven to 450°F. Don't bake until at least 20 minutes after the oven reaches the correct temperature. Fill a sprayer with water.

Lightly flour a peel (or the back of a baking sheet) and place it over the dough. Turn the bowl or basket over onto the peel (or baking sheet) and lift it and the cloth off the bread. Quickly slash the top of the loaf (see the photograph on page 149) with 4 long slashes to make a square, then transfer it to the hot stone or tiles or baking sheet. Immediately spray the oven and bread vigorously, then close the door. Bake for 30 minutes, spraying every 3 to 4 minutes for the first 15 minutes. Lower the heat to 400°F and bake for another 15 to 20 minutes, until the loaf is a rich golden brown all over. The bottom should sound hollow when tapped, and the bottom edges should be firm when pinched; if not, bake for another 5 to 10 minutes, then test again.

When it is done, place the bread on a rack to cool for at least 30 minutes before slicing it.

chickpea spice breads

Makes 2 low, golden brown oval loaves for slicing, or 1 loaf and 6 baking sheets' worth of thin aromatic crackers

The Minoan civilization in Crete existed more than 3,500 years ago, and after the Minoans came the Mycenaeans, Greeks from the mainland. Archaeologists can't tell us in great detail about daily life in those times, as they were followed by several centuries of "dark ages" before the rise of classic Greek civilization. But one of the things we do know, from digs and the deciphering of inscriptions, is that barley and wheat were the staple grains. (Other important foods produced on the island were olive oil and grapes for wine.) It's humbling to think that we can connect with those long-ago times, in however small a way, by making and eating these naturally leavened wheat and barley breads from Crete.

Like any staple food, the bread is very makable in a home kitchen; it just takes a little time. You start with chickpeas, and use their fermentation to make a natural starter that is the only leavening in the dough. The whole dough is perfumed with bay leaf as well as anise, coriander seed, cinnamon, and pepper. Though the bread is often baked into rusks called paximadia, *we prefer it either as bread for slicing or as crackers. Instructions for all three are given.*

Note on Timing: *Allow about 36 hours from start to finish: 3 hours soaking time for the chickpeas; 8 to 12 hours for the first ferment; 8 to 10 hours for the second ferment; 5 hours fermentation for the dough: 4 hours proofing; 40 minutes for the shaped loaves to bake.*

STARTER

½ cup organic chickpeas

About 6½ cups springwater

10 to 12 bay leaves

½ cup organic barley flour or organic whole wheat flour

¼ teaspoon fine sea salt

BREAD

½ cup organic barley flour

½ cup whole wheat flour

4½ to 5½ cups all-purpose flour

2 tablespoons sugar

½ teaspoon anise seeds, ground

½ teaspoon cinnamon

½ teaspoon coriander seeds, ground

¼ teaspoon freshly ground black pepper

1 tablespoon salt

Sesame seeds for topping (optional)

Make the starter at least 18 hours before you want to make the dough: Soak the chickpeas in about 2 cups lukewarm springwater for 3 to 4 hours.

Drain the chickpeas, leaving just a little water to make processing easier. Place in a processor or blender and mix to break the chickpeas into smaller pieces, about 1 minute; you'll have about 1 cup of chopped chickpeas. Transfer to a medium bowl and set aside.

Meanwhile, place about 4½ cups springwater in a pot with the bay leaves and bring to a boil. Simmer half covered for about 10 minutes, to infuse the water with the bay laurel aroma. Let cool to lukewarm.

Add 1¼ cups of the lukewarm laurel water to the processed chickpeas; cover the remaining water and set aside. Add the barley flour and salt and stir to blend thoroughly. Cover well with plastic wrap and place in a warm, draft-free place (70° to 75°F) for 8 to 12 hours (overnight is easiest); stir the mixture halfway through if convenient. When the starter is ready, there will be small bubbles and a little liquid at the surface.

To make the dough, place the starter in the processor or blender and whiz to reduce the chickpeas to a finer texture. Add 2 more cups of the bay leaf–infused water, the barley flour, whole wheat flour, and 2½ cups of the all-purpose flour. Stir vigorously with a wooden spoon, always in the same direction, for about 5 minutes. Cover well with plastic and set the bowl in a warm place for 8 to 10 hours. Again, there will be bubbles on top.

(If you wish to set some starter aside for later use, remove 1 cup and store well sealed in the refrigerator. Reduce the salt in the recipe to 2½ teaspoons and use a scant measure for the spices, sugar, and remaining flour.)

Sprinkle the sugar, spices, and 1 cup all-purpose flour over the dough. Turn and stir to blend. Sprinkle on the salt and 1 cup flour, and stir and turn. Turn out onto a lightly floured surface and knead for 10 minutes, or until smooth. The dough will be soft and a little sticky.

Place the dough in a clean bowl and cover well with plastic. Let rise for about 5 hours.

Turn the risen dough out onto a lightly floured surface. Divide the dough into 2 equal pieces. Shape 1 into an oval loaf about 9 inches long and set aside on a floured surface. Cover with plastic and let rise for 4 hours. Repeat with the remaining dough (or use it to make crackers or rusks; see the variations).

Place a baking stone or unglazed quarry tiles, if you have them, (or a baking sheet) on a rack in the center of the oven. Preheat the oven to 450°F. If using a baking sheet, preheat for about 5 minutes on the rack.

Rub a peel (or the back of another baking sheet) with flour. Use a large flat blade, such as a dough scraper, to transfer a loaf to the peel. If you wish to top it with sesame seeds, spritz with water and sprinkle on seeds. Use a sharp knife to slash the loaf lengthwise from end to end, then place on one side of the preheated surface in the oven, leaving room for the other loaf. Spritz four or five times with water. Repeat with the second loaf. Bake for about 40 minutes, spritzing again after the first 5 minutes, until a dark golden brown. The loaves should sound hollow when tapped on the bottom. Remove from the oven to a rack to cool for at least an hour before slicing.

SPICED CRACKERS Use half the risen dough and divide it into 6 pieces. Let the dough rest, covered with plastic wrap, for about 20 minutes.

Meanwhile, place two racks just above and below the center of the oven. Preheat the oven to 450°F. Lightly grease two large baking sheets with oil.

Work with 2 pieces of the dough at a time, on a very lightly floured surface. Flatten each into an oval, then begin rolling out thinner with a rolling pin. Eventually you will be able to pick each piece up on the back of your hands and stretch it even thinner into a large rectangle (see Semolina Crackers, page 326, for detailed instructions).

Place each piece of stretched dough on a baking sheet. Spritz lightly with water, sprinkle on a little coarse sea salt and/or sesame seeds, and use a pizza cutter or sharp knife to cut into crackers. Place one sheet on each oven rack, and bake until touched with brown, about 5 minutes (this will vary depending on how thin you rolled your crackers). Turn out into a large bowl. Repeat with the remaining pieces of dough. The crackers will crisp up as they cool. Let cool for at least 4 hours before placing in a tin or sealed bag to store.

SPICED RUSKS Use half the dough and divide it in half. Shape each half into a mound about 5 inches long and 1 inch high and place them side by side on a baking sheet. Score each loaf into ½-inch slices, cutting about halfway through the dough. Let proof, covered, for about 4 hours. Bake in the center of a preheated 400°F oven until browned, about 35 minutes. Let cool on a rack before slicing through. Bake the slices flat on a baking sheet or stone at 250°F for about 2 hours, or until they are crisp and dry. Turn the slices over halfway through the baking. Soften well with water or oil before eating (see Friselle dell'Orzo, page 320).

FOLLOWING PAGES: *Loaves rising and readying to bake, Chaniá, Crete, Greece. Salt beds where salt and* fleur de sel *are harvested near Guérande, France.*

Wet bread At a bakery in Specchia Gallone, near Puglia's Adriatic coast, there's a charming baker who has a bad stammer and very deft hands. He makes a remarkable bread called *pitilli* from a dough that's extremely wet. The dough is slippery; after a first rise, it gets shaped with wet hands and dropped onto a wet peel, then spilled directly onto the hearth of the bake oven. The wood-fired oven holds about a hundred loaves, and I watched, mesmerized, as each bread was shaped, dropped onto the wet peel, slipped off onto the hot stone floor of the oven, and then again. . . .

It turns out that this bread is a local tradition, home-baked in a wood-fired oven (see Pugliese Sponge Breads, page 188). The baker had used a commercial-sized dough hook to mix his huge dough, but I wondered how people did it at home. "Like this, of course," he said, moving his hand and forearm in a vigorous beating motion.

Once the oven had been filled and the door closed for the bake, there was a little dough left over. The baker invited us (I was there with several friends) to try working with it. I picked up a little and tried to mimic his gestures, passing it from one hand to the other and tucking the edges under to pull the top surface a little taut. I could feel the strands of gluten that made up the dough's structure, but it took a good moment to get a feel for the slithery, elusive mass in my hands. Then suddenly I tuned in. I could feel I was working with the dough rather than just handling it. I looked up from my hands to see the baker smiling, and behind him a small crowd of older women from the village, all in black, nearly doubled over with laughter.

OPPOSITE: *Farmer haying in Puglia, Italy, with typical cone-shaped* trulli *in the background.*
ABOVE: *Country woman, Minho, Portugal.*

galician hearth bread with whole corn

Makes 2 large, fairly dense, domed hearth breads with an attractively slashed and torn crust and a crumb dotted with corn kernels

PHOTOGRAPH ON PAGE 180 *Broa is the Portuguese and Galician word for "bread." It originally meant millet, which at one time was the staple grain in many hard-scrabble places all over Europe. Used on its own, millet makes dense heavy bread. The arrival of corn from the New World after 1492 changed many Europeans' diets; corn displaced millet in many poorer regions. In recent times, wheat has become more available in those remote areas. These days in rural Portugal, broa generally means a round loaf made of a mixture of flours—corn with wheat, and often rye too.*

Only in Spanish Galicia did I see a broa like this one, made with corn kernels as well as cornmeal. It's beautiful, with a welcoming fresh grain aroma and flavor. The bread keeps well, slices well, and is good for sandwiches.

RYE POOLISH

2 cups light rye

2 cups water

¼ teaspoon active dry yeast

1 teaspoon salt

BREAD

½ cup dried yellow cracked corn

2 cups water

2 teaspoons active dry yeast

1 tablespoon salt

1 cup white corn flour

4 to 5 cups all-purpose flour

Cornmeal for dusting

Make the poolish 15 to 20 hours before you wish to bake: In a large bowl, stir the poolish ingredients into a smooth batter. Cover with plastic wrap and set aside at cool room temperature for 8 to 12 hours, or overnight.

Meanwhile, place the cracked corn and water in a pot. Bring to a boil and cook until the kernels are soft but not mushy (about 20 minutes). Drain, reserving the cooking water. Measure 1 cup of the corn water (add extra water if necessary) and let cool to lukewarm. Set the kernels aside.

When ready to proceed, dissolve the yeast in the reserved lukewarm water. Add the mixture to the poolish and stir in. Add the reserved corn, sprinkle on the salt and corn flour, and stir in. Gradually, add 3 cups of the all-purpose flour, stirring and turning to combine.

Turn the dough out onto a surface floured with about 1 cup more all-purpose flour. Knead, adding a little more flour if necessary, until smooth, 3 to 5 minutes. The dough will still be a little tacky.

Place the dough in a clean bowl, cover, and let rise until almost doubled, about 4 hours.

Turn the dough out onto a lightly floured surface. Cut it in half and shape each piece into a round boule. Rub flour into two cotton cloths and use them to line two 9- or 10-inch wooden bowls or baskets. Place each boule seam side up in a bowl, cover loosely, and let proof for 1 hour. When ready, the breads will not have doubled, but if you press your fingers into the dough, they'll leave a depression.

Meanwhile, place a baking stone or unglazed quarry tiles, if you have them, (or a baking sheet) on a rack in the center of the oven and preheat the oven to 400°F. Fill a sprayer with water.

Flip one loaf out onto a cornmeal-dusted peel. With a sharp knife or razor blade, deeply slash it once across. Place on one side of the baking stone or the tiles (or the sheet), leaving room for the other loaf, and spritz with water. Repeat with the other loaf. Bake for 15 minutes, spritzing several more times in the first 5 minutes. Then lower the heat to 375°F and bake for another 40 minutes, or until the loaves are golden and sound hollow when tapped on the bottom. Each will have an attractive tear as well as the slash on top. Let cool completely on a rack, preferably overnight. The bread texture is best the day after baking.

OPPOSITE: *Grape harvest offering, near Soajo, Minho, Portugal.* FOLLOWING PAGES: *Fields of ripening wheat near Pésc; stone windmill east of the Danube; loading hay on a wagon, all in Hungary.*

The miller's tale As I traveled through Hungary—avoiding cities, sticking to small roads, and

stopping at bed-and-breakfasts in small towns or villages—I kept looking for bakeries where I could find

the good Hungarian bread I'd read so much about. There was bread in the grocery stores, but village

bakeries were hard to find. Two generations of Communist government had left milling and bread

making very centralized and industrialized, it seemed. Yet in southern Hungary, especially just east of

the Danube, the half-ruined towers of old windmills, rounded and graceful stone towers, still stand,

evidence of an earlier era when grain was locally milled. Old books on Hungary talk of incredible breads,

large white domes and hearty rye breads, made in households and baked in farm ovens and small village

bakeries. Where are they now? I wondered. Why were almost all breads I saw the same featureless white

loaves, with little flavor or staying power?

And then I met a miller, in his early eighties, working at an old water mill that had been turned

into a small museum. He was strong and lively, with big gnarled hands and a weathered face. He laughed

as he joked about the reputation of millers: The story goes that they always had large families because the

miller's work, unlike the farmer's, was so light that he had time on his hands for recreation!

He confirmed that bread habits, in his part of Hungary at least, had changed dramatically since the

1930s. "Now the bread has no taste. We don't grow any rye flour around here, and people have stopped

baking at home," he explained. Before the Second World War, most people outside the cities and towns

made their own bread from a blend of rye and wheat flours, using a starter saved from the previous batch of

baking. They baked it in traditional wood-fired ovens. Whiter, lighter loaves made entirely of wheat flour

were for special occasions, the rye blend for every day. "And the bread made us strong!" he said, proudly.

smooth onion rye

Makes 2 torpedo-shaped rye-and-wheat-flour loaves (each weighing about 1½ pounds) with a soft, smooth crumb

For several years we were in and out of Hong Kong fairly frequently, and the one place we would go on every visit was a bakery in the basement of the Holiday Inn on Nathan Road in Tsimshatsui. The bakery made twelve to fifteen different German and Austrian breads, some wheat and some rye, and all extremely good. If we were heading into China, which we often were, we would buy three or four different breads and take them with us. Like all good German breads, the loaves would last us anywhere from a week to ten days without getting stale.

This onion rye is a bread that we began making at home based upon one of the breads from the bakery in Hong Kong. It's very like flavored breads we encountered when we were in Schleswig-Holstein, the area in north Germany at the "neck" of the Danish peninsula.

Rye sours (see page 112) are special, rather mysterious agents of flavor and leavening. Timing is more critical than with wheat poolishes or old doughs, because rye ferments very quickly. The aroma of the onions baking in the slightly soured rye and wheat flour dough makes our kitchen smell terrific, and we think the bread tastes even better than it smells.

POOLISH

Pinch of active dry yeast

1 cup lukewarm water

1 cup unbleached all-purpose flour

RYE SOUR

½ cup lukewarm water

½ cup light rye flour

BREAD

5 to 6 cups unbleached all-purpose flour

1½ cups light rye flour

1½ cups lukewarm water

½ teaspoon active dry yeast

2 teaspoons salt

1 tablespoon unsalted butter, softened, or olive oil

1 cup coarsely grated onions (just under ½ pound)

Cornmeal for dusting (optional)

Make the poolish at least 12 hours before using it: Stir the yeast into the lukewarm water to dissolve it. Stir the flour in to make a smooth batter. Let stand, covered, for 12 to 36 hours.

To make the rye sour, stir the water into the poolish, then stir in the rye flour. Cover with plastic and let stand for 12 hours, or overnight.

When ready to proceed, make the dough.

Using a stand mixer: Place 2 cups of the all-purpose flour, the rye flour, and the rye sour in the bowl of a mixer fitted with the dough hook. Mix briefly. In a small bowl, stir together the water and yeast to dissolve the yeast. Add to the flour mixture. Mix at the lowest speed for 2 minutes. Sprinkle on the salt, add the butter or oil, and mix briefly. Add the onions and 2½ more cups all-purpose flour and mix for 5 minutes. Turn out onto a well-floured surface and knead for about a minute. The dough will be a little sticky (because of the rye) but fairly firm.

By hand: In a large bowl, stir together the water and yeast. Add the rye sour and stir to break it up into the liquid. Add 2 cups of the all-purpose flour and the rye flour and stir well, about a minute, always in the same direction. Sprinkle on the salt, add the butter or oil, and stir in. Add the onions and stir in. Add 2 more cups all-purpose flour, a cup at a time, turning and folding the dough. When it gets too hard to manipulate with a spoon, turn the dough out onto a well-floured surface and knead, incorporating flour as needed, for 10 minutes, or until firm but still a little sticky.

Place the dough in a large, clean bowl and cover with plastic wrap. Let rise for 4 hours. It will not quite have doubled but will be soft and raised.

Turn the dough out onto a lightly floured surface and cut it in half. Shape into two bullet-shaped loaves: Flatten each piece out to an oval or rectangle, then roll up from a short side. Pinch the seam to seal and place seam side down on a lightly floured surface in a warm (70° to 75°F) place. Cover loosely with plastic wrap and a cotton cloth to keep warm, and let rise for 1½ hours. The loaves will be a little tacky and soft when ready, and, if pressed lightly with a fingertip, the dough will stay indented.

Meanwhile, place a baking stone or unglazed quarry tiles, if you have them, (or a baking sheet) on a rack in the lower third of the oven, and preheat the oven to 450°F. Fill a sprayer with water.

Transfer one loaf to a cornmeal- or flour-dusted peel (or the back of a baking sheet). Make 3 diagonal slashes in it with a straight razor or a sharp knife, then transfer to the baking stone, tiles, or sheet, jerking the peel out from under it. Repeat with the other loaf. Spritz generously with water. Bake for 15 minutes, repeating the spritzing four or five times in the first 10 minutes.

Lower the heat to 400°F and bake for 15 or 20 minutes longer. To test for doneness, tap the bottom of each loaf—it should sound hollow. Let cool completely on a rack, at least 2 hours. The loaves are best left unsliced until the next day.

NOTE This bread freezes well: Let cool for 12 hours, then seal in a plastic bag and freeze. To defrost, let stand overnight at room temperature.

pepper-bacon ring

Makes 2 ring-shaped loaves (about 1¼ pounds each), flavored with black pepper and small chunks of bacon

PHOTOGRAPH ON PAGE 212 *Inspired by a bread at A & G Bakery in Brooklyn, New York, these bread rings (couronnes) are simple to make and loaded with flavor. Small pieces of bacon dot the moist, well-structured crumb. Their salty richness is complemented by a healthy dose of black pepper in the dough. The crust is thin and softens as the bread cools. Serve it in slices, plain, or with a smooth, fresh cream cheese or goat cheese.*

BIGA

¼ teaspoon active dry yeast

1 cup lukewarm water

2 cups all-purpose flour, preferably unbleached

BREAD

1 cup lukewarm water

1 teaspoon active dry yeast

2½ to 3½ cups all-purpose flour, preferably unbleached

½ pound bacon (preferably not sweet-smoked),
   chopped (about ½ cup) and cooked until slightly crisp

2 teaspoons salt

1½ teaspoons black pepper (fine- or medium-ground)

Cornmeal for dusting

2 tablespoons melted lard, bacon drippings,
   or olive oil for brushing

Make the biga 24 hours before you wish to bake: Stir the yeast into the lukewarm water until dissolved. Stir in 1 cup of the flour to make a smooth batter. Sprinkle on the remaining 1 cup flour, stir to incorporate, and then knead the dough in the bowl until smooth, 3 to 4 minutes. Set aside in a clean bowl or on a floured counter, covered with plastic wrap, to ferment for 24 hours. (Or seal in a plastic bag, leaving room for expansion, and store in the refrigerator for up to 4 days. Bring to room temperature before using.)

Cut the biga into 4 or 5 pieces. Place in a large bowl or the bowl of a stand mixer. Add the lukewarm water and stir in the yeast to dissolve it.

By hand: Break up the biga with your fingers in the water. Add 1 cup of the flour and stir well to make a batter. Sprinkle on the bacon, salt, and pepper and stir in. Add about 1 cup flour and stir to incorporate it. Flour your work surface generously and turn out the dough. Knead until satiny, about 8 minutes.

Using a stand mixer: Fit the mixer with the dough hook. Add 1 cup of the flour to the bowl and mix on low speed for 1 minute. Sprinkle on the bacon, salt, pepper, and another 1½ cups flour and mix on low speed for 5 minutes, or until the dough is smooth.

Place the dough in a clean bowl, cover well with plastic, and let rise for 3 hours.

Turn the dough out onto a lightly floured surface and cut it in half. Gently roll each piece under your palms into a cylinder about 18 inches long. Shape each piece into a circle, with a good overlap of the ends, and pinch them to seal. Place the breads on a well-floured surface and cover with plastic. Let rise for 30 minutes.

Meanwhile, place a baking stone or unglazed quarry tiles, if you have them, (or a baking sheet) on a rack in the center of the oven and preheat the oven to 400°F. Fill a sprayer with water.

Dust a peel (or the back of a baking sheet) with cornmeal. Transfer one bread onto the peel or sheet, brush the top generously with half the fat or olive oil, and place on the hot baking stone or tiles (or baking sheet), leaving room for the other bread. Repeat with the second bread. Bake for 25 to 30 minutes, spritzing several times during the first 5 minutes, until touched with gold and crisp on the bottom.

Place on a rack to cool for 30 minutes or more before slicing. Serve warm or at room temperature.

hazelnut-currant boule

Makes 1 beautiful domed bread (weighing just over 2 pounds) with hazelnuts and currants scattered in a moist crumb

We came across a bread like this long ago at a boulangerie in Paris. Hunks of it were being cut from a huge loaf and sold by weight. It was fine-textured, a little enriched, and studded with black currants and hazelnuts—a real cross between bread and cake, but definitely on the bread side. Here's a home-style version, made into a single attractive boule and baked on a baking stone. It's delicious on its own or with hard cheese.

2 cups lukewarm water

1 teaspoon active dry yeast

2 cups whole wheat flour, plus extra for dusting

½ cup light or medium rye flour

2 teaspoons salt

3 tablespoons unsalted butter, softened

½ cup toasted hazelnuts, finely chopped

½ cup dried currants

2 to 3 cups all-purpose flour, preferably unbleached

Place the water in a large bowl, sprinkle on the yeast, and stir to dissolve. Stir in the whole wheat flour. Stir for 1 minute, always in the same direction, to make a smooth batter. Cover and let stand for 2 hours.

In a medium bowl, mix together the rye flour and salt. Add the butter and rub it into the flour with your fingertips until the texture of fine meal. Alternatively, mix the rye flour and salt together in a food processor, add the butter, and process to a fine meal.

Add the rye-butter blend to the yeast batter and stir in thoroughly. Sprinkle on the hazelnuts and currants and stir in. Add 2 cups all-purpose flour, a cup at a time, and stir and turn to blend into the stiff dough.

Flour a work surface generously with all-purpose flour and turn the dough out. Knead until smooth, about 8 minutes, incorporating more flour only as necessary to prevent the dough from sticking.

Place the dough in a large clean bowl, cover with plastic wrap, and let rise for about 2 hours. The dough will about double in volume, and when you press two fingers into the dough, it will not spring back.

Pull the dough away from the sides of the bowl and turn out onto a lightly floured surface. Form into a round loaf about 8 inches in diameter: Stretch the round under your palms and tuck the edges under all around, pinching the edges together on the underside to give a smooth stretched top surface.

If using a baking stone or unglazed quarry tiles, line a shallow round 8-inch basket or wooden bowl with a cotton cloth. Dust it generously with whole wheat flour, rubbing some of the flour into the cloth. Place the shaped bread seam side up on the cloth. If using a baking sheet, grease it lightly with butter and place the bread on it. Cover loosely with plastic wrap and set aside to rise until almost doubled (about 50 minutes).

Meanwhile, place a baking stone or unglazed quarry tiles, if you have them, (or a baking sheet) on a rack in the center of the oven. Preheat the oven to 425°F. Fill a sprayer with water.

If the bread proofed in a basket or bowl, dust a peel (or the back of a baking sheet) with flour. Place it on top of the bread, flip it onto the peel or sheet, and lift off the basket or bowl and cloth. Use a razor blade or a sharp knife to cut a crisscross pattern in the top of the bread, 2 or 3 cuts in each direction. Spritz with water and place the bread on the baking stone or tiles. If baking on a baking sheet, dust the top of the bread with a little whole wheat flour, then cut a crisscross pattern on top as described above, spritz, and place in the oven.

Bake for about 50 minutes, spritzing a few times in the first 5 minutes, until it is brown and sounds hollow when tapped on the bottom. Place on a rack to cool before slicing. Serve warm or at room temperature.

OPPOSITE: PEPPER-BACON RING (*page 210*).
ABOVE: *Field of grain, Brittany, France.*

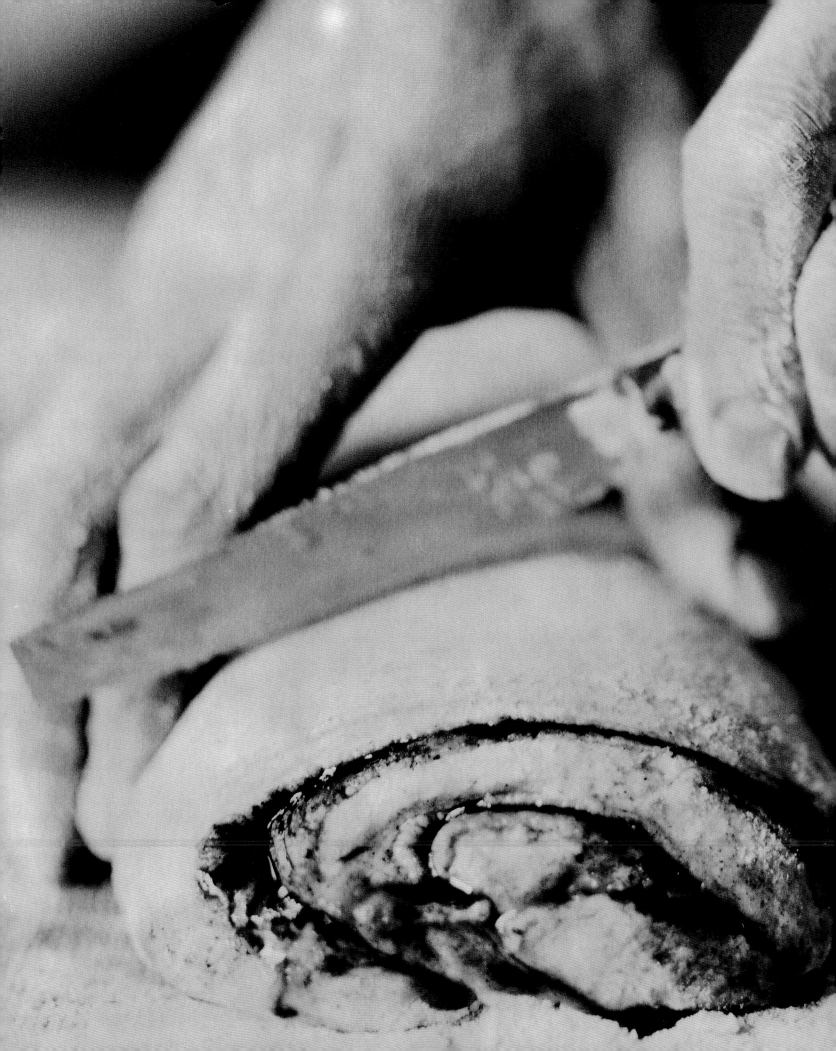

THREE | SMALLER BREADS

Rolls, Bagels, and Sweet Buns

Skillet Breads and Pancakes

Flatbreads and Crackers

ON THAT GREAT CONTINUUM OF BREAD, all the way from simple tortillas to hearth loaves, here we focus on the vast array of smaller breads, savory and sweet: rolls, flatbreads, pancakes, and sweet buns. If breads were people, in this section you would find the painters, the magicians, the actórs, the street musicians, and mimes. Here idiosyncrasy is the rule, a certain twist, a particular shape, or a quirky technique.

Rolls and flatbreads are smaller than loaf breads, so they cook more quickly, and often at higher temperatures. They're also more flexible, less demanding, for example, of steady, even oven temperature. Stove-top breads and pancakes don't need an oven at all.

Many of these breads come from areas of the world where cooking fuel can be scarce and expensive, making it important for the bread to cook quickly in an energy-efficient way. And because they cook quickly, many of these breads are a versatile way to turn flour into food. They're especially useful on occasions when the weather is so hot that turning an oven on indoors is very unappealing.

Other small breads, such as rolls, sweet buns, and bagels, have evolved out of loaf-bread traditions, perhaps as a way of making a sweet treat on baking day or adding diversity to the daily bread.

Language and Technique

We approach rolls, bagels, sweet buns, and flatbreads in the same way we approach loaf breads. It's just as important to develop good taste and texture, even if the dough is to be baked quickly as dinner rolls or flattened, brushed with butter and cinnamon, rolled up, cut into cinnamon buns, and baked as individual coils. As with loaf breads, to achieve good taste and texture, we give the dough a long, slow period of fermentation. Traditional techniques using a starter dough or batter such as a biga or poolish (see page 111) can also add flavor and character to the dough.

And with smaller breads and flatbreads, shape determines texture and that in turn affects taste. If you use the same dough to make a loaf and a flatbread and rolls, you'll see what we mean. Several of the bread recipes set out such possibilities (see Challah, page 118, and Tender Potato Bread, page 152, for example). Similarly, some of the doughs used for rolls or flatbreads in this section could very well be used to make loaves, hearth breads, or pan breads.

A big part of making rolls and sweet buns is learning different shaping techniques. Shaping not only creates a distinctive look for each roll or bun, but it affects the taste as well, adding to what we think of as the fun factor of a bread. Unrolling a cinnamon roll, for example, is a big part of the delight of eating it. The outside might be crusty, and then with each successive sugary-sweet peel off the roll, the texture becomes softer, the taste more intense. When shaping the dough to make cinnamon rolls, you can roll your "jelly roll" with tight, thin spirals, or you can make them fat and wide. The choice is yours, depending upon what you like most to eat, and shaping is the key.

Classic round rolls are shaped under a cupped hand on an unfloured surface. You cup the piece of dough, pressing down slightly, then rotate your hand in a circular motion. This encourages the dough into a round shape with a smooth top surface. The only danger when shaping rolls is the temptation to worry too much about uniformity. Yes, a baking sheet of dinner rolls looks pretty when they're all the same size and a uniform color, but in fact it's variety of size and texture that makes rolls and flatbreads more interesting. If you watch people at a bakery choosing rolls from a basket (see Last Easter at the Bakery, page 399), you'll notice them studying the selection, looking for just the right one. It's a wonderful bit of human nature, looking for just the right one. And we as home bakers can satisfy everyone by maintaining variety. For fun, take a batch of dough and see how many different shapes of rolls you can make. Sprinkle some with sunflower and sesame seeds; egg wash some and "water wash" others.

With flatbreads, this notion of variety of texture becomes even more important. At bakeries in Turkey and Afghanistan, each nan is unique as it gets pulled hot from the oven. Some will have a thick, round outside crust, others a narrow, stretched crust. Some will be dotted with dark, nearly burned areas, and others will have an even pale golden color. The irregularity is part of the process, part of the character of the bread.

Crackers take irregularity and unpredictability of texture to another level. We love crackers for their versatility, their snack-on-me-anytime quality, and their direct grain taste. Some crackers are individually shaped, but many are cut with a pizza cutter into diamonds or whatever shapes you wish. Thinness affects texture: The thinner the cracker dough is rolled, the more it will melt in your mouth when you eat it. Uneven edges will be crispy, browned, and interesting; thicker crackers will be paler, with more bite.

Tools to Have on Hand

All these smaller breads start with a dough that gets divided into smaller pieces. The easiest way to divide a dough into eight or sixteen equal pieces is to cut it in half and then half again and so on, using a **sharp knife** or a **dough scraper** (see the photograph on page 220). We've tried to make recipes divisible by eight to make things easier, but some make a dozen. That requires cutting the dough in half and half again, then each piece into thirds.

Dough scrapers are invaluable not just for cutting, but for keeping your work surface clean. A clean surface is especially important when you're rolling out doughs, for if there is any crusty bit of dough sticking to the surface, it will catch on your bread. Just slide the scraper across your work surface several times and presto! It will be smooth. Then dust it lightly with flour and start rolling out.

To roll out doughs for skillet breads or for crackers, use a **rolling pin.** We have a drawer full of rolling pins (also used for pastry and for cookies, of course), from small dowellike pins used for rotis to large, heavy rolling pins with big handles at either end. We've come to prefer the style of pin that's tapered at the ends. Make sure your rolling pin is smooth, with no rough places to catch on the dough, and rub a little flour onto it when you start to to help keep it from sticking to the dough. Roll from the center outward and rotate the dough a little between each stroke to make sure it isn't sticking to your work surface. If it does stick, detach it gently, using your dough scraper, then dust the surface (*not* the bread) lightly with flour and continue.

The most important element in cooking skillet breads and pancakes is an even heat, usually not too hot, so the bread or pancake has time to cook through before the outside surface gets too crisped. A good heavy **cast-iron skillet** holds the heat well and transmits it evenly, with no hot spots. Together with a good dependable wok (which can be great fun with breads, see Lebanese Sajj Bread, page 271), a cast-iron skillet is among our favorite pieces of cookware.

For baking most rolls and sweet buns, you'll need only a **baking sheet**. Some we bake instead in a standard 9-by-5-inch bread pan or a 13-by-9-inch baking pan or a 9-inch cast-iron skillet. As with larger breads, we find it useful to keep a **baking stone** in the oven to help maintain an even heat and to help keep the temperature up when the door is opened.

For baking flatbreads in the oven, you need many of the same tools used for hearth breads (see page 114). A **baking stone** or a **set of unglazed quarry tiles** that fit together on your oven rack to make a baking surface is really essential. Tandoor-style breads get laid directly on the porous clay surface, just as hearth breads do. It gives them a good bottom crust. You can use a **peel** (or the back of a baking sheet) to help place the breads on the hot surface, or you can place them in the oven by hand. For several breads, we use **parchment paper** for either shaping or baking. It is available in specialty stores; waxed paper can be substituted, though it is narrower and not as strong. To remove flatbreads from the oven, use a **large metal spatula** or, with some of the larger or heavier flatbreads, oven mitts, as you would do for large loaves.

Crackers are rolled out very thin and then baked on baking sheets or directly on a baking stone or tiles. Many crackers are rolled into a large thin sheet, then cut into shapes using a **pizza cutter** (or you can use a sharp knife). A pizza cutter has a wooden handle attached to a metal circle with a cutting edge. The circle rolls across the dough, cutting through it. It's very easy to make good, clean, straight cuts in crackers if you have a large, strong pizza cutter.

BEIRUT TAHINI SWIRLS (*page 244*)

ROLLS, BAGELS, AND SWEET BUNS

olive panini

Makes 12 attractive low, round rolls, 5 to 6 inches across, generously dotted with olives

PHOTOGRAPH ON PAGE 224 *Puglia, in Italy's heel, is surrounded on three sides by the sea, and in many ways it is a region apart. Unlike the rest of Italy, its food is loaded with onions but no garlic, and the landscape, with olive groves and low stone walls and glimpses of the blue, blue sea, are reminders of Greece, just across the Ionian Sea. In a few small villages in the Salentine (the peninsula that forms the heel of the boot), people still speak a form of Greek, for the Greeks had a long presence there.*

These small olive-studded Pugliese breads, called puccie, *like the* pitilli *loaves on page 188, are made with a very wet dough. You can make the dough by hand or in a stand mixer. Many of the breads in Puglia are made with* semola *("semolina"), an indication that Puglia produces good hard durum wheat, the kind used mostly for pasta making. We use a blend of semolina and unbleached white flour here.*

One of our favorite versions of puccie, *from Lecce, had a mix of small green and black olives. Be sure to use good Mediterranean olives.*

BIGA (see Note)

¼ **teaspoon active dry yeast**

½ **cup lukewarm water**

1 **cup all-purpose flour, preferably unbleached**

BREAD

2½ **cups lukewarm water**

½ **teaspoon active dry yeast**

1½ **cups coarse semolina (not semolina flour; see Glossary)**

1 **tablespoon salt**

2 **tablespoons olive oil**

Generous 1 **cup pitted Mediterranean olives—green or black**
    or a mixture, coarsely chopped if large

3 to 4 **cups all-purpose flour, preferably unbleached**

Make the biga at least 1 day before you wish to bake: Stir the yeast into the water until well dissolved. Stir in ½ cup of the flour until smooth, then add the ½ cup remaining flour and knead briefly in the bowl or on a work surface until smooth. Cover with plastic and let rise overnight, or for up to 36 hours; refrigerate after 12 hours.

When ready to proceed, place the 2½ cups water in a medium bowl or the bowl of a stand mixer and stir in the yeast to dissolve it. Cut the biga into 5 or 6 pieces, add to the bowl, and use your fingers to break it up into the water.

By hand: Stir the semolina thoroughly into the biga mixture to make a batter. Sprinkle on the salt and stir in. Add the olive oil and olives and stir. Add 2½ to 3 cups of the all-purpose flour, a cup at a time, turning and stirring. Flour a work surface with about ½ cup flour and turn the dough out. Knead, incorporating the flour, until you have a soft dough, about 5 minutes.

Using a stand mixer: Fit the mixer with the dough hook. Add the semolina to the biga mixture and mix for 2 minutes or so on low speed, until the biga has dissolved into the dough. Add the salt, olive oil, olives, and 1 cup of the all-purpose flour and mix, still on low speed, for 1 minute. Add the 2½ cups flour more and knead for 3 to 4 minutes on low speed.

Place the dough in a clean bowl, cover with plastic, and let ferment for 3 hours. The dough will not double in volume, because it's so loaded down with olives and oil, but it will rise a little in the bowl to a dome shape.

About 30 minutes before the dough is ready, place a baking stone or unglazed quarry tiles, if you have them, (or a baking sheet) on a rack in the center of the oven and preheat the oven to 450°F.

On a floured surface, halve the dough. Return half to the bowl; keep covered. Divide the other piece of dough into 6 pieces; loosely cover 5 of them with plastic. Shape the remaining piece of dough into a loose mound and place it on the preheated stone or tiles (or the sheet), toward the back and to one side. (We find it easiest to place the breads directly on the stone or tiles, but you can use a semolina-dusted peel or another sheet to transfer the breads onto the hot surface.) Repeat with the other 5 pieces of dough. If you can't fit all the breads from this first batch onto your stone or tiles at once, you'll just be baking the dough in three batches rather than two.

Leave the remaining piece(s) of dough covered until ready to bake the next batch. Bake the breads for 15 to 20 minutes, until slightly spotted with brown but still rather pale. Repeat shaping and baking with the remaining dough. Each will bake into a low dome about 5 to 6 inches across. Let cool on a rack.

Eat plain or split open for sandwiches.

NOTE If you have a 1- or 2-day-old biga already, use about 1 cup of it in the recipe.

Olive breads, Lecce, Puglia, Italy

vietnamese minibaguettes

Makes 8 torpedo-shaped rolls, about 8 inches long, with a white crumb and brittle golden crust

The French colonial era in Vietnam, Laos, and Cambodia had many culinary consequences, among them this attractive fusion bread. Looking a little like a minibaguette but with a different texture, the bread is made in cities and sold in stacks at markets and in the occasional bakery. It's also the basis for the brilliant sub-style sandwiches of Southeast Asia (we call them Mekong subs) that are now available in many cities across North America.

Because wheat doesn't flourish in the tropics, wheat flour has to be imported and is relatively expensive. No doubt that's why it's diluted with a little rice flour in these breads. The rice flour, together with the wheat malt, gives them a very distinctive soft crumb, without the elasticity or flavor of a baguette, and a brittle crust. The breads can be made without the malt; they'll have just a little less loft. The breads hold up well when filled with moist fillings (Mekong subs start with butter and mayonnaise, which are topped with sliced meats and/or pâté, salad greens, pickled carrot shreds, chiles, herbs, and more) and are best eaten the day they're made.

1 cup rice flour (see Rice in the Glossary)

1 cup pastry or cake flour, or substitute

¾ cup all-purpose flour

2 teaspoons baking powder

2 cups lukewarm water

1 tablespoon active dry yeast

1 tablespoon wheat malt syrup (see Glossary),
   or 1½ teaspoons sugar

1½ teaspoons salt

About 4 cups all-purpose flour

Combine both flours and the baking powder in a bowl; set aside.

Using a stand mixer: Place the water in the bowl of a mixer fitted with the dough hook and use a spoon to stir in the yeast to dissolve. Add the malt syrup or sugar and the rice flour mixture and mix briefly. Sprinkle on the salt and 3½ cups of the all-purpose flour, and knead for 3 minutes at low speed. Turn the dough out onto a lightly floured surface and knead for another minute.

By hand: Place the water in a medium bowl and stir in the yeast to dissolve well. Add the malt or sugar and the rice flour mixture and stir until smooth. Sprinkle on the salt and 1 cup all-purpose flour and stir in. Add 2½ cups more all-purpose flour, ½ cup at a time, and turn and fold with a spoon to incorporate. Turn the dough out onto a lightly floured surface and knead for about 5 minutes, incorporating flour as necessary, until smooth.

Place the dough in a clean bowl, cover with plastic wrap, and let rise for 1½ hours, or until more than doubled in volume.

Turn the dough out onto a lightly floured surface and divide it in half, then cut each half into 4 equal pieces (each piece will weigh about 6 ounces). Roll each under your palm into a ball, then flatten slightly. Cover and let stand for 5 to 10 minutes.

Line two baking sheets with parchment paper and place near your work surface.

To shape the rolls, work with one piece of dough at a time, leaving the rest loosely covered. Flatten the dough with the palm of your hand into an oval, and then use a rolling pin to roll it out to a pointed oval 8 inches long and 6 inches across at the widest point. Roll up into a cylinder, starting from one pointed end

PRECEDING PAGES: OLIVE PANINI *sandwiches (page 222). Olives, Taroudannt, Morocco.*

and stretching the dough crosswise as you roll, to make a minibaguette about 8 inches long. The seam should be a clearly visible V-shape on the bread. Place on a baking sheet with the point down. Repeat with the remaining dough, leaving about 1½ inches between the breads on the baking sheets. Cover and let stand in a warm place to rise for 30 minutes, or until approximately doubled in volume.

Meanwhile, place two racks just above and below the center of the oven and preheat the oven to 425°F. Fill a sprayer with water and place it near your oven.

Bake the breads for about 20 minutes, spritzing them two or three times in the first 10 minutes and rotating the pans after 10 minutes, until they are golden and sound hollow when tapped on the bottoms. Transfer to a rack to cool completely.

NOTE If you have leftover breads, freeze them. If you leave a few of them out, they'll be dry by the next day and you can use them to make Vietnamese Bread Pudding (page 147).

LEFT TO RIGHT: *Curbside minibaguettes, Siem Reap, Cambodia; market sandwich vendor.*

rum-raisin rolls

Makes 32 slightly sweet, tender round rolls, golden on top and dotted with raisins

When you make rolls with raisins that have been soaked in rum, you really can't go wrong. The raisins hold on to all that flavor when they're baked, so the final result is just the best, especially for anyone who loves dried fruit in bread (see also Papaya-Almond Whole Wheat Bread, page 168).

2 cups dark raisins

½ cup dark rum

1½ cups whole or reduced-fat milk

½ cup packed light brown sugar

1½ cups water

2 teaspoons active dry yeast

½ cup whole wheat flour

About 8 cups all-purpose flour

1 tablespoon salt

1 medium egg, whisked with 1 tablespoon water,
for egg wash

Place the raisins and rum in a medium saucepan and set over low heat, stirring to moisten the raisins, until warm but not boiling. Transfer to a bowl, cover, and let soak for 2 hours, or overnight, whatever is more convenient.

When you are ready to make the dough, heat the milk until steaming but not quite at the boil. Pour into a large bowl, or the bowl of a stand mixer, and stir in the brown sugar, then the water. Let stand until just lukewarm.

Drain the raisins and set aside.

Sprinkle the yeast over the milk mixture and stir until it has dissolved.

By hand: Stir the whole wheat flour into the yeast mixture, then add 3 cups of the all-purpose flour, 1 cup at a time, stirring well after each addition, and always in the same direction. If you have the time, cover and let stand for 30 minutes, or for up to 3 hours; otherwise, continue with mixing. Sprinkle with the raisins and salt, then turn and stir to mix well. Mix in the remaining 5 cups or so all-purpose flour, 1 cup at a time, until the dough becomes too difficult to stir. Flour a work surface and turn the dough out. Knead, gradually incorporating more flour as necessary to prevent sticking, until smooth and elastic.

Using a stand mixer: Fit the mixer with the dough hook. Add the whole wheat flour and 3 cups of the all-purpose flour to the yeast mixture and mix on the lowest speed until smooth, then mix for another minute. If you have the time, cover and let stand for 30 minutes, or for up to 3 hours; otherwise, continue mixing the dough. Sprinkle with the raisins and salt and mix briefly, then add 3 cups more of the all-purpose flour and mix in. Add another 2 cups flour, then mix for 4 minutes. Sprinkle a work surface with flour, turn the dough out, and knead briefly.

Place the dough in a large clean bowl, cover with plastic wrap, and let rise until doubled in volume, about 3 hours.

Lightly grease an 18-by-12-inch baking sheet or two smaller sheets with butter or olive oil.

Turn the dough out onto a lightly floured surface. Use a dough scraper or heavy knife to cut it in half, and then in half again. Set 3 pieces aside, loosely covered, and cut the fourth into 8 equal pieces.

To shape the rolls, cup the palm of your hand over 1 piece of dough and gently press it downward. Move your hand in a short circular motion, rotate the dough about ten times, pressing downward lightly as you do so: This will help tighten the top of the roll and make a ball shape. Place the roll on the baking sheet and repeat with the remaining 7 small pieces, placing the rolls about ½ inch apart. Keep the shaped rolls loosely covered with plastic as you work. Divide and shape the remaining dough, to make a total of 32 rolls. Set the rolls aside, well covered, to rise for 45 minutes. The rolls will rise and then bake together.

Meanwhile, place a rack in the upper third of the oven and place a baking stone or unglazed quarry tiles, if you have them, (or a baking sheet) on the rack. Preheat the oven to 400°F.

Just before baking, brush the tops of the rolls with the egg wash. Bake for 20 to 25 minutes, until the tops of the rolls are golden and the bottoms sound hollow when tapped.

Transfer to a rack to cool slightly. Serve warm or at room temperature.

baker's sign pretzels

Makes 8 rich, brown, small- to medium-sized twisted pretzels

The traditional sign of the baker in Germany and Austria is a pretzel (pretsel in German); bakeries all hang a large pretzel sign out over the shop door (see The Baker's Wife, page 154). Pretzels are an old form of bread, a length of leavened dough shaped into a twist or a round, and dropped into a hot water bath before baking. (Bagels are a specialized version of pretzel.) All pretzels, even the dried packaged ones, have a distinctive back taste when you chew them that comes from the baking soda in the water bath.

This yeasted pretzel dough is enriched with milk and butter and sweetened with a little malt syrup. The dough does a quick first rise before being shaped, bathed, and baked.

Shaping is simple: You hold a long string of dough in two hands to make a loop, then twist several times, lay the loop down, and trail the ends up onto it.

LEFT TO RIGHT: BAKER'S SIGN PRETZELS; *baker's sign, Austria.*

1 cup milk, scalded and cooled to lukewarm

2 teaspoons active dry yeast

1 tablespoon wheat malt syrup or barley malt syrup
(see Glossary)

2½ to 3 cups all-purpose flour

1 teaspoon salt

2 tablespoons unsalted butter, cut into pieces, softened

SHAPING AND BAKING

¼ cup baking soda

1 egg yolk, beaten with 2 teaspoons milk, for egg wash

Place the milk in a medium bowl and stir in the yeast to dissolve it well. Add the malt syrup and 1 cup of the flour and stir until you have a smooth batter. Sprinkle on the salt, add the butter, and stir well to incorporate. Add 1¼ cups more flour and stir and turn the dough to incorporate it. Turn out onto a floured surface and knead for 5 minutes, incorporating more flour as necessary.

Place the dough in a clean bowl, cover with plastic, and let rise for 1½ hours, or until smooth, softened, about doubled in volume.

Place a rack in the upper third of the oven and place a baking stone or unglazed quarry tiles, if you have them, (or a baking sheet) on it. Preheat the oven to 450°F.

Turn the dough out onto a very lightly floured work surface. Cut it into 4 equal pieces and cut each piece in half. Place a parchment paper–lined baking sheet next to your work surface.

Work with 2 pieces of dough at a time, keeping the remaining pieces covered with a cotton cloth. Roll each piece of dough out under your palms to a long skinny rope, 24 to 30 inches long, slightly fatter in the middle and very thin at the ends. Press down lightly and push outward toward the ends with both hands as you roll, encouraging the dough to lengthen and stretch. You will find the dough very elastic, and that it springs back and shortens after you let it go, so switch back and forth between the two pieces. This will give the gluten strands in the dough an opportunity to relax a little.

Once you have a long rope, pick up one end with each hand and twist one around the other once or twice about 2 inches from the ends, then lay the dough down in a curve on the baking sheet and lay the ends onto the fatter center of the curve to make the classic pretzel shape. Cover lightly while you shape the remaining pretzels. Let the pretzels rise for about 10 minutes.

Meanwhile, heat 1 cup water in a large saucepan until almost boiling. Add the baking soda and stir well to dissolve. Keep the water simmering until just before ready to use. Have a flour-dusted peel (or the back of a baking sheet) near your work surface, and a razor blade or sharp knife for slashing the dough.

Lift up one pretzel with a wide spatula and place it briefly in the hot soda-water bath, leaving it on the spatula. Remove it after 20 seconds and let the water drain off the spatula, then brush the pretzel top with the egg wash and place the pretzel on the peel. Make a deep 1- to 2-inch slash in the top of the fattest part of the pretzel, then immediately slide it off the peel (or sheet) onto the hot stone or tiles (or baking sheet). Repeat with the remaining pretzels. (If your stone or oven is small, you may have to bake them 4 at a time.)

Bake the pretzels for 10 to 12 minutes, until a deep golden brown on top. Place on a rack to cool. Serve warm or at room temperature.

NOTE If you'd like a little coarse salt on your pretzels, sprinkle on a pinch right after you slash each one.

montreal bagels

Makes 32 low-rise bagels, coated with sesame seeds or poppy seeds, with a chewy texture

PHOTOGRAPH ON PAGE 234 *The world of bagel lovers is sharply divided: Some love the fat, rounded New York–style bagel, others swear by the smaller, chewy Montreal bagel. In Montreal, these bagels are made twenty-four hours a day, in wood-fired ovens. After their immersion in hot water, they go into the oven on very narrow, long wooden peels, all in a row, then get pulled out and tossed into a bin. On a winter night, there's likely to be a line of people waiting for fresh bagels, all talking hockey, and steam on the windows. And always there's hungry expectation.*

For the purists among the Montreal partisans, there's one big problem: True Montreal bagels are available only at bakeries in Montreal, and they don't taste the same once they've spent more than four hours out of the oven (they're edible, but they're not at their best). Montrealers who have relocated to New York or Toronto or L.A. may be happy with their lives, but they still consider themselves deprived in an important respect.

We thought it should be possible to make Montreal bagels at home, in our kitchen in Toronto. We asked for advice, experimented, and finally came up with bagels that met the exacting standards of our bagel-loving friends from Montreal. We still feel triumphant about it. The bagels aren't hard to make, and they certainly are rewarding, especially if you make them for a crowd of hungry believers.

2 teaspoons sugar

1 cup lukewarm water

1 tablespoon active dry yeast

2 tablespoons wheat malt syrup (see Glossary)

½ cup warm water

1 large egg

1 tablespoon vegetable oil

2 teaspoons salt

About 4 cups all-purpose flour

FOR SHAPING AND TOPPING

3 tablespoons honey

About 1 cup hulled sesame seeds or black poppy seeds
 or some of each

In a medium bowl or the bowl of a stand mixer, dissolve the sugar in the 1 cup lukewarm water, then stir in the yeast. In a small bowl, dissolve the wheat malt in the ½ cup warm water. Stir in the egg, oil, and salt; set aside.

By hand: Add 1 cup of the flour to the yeast mixture and stir in. Add the wheat malt mixture and then 2 more cups flour and stir, always in the same direction, until a smooth, moist dough forms. Add 1 more cup flour and stir and turn to blend it in. The dough will be quite stiff. Turn the dough out onto a lightly floured surface and knead for 5 to 10 minutes, until smooth and elastic.

Using a stand mixer: Fit the mixer with the dough hook. Add 2 cups of the flour to the yeast mixture and mix on low speed for 1 minute. Add the wheat malt mixture and 2 more cups flour and mix for 3 to 4 minutes on the lowest speed. Turn the dough out onto a lightly floured surface and knead briefly.

Place the dough in a clean medium bowl and cover with plastic wrap. Let rise for 1¾ to 2 hours, until the dough is soft and has doubled in volume.

Gently punch the dough down, cover, and let rise again for 1 to 1½ hours.

Meanwhile, place a baking stone or unglazed quarry tiles, if you have them, on a rack in the upper third of the oven. Preheat the oven to 450°F.

Cut the dough into quarters and work with 1 piece at a time, leaving the others covered with plastic wrap. Cut the piece of dough into 8 equal pieces (each will weigh about 1½ ounces). Roll each small piece out under your hands into a very skinny rope 10 to 12 inches long: Press on the dough and roll it back and forth, pushing out lightly toward the ends in order to encourage it to lengthen and thin. The dough is very elastic; it will shrink back after you roll it out. You may want to work with 2 pieces at a time, rolling out 1 and then letting it rest while you start rolling out another, then coming back to the first.

Lay the dough rope over one hand, with one end lying across your palm and the other hanging down. Wrap this other end around your hand so that the ends overlap by a good inch on your palm. Pinch the overlapping ends together, then, with your hand still in the dough loop, place your hand palm down on your work surface. Press down slightly as you roll the seam under your palm to encourage it to stick together. Place the bagel on a baking sheet or on a work surface by your stove top and shape the remaining 7 small pieces of dough. Cover with a cotton cloth and let stand for 10 to 15 minutes.

Meanwhile, bring 8 cups of water to a boil in a wide 4- to-6-quart pot. Add the honey and stir to dissolve. Have a slotted spoon ready. If using a baking stone or tiles, have a peel (or a baking sheet to use as a peel) nearby. If not using a baking stone, place a parchment paper–lined baking sheet by your work surface. Put the sesame seeds or poppy seeds on a large plate, or put out a plate of each.

Gently slide 4 bagels into the boiling water. They will sink and then rise to the surface within 10 seconds or less. Use the back of the slotted spoon to gently press them down into the water occasionally and let boil for about 45 seconds, puffing and growing a little, then use the spoon to remove them one by one and lay them on the seeds. Roll each bagel in the seeds, coating both sides, then place them on your peel or the paper-lined baking sheet, leaving an inch or more between them. When all 4 are ready, use the peel to transfer them onto the baking stone or tiles, or place the baking sheet into the oven. Repeat with the remaining 4 bagels, placing them beside the first 4.

Bake for about 8 minutes, then use a long-handled spatula to turn them over and bake for another 5 to 7 minutes, until golden brown.

As soon as you put the bagels in to bake, start shaping the next batch of 8. Remove the baked bagels from the oven when done and repeat with the remaining dough until all of the bagels have been boiled and baked.

Bagels are best eaten warm, or at least within 24 hours of being baked. If you make a larger batch than you can consume in 24 hours, let extras cool to room temperature, then slice crosswise in half and freeze in a well-sealed plastic bag. Reheat in the toaster or the oven.

FOLLOWING PAGES: MONTREAL BAGELS. *Austrian bannetons.*

sweet potato dinner rolls

Makes 16 medium-sized soft dinner rolls with very browned tops and a beautiful pale orange crumb

"There are only two things I don't like," my father always used to tell us. "I don't like eggplant and I don't like sweet potatoes." When I got older and started making bread, I came across sweet potato rolls in James Beard's wonderful book Beard on Bread. I tried them out at the restaurant in Laramie (see Making Rolls, page 238), then one day tried them out on my father. The rolls are a beautiful pale tangerine color, and soft and tender as can be. Of course, he just loved them. And of course I had the pleasure of saying, "See, you like sweet potatoes after all."

These are an American classic, and deservedly so. Our version is a little different from James Beard's—less yeast and fewer eggs.

¾ pound (1 large) sweet potato, peeled and cut into chunks

1 teaspoon active dry yeast

¼ cup packed light brown sugar

3½ to 4½ cups all-purpose flour

About 2 tablespoons unsalted butter, softened

1 tablespoon salt

2 large or extra-large eggs

1 egg, whisked, for egg wash

Put the sweet potato in a saucepan with about 2 cups water and bring to a boil. Cook for about 15 minutes, until tender. Drain, reserving the cooking water. Mash or puree the potato (you should have about 1¼ cups), and place in a large bowl. Let the potato and cooking water cool to lukewarm.

Measure out 1 cup of the lukewarm cooking water and stir in the yeast to dissolve thoroughly. Add the yeast mixture to the potato, then stir in the brown sugar and 1 cup of the flour. Add the butter and salt and stir, then add the 2 eggs and mix well. Add 2 more cups of flour, a cup at a time.

Dust a work surface generously with flour and turn out the dough. Knead for about 5 minutes, until soft, smooth, and somewhat elastic.

Place in a clean bowl, cover with plastic wrap, and let rise until doubled, about 4 hours.

Pull the dough away from the sides of the bowl and turn out onto a lightly floured surface. Lightly grease an 18-by-12-inch baking sheet with butter.

Use a sharp knife or a dough scraper to divide the dough into 16 pieces (cut it in half, then cut in half again and again). Using your cupped palm, pressing the dough lightly into your work surface, roll 1 piece into a round roll by rolling it in a short circular motion about ten times. Place the shaped roll on the baking sheet. Continue with the remaining dough, placing the rolls about ½ inch apart on the baking sheet (4 rows of 4 rolls each). Cover with plastic wrap and let rise for 30 to 40 minutes.

Place a rack in the center of the oven and preheat the oven to 400°F.

Just before baking, brush the tops of the rolls with the egg wash. Bake for 30 minutes, or until the rolls are a deep brown on top and a golden orange at the sides. They will be nested together, touching.

Let cool for 10 minutes before serving. Store, once completely cooled, in a well-sealed plastic bag.

Shaped dough rounds proofing, Bekaa Valley, Lebanon

Making rolls One of the best jobs I ever had—and I had the job twice—was making lunch rolls for a restaurant in Laramie, Wyoming. I had lots of freedom in both places, just so long as the rolls were ready and warm when the food was served. I'd start early in the morning, mixing and stirring a sponge, drinking my coffee, contemplating my day's rolls. Would I make rye and walnut, or carrot and raisin, or beautiful tangerine-colored sweet potato rolls? Would I make them hearty and healthful with whole wheat flour, or would they be soft and golden with an egg wash and a sprinkle of sesame seeds?

As I'd make the dough, I'd listen to music and daydream about faraway places—about hiking in the mountains in Nepal, about watching the sunset on a long white sandy beach in south Thailand. By mid-morning, as the dough was rising and I was looking after other chores in the restaurant bakery, my friend Rick would drop by, or Mark, and we'd drink another cup of coffee, happy to be there with the smell of the dough and the sunshine streaming through the windows.

By late morning, the bakery was no longer a peaceful place. Cooks were in and out, reaching for

supplies, waiters were in and out fussing, everyone was asking about the rolls: Would they be ready? What

kind were they? Was I sure I was making enough? I'd have my ovens hot, my rolls rising, I'd feel that

wonderful restaurant adrenaline, and then into the oven the rolls would go, tray after tray. The bakery

would fill even more with good smells, and the smells would mix with the smells of food from the

restaurant, and the good cheer. When at last the rolls were ready, I'd pull them out and separate them one

from another, and the air would fill with luscious hot steam. And my workday was over.

I love rolls.

Rolls cooling, Della Fattoria, Petaluma, California

bran muffins

Makes 10 medium-to-large tender, richly flavored bran muffins

What makes us love bran muffins? The moist texture? The feeling that there's something of substance, not just air and sugar, in them? Whatever the attraction, it's a strong one. And along with it go very clear—and sometimes widely divergent—views about what constitutes a good bran muffin.

We've spent a lot of time exploring that question, baking with wheat bran and oat bran, taking a low-fat approach and a full-fat one too. We've emerged from all that testing with this recipe made with wheat bran, sour cream, and whole milk. The muffins are not particularly sweet, but they have a good deep flavor thanks to the combination of molasses and brown sugar.

1 cup sour cream (full-fat)

1½ cups wheat bran

1 large egg

½ cup whole milk

1 tablespoon blackstrap molasses, or a scant tablespoon regular molasses

¼ cup packed light brown sugar, plus (optional) 2 tablespoons for sprinkling

1 cup all-purpose flour

1 teaspoon baking powder

½ teaspoon baking soda

½ teaspoon salt

Place the sour cream in a medium bowl and stir in the bran. Add the egg and milk and beat to blend. Let stand for 30 minutes to 1 hour so that the bran can soften and absorb the liquid.

Place a rack in the lower third of the oven and preheat the oven to 350°F. Set out one 12-cup or two 6-cup regular muffin tins; if they are not nonstick, lightly grease 10 of the cups with butter or oil.

Stir the molasses and brown sugar into the bran mixture. In a small bowl, whisk together the flour, baking powder, baking soda, and salt. Add to the wet mixture and fold and stir to just blend in and completely moisten the dry ingredients. You will have a thick, scoopable—not pourable—batter.

Ladle the batter into 10 muffin cups to fill them just below the top edge. If you wish, sprinkle the top of each muffin with a little brown sugar. Bake for about 25 minutes. The muffins will have pulled away from the sides of the cups and a skewer inserted into the center will come out clean.

As soon as they are baked, turn the muffins out of the tin onto a wire rack to cool and firm up.

rice flour muffin-cakes

Makes 12 small- to-medium-sized, fine-textured moist muffins, pale golden–colored and gluten-free

Having met people with wheat intolerance, as well as those who are allergic to gluten (celiacs), we're always on the lookout for baked goods that use only rice or sorghum or corn flour.

We discovered a bare-bones recipe for plunkets (we don't know the origin of the name) in André Simon's Cyclopedia of Gastronomy *(see Bibliography). We've played with the recipe until it is now clear and reliable. It yields small rich muffins using only rice flour. The proportions are like those of a classic pound cake: equal weights of eggs, butter, sugar, and flour. Though the muffins are unleavened, they have a fine, moist, cakelike texture that holds together well even when we dunk them in tea or coffee.*

4 large eggs, separated

¼ teaspoon salt (reduce to ⅛ if using salted butter)

11 tablespoons (1⅓ sticks) unsalted butter, softened

¾ cup sugar

1½ cups rice flour (see Rice in the Glossary)

¼ teaspoon pure vanilla extract

Place a rack in the center of the oven and preheat the oven to 350°F. Lightly grease 12 regular muffin cups.

Combine the egg whites and salt in a bowl and beat with a hand mixer (or use a stand mixer fitted with the whisk attachment) until stiff. Set aside.

Place the butter and sugar in another bowl and cream them together until smooth and pale. Add the egg yolks and beat until smooth. Gently stir in the rice flour and vanilla, then fold in the beaten whites.

Spoon the batter into the prepared muffin cups, filling them half to three-quarters full. Bake for about 20 minutes, until puffed in the center, with a golden brown rim around the edge.

Let stand for 5 minutes to firm up, then turn out the muffins onto a wire rack to cool.

sweet anise bagels

Makes 20 to 24 golden brown rings, with a tender crumb, flavored with anise and sugar

Around the time Tolstoy was writing his masterpieces, another Russian author was also breaking new ground. Elena Molokhovets's comprehensive cookbook A Gift to Young Housewives *was first published in 1861. The book enjoyed more than twenty editions, with extensive revisions and additions. We feel very fortunate that historian Joyce Toomre has translated and annotated many of the recipes in a volume called* Classic Russian Cooking *(see Bibliography). It offers a fascinating and evolving picture of life and food in the wealthier layers of Russian society in the second half of the nineteenth century. There are many treasures in the book.*

Intrigued by a recipe for bagellike buns flavored with anise (translated as "quick pastry rings for coffee"), we experimented to figure out a modern equivalent. The "bagels" are made from a soft soda-raised sweet, rich dough, flavored with toasted crushed anise. (For a milder anise taste, use ³⁄4 teaspoon seeds; for a more forward taste, use 1 teaspoon.) The dough is shaped into rings and dropped briefly into simmering milk, just as bagels are briefly boiled in water (see Montreal Bagels, page 232), then the rings are slow-baked for about two hours, until golden brown and firm. The beautiful rings have a close, tender crumb, aromatic with anise and only slightly sweet: delicious surprises from the past.

2 tablespoons unsalted butter, softened

2 tablespoons honey

4 large egg yolks

½ cup sour cream (full-fat)

2 to 2½ cups all-purpose flour

1 teaspoon baking powder

¼ teaspoon baking soda

³⁄4 to 1 teaspoon anise seeds, toasted and crushed

About 3 cups milk for simmering the bagels

Place a rack in the lower third of the oven and preheat the oven to 300°F.

In a medium bowl, beat together the butter, honey, egg yolks, and sour cream. In a separate bowl, combine 1¾ cups of the flour, the baking powder, baking soda, and anise seeds. Stir the sour cream mixture into the dry ingredients until smooth.

Turn the dough out onto a well-floured surface and knead briefly until less sticky. Set aside, loosely covered.

Pour an inch of milk into a wide pot and bring to a boil. Lower the heat to maintain a strong simmer. Skim off any scum and discard. Place a slotted spoon and a baking sheet lined with parchment paper or wax paper near your stove top.

Cut the dough into 4 equal pieces and set 3 of them aside, loosely covered. Roll out the remaining piece of dough under your palms to a rope about as thick as your little finger (about ⅓ inch). Cut off a 5-inch length, form it into a loop, overlapping the ends, and pinch them together firmly. Drop the ring into the hot milk: It will sink to the bottom, then rise back up in about 10 seconds. Let it float for another 10 seconds or so, then use the slotted spoon to transfer it to the paper-lined baking sheet. Prepare 2 or 3 more rings in the same way—the number you cook at one time will depend on how large your pot is—leaving a 1-inch or slightly larger space between the rings on the baking sheet. Repeat with the remaining dough, rolling any short leftover ends of rope together to form another ring or two.

Place the baking sheet in the oven and bake for 45 minutes to 1 hour. The rings will puff up and become golden and firm. Remove from the oven.

Line a second baking sheet with parchment or wax paper. The rings will have stuck to the first sheet of paper, so lift it up and lay it, upside down, on the second baking sheet. The first paper will still be (rather unattractively) stuck to the rings—don't worry, just leave it there.

Place the rings back in the oven to bake until firm, about another hour. The paper will detach easily by the time they are fully baked. Place on a rack to cool slightly before eating.

NOTE The original recipe, as translated by Ms. Toomre, called for sweet cream and "birch lye" (as a leavening). We substituted sour cream and baking soda with a little baking powder, then adjusted the proportions of the other ingredients. The original calls for the rings to go onto a wooden plank in the oven and then for the plank to be turned over; the translator wasn't sure why. We realized after making these rings that it was because the half-cooked rings stick to the surface they're on, coming off only when they're fully baked. The modern option, of parchment or wax paper, is much easier to handle than a wooden plank!

The domes of St. Basil's Cathedral, Red Square, Moscow, Russia

beirut tahini swirls

Makes 6 golden brown, flaky-textured coiled rounds, about 6 inches wide, filled with sesame paste and sugar

PHOTOGRAPH ON PAGE 218 *Beirut has a lot of good food at every level, from fancy restaurants to local eateries, from home cooking to quality market shopping. And for a curbside snacker like me, it's paradise. There are sesame-covered flatbreads, grilled meats, and sweet and not so sweet cookies; there's always something nearby to eat. One afternoon, I wandered around an antiques store neighborhood on the Muslim side of the old Green Line (which divided Beirut from the mid-seventies to the late eighties during the years of fighting) and as I window-shopped, I snacked nonstop. My idea of a perfect afternoon.*

These tahini swirls, called sukkar bi tahin *in Arabic, are flattened flaky rounds flavored with tahini and sugar, not too sweet, not too strong tasting. Serve them warm or at room temperature—they're just right either way.*

½ **teaspoon active dry yeast**

1 **cup lukewarm water**

About 2½ cups all-purpose flour

2 **teaspoons sugar**

1 **tablespoon olive oil**

FILLING

¾ **cup tahini (see Glossary)**

¾ **cup sugar**

In a medium bowl, dissolve the yeast in the lukewarm water. Stir in 1 cup of the flour, then add the sugar and oil and stir in. Incorporate a second cup of flour, then turn the dough out onto a well-floured surface and knead for 5 minutes, or until smooth.

Cover the dough with plastic wrap and let rise for 2 to 3 hours, until doubled in volume.

Meanwhile, place a baking stone or unglazed quarry tiles, if you have them, (or a baking sheet) on the middle oven rack and preheat the oven to 375°F. Mix together the tahini and sugar and stir until smooth. Set aside.

Cut the dough into 6 equal pieces. Work with 3 at a time, keeping the others covered. Flatten each out on a lightly floured surface, then roll each out to a rectangle about 5 inches by 10 inches. Spread the top surface with 2½ tablespoons of the filling mixture, spreading it almost to the edges. Roll up the rectangle from a long side into a cylinder, which will stretch as you roll to about 20 inches long. Anchor one end and coil the bread around itself, then tuck the end in. Flatten with the palm of your hand, then set aside, covered, while you fill and shape the other 2 rectangles.

Return to the first coil and roll out gently with a rolling pin. Roll the other 2 out a little and then return to the first one and roll it out a little more thinly, and so on, until you have rolled each to a round about 6 to 7 inches in diameter. A little filling may leak out—don't worry, just leave it.

Place the breads on the hot baking stone or tiles (or baking sheet) and bake for 15 to 20 minutes, until golden brown and flaky. Transfer to a rack to cool.

Shape and bake the remaining 3 pieces of dough. Serve warm or at room temperature.

cranberry-chocolate sweet buns

Makes 2 loaves of 8 soft rolls each, dotted with cranberries and semisweet chocolate chips

PHOTOGRAPH ON PAGE 246 *These large buns take less than three hours from start to finish. They bake together in a loaf pan or cake pan to form two attractive hillocky loaves, inviting and delicious. They're designed to be pulled apart into rolls and eaten out of hand, rather than sliced, though you can cut them if you like.*

The tartness of the cranberries scattered throughout the dough is a bit direct and unsweet for most children; these are adult breads. The taste of the semisweet chocolate chips marries well with the cranberries, especially once the bread has cooled. The buns make a great next-morning treat with coffee.

Use the smallest cranberries in the bag, straight from the freezer (or well-chilled fresh cranberries), and cold chocolate chips, too. Let the buns cool before eating—if you can.

2 cups milk, heated until lukewarm

2 teaspoons active dry yeast

About 5 cups all-purpose flour

2 tablespoons unsalted butter, cut into very small pieces, plus a little butter for shaping the buns

2 tablespoons sugar

1 large egg, beaten

¼ teaspoon salt

¾ cup semisweet chocolate chips, chilled

½ cup frozen cranberries or well-chilled fresh cranberries

TOPPING

1 egg, whisked with 2 tablespoons warm water, for egg wash

About 3 tablespoons granulated or pearl sugar (see Sugars in the Glossary)

Place the milk in a medium bowl and stir in the yeast. Let stand for several minutes, then stir in 1 cup of the flour. Add the butter, sugar, egg, and salt and stir to incorporate. Add 2 more cups flour and stir, always in the same direction, until smooth. Add the cold chocolate chips and cranberries, together with ½ cup more flour, and stir and turn to incorporate.

Turn the dough out onto a generously floured surface and knead gently, folding the dough over on itself without pushing down too hard (you don't want to break open the cranberries) and incorporating flour as needed, until the dough is only slightly sticky, about 4 minutes.

Place the dough in a clean bowl, cover with a cloth, and let rise until doubled, about 1½ hours.

Turn the dough out onto a lightly floured surface. Cut in half, then cut each half into 8 pieces, and lightly cover them. Lightly butter two 9-by-5-inch bread pans or two 8-inch round cake pans.

Grease your palm with a little butter, then roll one piece of dough lightly under your hand to shape it into a rough ball. Place it in one of the pans. Continue with the remaining pieces of dough, placing 8 balls in pairs side by side in each rectangular pan, or placing 8 balls in a circle, starting from the outside edge and working in, in each cake pan. Cover with a cloth or plastic and let rise for 30 minutes.

Place a rack in the center of the oven and preheat the oven to 400°F.

Just before baking, brush each loaf with the egg wash. Sprinkle the sugar over them and bake for 30 to 40 minutes (the timing will vary with the shape of the pans; they usually bake more quickly in cake pans), until puffed and golden brown. Immediately remove from the pans; let cool on a rack. These are best after they've cooled almost to room temperature. Tear off rolls, or slice like a loaf if you prefer.

chelsea buns

Makes 16 to 20 coiled buns, dotted with currants and sweetened with brown sugar

When I was a student in London, I came to understand why the buns and cakes in England and Scotland are rich and plentiful. The damp months of winter are so chilling that the only way to chase the cold is to drink lots of hot tea and thicken the blood with stacks of butter-rich treats. It may not be what the doctors order, but that's a different issue. On a cold tired day, foods like these are such a pick-me-up.

Chelsea buns are coiled rolls: A yeasted dough, enriched with eggs and butter, is shaped around a butter, currant, and brown sugar filling. These days, Chelsea buns are usually outsized and very sweet. We prefer small ones that are easy to get your mouth around and that invite you to eat them two at a time.

4 to 5 cups all-purpose flour

½ pound (2 sticks) unsalted butter, softened

2 tablespoons sugar

1 teaspoon cinnamon

1 teaspoon salt

2 large eggs

2 teaspoons active dry yeast

1 cup whole milk, heated until just lukewarm

FILLING, TOPPING, AND GLAZE

Scant 8 tablespoons (1 stick) cold unsalted butter, cut into small cubes

½ cup currants, soaked in a little warm lemon juice or water until softened, if necessary

½ cup packed light brown sugar

5 tablespoons granulated sugar

1 tablespoon milk

Place 4 cups flour in a large bowl. Blend in the butter, using your fingers or a pastry cutter to blend it to a coarse meal texture. Stir in the sugar, cinnamon, and salt. Whisk the eggs, then add to the flour. Stir the yeast into the warm milk until well dissolved, then add to the dough and stir and knead in the bowl for several minutes, until a smooth dough forms. If the dough is sticky, knead in extra flour; the dough should be firm but pliable.

Place the dough in a clean bowl, or on a counter, cover with plastic wrap, and let rise for 3 hours. It will be puffy and moist but not quite doubled.

Lightly butter an 18-by-12-inch baking sheet.

Knead the dough briefly on a floured surface and cut it in half. Flatten one piece out into a rectangle about 8 inches by 12 inches. Sprinkle on half the butter cubes, then half the currants and half the brown sugar. Fold the

PRECEDING PAGES: CRANBERRY-CHOCOLATE SWEET BUNS *(page 245). Dairy cattle, Brittany, France.*

dough in thirds like a business letter, folding one end over the center, then folding the other end over that. Rotate the dough 90 degrees. Use a rolling pin to flatten it out into a rectangle 8 inches by 12 inches again. Roll up from one narrow end like a jelly roll and pinch to seal the seam. Use a sharp knife moistened with cold water to cut the roll into ½-inch-wide slices. Lay the slices on the prepared baking sheet, leaving about ¾ inch between them. Cover with plastic wrap while you repeat with the second piece of dough. (If you can't fit all the buns on one sheet, butter a second. Bake one sheet at a time.)

Set aside, covered, to rise for about 1 hour. The rolls will expand until almost touching.

Meanwhile, place a rack in the upper third of the oven and preheat the oven to 425°F.

Sprinkle 3 tablespoons of the sugar over the buns (it gives a sheen and a little texture) and place the baking sheet in the oven. Bake for 15 minutes, or until lightly golden.

Just before the rolls are done, mix together the milk and the remaining 2 tablespoons sugar in a small saucepan. Bring almost to a boil, stirring to prevent scorching; you want the mixture to be very hot when the buns come out of the oven.

Brush the milk glaze over the buns as soon as they come out of the oven. They are delicious hot from the oven, and also once they've cooled and firmed up. Place on a rack to cool.

NOTE These keep well for 3 to 4 days. Let cool completely before wrapping in plastic.

FOLLOWING PAGE: *Flo, the waitress at Johnson's Corners, near Loveland, Colorado.*

Cinnamon rolls and dog races My dad's a gambler. He plays the dogs, the horses, and the occasional game of poker—but mainly the dogs. He's been playing the dogs since I was born, but in our town we didn't have a track, so on Friday nights he and I would drive an hour south to a bigger town, Fort Collins, Colorado, and go to the dogs.

Kids weren't allowed inside the track, so I'd stand outside the barbed-wire fence and watch from there. I couldn't see the entire race, but I could see the trainers put their greyhounds into the starting gate, I could hear the mechanical rabbit, Rusty, coming around the track—and then, *whoosh,* they were off. Between races, Dad would come by and we'd confer, then he'd head back to place his bets. I loved the dogs, just as Dad did.

After the races, after all the other cars had left the parking lot, we'd sleep in the back of our Rambler station wagon. Next morning, bright and early, we'd tidy up the car, then drive down to Johnson's Corners, a truck stop a few miles away, to eat cinnamon rolls—big fat cinnamon rolls. They'd come hot to our table, or to the counter, where we often sat, along with farmers stopping in for a morning cup of coffee, or long-distance truckers looking for a hearty breakfast.

We actually had three different places not far from the dogs where we would go for cinnamon rolls—or I should say that Dad had two places, and I had three. There was Vern's, where the rolls were even bigger than those at Johnson's Corners, but they were not as sweet, not as goopy. And Vern's wasn't nearly as sunny as Johnson's Corners, which is important after a night's sleep in the back of a car.

The third place, the Rainbow, didn't appear until a little later. It was a late-sixties, early-seventies place, not far from the university, a place where boys wore their hair in ponytails and girls dressed in long Indian block-print cotton skirts. The Rainbow made my favorite cinnamon rolls, one hundred percent whole wheat, smothered in honey, and topped with pumpkin and sunflower seeds.

Dad was never particularly fond of the Rainbow's cinnamon rolls—they reminded him of the Great Depression and World War II, when all there was was whole wheat; his first choice was Johnson's Corners—but he'd drop me off and come back for me an hour or so later. He knew how much I loved them and he knew how important these things can be.

After breakfast, what we did would depend on whether there was a Saturday matinee at the track. If there was, we'd do a few errands, perhaps buy a big bag of red-and-white hard-candy peppermints at a discount store, then head on over. If there wasn't, and if it happened to be summertime, we'd go looking for a swimming pool.

When the races were over the second night, which was usually well past midnight, we'd drive home. But first we'd stop at Johnson's Corners, open twenty-four hours. Maybe we'd have a milk shake, maybe another cinnamon roll. We'd talk about the races; we'd be happy if we'd won, a little gloomy if we'd lost. Dad would usually give me a small take of any winnings, though always with the same don't-tell-your-brothers-and-sister look. Then we'd drive home through the night, replaying every race, sucking on red-and-white hard-candy peppermints.

taipei coconut buns

Makes 12 hot dog bun–shaped rolls with a sweet coconut filling

We have no idea where the Chinese bakery tradition of soft white filled buns comes from, but in Taiwan, in Hong Kong, and even here in each of Toronto's Chinatowns, we can always find a bakery with a dazzling array of them.

The first bun shops I ever saw were in Taipei; they're still my favorites. I'd already been living in the city for three or four months when my friend Rick (alias Cinnamon Roll Rick) arrived for a visit. Within a day, he'd found the bun shops and came running to find out which buns were my favorite. I'd never noticed the bun shops and I thought he was crazy. But he was right. And for the next six months, we ate a ton of sweet buns.

These coconut buns are our take on my favorites. The filling is an easily prepared paste of dried coconut and brown sugar. Make it immediately after the dough is first kneaded and left to rise, or even earlier, up to two days before you make the dough. The filling firms up to an easy-to-handle pastelike texture if well chilled.

2 tablespoons sugar

⅔ cup lukewarm water

2 teaspoons active dry yeast

⅔ cup pastry or cake flour, or about another
    ½ cup all-purpose flour

⅔ to ¾ cup all-purpose flour

¼ cup vegetable oil

1 teaspoon salt

FILLING

½ cup plus 2 tablespoons dried unsweetened shredded
    coconut, or ⅔ cup sweetened shredded coconut and
    reduce the sugar by 2 tablespoons

¼ cup boiling water (if using dried coconut)

½ cup packed light brown sugar

2 tablespoons cornstarch

1 tablespoon unsalted butter, shortening, or lard

In a large bowl, dissolve 1 teaspoon of the sugar in the warm water, then stir in the yeast. Stir in the pastry or cake flour and let stand for 15 minutes.

Add the all-purpose flour, the remaining sugar, the oil, and salt and stir and turn to mix together. Lightly flour your work surface and turn the dough out. Knead it for 3 to 5 minutes. The dough will be somewhat sticky when you begin, but it will become smooth and no longer sticky.

Place in a clean bowl and cover with a cloth or plastic wrap. Let rise for 1½ hours, or until more than doubled in volume.

Meanwhile, make the filling: If using dried coconut, place the ½ cup of coconut in a bowl and pour over the boiling water. Let stand for 10 to 15 minutes.

In a small bowl, mix together the sugar and cornstarch, then stir into the coconut mixture; or combine ½ cup of the sweetened coconut with the sugar and cornstarch in a bowl. Melt the butter or fat in a saucepan over medium-low heat. Add the coconut-sugar mixture and cook for about 2 minutes, stirring occasionally to prevent burning or sticking, until the mixture thickens. Set aside to cool, then refrigerate, covered.

About 30 minutes before the dough is ready, take the filling out of the refrigerator. The mixture hardens as it cools, but stirring it with a wooden spoon will soften it. Stir the remaining 2 tablespoons coconut into the softened paste and set aside.

Line a large baking sheet (or two smaller sheets) with parchment paper. Turn the risen dough out onto a lightly floured surface. Cut it into 2 pieces and set 1 aside, loosely covered. Flatten the other piece with your hands and then roll it out to a thin rectangle 12 to 14 inches long and 6 to 7 inches wide. Cut it lengthwise in half, making 2 long thin strips.

Place a scant packed ¼ cup filling lengthwise down the center of each piece of dough in a compact strip. (The filling should have a fairly dry pastelike texture; if there is any liquid, avoid transferring it to the dough.) Pull one side of one strip of dough over the filling, then pull the other side over to overlap slightly. Pinch to seal the dough and enclose the filling, then gently roll the tube

over so the seam is on the bottom. Use a sharp knife or dough scraper to cut the tube into 3 equal pieces. Pinch the ends of each roll closed to seal in the filling, pushing the filling in from the ends a little to give you enough dough to work with so that each end of each roll is well sealed. Transfer the buns to the parchment paper–lined baking sheet, leaving at least 1½ inches between them, and repeat with the remaining strip of dough. Then roll, cut, fill, and shape the remaining dough.

Cover the buns with a cotton cloth or plastic and let rise for 35 to 45 minutes. The buns are ready when they have increased slightly in volume and when the indent of a lightly pressed fingertip stays in the dough.

Meanwhile, place a rack in the center of the oven and preheat the oven to 375°F.

Bake the buns for 15 to 18 minutes, until golden brown. (If using two baking sheets, bake on two racks and rotate the pans after 8 minutes to ensure even baking.) Transfer to a rack to cool. Eat warm or at room temperature.

truck-stop cinnamon rolls

Makes 12 large bready cinnamon rolls, about 2 inches tall and 4 to 5 inches across

Everyone's idea of the perfect cinnamon roll differs: Some like them flaky, like Danishes, while for others they're a special form of bread. We fall squarely in the second category. These cinnamon rolls, inspired by those at Johnson's Corners, near Loveland, Colorado (see Cinnamon Rolls and Dog Races, page 250), are very large crusty breads flavored with cinnamon and sugar. If you want them softer, wrap them in plastic overnight. To make smaller ones, slice the rolled-up dough thinner, into eighteen rolls.

1 tablespoon dried yeast

5 cups warm water

½ cup light or dark brown sugar

2 tablespoons salt

About 13 cups all-purpose flour, preferably unbleached

FILLING

¼ cup vegetable oil

About 1½ cups light brown sugar or granulated sugar

¼ cup ground cinnamon

Dissolve the yeast in the water in a large bowl. Stir in 6 cups of flour, 1 cup at a time, always stirring in the same direction. Then stir for about another minute, in the same direction. Let the sponge rest for 2 hours, covered.

The sponge will be lively and will have grown. Gently stir it, then sprinkle on the sugar and salt and stir in. Add about 6 cups flour, a cup at a time, stirring and turning as a dough begins to form. When the dough becomes too difficult to turn with the spoon, turn it out onto a well-floured work surface. Knead for 8 to 10 minutes, incorporating more flour as needed, until smooth and elastic.

Place the dough in a large lightly oiled bowl. Cover the bowl with plastic wrap and let the dough rise until doubled in volume, 1½ to 2 hours.

Pull the dough away from the sides of the bowl and transfer to your work surface. Flatten it to a square approximately 24 inches across. Pour on the oil and rub it around to completely cover the surface of the dough. Sprinkle on the sugar and then the cinnamon. Roll up the dough into a jelly-roll shape, then cut into 12 rounds.

Lightly grease a large baking sheet. Lay the cinnamon rolls on the baking sheet, placing them approximately ½ inch apart. Cover with plastic wrap and let rise for 30 minutes.

Meanwhile, place a rack in the upper third of the oven and preheat the oven to 400°F. Bake the rolls for 35 to 40 minutes, until they are a beautiful brown color. Lift the rolls off the sheet and transfer to a rack to cool. To soften the crusty tops, cover loosely with a cotton cloth after 10 minutes.

chocolate bread batons

Makes 24 long rolls, flecked with chocolate (nearly 4½ pounds altogether)

The day we made these chocolate-flecked minibreads for the first time, we all dived for them—tender bread with just the right amount of dark chocolate through it. One thing to know is that occasionally bits of dark chocolate fall like crumbs as you eat. So, as Jeffrey said, "We'd better tell people NOT to eat these while sitting on a white sofa!"

POOLISH

1 cup lukewarm water

⅛ teaspoon active dry yeast

1 cup all-purpose flour

BREAD

2 cups milk

1 cup warm water

1 teaspoon active dry yeast

2 cups pastry or cake flour, or about another
    1½ cups all-purpose flour

4½ to 6 cups all-purpose flour

4 teaspoons salt

Two 3½-ounce bars 70% bittersweet chocolate,
    chilled

Make the poolish 12 to 30 hours before you wish to bake: Mix the water, yeast, and flour into a smooth batter. Cover with plastic wrap and let ferment for 8 to 24 hours. (If keeping it longer than 12 hours, refrigerate; bring to room temperature before using.)

Mix the milk and water in a large bowl. Sprinkle on the yeast and stir to dissolve it. Add the poolish and stir in, then add the pastry or cake flour and 1 cup of the all-purpose flour and stir to make a wet batter. Sprinkle on the salt and stir in, then add 3½ to 4 cups all-purpose flour, a cup at a time, stirring to incorporate it, until a wet dough forms.

Generously flour a work surface and turn the dough out onto it. Knead for 5 minutes or more, incorporating flour only as necessary to prevent sticking: Work toward a soft moist dough rather than a stiff one—the dough should be smooth and soft.

Place the dough in a clean bowl and cover with plastic wrap. Let rise for 3 to 4 hours at room temperature, or if more convenient, for as long as 8 hours or overnight, in a cooler place.

When ready to proceed, turn the dough out onto a lightly floured surface and cut it into 2 equal pieces. Let rest for a few minutes while you lightly butter (or line with parchment paper) an 18-by-12-inch baking sheet or two 12-by-9-inch sheets. Use a large knife or cleaver to cut the chocolate bars crosswise into very thin, stick-like slices, then cut the slices in half; set aside.

Flatten 1 piece of dough into a rectangle about 20 inches long and 8 or 9 inches wide. Sprinkle half the chocolate pieces (about ¾ cup) over the dough. Roll up the dough loosely from a short end, pulling a little on each side to stretch it wider as you roll, so you have a roll about 18 inches long. Flatten it with lightly floured palms to a rectangle about 5 inches wide; don't worry if a little of the chocolate is showing or pushing out of the dough.

Use a sharp knife or a dough scraper to cut the dough crosswise into 12 pieces. Pick up one piece by the ends and give it a twist while stretching it lengthwise a little, then place it on a prepared baking sheet. Repeat with the remaining pieces, laying them side by side in two rows, leaving a ½-inch space between them. Set aside, covered, while you repeat with the second half of the dough to make another 12 rolls. Cover with plastic wrap and let rise for 1 hour before baking.

Meanwhile, place a baking stone or unglazed quarry tiles, if you have them, (or a baking sheet) on a rack in the middle or lower third of the oven and preheat the oven to 450°F. Fill a sprayer with water.

Bake for 5 minutes, spritzing the rolls generously with water three times. Lower the heat to 425°F and bake for about 15 minutes longer. The rolls should be lightly golden. They will have baked together, creating a soft place along the sides of the rolls where they touch. Transfer to a rack to cool. The rolls keep well for 2 days, though they rarely last that long.

SUPER-CHOCOLATE BREAD BATONS You can increase the amount of chocolate to 3 bars, or even use 4, giving a very chocolatey bread. We like the balance of bread and chocolate in this recipe, but we know that for some people, there's no limit to how much more chocolate tastes even better.

rich and sticky buns

Makes 12 large, soft sweet buns with a gooey butter-and-brown-sugar topping

Cinnamon rolls and sticky buns are like two siblings, similar in so many ways and yet so different. It all comes down to texture. Sticky buns are . . . well, sticky and gooey; cinnamon rolls are relatively dry. Our friend Dina occasionally stops by on a weekend morning with fresh sticky buns from Harbord Bakery, an institution in downtown Toronto. They're great; they're the ones we most tried to replicate in the following recipe—no nuts, no raisins, just butter and brown sugar and a tender yeasted brioche dough. They look as if they're bursting out the top of the cake pan they're baked in (see Note).

Remember to turn them out of the pan, sweet bottom side up, as soon as they're baked. They'll keep well for several days, but that's never a problem—they're grabbed and eaten immediately.

2 teaspoons active dry yeast

2 tablespoons water

2¾ to 3½ cups all-purpose flour

1 cup pastry or cake flour, or about another
  ¾ cup all-purpose flour

6 large eggs

¼ cup sugar

1½ teaspoons salt

¾ pound (3 sticks) unsalted butter, very soft
  (so it can be squeezed through your fingers)

TOPPING

8 tablespoons (1 stick) unsalted butter

1 cup packed light brown sugar

Dissolve the yeast in the water in a small cup. Pour the mixture into the bowl of a mixer fitted with the dough hook. Add 2¾ cups of the all-purpose flour, the pastry or cake flour, eggs, sugar, and salt and mix on low speed for 5 minutes, stopping occasionally to pull the dough down off the dough hook. The dough will be quite stiff; add up to ½ cup more flour if it seems very soft.

Leaving the mixer on low speed, toss in approximately 2 tablespoons of the softened butter and mix until incorporated, then toss in another 2 tablespoons. Repeat until

all the butter has been incorporated, then continue mixing for another 3 to 5 minutes, until the dough is soft, almost gooey, and climbing up the dough hook; it should also be pulling away from the sides of the bowl.

Cover the bowl with plastic wrap and let the dough rise until doubled in volume, 1½ to 2 hours.

Pull the dough away from the sides of the bowl and transfer to a plastic bag. Flatten the dough and seal the bag, then refrigerate for at least 6 to 8 hours, or as long as 18 hours.

Prepare the topping before removing the dough from the refrigerator: Place the butter and sugar in a heavy saucepan and melt them over low heat, stirring occasionally to prevent burning. Scoop out about ¼ cup of the mixture and set aside. Pour the remaining mixture into a 13-by-9-inch nonstick cake pan (see Note) or two 9-inch round cake pans.

Turn the chilled dough out onto a lightly floured surface. Cut it into quarters and then cut each into 3 pieces. (Each piece will weigh approximately 3 ounces.) Work with 1 piece at a time, leaving the rest covered with plastic wrap. Roll the dough under your palm to a thin rope about 16 inches long. Twine it into a figure eight, tucking in the ends. Lay on the syrup in the pan. Repeat with the remaining pieces, placing them tightly in the

pan in 3 rows of 4 buns each; or, if using round pans, place 2 in the center and 4 around the outside.

Cover the buns with plastic wrap and let rise for about 1½ hours, until approximately doubled. The buns will have puffed up and fattened; when gently pushed with a fingertip, the dough will stay indented.

Meanwhile, place a rack in the center of the oven and preheat the oven to 375°F.

If the reserved topping has solidified, warm it gently until it is just liquid. Drizzle it over the buns, spreading it with the back of a spoon or with a pastry brush. Bake the buns for 20 to 25 minutes, until a rich golden color. Immediately invert them onto a baking sheet (if you delay, some of the bottom "stickiness" will remain in the pan rather than staying on the buns as a gooey topping). Let stand for an hour to firm up before serving.

NOTE We have also baked these in an 12-by-8-inch pan. It was a tighter fit, so the buns rose taller. In other words, pan size is flexible.

Boulangerie, *near Grenoble, France*

SKILLET BREADS AND PANCAKES

cardamom-scented sweet potato roti

Makes 8 round flatbreads, about 7 inches across, lightly brushed with butter

PHOTOGRAPH ON PAGE 264 *Roti is a Hindi-Urdu word used throughout the north of India and in Pakistan to describe a great variety of flatbreads. It can mean the same as* chapatti, *thin flatbreads that are dry-cooked on a skillet or griddle, or it can refer to bread that is baked in a tandoor oven (and is then usually called* tandoor roti). *Rotis can be made with wheat, corn, millet, sorghum, or even with flour from ground chickpeas (besan). They can be plain, or they can be seasoned with fresh herbs or spices, or with garlic or onion. In the region, there is unlimited ingenuity when it comes to making flatbreads.*

In this cardamom-scented roti, cooked pureed sweet potato is mixed with wheat flour and sweetened with a little brown sugar. The breads are rolled out thin and cooked on a lightly oiled skillet or griddle. They turn a beautiful pale tangerine color that deepens if they are brushed with a little melted butter after baking. Serve warm.

1 medium-large (¾ pound) sweet potato,
 peeled and coarsely chopped
Water
1 cup whole wheat flour
1 tablespoon light brown sugar
½ teaspoon salt
Seeds from 1 green cardamom pod, ground
Melted butter for brushing

Place the sweet potato in a saucepan with water to cover and bring to a boil. Simmer until the potato is soft. Drain, reserving the cooking water, and let cool for a few minutes.

Transfer the potato to a food processor and puree. Add the flour, sugar, salt, and cardamom and process: A ball of dough may form, but you will probably have to add 2 to 4 tablespoons of the reserved cooking water (through the feed tube) in order to moisten the mixture enough for a dough to form. Once you have a ball of dough whirling around, process for 15 seconds longer, then turn out onto a lightly floured surface.

Knead the dough briefly, then set it aside, covered with plastic wrap, to rest for 30 minutes to 1 hour.

Divide the dough into 8 pieces. Flour both sides of all the pieces generously, then set aside, loosely covered to prevent drying out. Roll out 2 breads at a time. Flatten each with the palm of your hand. Roll 1 out to about 5 inches in diameter, and repeat with the other. Roll the first one and then the second one out to about 7 inches in diameter. The dough is tender and a little sticky, so roll with a light touch and rotate the bread after each stroke.

Place a cast-iron or other heavy skillet over medium heat and rub with an oiled cloth. When the skillet is hot, place a bread top side down in the skillet for 15 seconds, then gently flip it over and cook the second side for about 2 minutes, until touched with brown. Flip back over and finish cooking the first side. The roti will start to balloon. Press lightly on the puffing area with a cotton cloth to encourage the air to move into the parts that are still flat, and keep the roti moving around on the surface so it doesn't stick or develop hot spots.

Turn out into a basket or bowl lined with a cotton cloth. Brush the top with melted butter, and cover loosely to keep warm and to prevent it from drying out. Repeat with the remaining breads, rolling more out as you bake, then stacking them in the basket or bowl.

baja wheat flour tortillas

Makes 16 fine wheat tortillas, about 8 inches in diameter

Mary's Tortillas, a shop on a side street of Ensenada, in Baja California, was airy and filled with light. Women were laying freshly cooked tortillas on mesh racks to air-dry a little before being packaged. The tortillas were so fine they seemed almost transparent. And when I tore one and then bit into it, it was extraordinary—supple, light but substantial.

The tortillas I brought home from Ensenada kept for four days and came back to life when heated quickly on a hot skillet or over a fire. Mary's secret ingredient isn't just good lard; it's also a little baking powder. Try making them and see for yourself.

½ cup lard or vegetable shortening

3 cups all-purpose flour

1 teaspoon salt

1 teaspoon baking powder

About 1 cup lukewarm water

Combine the lard and dry ingredients in a food processor and process for 20 seconds, then pulse several times, until the texture of fine meal. With the machine running, pour the water through the feed tube until a ball forms, then process for another 15 seconds. Turn out onto a very lightly floured surface and knead briefly. The dough will be soft and very smooth.

Cut the dough in half, then cut each half into 8 equal pieces (each will weigh just over 1¾ ounces). Roll each into a ball under your palm and place on a lightly floured counter or baking sheet. Cover well with plastic to prevent drying out and set aside for at least an hour. (You can, if you like, bake some after an hour and leave the remaining balls to be baked as long as 12 hours later.)

Heat a 10-inch or larger ungreased cast-iron skillet over medium heat. (The heat should not be higher, or it will result in hard patches on the tortilla as it cooks.) Flatten one ball in a little flour, first on one side and then the other, to make a floured disk. Roll it out with a rolling pin, using very firm light strokes, working from the center outward. Rotate the tortilla between strokes—this helps keep it from sticking and also makes it easier to get a perfectly round shape—but do not turn it over. The tortilla will eventually be a very fine and supple round about 8 inches in diameter.

When the round is as thin as you want it, put it top side down in the skillet. Watch it as it cooks, for about 15 seconds or until the first side has spots of pale brown, then turn it over. Cook very briefly on the second side for 20 seconds or so, then turn it back to the first side and cook briefly.

Wrap the cooked tortilla in a cotton cloth to keep it soft and warm and continue rolling out and baking the remaining balls of dough. Serve warm.

NOTE If you make the tortillas ahead, or have leftovers, seal them, once completely cool, in a plastic bag. They will keep for 2 to 3 days in a cool place. To reheat, place in a medium-hot skillet for about 10 seconds a side or on a grill for a moment on each side, or see page 333 for Oven-Baked Chips.

SKILLET QUESADILLAS To make quesadillas, sprinkle a handful of Oaxacan string cheese or grated Monterey Jack or fresh Salvadoran cheese (see Glossary) on half of a fresh tortilla. Fold over, to make a half-moon, and place in a hot skillet for about 10 seconds a side, pressing down to heat it through. (You can also use a microwave to heat and melt the cheese in the quesadilla.)

OPPOSITE: CARDAMOM-SCENTED SWEET POTATO ROTI *(page 262)*.

ABOVE: *Tortillas drying on a rack, Ensenada, Baja California, Mexico.*

welsh cakes

Makes about 12 currant-dotted, round butter-rich scones, 3 to 3½ inches across

In Welsh, the word for griddle is planc. *In Welsh houses, food was traditionally cooked over an open fire, either in a large pot or on an iron planc set over the coals. A cast-iron or other heavy skillet on your stove top is a successful substitute for cooking these sconelike griddle cakes. The heat must be moderate so the cakes have time to cook through before the outside gets too crisp. They're also easy to make over a campfire, as long as you place the skillet over coals or at a distance from the flame so it doesn't get too hot.*

12 tablespoons (1½ sticks) cool unsalted butter

1½ to 2 cups all-purpose flour

⅓ cup sugar

¼ teaspoon salt (scant if using salted butter)

Pinch of grated nutmeg

⅛ teaspoon ground black pepper

⅛ teaspoon cinnamon

⅛ teaspoon powdered ginger

Pinch of ground cloves

½ cup currants

2 extra-large eggs

By hand: Cut the butter into small pieces. Place 1½ cups of the flour in a bowl. Add the butter and cut with a knife or a pastry cutter to blend together into the texture of coarse meal.

Using a food processor: Cut the butter into several chunks, place in a processor bowl with 1½ cups flour, and process to the texture of coarse meal; turn out into a bowl.

Add the sugar, salt, spices, and currants to the flour mixture and stir to mix. Break the eggs into a bowl and beat briefly with a fork to blend, then add to the mixture. Turn and stir to moisten so it comes together as a firm, moist dough.

Turn the dough out onto a lightly floured surface and flatten under your palms, or use a lightly floured rolling pin to roll it out to about ¼ inch thick. Use a round 3-inch cookie cutter to cut out cakes. You should be able to get 12 or 13 from the dough.

Heat a heavy skillet over medium heat. When it is hot, rub the cooking surface with a lightly buttered paper towel, then lower the heat to medium-low. Wait several minutes, then place 3 or 4 rounds top side down in the skillet and cook for about 2 minutes. Flip them over and cook on the other side for 3 minutes. Both sides will be touched with brown and a little black; the cakes will have risen a little, and their sides will still be moist looking. Turn back over and cook on the first side for another minute or so. Lift out and onto a rack to cool and set for 10 minutes or more before eating. Cook the remaining cakes the same way. (If you have two skillets, once you're comfortable with the timing, you can work with both.)

cathead skillet biscuits

Makes 12 tender flat biscuits, touched with gold

Dawnthebaker has a recipe for cathead biscuits (we don't know where the name comes from) from her grandmother, who was born and raised in the southern United States. The biscuits are flat, tender-flaky, and oven-baked. But when our oven broke as we were busy developing and testing recipes for this book, we cast around for stove-top breads and decided to try making the biscuits in a skillet. What a good idea that was! They're a great option when it's too hot to turn on the oven, or for campfire cooking, or even for that unexpected disaster when the oven stops working.

So here they are, quick to make and very quickly eaten. Make them up just before putting dinner on the table, about twenty minutes before you're going to serve the meal, then bake them quickly on a hot skillet in several batches, or in the oven in one batch. When skillet-baked, the biscuits are unevenly browned, touched with gold-to-brown patches, and once they cool, they're a little more brittle than oven-baked biscuits.

2¼ cups pastry or cake flour, or 1½ cups all-purpose flour
plus ¼ cup pastry or cake flour

1 teaspoon salt

1 tablespoon baking powder

¾ cup vegetable shortening

¾ cup warm milk

Combine the dry ingredients in a bowl. Cut in the shortening until you have a crumbly meal. Add the milk and stir with a wooden spoon, or your hand, just until smooth. The dough will be moist and a little sticky.

Turn out onto a lightly floured surface and cut into 12 pieces (each will weigh just under 1½ ounces). Moisten your hands with water, then flatten each piece of dough to a round 4 to 5 inches in diameter and less than ¼ inch thick.

Heat a heavy skillet over high heat until hot. Wipe quickly with an oiled paper towel and lower the heat to medium-high. Add as many biscuits as will fit in the skillet without touching. Cook until lightly browned on one side, 1 to 2 minutes, then turn over and cook another 1 to 2 minutes on the other side. Turn back over and cook a little longer, until more touched with brown, then use a spatula to transfer the biscuits to a plate. Cover the cooked biscuits loosely with a cloth to keep warm and soft while you bake the remaining rounds. Serve hot.

NOTE To bake the biscuits in the oven, preheat the oven to 450°F. Lightly grease a baking sheet. Place the biscuits about ½ inch apart on the baking sheet and bake in the center of the oven until touched with gold, about 10 minutes. Serve hot.

Mountain women The Wakhi people live in the upper part of the Hunza Valley and also on the other side of the mountains in Afghanistan and western China. They live in settled villages in this high country, but they are seminomadic still, moving up to high pastures with their herds when spring comes. We once bicycled from China into Hunza along the Karakoram Highway. The day after we crossed into Pakistan, we pedaled into a small village called Khaibar. The valley we were bicycling down was narrow and steep-sided, hot and dry, and like the inside of a giant quarry, all sand and gravel. But when we reached the village, there was an oasis of wonderful green, with young wheat growing and fruit trees neatly tended, watered by careful irrigation channels that guided glacial stream water through the cultivation.

Hunza Valley, Pakistan

Kids came running up and gestured for us to follow them. We were taken inside a house by several women, who sat us down by the fire, poured us some tea, and started making breads. The breads were huge unleavened roti, rolled and patted very thin and cooked on a cast-iron surface over the fire.

Jeffrey had long hair at the time, and only when he spoke did they realize he was a man. There were no other men around—gone, they told us in gestures, to take the animals up into the mountains. They were surprised and a little embarrassed to have invited a man in, but they didn't seem really worried by it, and soon they were laughing about their mistake. They plied us with tea and bread and yogurt, tried on our boots, played with our zippers, and, when we left, accepted our thanks with grace and humor and waved us down the road.

bahian kisses

Makes 7 or 8 flat lacy breads, about 4 inches across, or 3 larger (6 inches in diameter) breads with a slightly chewy texture, folded over a melted cheese or sweet coconut filling

Beiju means "kiss" in Portuguese—a perfect name for these light snacks from the Bahia region of Brazil (see Kisses from Brazil, page 275). They're made of tapioca starch (available from Thai and Vietnamese groceries) that's moistened with water, then sprinkled into crumbs. The crumbs come together as they cook and the final bread is pale, touched with gold, and folded over a sweet or a savory filling; melted cheese is our favorite, like a Brazilian form of quesadilla.

Note: The one special tool you'll need to make these is a metal ring that you can lay in your skillet to make a rim for the bread. In Brazil, the rings are about 7 inches across; we use a much smaller one, a cookie cutter about 3½ inches in diameter.

½ cup tapioca starch (see Glossary)
3 tablespoons water

TOPPING
Grated cheese or a little grated coconut and
   some sweetened condensed milk

Place the tapioca starch in a small bowl and add the water. Mix them together with your hands. The mixture will feel hard and lumpy; don't worry. Place a sieve over another bowl. Crumble the tapioca mixture into the sieve and use the back of a wooden spoon to press it through the sieve. You'll have a heap of tapioca crumbs or flecks. Set aside.

Heat a heavy skillet over medium heat and rub it with an oiled paper towel. Place a metal ring (see Note above) in the hot pan: If your ring is 3 to 4 inches across, use 1 tablespoon crumbs per bread; if it is 4 to 6 inches, use 1½ to 1¾ tablespoons; if it is 6 to 7 inches across, use a generous 2 tablespoons. Place the measured tapioca crumbs inside the ring, then use the back of a spoon to spread them out to the rim and to flatten them. The crumbs should just barely cover the surface in a slightly lacy pattern (if your first one is too thick, use less tapioca for the next one). The gaps will fill in as you press down with the spoon and as the bread cooks; flatten it well. Lift the ring off after less than a minute and set aside, then use a spatula to flip the bread over and cook on the other side for about a minute, pressing down on it again to flatten. Flip over once more; there should be a slight golden tinge to the edges. (The kisses actually puff up like rotis once they've cooked on two sides—astonishing.)

Sprinkle on a little cheese, or some grated coconut and a drizzle of sweetened condensed milk, fold in half, press down, lift out of the pan, and serve. Repeat to make more breads.

lebanese sajj bread

Makes 8 large, supple wheat flour flatbreads

Lebanon is a relatively small country, but it has a great many different breads. It has a bread for this, a bread for that, a bread that is made only here, a bread that is made only there. And as many breads as I was shown and told about in two weeks traveling across the country, I'm sure there are many, many more.

Sajj bread is, as its name indicates, made on a sajj, a large metal surface (like a wok, only wider and a little flatter; see the photograph on page 314) that is set over a fire dome side up. The large surface area enables the baker to make the bread extra big, and because it is a very thin bread, it comes out looking (and tasting) a lot like Armenian lavash. Like lavash, it tends to dry out quickly (and is then used broken up into soups, stews, and salads).

When hot and fresh, these breads are soft and supple, great for wrapping around cheese and tomato or whatever combination you choose.

1½ cups lukewarm water

1 teaspoon active dry yeast

3½ to 4 cups unbleached all-purpose flour

1 teaspoon salt

Place the warm water in a medium bowl, sprinkle the yeast over, and stir to dissolve. Gradually add 2 cups of the flour, stirring in the same direction. Stir for 1 more minute in the same direction, then set aside, covered, for several hours, if you have the time. Or just proceed with the recipe.

Sprinkle on the salt and continue to stir in the flour. When it is too stiff to stir, turn the dough out onto a lightly floured surface and knead until smooth and elastic, about 7 minutes, adding more flour only as needed.

Place the dough in a clean bowl and cover it with plastic wrap. Let rise for 1½ to 2 hours, until doubled in volume.

Punch down the dough and let rest for 10 minutes.

Turn the dough out onto a lightly floured surface and cut into 8 equal pieces. Flatten each piece between floured palms. To roll out the dough, work with 2 pieces at a time, and keep the other pieces covered. Roll out one dough to 6 to 7 inches in diameter, then switch to the other dough. (In rolling out yeasted doughs, it is important to roll them out only so far, and then to let

them rest before rolling out more. The gluten is stretched, and once it gets accustomed to its new shape, it can be easily stretched some more.) Alternate between the two doughs until each is very thin and about 13 to 14 inches across.

If you have a large spun steel wok (or a sajj), and a gas stove, turn the wok (or sajj) dome side up over a burner. Turn the burner on to high heat. Lightly oil the dome with a paper towel, and let it get hot before putting on a bread. (An oven-baking method follows.)

The rolled-out bread will be a little fragile at this point and can be torn while being transferred to the wok. To carry it easily, roll it up on the rolling pin, then lay one edge on one side of the hot wok and gradually unroll the rest of the bread on the hot surface. Cook for about 1 minute, until you see the center starting to brown from underneath. Flip over and cook for 20 seconds Remove the bread and wrap it in a clean kitchen towel to keep it warm and soft. Continue rolling out and cooking the breads until all are finished.

BAKED LEBANESE WRAPPING BREAD Place a baking stone or unglazed quarry tiles, if you have them, (or a baking sheet) on a rack in the middle of the oven and preheat the oven to 450°F. Bake each batch for 2 to 2½ minutes.

mountain women's roti

Makes 4 very large, thin flatbreads, about 15 inches in diameter

We make these flatbreads on our stove top using a pizza pan over two burners set to a moderate heat, rotating the pan or the bread frequently for even cooking. A campfire or other larger source of heat is an ideal cooking situation, as long as it isn't too hot, and you have a heavy piece of iron or steel to distribute the fire's heat, just like the Wakhi women had in Khaibar in the Hunza Valley (see page 268). Leftover roti make great crackers (see page 333).

4 cups atta flour (see Glossary)

2 teaspoons salt

Scant 2 cups lukewarm water

Make the dough.

Using a food processor: Place the flour and salt in the bowl of the processor. Start the machine and add water through the feed tube until a dough ball forms. Process for another 15 seconds or so. Turn out on a lightly floured surface and knead for a minute, or until very smooth.

By hand: Mix the flour and salt together in a large bowl. Make a hollow in the center and add 1¾ cups water. Use your hands or a wooden spoon to blend the water into the flour, adding a little more water if necessary. Turn the mass of dough out onto a lightly floured surface and knead for 5 minutes, or until very smooth.

Set the kneaded dough aside on a floured surface or in a bowl, well covered with plastic wrap, for 30 minutes to 1 hour.

Cut the dough into 4 equal pieces. On a floured surface, shape each into a ball under the cupped palm of your hand, then flatten each one, flouring both sides generously. Set aside, covered, for a moment.

Place a 16-inch pizza pan over two burners set to medium-low heat.

Start rolling out a bread with a rolling pin, using light strokes and rolling from the center outward (don't turn the dough over), until 15 to 16 inches in diameter and very thin. Pick up one edge, slide the rolling pin under it, and use the pin to transfer the bread to the pan. Lay the top of the bread onto the hot pan, first laying one edge down and then gently draping it onto the pan. Flip the bread over after 15 seconds, then cook the second side until set, about 1½ minutes. Keep moving the bread a little on the pan so all of it is exposed to the heat; move the pan around too. If you get hot spots, lower the heat a little. Flip the bread over again to finish cooking the first side, another minute or so. Transfer immediately to a cotton cloth. Fold into quarters and wrap well to keep it supple while you cook the remaining breads.

tibetan overnight skillet breads

Makes 16 round, soft, slightly sweet flatbreads, about 4 inches in diameter

We came across a recipe for these breads in a small Tibetan cookbook written by two women, one Tibetan and one Nepali, called Tibetan Cooking, *published in Kathmandu. Intrigued, we tried it and were amazed to discover the distinctive taste of skillet breads we'd eaten in Lhasa, in Tibet. The breads, called* kogyum *in Tibetan, have an unusual mix of sweet and savory taste, very pleasing. We've adapted the recipe, but the results are still a spot-on taste of faraway.*

These make great panini, crosscultural sandwiches, split in half and filled with tomato and lettuce and salami.

About 4 cups all-purpose flour

¼ cup sugar

1½ teaspoons baking soda

About 1½ cups lukewarm water

1 teaspoon salt

Peanut or vegetable oil for cooking

Combine the flour, sugar, and baking soda in a food processor and process briefly to mix. With the machine on, pour the water through the feed tube. A ball of dough will form. Process for another 15 seconds, then turn the dough out onto a very lightly floured surface and knead briefly.

Place the dough in a bowl, cover with plastic wrap, and let stand for 12 to 24 hours to rise very slightly.

Turn the dough out onto a floured surface, flatten it, and sprinkle with the salt. Roll up and knead briefly. Cut the dough in half and set one half aside, covered with plastic wrap. Cut the other piece of dough into 8 equal pieces. Roll each into a ball under your cupped palm, then flatten each into a small disk. Press both sides of each disk onto a floured surface to flour them lightly.

Working on the lightly floured surface, roll out 2 disks at a time, alternating between them to give the dough a chance to relax and stretch. Roll out, without turning the dough over, to 4 inches in diameter. Once all 8 are rolled out, cover loosely with plastic wrap.

Heat a cast-iron or other heavy skillet or griddle over medium-high heat. Once it is hot, pour on a little peanut or vegetable oil, spread it all over to grease the surface well, and then wipe off excess with a paper towel or cotton cloth. Reduce the heat to medium or medium-low. Roll out one bread a little more, to nearly 5 inches in diameter, and place top side down on the skillet. Cook for 10 seconds, then flip over. Cook for 2 to 3 minutes, until golden and touched with darker brown on the second side, then flip back over to finish cooking the first side, about another 2 minutes. You'll see the bread lift up as it cooks, much as a leavened pancake does, but these breads hold their loft. When cooked, the bread will be pale brown all over. Transfer to a rack or a cloth-lined basket, and repeat with the remaining breads, adding more oil if necessary between breads. Once you get comfortable with the process, you'll be able to cook 2 breads at once if your skillet is large enough, or if you have two skillets to work with.

Once you've cooked the first 8 breads, wrap them well in a cotton cloth to keep warm while you shape and bake the other 8. Alternatively, set the remaining dough aside and bake it later, perhaps for another meal that day or next morning. (You can keep the dough wrapped in plastic wrap for up to another 24 hours before baking; the breads will be a little lighter textured with the natural fermentation.)

Kisses from Brazil My E-mail from Brazil to Jeffrey and the kids read: "They make a thing called *beiju* here, a street food that is just manioc flour cooked on a skillet surface in a ring to hold it. Makes a kind of tortilla, smallish, which is folded over simple fillings. Very good."

In the coastal capital of Bahia, a Brazilian state nearly a thousand miles north of Rio, everything was unknown to me: cakes and skillet breads and puddings made from manioc (see Glossary) in all its forms; steamed corn cakes; fruits of every color and description; a street food called *acaraje* that looked like filled buns but was actually a patty made from beans, deep-fried and filled with a spicy shrimp paste. I was completely ignorant about even the staple foods that everyone there, from market vendors to home cooks, takes for granted and that even the smallest child knows how to prepare. Luckily, there were people to take me in hand.

The simple-looking skillet bread known as *beiju* ("kiss" in Portuguese) is made from tapioca flour (*tapioca* and *manioc* are two words for the same thing) and folded over a little filling, quesadilla style. I encountered it first in Cachoeira, a small town of faded beautiful buildings that was once rich from the tobacco trade. It was evening, and the tree-filled square near the river was alive with music and the voices of people sitting at small tables sipping beer and talking and laughing.

The vendor stood by her hot grill and deftly formed and cooked beiju for a stream of passersby. She placed a metal ring on her griddle, sprinkled the moistened crumbs of tapioca flour inside it, and quickly tamped and flattened it. Once the crumbs set, they seemed to stick together to make a continuous surface. She lifted off the metal ring and flipped the round skillet bread over. Now the top side was a smooth white cooked surface. She used her spatula to press down on the round, then flipped it over, sprinkled on a little cheese, or grated coconut and sweetened condensed milk, and folded it in half. She wrapped the beiju in a piece of paper and handed it to the customer.

Like all practiced street vendors, she made it look effortless. And her breads were amazing—skillet flatbreads made with only tapioca starch and a little water.

At the main market, Salvador, Bahia, Brazil

russian apple pancakes

Makes 2 large apple-filled pancakes with caramelized surfaces; serves 6 to 8

Yeasted pancakes, like sourdough pancakes, have a moist texture and an airiness that we love. These are apple pancakes with a difference, a version of the yeasted Russian pancakes called olad'ye. *We make them as a dessert. Rather than including sliced apple in the batter, this recipe calls for cooking the apples separately, then pouring the batter over them. The apple slices caramelize, like a pancake version of tarte Tatin; then the pancake's top surface is caramelized, either in a skillet or under the broiler.*

We call for a blend of whole wheat and white flours. Use the proportion you wish (we like both versions equally and can't decide between them), and adjust the quantity of milk as directed. Make the batter at least six hours ahead, then cook the pancakes quickly, just before serving.

Serve hot for breakfast or brunch, plain or with maple syrup. Or, if serving for dessert, offer heavy cream or vanilla or nut-flavored ice cream as an accompaniment. You can serve the cakes on a platter and let guests slice off wedges as they wish, or you can cut them beforehand into individual servings. Allow a third to a half of a skillet cake per person for breakfast, depending on the appetite, and a quarter per person for dessert.

1 cup whole or reduced-fat milk (plus 2 tablespoons if using
   ¾ cup whole wheat flour), heated to lukewarm

½ teaspoon active dry yeast

1½ cups flour: ¾ cup each whole wheat and all-purpose,
   or ½ cup whole wheat and 1 cup all-purpose

¼ cup sugar

1 large egg

1 teaspoon salt

2 tablespoons unsalted butter, melted and cooled
   to room temperature

2 tablespoons unsalted butter

2 medium to large tart apples, peeled, cored,
   and thinly sliced

About 2 tablespoons cinnamon sugar (½ teaspoon cinnamon
   to 2 tablespoons sugar)

Place the milk in a medium bowl and stir in the yeast, then stir in the flour and 2 tablespoons sugar. Stir for 1 minute, then set aside for 30 minutes to 2 hours, whichever is most convenient.

When ready to proceed, add the egg, salt, and melted butter and mix thoroughly. Cover with plastic wrap and let stand for 6 to 8 hours, or overnight. (If keeping the batter for longer than 8 hours, or if the temperature is very warm, refrigerate the batter until 2 hours before using.) The batter should be bubbly when ready.

Before cooking the pancakes, decide which method you wish to use to caramelize the pancakes: If using a broiler, turn on the broiler and use an ovenproof 8- to 9-inch skillet. Otherwise, put out two heavy 8- to 9-inch skillets.

Heat a heavy 8- to 9-inch skillet over medium heat, and melt 1 tablespoon of the butter. Add half the apples and sauté until soft but not brown. Spread the slices well over the bottom of the pan, sprinkle on 1 tablespoon sugar, and lower the heat to medium-low. Pour on a scant 1½ cups batter and spread it to the edges of the skillet. Cook until the top is spongy and dull, no longer liquid and shiny, about 5 minutes (be patient). Meanwhile, if using two skillets, butter the other one lightly and place over medium-high heat.

Sprinkle the top of the pancake generously with cinnamon sugar (about 1 tablespoon). Place the skillet under the broiler and broil until the cinnamon sugar melts, about 1 minute; or flip the pancake into the other skillet and cook for 1 to 2 minutes. Transfer the pancake to a platter apple side up.

Repeat with the second pancake. Serve hot.

my grandmother's crepes

Makes about 12 crepes; serves 4 to 6 for breakfast, 6 to 8 for dessert

My grandmother (see Grandmum, page 406) made pancakes for dessert, not for breakfast. They were really crepes, fine and pale yellow with egg, made with no leavening. We ate them with a spoon and fork, English style, after dusting them with granulated sugar, squeezing on some lemon juice and rolling them up neatly. They were a rare pleasure, served at the scrubbed pine kitchen table of my grandparents' log house in northern British Columbia.

Serve these sustaining yet elegant pancakes for a special breakfast treat or a simple dessert. Serve singly, flat or rolled up, or in stacks of two or three, generously drizzled with maple syrup. Accompany them with several wedges of lemon or lime so guests can squeeze on fresh flavor to temper the sweetness of the syrup. Alternatively, the classic English way of serving crepes is dotted with butter, sprinkled with confectioners' sugar or spread with a thin layer of jam, and topped with a squeeze of lemon juice, then rolled up and eaten with a spoon and fork.

1½ cups all-purpose flour

2 teaspoons sugar or vanilla sugar

    (see Sugars in the Glossary), or more if you wish

Scant ⅛ teaspoon salt

3 large or extra-large eggs (see Notes)

¾ cup whole or reduced-fat milk

About ¾ cup warm water

Unsalted butter or vegetable oil for cooking

In a medium bowl, mix together the flour, sugar, and salt; set aside. In another bowl, whisk the eggs until smooth, then add the milk and water and whisk briefly to blend. Pour the liquids into the flour mixture and whisk until smooth, about 1 minute. Cover and set aside for 30 minutes to 1 hour. (The batter can be set aside for up to 12 hours; refrigerate until 30 minutes before using.)

When ready to proceed, place a cast-iron or other heavy skillet, 10 inches or more in diameter, over high heat. Add about 1 teaspoon butter or oil and swirl to coat. Lower the heat to medium-high and use a paper towel or cotton cloth to wipe the excess fat from the pan.

Stir the batter very well. It should be a smooth liquid that flows easily on the surface of the pan; if it is too thick, add a little water to thin it to the desired consistency (see also Troubleshooting Note).

Before cooking the first crepe, drip several drops of batter into the pan. They should sizzle very slightly, indicating the pan is hot enough, but should not sizzle briskly or burn (if this happens, lower the heat slightly and wait 30 seconds before proceeding). Using a small ladle or cup, scoop up a scant ¼ cup of batter (see Notes). Begin pouring it onto the center of the skillet in a circular motion as you lift the skillet off the heat with the other hand and tilt it to get the batter to form a circle about 7 inches in diameter. Don't worry if the circle isn't perfect. Place the pan back on the heat and let the crepe cook for about 1 minute, until the bottom has golden spots. Flip over and cook the other side for about 45 seconds, or until slightly golden. Lift the crepe onto a warm plate. Cover with a cotton cloth to keep warm, and cook the remaining crepes. The crepes can be stacked one on top of the other until all are cooked, or served in ones, twos, or threes, as they come from the skillet. If you wish, keep cooked crepes warm in a 150°F oven, covered, while you cook the remaining crepes.

NOTES If you wish to cut back the eggs to 2, increase the milk by about ⅓ cup.

If you have extra batter, store it covered in the refrigerator for up to 36 hours. Leftover cooled crepes can be wrapped in plastic wrap and stored in the refrigerator for no more than 2 days. Reheat on a medium-hot griddle, touching each side to the pan for about 20 seconds. Leftovers make great wrappers for anything from cheese with fresh herbs to wildflower honey.

TROUBLESHOOTING NOTE *If the batter skids on the pan when you pour it in,* either the pan is not hot enough or there is too much oil. Wipe the pan out with a paper towel if necessary to remove any excess oil, and heat again over medium-high heat.

If the crepes are too thick, thin the batter with warm water or with milk, stirring in 2 tablespoons at a time until the right pourable consistency is reached. You want the batter to flow smoothly over the surface of the pan, thus giving a larger, thinner, finer crepe.

SAVORY CREPE WRAPPERS To make savory crepes, omit the sugar and increase the salt to 1 teaspoon. Use them to make savory roll-ups.

Crepes for sale, Brittany and Normandy, France

St. David's Head I was eighteen when I made my first trip overseas to Wales. Having grown

up in a small town in Wyoming, I was terrified of being in a city, so I flew into London on a Sunday and

immediately caught a train out to Bath. I bought a bicycle in a secondhand store, a five-speed Claude

Butler, and two days later I headed off across the Severn to Wales. I'd never ridden a bicycle cross-country

before, so I stupidly rode with a backpack on my back. I must have been a silly sight. It was May and it

rained every day. At night, I'd pitch my little pup tent, and the rain would drip inside and onto my down-

filled sleeping bag. I was miserable and horribly homesick. It went on that way for two solid weeks.

One day, the sun finally came out, and I hit the Atlantic; suddenly it all seemed worthwhile. I pedaled

into a little village called St. David's Head and stopped for an ice cream, then asked if there was anyplace

to stay. A half hour later, I was in a youth hostel looking out over tall cliffs and a beautiful treeless

landscape. I was the only one there, except for the young couple who ran the place, but I was happy and

dry. Next morning, they asked me if I wanted work, and I said sure. So off we went high up on the cliffs,

picking tiny new potatoes from deep rich soil. I was a very slow picker, but they were nice and didn't seem

to care. At lunchtime, we stopped and sat on a blanket thrown down on the field, a beautiful view in all

directions. We ate boiled potatoes with salt and pepper and freshly made home-baked Welsh cakes with

butter. And we drank tea, of course, poured from a thermos into teacups with saucers.

I stayed awhile in St. David's Head, my first home away from home. The couple bought my Claude

Butler for what I had paid for it, and from there on I hitchhiked, carrying a big bag of new potatoes in

my backpack.

buckwheat crepes

Makes about 30 crepes

Buckwheat crepes are originally from Brittany and parts of Normandy (see Crepes in Hard Times, page 288). Buckwheat is called blé noir in Brittany, and sarrasin *in the rest of France.*

There's no agreement about what a "real" crepe is made of. The original peasant version was made of buckwheat flour, water, and salt. But buckwheat batter is much easier to handle if it has a little wheat flour or an egg in it, so most modern recipes call for one or both. We've tried many combinations; two follow: The first is a simple "pure" version; the second is a more modern blend, easier to handle on the griddle. For either, try using two griddles, because flipping the crepes over can be tricky.

Like many basic food techniques, crepe making takes practice to master. The happy news is that we "outsiders" can, with a little effort, turn out good-tasting crepes that are a pleasure to eat, even if they aren't as fine and perfect as those of a crepe master. You can make the batter by hand or in a stand mixer or food processor. Before you begin to cook, put out an offset spatula or a large ladle for spreading the batter. And make sure your griddles are well seasoned and smooth.

BASIC BUCKWHEAT CREPES

4 cups buckwheat flour

1 teaspoon salt

About 1½ cups lukewarm water

Butter for serving

By hand: Place the flour and salt in a bowl, add 1 cup water, and stir with a wooden spoon or your hand until smooth and stiff. Add more water, stirring, until you have a batter with the consistency of mayonnaise. Beat for 10 minutes.

Using a stand mixer or a food processor: Place the flour, salt, and water in the bowl and mix or process for 5 minutes.

Cover the batter while you heat two griddles or heavy skillets over medium-high heat. Wipe the cooking surfaces with a lightly oiled paper towel or cotton cloth.

Scoop up 2 to 3 tablespoons batter and dribble it in a spiral on one griddle, then immediately spread it from the center outward, using the back of a large ladle or an offset spatula. (Your first few crepes will be a little thick and uneven as you experiment with temperature and quantity and as you work out a system for spreading the batter.) Cook the first side for about 1 minute, then flip the crepe onto the other griddle and cook until set, about 1 minute. Put a little butter on top and, when it melts, fold the crepe in half and serve it. Repeat with the remaining batter.

MODERN CREPES

4 cups buckwheat flour

½ cup all-purpose flour

1 teaspoon salt

1 large egg

About 1½ cups lukewarm water

Butter for serving

By hand: Place the flours and salt in a bowl and mix well. Add the egg and 1 cup water and mix with a wooden spoon or your hand until a smooth, stiff dough forms. Add more water, stirring, until you have a smooth batter; do not beat.

Using a stand mixer or a food processor: Combine the flours, salt, egg, and water in the bowl and mix or process to a smooth batter.

Heat two griddles and cook the crepes as directed on page 282.

EGG-TOPPED CREPE Once you've flipped the crepe over, you can break an egg onto it in the center. Use a fork to scramble it, or just spread the white. Top with a little butter and season with salt and pepper. Cook until the egg sets, then fold the four edges over to cover the egg. Serve with a little pat of butter on top.

NOTE In upper Brittany, *galette* is the word for buckwheat crepes and the word *crepe* is used only for the more recent (in the last one hundred years or so) wheat flour crepes. In lower Brittany, around Quimper and the Bay of Douarnenez, the whole range of the species, savory or sweet, made with buckwheat or wheat flour or a combination, is known as crepes.

czech potato pancakes

Makes about 15 small, golden savory pancakes; allow 2 or 3 per person

South of Prague and north of Linz lies Bohemia, a verdant rolling country, part of the Czech Republic. My first time there was in 1970, two years after the Soviet invasion. The landscape at the border was scarred with a high-wire fence designed to prevent Czechs from leaving. The towns were bleak, with little in the shops and no activity in the streets.

When I went back thirty years later, the picture was wonderfully different. The jewels of Bohemia—towns like České Budějovice and Český Krumlov—were being restored. Their main squares were lively; locals and tourists of all ages were strolling in the streets, hanging out in cafés, and spending money in shops and restaurants. At the border, both going in and going out, I was waved through.

These potato pancakes are called bramborak. *Like* latkes, *the Jewish potato cakes, and Irish Potato Breads (page 317), they're made with grated potato. The potato is moistened with milk and egg, then turned into an easily managed batter with a little flour. Traditionally the pancakes are cooked in a good quarter inch of hot oil or lard; we like the crispness that comes from using just a generous covering on a hot, heavy skillet. You can also cook them in bacon grease for a salty diner-style griddle pancake. Serve for lunch, with wilted greens or a salad or a fresh salsa; or for a hearty breakfast, with eggs, fried tomatoes, and toast.*

About 1 pound floury (baking) potatoes, peeled and grated (3 packed cups)

¼ cup milk, heated until hot

1 large or extra-large egg

1 to 2 teaspoons minced fresh chives, or ½ teaspoon dried chives

½ teaspoon salt

Grinding of black pepper, or to taste

½ cup all-purpose flour

About ¼ cup peanut oil, lard, or bacon grease for frying

Place the potatoes in a sieve and press out excess liquid. Transfer them to a bowl and stir in the hot milk. Whisk the egg, then stir it in. Add the chives and seasonings, then stir in flour to make a batter. Set aside.

Heat 2 to 3 tablespoons oil or fat (you want to start with enough oil to thoroughly cover the pan) in a heavy skillet over high heat. Once it is very hot, lower the heat to medium-high. Scoop up about 2 tablespoons batter and place it gently in the hot oil. Use the back of a spoon or cup to help it flatten out to a round just over 2 inches across. Repeat until the skillet is fairly full (3 or 4 more pancakes, depending on the size of your skillet). Cook until golden on the first side, 2 to 3 minutes, then turn over, press down gently with your spatula, and cook until golden, another 2 minutes or so. Move the pancakes around if your skillet is not cooking them evenly. Turn out onto a paper towel–lined plate and blot any excess oil from both sides of the pancakes, then place on a plate in a warm oven while you cook the remaining batter. Be sure to bring the oil up to temperature before cooking the remaining pancakes, and add more oil to the pan if it starts getting dry after two batches.

NOTE We have tried using a food processor to make the equivalent of hand-grated potatoes. Unfortunately, any processor produces small chunks of potato that don't cook as evenly as the flat potato gratings that are ideal for these pancakes. Actually, once peeled, the potatoes can be quickly grated by hand on the coarse side of a box grater; like many tasks, it's a job that is less laborious than it sounds.

home-style dosa

Makes 15 to 20 lacy-edged, savory griddle crepes, 8 to 10 inches in diameter; allow 2 to 3 per person

PHOTOGRAPH ON PAGE 286 *South Indian dosa is made of a batter of soaked rice and urad dal. The two are soaked and ground smooth, then allowed to sour a little. There are sweet dosas, filled with a little jaggery (palm sugar), but the more common dosa is a huge, slightly crisp golden sheet served loosely rolled up, sometimes filled with curried potatoes or an onion mixture, and always served alongside fresh coconut chutney and a soupy dal called* sambhar. *Serve these smaller (easier to manage) savory dosa with a moist curry or with a chutney or salsa; tear off pieces of dosa and use them to scoop up the sauce.*

Until recently, the grinding of the dosa batter called for heavy labor. Now with electric grinders, mixers, and food processors, the work is easy. The other labor-saving trick is using rice flour rather than starting with raw rice.

¾ cup urad dal (see Dal in the Glossary), soaked overnight in water to cover

About 3½ cups cold water, preferably springwater

2 cups rice flour (see Rice in the Glossary)

1 teaspoon salt

1 tablespoon vegetable oil

Drain the dal and place in a blender with 1 cup cold water. Blend until smooth, stopping to scrape down the sides of the blender as necessary.

Heat ½ cup of the water in a small saucepan over low heat. Stir in 1 tablespoon of the rice flour and cook, stirring constantly, until the mixture begins to thicken, then remove from the heat and set aside.

In a large bowl, mix together the ground dal mixture, salt, the remaining rice flour, and 2 cups water. Stir well to make a thin batter. Stir in the thickened rice paste and mix well. Cover loosely and let stand for at least 6 hours, or as long as 12 hours, at room temperature.

Heat a large griddle (see Note) over medium-high heat. To oil it the traditional way, cut a potato in half, dip a cut surface into vegetable oil, and rub all over the hot cooking surface (you can instead rub it with an oiled paper towel). Stir the batter: It should be like a thin crepe batter. If it thickened a little as it rested, add a little water to thin it. Scoop up ½ cup batter and pour it onto the hot surface in a thin stream, starting at the center and moving out in a spiral pattern. Use a spatula to help spread the batter to the edges of the griddle, making the dosa as thin as possible. Cook for about 2 minutes on the first side, then turn and cook for about 1 minute longer, or until cooked through.

Place the dosa on a plate and cover with a cotton cloth to keep warm. Repeat with the remaining batter, stacking the cooked dosas to keep them warm.

NOTE Because the dosa is spread right to the edges of the griddle, a cast-iron skillet isn't practical, for its sides make it impossible to get a spatula under the edge of the dosa without tearing. You can use a heavy metal griddle that is designed to fit over two burners, or a low-sided cast-iron griddle made for cooking tortillas.

FOLLOWING PAGES: HOME-STYLE DOSA *served with potato curry. Rooftops of Český Krumlov, Bohemia, Czech Republic.*

Crepes in hard times The village of Brasparts lies on the slopes of Montagne-Saint-Michel, a half-hour's drive inland from the Atlantic coast of Finistère in western Brittany. The rolling countryside is green and gold in mid-June, with ripening grain in the fields, stone walls, and big skies swept with moving clouds. Life these days is much less harsh than a hundred years ago, when Brittany was known for its poverty and the Breton language was considered backward and uncivilized.

"The Germans requisitioned the wheat, but they weren't interested in the buckwheat. We had plenty of flour for crepes." The woman I was speaking with had lived her whole life in Brasparts, all eighty-some years of it, "and I expect to die here, of course," she said proudly. She told me that before and during the Second World War, villagers used buckwheat (*blé noir*) grilled and milled as a coffee substitute and as a thickener in soup. For breakfast, they'd tear up buckwheat crepes into a big bowl of the coffee with fresh milk (never in short supply, even during the war) and lots of sugar.

In the old days, in rural Brittany, before 1900 or so, crepes were made once a week, aired well, then folded, stacked, and wrapped in a linen sheet. The stack was left on the table so you could grab one anytime. The poorest had only crepes, the less poor had white bread more regularly. During the war, people in Brittany had to go back to those old ways, the woman told me, cooking the way it had been done around 1900, making crepes of buckwheat flour over an open fire in the chimney hearth. The woman of the house would kneel on a pillow in front of the fire and wipe a cast-iron griddle (a *bilig* in Breton) with an oiled cloth. Then she'd pour on some batter, smooth and spread it with a *rozell*, a T-shaped spatula, to a lacy thinness, and wait until the edges lifted a little, before using a spatula to flip it—all this in about one minute. (And all the while, she was also maintaining the fire at an even heat.) She'd spread the crepe with a little butter and transfer it to a plate, before starting all over with the next crepe.

OPPOSITE: *Breton village.* ABOVE: *Making crepes in Brasparts.*

savory bangkok waffles with dipping sauce

Makes about 15 attractive waffles or crepes, each about 7 inches across, flavored with lime juice, dried shrimp, and coriander leaves; allow 2 per person

PHOTOGRAPH ON PAGE 292 *In the bread museum in Ulm, in southern Germany, there are decorated cast-iron waffle irons that date back to the sixteenth century. Waffles—gauffres in French—are popular sweets in Germany, Belgium, Holland, and France, and, of course, in North America too.*

In Thailand, the waffle idea has been transformed, as many foreign food ideas are, in a creative and, we think, brilliant way. The "waffle iron" is two plain pieces of hot metal; between them is pressed a batter flavored with tiny dried shrimp, coriander leaf, and lime juice. The resulting skillet cakes are known in Thai as thong paen na goong, and look like small crepes. You can make them like crepes in a small heavy skillet, but we love the unusual look of them when we use a regular American or European waffle iron.

¼ cup rice flour (see Rice in the Glossary)

1 cup all-purpose flour

⅓ cup sugar

¾ cup canned coconut milk, plus a little more if needed

1 large egg yolk

¼ cup plus 2 tablespoons freshly squeezed lime juice

½ cup tiniest dried shrimp (see Note)

Peanut oil or vegetable oil for frying

20 to 30 coriander leaves

Place the flours and sugar in a medium bowl and stir in the coconut milk and egg yolk. Stir in the lime juice and beat to a smooth batter. Let stand for at least 20 minutes, or as long as 2 hours. (If leaving more than 30 minutes, cover and refrigerate until 10 minutes before using.)

Just before you wish to start cooking, stir the dried shrimp into the batter. The batter should be like crepe batter, smooth and pourable. If necessary, thin it with a little coconut milk.

Using a skillet: Place a heavy 8-inch or 9-inch skillet over high heat. When it is hot, lower the heat to medium-high and rub a paper towel oiled with peanut or vegetable oil over the cooking surface. Use a ladle or cup to scoop up a scant 3 tablespoons batter and drop a coriander leaf or two into it. Remove the skillet from the heat, pour the batter onto the center of the skillet, and spread it out with the back of your ladle or a spatula. Place the skillet back on the heat and let cook for 1 minute, or until lightly browned on the first side, then turn the crepe over and cook for 35 to 40 seconds on the second side, or until dotted with light brown spots. Turn out onto a plate and repeat with the remaining batter, wiping the skillet with an oiled paper towel between each one.

Using a waffle iron: Preheat the waffle iron. Brush it with oil, then use a ladle to pour the batter onto the center of the iron: Use the same amount of batter as you would for a regular waffle. Before you close the waffle iron, the batter should just cover about half the surface; when you close the iron, the batter will be pushed out to fill the whole iron. (The amount of batter you need to use for each waffle will vary with the size and style of waffle iron, so you may need to make one or two before you get amounts exactly right.) Cook until lightly browned on both sides. Turn out onto a plate and repeat with the remaining batter, brushing the iron lightly with oil between waffles.

Serve hot or warm, on their own or with a plate of lettuce leaves and an easy hot, sour, salty, sweet dipping sauce such as the one here. Or you could put out a spicy Mexican-style salsa instead. Invite guests to tear off a piece of crepe, wrap it in a lettuce leaf, and drizzle it with sauce or salsa before eating.

NOTE Use very small dried shrimp that look like feathery shreds and are a dark, rich color. A wide assortment of dried shrimp is available in Chinese and Southeast Asian groceries. If you can find only larger dried shrimp, mince them before using.

dipping sauce
Makes about $1/3$ cup dipping sauce

2 tablespoons Thai fish sauce

2 tablespoons rice vinegar

1 tablespoon water

1 teaspoon salt

1 small garlic clove, minced

1 bird or serrano chile, minced (less for less heat) (optional)

Mix all the ingredients together. Set out in a small bowl with a spoon to use for drizzling the sauce on.

FOLLOWING PAGES: SAVORY BANGKOK WAFFLES WITH DIPPING SAUCE. (LEFT TO RIGHT) *At the night market, Thap Sakae, Thailand; bunches of fresh coriander.*

ventry sourdough pancakes

Makes 6 to 8 large, airy pancakes

I never make these sourdough pancakes without thinking about our kitchen in Ventry, in Ireland (see page 135). It had windows on three sides and it looked out over Ventry Bay; it was probably the most beautiful kitchen I have ever cooked in. But in the winter, when I lived there, any cooking immediately fogged all the windows, the hot steam hitting the glass chilled by the cold ocean air outside. Sourdough pancakes were one of our staples, topped with blackberry apple jam and fresh cream from our landlady's milk cow.

In order to make these pancakes, you'll need to make a starter at least twelve hours ahead. It's like a basic poolish and relies on a pinch of yeast to get started. If you make pancakes regularly, you'll want to keep the starter going: Set aside ½ cup when you use the rest, then store and refresh it as directed below.

SOURDOUGH STARTER

¼ teaspoon active dry yeast

2 cups lukewarm water, preferably springwater

2 cups all-purpose flour, preferably unbleached

PANCAKES

2 large or extra-large eggs

¼ cup sugar

¼ cup vegetable oil

1 tablespoon salt

1 teaspoon baking soda

About 2 cups all-purpose flour

To make the starter, dissolve the yeast in the water, then add the flour and stir vigorously or whisk to make a smooth batter. Let stand, covered, for 12 to 24 hours at room temperature. (If leaving it any longer, refrigerate; it will keep for 5 more days in the refrigerator.)

Before using the starter, take out ½ cup and save in a well-sealed glass jar in the refrigerator for use at a later date (see Note).

Place the remaining 3½ cups starter in a bowl. Stir in the eggs, sugar, oil, salt, and baking soda and beat until smooth. Add the flour and stir until you have a thick, pourable batter.

Place a large 8- to 10-inch heavy skillet over medium heat. Wipe with an oiled cloth or paper towel. Scoop out about ½ cup batter and pour into the skillet, tilting the pan to encourage the batter to flow to the edges and make a round. Cook until the top surface shows bubbles all over, about 3 minutes, then turn the pancake over and cook until the second side is golden, about 2 minutes more. Turn out onto a warm plate and repeat with the remaining batter.

NOTE The day before you wish to make these pancakes the next time, or to use the starter in another recipe, refresh the reserved ½ cup starter: Add 2 cups water and 2 cups flour and stir well, then cover and refrigerate overnight. Bring back to room temperature and remove ½ cup before using.

sweet ramadan half-moons

Makes 12 to 15 half-moon–shaped cheese-filled sweet pancakes

Apart from the pleasure of eating them, the great thing about these little filled fried treats, called atayef, *is that they can be made and filled ahead and then quickly fried at the last minute. They're even more wonderful if you come to them hungry, whether from fasting—they're traditionally eaten in Lebanon and Syria to break the Ramadan fast—or to counter the distractions of the day. Serve them hot and fresh.*

PANCAKES

Scant ¼ teaspoon active dry yeast

1½ cups lukewarm water

1 cup plus up to ¼ cup all-purpose flour

Pinch of salt

Butter for cooking

Peanut or vegetable oil for frying

FILLING

⅔ cup coarsely grated kanefa, haloumi,
or ricotta salata cheese (see Cheeses in the Glossary)

Generous pinch of salt

2 tablespoons sugar

In a medium bowl, dissolve the yeast in the water. Add the flour and salt and stir well. Let stand, loosely covered, to ferment for 45 minutes.

Meanwhile, prepare the filling: Mix the ingredients in a bowl until you have a homogeneous mass. Set aside.

When ready to proceed, heat a small heavy skillet over medium heat for 5 minutes. Lightly brush the skillet with butter. Stir the batter well to blend. Scoop up about 2½ tablespoons batter and pour onto the skillet to make a 4-inch round or an oval about 4 inches long. Cook until bubbles appear on the top and the top has a matte dull surface, about 1 minute and 20 seconds. The underside will be just touched with the palest brown. Transfer to a plate cooked side down.

Scoop up 1 teaspoon filling and squeeze it in your hand into a firm oblong, then place it on the cooked pancake. Immediately fold the pancake over and pinch the edges together to make a sealed half-moon shape. (The trick with atayef is to fill them while the top of the pancake is still warm so the edges stick together well.) Set aside on a plate, and repeat with the remaining batter and filling. (Once you get comfortable with the sequence of steps, you may want to have two skillets going at once, to speed production. But even with only one person and one skillet, you can get all the atayef made in a short time.)

The filled pancakes can sit, loosely covered, for up to 3 hours before being fried.

When ready to proceed, pour about 1 inch of peanut or vegetable oil into a deep-fryer or stable wok or other deep-frying arrangement, and heat to 375°F. Use a thermometer to check, or the following test: Stick a chopstick vertically into the hot oil. If bubbles come rising up beside it, the oil is hot enough. Have a slotted spoon by your stove top as well as two paper towel–lined plates.

Slide the first half-moon into the hot oil. It should bubble a little. Then slide in another, and another. Each should cook for about 30 seconds, until lightly browned; turn each over in the oil after about 15 seconds. With the slotted spoon, transfer to a paper towel–lined plate. Fry the remaining half-moons in the same manner. Serve hot or warm, with tea or coffee.

thai tuiles

Makes about 100 two-bite sweet tuiles, filled with a blend of sweet meringue and savory herbs

These are some of our all-time favorite street snacks in Thailand. Vendors pour out a little batter on a griddle to make small, thin crepes, then paint them with toppings and fold them over partway to make tuiles. They're a fabulous surprise when you bite into them: In the middle of the slightly crisp and crunchy sweet tuile, in a pillow of sweet meringue, your mouth encounters minced scallion and coriander leaf. Altogether, they're one of the great hits of the Thai repertoire, and that's saying something. They need to be eaten fresh from the pan, so they're not practical for every day. But for a special occasion, a street fair, or a large party, they're a knockout.

In any case, practical or not, we were so delighted at having figured out how to make them that we couldn't resist including them.

TUILES

¼ cup rice flour (see Rice in the Glossary), sifted

¼ cup all-purpose flour

2 tablespoons sugar

⅛ teaspoon salt

½ cup coconut milk, canned or fresh

¼ cup vegetable oil

FILLING

1 cup Italian Meringue (see Meringue Choices, page 381)

½ cup minced scallions (white and tender green parts)

1½ cups coarsely torn coriander leaves

In a medium bowl, combine the flours, sugar, and salt. In another bowl, whisk together the coconut milk and oil, then stir the liquids into the flour mixture. Stir and beat until you have a very smooth batter. Set aside for 30 minutes or so. (If setting aside for longer than 1 hour, cover and refrigerate; the batter can be stored chilled for up to 48 hours. Bring back to room temperature and stir well before using.)

When ready to proceed, have the meringue and fillings near your stove top, together with a narrow metal spatula for spreading the meringue and a wide spatula for transferring the tuiles from the skillet.

Heat a heavy 9- or 10-inch skillet over medium-high heat. Rub the cooking surface with an oiled cloth or paper towel. Use a large metal spoon to drop about ½ teaspoon batter onto the skillet and spread it into a thin disk by brushing it lightly with the back of the spoon in a circular motion so it spreads out. This takes a little practice, but it does work.

Cook for about 45 seconds, until you see the edges browning and starting to lift off the skillet (if the tuile cooks too fast or starts to burn, lower the heat slightly). Quickly spread a scant ½ teaspoon meringue over the tuile, sprinkle on a pinch each of scallions and coriander, and fold over like a taco. Use the wide spatula to lift the tuile out of the skillet and onto a plate. These are best eaten immediately, or at least within 30 minutes. Proceed to make more tuiles. Once you get comfortable, you will be able to cook two or even three at a time, so the whole batch can be cooked in about 1 hour. (Or, you could perhaps make half one day, and half the next.)

eleonore's kaiserschmarren

Makes a generous heap of sugar-strewn airy pieces of pancake; serves 4

Kaiserschmarren is Austrian in origin, and it's usually translated as "king's omelette." This recipe is adapted from a fairly classic version of kaiserschmarren sent to us by a friend of a friend named Eleonore. It's a delicious dessert that's basically a skillet soufflé. If the word soufflé *makes you worry, don't—this is extremely easy. And once it's baked, you tear it into pieces to make a casual piled dessert dusted with confectioners' sugar. The traditional version sometimes includes a few raisins; we like the color and the surprise of dried cranberries, so we mix the two. Make it at the last minute and serve warm, on its own, or accompanied by fruit conserves or thick jam as well as, if you wish, several dollops of whipped cream. It will melt in your mouth.*

3 large eggs, separated

⅔ cup pastry or cake flour

Pinch of salt

½ cup whole milk

1 tablespoon unsalted butter, melted

About ¼ cup granulated sugar

2 tablespoons unsalted butter

Scant ½ cup raisins or dried cranberries,
    or a mixture (optional)

Confectioners' sugar for dusting

Whisk the yolks in a bowl, then sift the pastry or cake flour over and fold it in. Add the salt, milk, and melted butter and beat or whisk until smooth and thick. Set aside.

Use a stand mixer or hand mixer to whip the egg whites until foamy. Gradually add the sugar and then whip until the whites are thick and shiny.

Gently fold one-third of the whites into the yolk mixture. Repeat twice more. Set aside.

Heat a 9- or 10-inch skillet over medium-high heat. Add the 2 tablespoons butter to it. Place another 9- or 10-inch skillet over medium-low heat, and brush it with some of the melting butter.

Pour the batter into the first skillet, lower the heat to medium, and cook for 3 to 4 minutes. Sprinkle on the dried fruit, if using, and cook for 3 to 4 minutes more, or until the bottom is golden brown and the pancake is coming away from the sides of the pan. Place the second skillet upside down over the first, then turn both skillets over together, so that the pancake falls out of the first skillet and into the second. Place it over medium heat and cook until lightly browned on the second side, 3 to 4 minutes. Remove from the heat.

Use two forks to tear the cooked soufflé-pancake into large bite-sized pieces. Sift confectioners' sugar over generously, then serve immediately, piled onto individual plates. Put out a bowl of plum or raspberry jam or fruit conserve and, if you wish, some whipped cream. Invite guests to serve themselves.

FLATBREADS AND CRACKERS

snowshoe breads

Makes 8 flatbreads, about 3 inches wide and 16 to 18 inches long, with hollows along the length of the bread, an optional sprinkling of nigella or sesame seeds, and a well-browned bottom crust

This is one of our all-time favorite tandoor-baked breads, nan. It's common in Turkey, Iran, and Afghanistan, though it varies a great deal from place to place. In Afghanistan, it's made primarily with whole wheat flour, but in neighboring Iran, it's often made with white flour. The dough is first shaped into a flat disk, allowed to sit for fifteen minutes, and then "potholed" all over with very wet fingers. Then the wet dough is picked up and stretched, forming approximately the shape of a snowshoe, and immediately put into a hot oven.

We first wrote about this bread in Flatbreads and Flavors, *but since that time we've changed the way we make it. We now use a higher proportion of white to whole wheat flour and we bake the bread higher in the oven to achieve a top surface that browns beautifully. We've also learned to use even more water in shaping than before.*

These breads are so decorative, so easy to make and to eat, that in our house they're a favorite standby for parties as well as a frequent everyday bread.

2½ cups warm water

1 teaspoon active dry yeast

1 cup whole wheat flour

4½ to 5½ cups all-purpose flour, preferably unbleached

1 tablespoon salt

About 1 teaspoon nigella seeds (see Glossary), or

    1 tablespoon sesame seeds (optional)

Place the water in a large bowl, add the yeast, and stir to dissolve it. Add the whole wheat flour and 1 cup of the all-purpose flour and stir well, then stir for about 1 minute, always in the same direction. If you have the time, let stand for 30 minutes (or as long as 12 hours if it's more convenient), covered. The longer wait helps develop flavor.

Sprinkle on the salt, then add another cup of flour and stir. Continue adding flour and stirring until you can stir no longer. Turn the dough out onto a floured surface and knead, incorporating flour as needed, until the dough is smooth and easy to handle, about 10 minutes.

Place the dough in a large clean bowl, cover well with plastic wrap, and let rise until more than doubled in volume, 2 to 3 hours.

Gently push the dough down and turn it out onto a lightly floured surface. Place a baking stone or unglazed quarry tiles, if you have them, on a rack in the middle of the oven (or lightly oil an 18-by-12-inch baking sheet and set aside). Preheat the oven to 500°F.

Meanwhile, cut the dough into 8 equal pieces. Shape each into a flat oval approximately 5 inches wide by 8 inches long. Leave these disks out on your work surface, covered with plastic wrap, to rise for 15 to 20 minutes. Place a bowl of cold water by your work surface.

Ten minutes after the oven has preheated, begin shaping the first bread. (If you are using a baking sheet rather than a stone or tiles, place the sheet in the center of the hot oven.) Dip your fingertips in the bowl of water and then, beginning at one end of the disk of dough, make tightly spaced indentations all over the surface, pressing down firmly with your fingertips and rewetting them as necessary, until the dough looks pitted

and wet (see photograph above right). Stretch the dough gently into a long oval strip by draping it over the back of both hands and pulling them apart gently. The dough should stretch and give, and after several tries will extend to make an oval 16 inches long or more with attractive stretch marks along it. You can pull on one end to stretch it a little more. Don't worry if it tears a little—every irregularity makes the texture of the baked breads more interesting.

Place the bread back on the work surface and sprinkle with a pinch (less than ⅛ teaspoon) of nigella or about ½ teaspoon sesame seeds, if using. Pick up the bread with both hands and place it directly on the hot stone or tiles (or baking sheet). While the bread bakes, begin to shape the next bread. The cooking time for each bread is approximately 4 minutes; you will soon develop a rhythm so that you can bake two breads side by side, one going in when the other is half done. When done, the breads will have golden patches on top and a crusty browned bottom surface.

To keep the breads warm and soft, wrap them in a cotton cloth 5 minutes after they come out of the oven. Serve warm or at room temperature.

LARGE SNOWSHOE BREADS To make larger breads such as the large ones we've seen in Afghanistan, divide the dough into 4 or 6 pieces. Shape each bread so it is both longer and wider. (Makes 4 to 6 flatbreads.)

silk road non

Makes 12 round breads, approximately 8 inches in diameter, with stamped centers and puffed rims

PHOTOGRAPH ON PAGE 304 *In most of central Asia, from Uzbekistan to Afghanistan,* non *(also pronounced and transcribed* nan *or* naan*) means "bread," most often flatbread baked in a tandoor oven. In the bazaars of Samarkand and Tashkent, the best non are sold from small tables or from wooden wheelbarrows. Women bake them at home, then trundle them to market in a wheelbarrow. Lines form as the breads arrive, and soon stacks of them are leaving the market, tucked under buyers' arms. As each woman sells out, she takes her money to do the day's shopping at the bazaar.*

These breads are baked on a baking stone or on unglazed quarry tiles for a dense tandoor-breadlike bottom crust. The centers are pricked or stamped to prevent them from puffing, the rims are soft. Lamb fat, greatly prized in central Asia, flavors pilafs, adds richness to kebabs, and is used in flatbreads. Rendered lamb fat (it's an easy process) has very little smell or taste, and is creamy and smooth. It gives these home-style Uzbek breads a tender richness.

2 teaspoons active dry yeast

3 cups warm water

7 to 9 cups all-purpose flour, or 2 cups whole wheat flour,
   plus 4 to 6 cups all-purpose

1 tablespoon salt, plus extra for sprinkling

About ¼ cup rendered lamb fat (see Fat in the Glossary),
   melted, or 4 tablespoons unsalted butter, melted

In a large bowl, dissolve the yeast in the water. Add 3 cups of the flour (if using whole wheat flour, add it and 1 cup all-purpose), a cup at a time, stirring well until a smooth batter forms, then stir for another minute, always stirring in the same direction. If you have the time, cover your bowl with plastic wrap and let stand for 30 minutes, or as long as 3 hours, if more convenient.

Sprinkle on 1 tablespoon salt and stir in. Add 3 table-spoons of the lamb fat or butter and fold in. Continue to add the flour, a cup at a time, stirring and folding it in until the dough becomes too stiff to stir.

Turn the dough out onto a well-floured surface and knead until smooth and elastic, 8 to 10 minutes.

Place the dough in a clean bowl, cover with plastic wrap, and let rise until at least doubled in volume, about 2 hours. (For more flavor, set in a cool place to rise for 8 hours, or overnight.)

Place a rack in the upper third of the oven and place a large baking stone or unglazed quarry tiles, if you have them, (or a baking sheet) on it. Preheat the oven to 500°F.

Turn the dough out onto a lightly floured surface. Cut it in half and set one half aside, covered. Cut the remaining dough into 6 equal pieces. Shape each into a ball and then flatten with the floured palm of your hand. With a rolling pin, begin rolling it out into thin rounds about 8 inches in diameter. The dough may resist stretching, so work with 2 rounds at once to give the gluten in the dough time to stretch and relax. Roll out 1 round as far as it will easily go, then work on a second before coming back to the first to roll it out a little more. As you complete each round, set aside on a lightly floured surface, covered with a towel or with plastic wrap. Let rest for 15 minutes before baking.

To shape the breads for baking, warm the remaining 1 tablespoon lamb fat or butter until very liquid and place by your work surface, together with a pastry brush and salt. Lightly dust a peel (or the back of a baking sheet) with flour. Place a dough round on the peel, then stamp or prick the center of the round thoroughly and vigorously with a fork, leaving a 1-inch rim. Brush lightly all over with lamb fat or butter, then sprinkle the center with a generous pinch of salt. Transfer to the baking stone or tiles (or baking sheet), placing it to one side to leave room for another bread. Prepare the next bread, and slide into the oven beside the first.

Bake each bread for 5½ to 7 minutes, until well flecked with gold. Use a long-handled spatula to lift the bread out of the oven and place on a rack to cool for 5 minutes or so, then wrap in a cotton cloth to keep warm. Continue baking the remaining breads in the same way.

CHIVE-TOPPED NON If you can get them, sprinkle some finely chopped fresh garlic chives onto the center of each bread just before baking.

NOTE In central Asia, the center of this non is pricked with a dough stamp called a *chekitch*. Dough stamps vary, but most are made with a wooden handle attached to a wooden round, the bottom of which is covered with sharp nails. The stamp leaves circular (or other-shaped) imprints all over the center of the bread, thump, thump, thump. Recently, a friend brought us back a different version from Kashgar (in the west of Xinjiang Province in China). Instead of nails, the stamp was studded with sharpened quills and the handle was made of a bundle of feathers!

FOLLOWING PAGES: SILK ROAD NON. CIABATTA *(page 306)*.

ciabatta

Makes 4 flour-dusted rectangular flatbreads, 10 inches long and 4 inches wide, with an open, tender crumb

PHOTOGRAPH ON PAGE 305 *Ciabatta is a rectangular flatbread with a very tender, airy crumb and thin crust, eaten on its own or used for sandwiches. This wonderful northern Italian bread has become well known in North America in the last fifteen years largely because of Carol Field, author of* The Italian Baker, *a truly classic cookbook. This recipe, adapted from her original, uses less yeast, a poolish rather than a biga as a starter (see page 111), and different proportions of milk and water. The ingenious method of proofing the breads on paper is Carol's invention.*

If you don't have a stand mixer, you can mix this bread with a wooden spoon or with your hand, then knead it with moist hands to keep it from sticking. Because it's quite a wet dough, it will feel unusual at first, but it's really very manageable.

POOLISH

⅛ teaspoon active dry yeast

1 cup lukewarm water

1 cup all-purpose flour, preferably unbleached

BREAD

1 cup milk

½ cup hot water

½ teaspoon active dry yeast

5 to 6 cups all-purpose flour, preferably unbleached

1 tablespoon salt

1 tablespoon olive oil

Make the poolish at least 18 hours before you want to have breads out of the oven: In a small bowl, stir the yeast into the water until well dissolved. Stir in the flour to make a smooth batter. Cover and let stand overnight or for as long as 24 hours, at room temperature. (The poolish can be refrigerated, well sealed, at this point, for up to 24 hours more. Bring back to room temperature before using.)

When ready to make the dough, stir the milk and hot water together in the bowl of a stand mixer or another large bowl. When the mixture is lukewarm, stir in the yeast to dissolve it completely.

Using a stand mixer: Fit the mixer with the dough hook. Add the poolish and 2 cups of the flour and mix at low speed until smooth. Sprinkle on the salt and another 3 cups flour and mix for 1 minute. Add the oil and mix at medium speed for 3 minutes. The dough will be smooth, very moist, and soft.

By hand: Let the yeast mixture stand for a moment, then add the poolish and 2 cups of the flour, stirring until you have a smooth batter. Add the oil and stir in. Add the salt and then 2 more cups of flour, a cup at a time, turning and stirring to incorporate it. Sprinkle ½ cup flour on the dough and another ½ cup to 1 cup on your work surface, turn the dough out, and knead for about 6 minutes. Once most of the flour is incorporated, if you find the dough is sticking to your hands, wet them and continue kneading. Use a dough scraper to keep your work surface clean. The dough will be smooth, very moist, and soft.

Transfer the dough to a large clean bowl, cover with plastic, and let rise for 3 to 4 hours. It will double in volume, will not bounce back when prodded with a fingertip, and will probably have several large air bubbles on the top surface.

Turn the dough out onto a lightly floured surface. Use a dough scraper or a sharp knife to cut the dough into 4 pieces. Let rest a moment, loosely covered. Place four 12-inch lengths of parchment paper or wax paper on a work surface or on several baking sheets. Sprinkle each generously with all-purpose flour.

Flatten 1 piece of dough, then roll it up into a cylinder, jelly roll style. With the seam side down, flatten the dough back out into a rectangle about 10 inches long and 4 inches wide; you want it to have good square corners. Place seam side up on one sheet of parchment paper and dimple firmly all over with your fingertips. This will help the bread stay flattened and stretched. Cover with plastic wrap; roll and flatten the other pieces of dough, placing each on a sheet of floured paper. Let stand, well covered, for 1¾ to 2 hours, until puffy-looking.

Meanwhile, place a baking stone or unglazed quarry tiles, if you have them, (or a baking sheet) on a rack in the center or upper third of your oven. Preheat the oven to 425°F. Set a sprayer filled with fresh water and a bowl of water by your work surface.

Rub a peel well with all-purpose flour. Place the peel over one bread, then flip the paper over so the bread is resting on the peel. Lift off the paper (it will stick a little, so peel it off carefully). Wet your fingers well with water, then dimple the bread deeply all over with your fingertips. Place on the baking stone or tiles (or the sheet), leaving room for another bread. Repeat with a second bread. (Unless you have a double oven, you will have to bake these breads two at a time; the extra wait won't hurt the second batch.)

Spritz the breads with water two or three times in the first 5 minutes of baking. They will be ready in about 20 minutes, golden on top, thin crusted, and hollow sounding when tapped on the bottom. Transfer to a rack to cool. Repeat with the remaining breads.

When they're cool, cut crosswise in slices. Or, to use for sandwiches, slice crosswise in half, then split horizontally.

WHOLE WHEAT CIABATTA For a partly whole wheat version, substitute 1½ cups whole wheat flour for 2 cups of the all-purpose flour in the dough. Add the whole wheat first.

moroccan anise breads

Makes 4 slightly domed, soft-textured flatbreads, about 6 to 8 inches in diameter

In the steep stone lanes of the Fez medina (the old town and bazaar area) around eleven in the morning, it's easy to find the bakeries: Just follow the children who are carrying flat cloth-covered trays on their heads. Under the cloths are low rounds of dough made at home, ready to be baked in the neighborhood oven. Then, sometime between noon and one, the children head back to the bakery to pick up the warm loaves, called k'sra, and take them home for the family's midday meal.

Every household has a different version of k'sra, some with whole wheat or barley, some with semolina, some wide and others small, many flavored with anise. These breads are made with semolina and a mix of white and whole wheat flours, and scented with anise.

3 cups lukewarm water

2 teaspoons active dry yeast

2 cups whole wheat flour

1 cup coarse semolina (not fine semolina flour; see Glossary),
　　plus extra for dusting

1 tablespoon anise seeds

1 tablespoon salt

3 to 4 cups all-purpose flour

Put the water in a large bowl and sprinkle on the yeast. Stir to dissolve it, then stir in the whole wheat flour. Add the semolina and stir in, then stir for about a minute to make a very smooth batter. Set aside, covered, for 30 minutes or up to 3 hours, whatever is convenient.

Sprinkle on the anise and salt, then add 2½ to 3 cups all-purpose flour, ½ cup at a time. Turn the dough out onto a well-floured surface and knead until smooth, about 8 minutes. Try to incorporate only a little extra flour, so the dough stays moist and fairly soft. Set aside in a clean bowl or on a floured work surface, well covered with plastic wrap, to rise for approximately 1½ hours, until about doubled.

When ready to proceed, knead the dough briefly on a floured surface, then cut into 4 pieces. Shape each into a ball, then flatten under your palm to a round about 6 inches across. Press on the dough with your fingertips to flatten it further. Dust a surface with semolina and put the breads on it, cover with plastic, and proof for 30 to 45 minutes.

Meanwhile, place a baking stone or unglazed quarry tiles, if you have them, (or a baking sheet) on a rack in the middle of the oven. Preheat the oven to 450°F.

Place one bread on a peel (or the back of a baking sheet) dusted with semolina flour. Prick the top about 10 times with a fork. Transfer to the hot stone or tiles (or baking sheet). Repeat with the remaining breads—you may need to bake the breads in two batches, but don't worry; the second batch can sit longer with no ill effects. Bake for 12 to 15 minutes, until golden. Lift out one bread and tap on the bottom; it should sound hollow.

Place the breads on a rack to cool, covered with a cloth so the crust softens. Serve cut into 4 wedges each.

LARGE MOROCCAN FLATBREADS To make larger breads, divide the dough into only 2 pieces. Each bread will be 11 or 12 inches in diameter. Bake for 20 to 25 minutes. (Makes 2 flatbreads.)

Taking breads from the bakery home for lunch, Fez, Morocco. FOLLOWING PAGES: GEORGIAN BATON BREADS *(page 312).*
Authors' rolling pin collection.

georgian baton bread

Makes 8 boomerang-shaped breads

PHOTOGRAPH ON PAGE 310 *Georgia, a small country separated from Russia by the Caucasus Mountains, has a distinctive and rich culinary tradition. In some parts of the country, corn breads are the household staple, but where wheat flour is available, these long, irregularly shaped flatbreads, called* shotis puri, *are the everyday bread, made both in home ovens and at bakeries. We learned this shaping technique by watching a baker named Yanni in Tbilisi a very long time ago. His breads were longer and wider than these, which have been adapted to fit into a home oven.*

The recipe calls for a little whole wheat flour; you can instead make the dough using just all-purpose flour.

1 teaspoon active dry yeast

2½ cups lukewarm water

1 cup whole wheat flour

4½ to 6 cups all-purpose flour, preferably unbleached

1 tablespoon salt

In a large bowl, dissolve the yeast in the warm water. Stir in the whole wheat flour and about 2 cups of the all-purpose flour, always stirring in the same direction, until smooth. Stir for about 1 minute longer, in the same direction. Cover with plastic wrap and let stand in a cool place for at least 10 minutes, or as long as 3 hours, whatever is convenient.

Sprinkle on the salt and stir in. Gradually add 2 to 3 cups unbleached flour, stirring and folding it into the dough until the dough becomes too stiff to stir. Turn the dough out onto a lightly floured surface and knead for approximately 10 minutes, incorporating extra flour as necessary, until smooth and elastic.

Place the dough in a clean bowl, cover well with plastic wrap, and set aside in a cool place to rise until more than doubled in volume, about 2 hours. (Note: We generally prefer to give the dough a long cool rise overnight, so if that's more convenient for you, place the bowl in a cool place and leave it for 6 to 8 hours to rise. If you don't have time to bake in the morning, push the dough back down, place it in a plastic bag, leaving room for expansion, and seal tightly. Place it in the refrigerator until you can bake it, within the next 36 hours. Bring back nearly to room temperature before proceeding.)

Place a large baking stone or unglazed quarry tiles, if you have them, (or a baking sheet) on an oven rack in the middle or just below the middle of the oven. Preheat the oven to 475°F.

Turn the dough out onto a lightly floured surface. Cut into 4 equal pieces. Shape each piece into a ball by rolling it under your hands and tucking the bottom edges under. Cover the balls and let stand for 5 to 10 minutes.

Work with 1 ball at a time, on a very lightly floured surface, leaving the remaining balls covered: Cut the ball in half with a sharp knife and turn the cut surfaces face down onto your work surface. Flatten out each piece with the palm of your hand, to an oval about 6 inches long and 4 inches wide. Cover loosely, then cut and flatten the remaining pieces. You can proceed directly to shape the first 2 breads, but the dough will be easier to handle if you let the ovals rest for about 10 minutes.

Place a bowl of lukewarm water by your work surface and dust your peel (or the back of a baking sheet) lightly with flour. Using both hands, pull gently on opposite sides at the points of one oval of dough to begin to make "wings," or batons, on each side. Then wet your fingertips with water and press them firmly and repeatedly onto the wings of the bread, making dents. Again, pick up the edges of the wings and stretch them a little longer (from tip to tip the bread should be about 12 inches), then press dents into them with wet fingertips.

Place the shaped bread on the flour-dusted peel, leaving one wing dangling over the far edge a little. Transfer the bread onto the hot baking stone or tiles (or baking sheet), preferably on one side of your oven, on a slight diagonal to fit it in if necessary: Lay the edge of the dangling wing onto the stone near the back of the oven. It should catch on the hot surface, so you can then quickly slide the peel out. Repeat with a second bread, placing it alongside the first.

Bake each bread for about 5 minutes, or until lightly touched with color on top and with a good golden crust on the bottom. Take the breads out of the oven one by one as they are ready, and place on a rack to cool briefly; wrap in a cotton cloth if you wish to keep them soft. Repeat with the remaining breads.

Village bakery, Bojormi, Georgia

Handmade tools I bought a book on blacksmithing so that I could learn to make cookware and other things out of steel. There's something so appealing about utensils, tools, and hinges made by hand, something so elemental about making the steel red-hot, then pounding it with beautiful hammers and shaping it into useful forms. Before going to bed, I used to read about anvils and forges, fullers and hardies, blowers and tongs. I didn't understand half of what I read, and I'm certainly no closer to making anything, but enough seeped in to make me appreciate handmade tools even more than I had.

In the copper souks in Morocco and Syria, and in the brass cookware bazaars in India, we love watching the smiths working, making pots and skillets from hunks of metal, tinning the cookware, making objects that can last a lifetime. One of our favorite pieces of iron cookware is a *sajj*, a curved metal sheet that gets placed like a low dome over a fire. Ours is handmade, thin metal pounded into a flattened curve, from the bazaar in Jerusalem. Sajjs are used throughout western Asia, particularly by seminomadic people such as the Bedouin and the Kurds, for baking large, thin, pliable breads that cook quickly on the hot surface. It's a brilliantly economical way of baking over an open fire, lightweight and very portable.

OPPOSITE: *Making spun-steel* sajjs. ABOVE: *Hammering a large copper pot. Both in Aleppo, Syria.*

bannock & damper

Makes 1 large, round, oven- or stove-top–baked, low-rise quick bread

In North America, campfire bread—wheat flour, leavened with baking powder, enriched with lard for warmth—is called bannock. In Australia, it's known as damper. Damper has been tamed over the years, and is now more often made there in home ovens and leavened with baking powder. But in the early days of European settlement in Australia, it was as bare and spare a form of bread as you could get, made by "swagmen" on an open fire and eaten with tea cooked in a "billy." In the aboriginal culture section of the museum in Adelaide, several displays mention that the aboriginal people used to make damper out of rush millet ground to a coarse flour, then moistened into a dough, and cooked over a fire.

Here's a basic campfire bread—call it bannock or damper, or quick bread, as you please. It can be baked in the oven or cooked on a stove top or over a fire (see Note). It has plenty of lard (or other fat) in it for warmth, necessary calories for people working hard and living out-of-doors most of the time.

3 cups all-purpose flour

1½ teaspoons salt

1 tablespoon baking powder

¼ to ⅓ cup lard, or 4 to 5 tablespoons unsalted butter,
  plus 1 to 2 tablespoons for greasing the pan

About 1¼ cups lukewarm water

If baking in the oven, place a rack in the center of the oven and preheat the oven to 425°F.

Put the flour, salt, and baking powder in a bowl and stir to mix. Add the lard or butter and cut in. Make a well in the center and pour in the water, mixing as you do. Continue to stir until all the flour is moistened, turning and folding the dough to make sure it's well mixed.

Heat an ovenproof cast-iron skillet over medium-high heat. Add 1 or 2 tablespoons of lard or butter. When the fat has melted, transfer the dough to the pan. Wet your hands and pat the batter out to flatten it and fill the skillet.

To oven-bake the bread, transfer the skillet to the oven and bake until lightly touched with brown, and the center feels firm when pressed with your fingers, about 25 minutes. *To bake on the stove top,* cover tightly with a heavy lid, lower the heat to medium, and cook for 20 minutes. Remove the lid, turn the bread over (use the lid to help flip the bread over), cover, and cook until the second side is browned and the bread is cooked through: Stick a sharp knife or a skewer into the center of the bread—it should come out clean.

Transfer to a rack to cool. Cut the bread into wedges and serve warm or at room temperature for breakfast, or to accompany any meal.

NOTE To cook the bread over an open fire, you'll need a cast-iron skillet. Follow the stove-top directions, but in addition, you'll need to keep moving the skillet on the fire so that the bread cooks evenly.

irish potato breads

Makes 8 golden 7-inch round flatbreads, each marked into 4 farls (wedges) with a chewy golden crust

Boxty—potato flatbread—is an Irish classic. It's very easy to make and is like a meal in one, with flavors of potato and butter, black pepper, and salt. The outside is chewy and golden, the inside very moist. The breads are made of a combination of cooked potato and grated raw potato, as if, long ago, a cook who wanted to make breads from leftover cooked potato found she needed a little extra, so grated in some raw.

These are great breads to put out when you have a crowd to feed, as a snack, or to accompany soup or stew.

1 pound (about 3 medium) preferably floury (baking)
    potatoes, peeled and coarsely grated
1½ cups well-mashed cooked potatoes
8 tablespoons (1 stick) unsalted butter, melted,
    or ½ cup bacon drippings
2 teaspoons salt (1½ teaspoons if using drippings)
Generous grinding of black pepper
About 3½ cups all-purpose flour

Place the grated potatoes in a sieve or colander placed over a bowl. Press and squeeze the potatoes to press out liquid. Set the potatoes aside. Let the liquid settle in the bowl for 10 minutes, then pour off the water and set aside the potato starch.

Mix together the mashed potatoes, butter or drippings, salt, and pepper in a large bowl. Add the potato starch and grated potatoes and mix together. Add 3 cups of the flour and turn and stir with a spoon until a dough forms. Transfer to a well-floured surface and knead the dough for 5 or 6 minutes. It will start out wet and sticky but will soon turn into a kneadable dough. Let the dough stand for 30 minutes to 1 hour, covered with plastic wrap.

Place two racks just above and just below the center of the oven and preheat the oven to 325°F. Lightly butter two baking sheets.

On a floured surface, cut the dough into 8 pieces (each will weigh about 4½ ounces). Flatten each to a round approximately 7 inches in diameter and ¼ inch thick, and mark the tops, using a knife or dough scraper, with a cross. (Once baked, the bread can be broken along these lines into *farls,* or quarters.) Place on the buttered baking sheets, leaving ½ inch of space between the breads.

Bake until golden brown, about 45 minutes, switching the baking sheets after about 20 minutes. The breads will be slightly crusty on the outside and moist inside. Serve hot. Split the farls open if you wish and butter them.

NOTE Leftover breads freeze well: Let cool completely, then seal in plastic bags and freeze. Reheat in a warm skillet for a few minutes.

THICKER BOXTY Sometimes boxty is made thicker, about ½ inch thick, but we find these fairly thin (¼ inch) breads more of a pleasure to eat; they also have a shorter baking time. To make thicker breads, divide the dough into only 4 pieces and bake for about an hour, until browned and cooked through. (Makes 4 breads.)

flaky chinese sesame breads

Makes 16 to 20 flaky strip breads, each 5 to 6 inches long and about 2 inches wide, coated with sesame seeds

These small unleavened flatbreads, tender and usually coated with sesame seeds, are known in China as shao bing. *They're among our favorites. We've seen them being baked on a shallow cast-iron wok over a fire as well as on the inside walls of a barrel oven, tandoor style. We think of them as fusion food, a central Asian idea (tandoor-baked flatbreads) translated centuries ago into Chinese cuisine.*

The breads are flaky because the dough is rolled thin, coated with lard, and folded many times, like savory puff pastry dough. Some of the lard also goes into the dough, making it tender. You'll notice that the dough isn't seasoned directly; instead, salt and pepper are added to the lard, which then flavors the dough.

¼ cup lard (see Note), or a blend of 3 tablespoons
    shortening and 1 tablespoon bacon drippings
6 to 8 Sichuan peppercorns, finely ground
Grinding of black pepper
1½ teaspoons salt (a little less if using drippings)
About 1½ cups all-purpose flour
1½ cups pastry or cake flour
Scant 1¼ cups lukewarm water
1½ to 2 tablespoons sesame seeds

Place the lard or shortening mixture in a bowl. Stir in the peppers, if using, and the salt to blend well. Set this flavor paste aside.

Using a food processor: Place both flours in the processor and pulse to blend well. With the machine running, add 2 tablespoons of the flavor paste, wait until it is blended in, then slowly add the water just until a ball of dough forms. Process for another 10 seconds or so, then turn out onto a lightly floured surface and knead for a minute or so, until soft and very smooth.

By hand: Place the flours in a medium bowl and stir well. Add 2 tablespoons of the flavor paste and blend it in, using a pastry cutter or your fingertips, until the texture of fine crumbs. Slowly add the water, stirring as you do so, just until a dough forms. Mix well, then turn out onto a very lightly floured surface and knead for 4 to 5 minutes. The dough will be soft and very smooth.

Cover the dough well with plastic (in a bowl or on a counter) and let rest for 1 hour, or as long as 3 hours, whatever is more convenient.

Meanwhile, place a baking stone or unglazed quarry tiles, if you have them, on a rack in the upper third of the oven and preheat the oven to 425°F. If you don't have a stone, lightly grease a large baking sheet and set aside. Put out a sprayer of water.

Lightly flour a large—20 inches by 30 inches—work surface. Turn the dough out and flatten and stretch it, using your hands and then a rolling pin, to a rectangle approximately 25 by 16 inches (roll from the center outward with the rolling pin). Use a spatula to spread the remaining flavor paste on one half of the dough, making a rectangle about 16 inches by 12 inches. Fold the bare dough over the flavored half, to make a 16-by-

12-inch rectangle. Fold it in thirds like a business let-ter, folding one short end over the center and then the other end over. Roll up, from a short side, like a jelly roll. You'll have a mound about 6 to 8 inches wide; flat-ten it a little, then let it stand a moment to rest.

Use your palms and then a rolling pin to flatten the dough out again. Be gentle with it, stroking lightly from the center outward to make a rectangle about 24 by 12 inches. Don't worry if the edges are a little uneven. Spritz the top with water, then sprinkle on the sesame seeds to make a light dusting all over.

Use a sharp knife to cut the dough into individual breads: Cut the rectangle lengthwise into 2 strips, about 6 inches wide, then cut crosswise into 2½- to 3-inch-wide strips. Use a spatula to help you transfer them onto the baking sheet, or directly onto the baking stone or tiles, placing them sesame side down and not quite touching. Bake for about 10 minutes, then flip over and bake for another 8 minutes or so, until pale golden on both sides. Transfer to a rack to cool, and bake the remaining breads. Serve warm or at room tempera-ture—delicious, and a little more crackery the next day.

NOTE Lard is sold by butchers and in many delicates-sans. Pure lard should be very mild tasting and almost odorless. You can also render your own very easily (see Fat in the Glossary).

SKILLET-BAKED SESAME BREADS You can also bake these in a large cast-iron or other heavy skillet. We usu-ally bake most of the batch in the oven, and skillet-bake the remaining few that don't quite fit on the baking stone or sheet, on the stove top. Heat the skillet over medium-high heat. When it is hot, put in the breads sesame side down and lower the heat slightly to prevent scorching; we find they do well on medium heat. Cook for about 6 minutes on the first side, then turn over and press down on the breads with a flat spatula as they cook, to encourage the center to cook through, until golden brown on both sides.

friselle dell'orzo

Makes 16 round barley rusks, 5 to 6 inches across, dry and golden

Friselle are Italian twice-cooked breads, a form of rusk. The first baking yields flat coiled buns that are then sliced horizontally in half and baked again until light and crisp. Traditionally fishermen would take them out on their boats, rehydrating them by dipping them in seawater to soften them, and shepherds used them as lightweight traveling food. Now they're sold in packages in many parts of Italy.

We came across barley friselle in Puglia. The biga (see page 111) is made of wheat flour, but the dough itself uses only barley flour. The rusks dry out in the second bake and become very hard; they must be moistened well with water to soften them before being eaten. They're best topped with a drizzle of olive oil and spread with chopped fresh tomatoes or cucumber, well seasoned with salt and pepper

Ancient olive tree, rural Puglia, Italy

BIGA

⅛ teaspoon active dry yeast

½ cup lukewarm water

About 1 cup unbleached all-purpose flour

BREAD

3 cups lukewarm water

1 teaspoon active dry yeast

5 to 6 cups barley flour

1 tablespoon salt

TOPPINGS

Extra virgin olive oil

Chopped tomatoes

Salt and freshly ground black pepper

Capers or basil leaves (optional)

Make the biga at least 1 day before you wish to bake the friselle: In a small bowl, sprinkle the yeast over the warm water and stir to dissolve. Add the flour and stir and fold to incorporate it. Knead briefly in the bowl until smooth, then cover with plastic and set aside to ferment for 12 to 24 hours. (Or, if leaving for longer—up to 5 days—store in the refrigerator. Bring back to room temperature before using.)

Pour 2½ cups of the lukewarm water into a large bowl, add the biga, and use your hands or a wooden spoon to break it up in the water. Dissolve the yeast in the remaining ½ cup warm water, stirring well, and add to the biga mixture. Add 3 cups of the barley flour, a cup at a time, always stirring in the same direction, then stir 100 times. Let stand, covered with plastic, for at least 30 minutes, or as long as 3 hours.

Add the salt and stir. Add 2 more cups barley flour, 1 cup at a time, and stir well. Turn the dough out onto a well-floured surface and knead, incorporating more barley flour as necessary, for 8 to 10 minutes, until the dough is smooth and no longer sticky. Dust a clean bowl with barley flour, place the dough in the bowl, cover with plastic wrap or a wet towel covered with plastic wrap, and let rise for 2 hours.

Pull the dough away from the sides of the bowl and turn out onto a lightly floured surface. Let rest briefly. Place a rack in the center of the oven and place a baking stone or unglazed quarry tiles, if you have them, on it. Preheat the oven to 425°F. Lightly oil a large baking sheet.

Divide the dough into 8 pieces. Working with 1 piece at a time and leaving the rest covered with plastic wrap, roll the dough under your palms until it forms a rope 8 to 10 inches long and ½ to ¾ inch thick. Anchor one end of the rope on the lightly floured surface and coil the length of rope loosely around it, so that it makes about 1½ turns. Tuck the end in or press it against the side of the coil and flatten the bread slightly with the palm of your hand: It should still be close to ½ inch thick. Transfer the bread to the baking sheet, placing it top side down. Proceed to shape the remaining breads in the same way, leaving about ½ inch of space or more between breads; if necessary, use two baking sheets. Cover the breads with plastic wrap and let stand for 10 to 15 minutes before baking.

Bake directly on the stone or tiles (if you don't have a baking stone, leave on the baking sheet to bake) for about 20 minutes. When done, the breads will be golden and firm on the bottom and still slightly soft on top. Let cool for 10 minutes on a rack. Lower the oven heat to 275°F.

Slice each bread horizontally in half, to create 16 rounds. Place the breads back in the oven, directly on the stone or tiles (or baking sheet) in the center of the oven, making sure each bread is lying flat so it keeps its shape as it rebakes. Bake for 20 to 30 minutes; when done, the breads will be very light because all the moisture will have evaporated. Place on a rack to cool thoroughly, then store in a plastic bag.

To use, dip in water, or hold under a running tap, then shake off excess water. Do make sure the bread is well moistened, so it's not a tooth-breaker. Top with a drizzle of extra virgin olive oil and some freshly chopped tomato. Sprinkle with salt and pepper to taste, and, if you wish, capers or torn basil leaves.

sweet farsi tandoor bread

Makes 4 large round or oval breads (each weighing about 1 pound), soft, puffed, and very tender

I was shown how to make these yeasted flatbreads, called kulchay, *at a Farsi home outside the Ashkhabad oasis in Turkmenistan, very close to the Iranian border. My hosts were Farsis who had fled from Iran to Turkmenistan forty years before. They had kept their own style of tandoor, of breads, and of clothing. Their garden was lush with herbs.*

These breads are traditionally baked in a tandoor oven, for which we substitute baking on a baking stone or on unglazed quarry tiles. If you have neither, you can bake them on baking sheets; they'll take several minutes longer and will have a softer bottom crust.

2 cups milk, heated to lukewarm

1 teaspoon active dry yeast

6 to 7 cups all-purpose flour

¼ cup sugar

2 large eggs

½ cup full- or reduced-fat plain yogurt

2 teaspoons salt

1 teaspoon baking soda

Scant 1 teaspoon nigella seeds (see Glossary) (optional)

Place the milk in a small bowl, sprinkle on the yeast, then stir to dissolve. Place 2 cups of the all-purpose flour and the sugar in a large bowl. Pour in the milk-yeast mixture and stir to mix.

In another bowl, beat together the eggs and yogurt. Add to the yeast mixture and stir in. Sprinkle on the salt and baking soda and stir to blend in. Add 3 more cups flour, a cup at a time, stirring and folding to incorporate it. Turn the dough out onto a well-floured surface and knead until smooth and soft, incorporating flour as necessary, about 5 minutes.

Put the dough in a clean bowl (or set aside on your work surface), cover well with plastic wrap, and let rise for 2 hours.

Meanwhile, place a baking stone or unglazed quarry tiles, if you have them, on a rack in the center of the oven. Preheat to 450°F. Fill a sprayer with water.

Turn the risen dough out onto a floured surface and cut into 4 pieces. Roll each 1 out to a thick 9-inch round or to an oval 11 to 12 inches long and 5 to 6 inches at the widest part. (Place the breads on flour-dusted baking sheets if you don't have room on your work surface for all 4.) Wet the end of a dowel or the handle of a wooden spoon (or any round wood about the diameter of your little finger, up to ½ inch across) and punch holes all over the breads, punching vigorously and many times right through to the work surface, spacing the holes about an inch apart. Let the breads stand, covered, for 15 to 20 minutes.

Just before baking, spritz the breads with a little water and, if you wish, sprinkle on a few nigella seeds (about ¼ teaspoon or less per bread). Use a flour-dusted peel (or the back of a baking sheet) to transfer 2 breads to the hot stone or tiles. (Or, if you have no stone or tiles, bake on a baking sheet.) Bake until well touched with golden brown and puffed, about 10 minutes. Place on a rack to cool for 10 minutes, then wrap in a cloth to keep them soft and warm while you bake the second pair of breads.

NOTE These focaccialike loaves make good sandwiches: Cut crosswise in half, then split horizontally in half.

spicy dal crackers

Makes 4 pizza pans' worth of thin spicy crackers (a good bowlful), aromatic with cumin and coriander

Baking can be full of good surprises. We were trying to make Rajasthani spiced rotis, but when we rolled the dough very thin, suddenly we had a dynamite knock-out cracker with a wild array of flavors, from dal and wheat to cumin, chile pepper, and onion—like a meal in every bite. The crackers are great with a mild yogurt dip or guacamole, or just on their own, full of flavor.

1 cup yellow moong dal (see Dal in the Glossary),
    soaked overnight in warm water to cover
½ teaspoon chile powder
½ teaspoon cumin
½ teaspoon coriander
1½ teaspoons salt
1 small red onion, minced
2 cups atta flour (see Glossary), plus extra for dusting
½ cup warm water

Drain the dal, transfer to a food processor, and process to a paste. Add the spices, salt, onion, and flour, and process for 1 minute to blend well. With the processor on, pour the water through the feed tube, until a ball of dough forms. Keep processing for another 20 seconds or so, then turn the dough out onto a lightly floured surface and knead briefly. The dough will be soft and smooth, with small pieces of onion in it.

Cover the dough with plastic and let rest for 30 minutes to 2 hours, whatever is most convenient.

Meanwhile, place a rack in the upper third of the oven and preheat the oven to 450°F. Fill a sprayer with water. When ready to proceed, divide the dough into 4 pieces. Flatten each into a 4-inch disk and flour both sides of each liberally.

Work with 1 piece at a time, keeping the others covered with plastic wrap. Roll the dough out to a 15- or 16-inch round and transfer the rolled-out dough to a 16-inch pizza pan. (The easiest way is to drape the dough over your rolling pin and lay it on the pan. You can also use a baking sheet and roll the dough to a rectangle.) Spritz with water. Use a pizza cutter or sharp knife to cut into rectangles of any size you please; ours are usually about 1 inch by 2 inches (and you have interesting irregular crackers at the edges of your round). Bake until touched with brown, 3 to 6 minutes. Repeat with the remaining dough. Let cool on a rack until crisp. Store in a well-sealed container.

SPICY SKILLET BREADS To make skillet breads with the dough, divide the rested dough into 8 pieces. Follow the instructions for rolling out and cooking Mountain Women's Roti (page 272), rolling the rounds to about 8 inches across and cooking them in a lightly oiled 10-inch cast-iron skillet. The breads have a much milder flavor than the crackers.

The smell of juniper On my first trip to Asia, I met a guy from Austria in Iran. He was

hitchhiking to India, while I was traveling by local buses, and it was his second trip, so I was impressed.

"Why are you going to India?" I asked.

"To work in a restaurant," he replied. "Same as last year. I make breads, *chapattis*. I love bread."

"Do you get paid?" I couldn't help but ask.

"Eight rupees a day."

Eight rupees a day in 1977 was a dollar. A dollar a day. It seemed a bit mysterious to me, traveling to

India to make bread. But then a lot of things seemed mysterious to me, that first time in Asia.

A few days later, on a bus, I met two other travelers. Paolo was a biochemist going to India to escape

political violence in Argentina. And Arthur, from California, traveling with his violin, was headed to

India to live in a yoga ashram. All three of us were traveling overland through Turkey, Iran, Afghanistan, Pakistan, for the first time. We all became friends.

We went first to Herat, then to Qandahar, then to Kabul. In Kabul, we found a hotel just off Chicken Street, the center of the cheap hotel district, and checked into a room with a balcony looking out over the neighborhood. A boy came to our door selling hashish, then another bringing hot black tea poured into tiny glasses half full of sugar, Afghan style. The high-altitude air was dusty but still fresh, and the strong angled October sun-dried our laundry almost as quickly as we hung it out. Chicken Street was full of street vendors selling carpets and beautiful lapis lazuli.

Near our hotel was a lively restaurant on the corner, windows all around. A big, bearded Afghan man, a money changer, sat in the restaurant all day—same table every day—stacks of paper currencies from all over the world set out on the table in front of him. He looked like a banker in a big-time Monopoly game. As we'd sit eating at a nearby table, people would come and go, exchanging Jordanian dinars, Filipino pesos, Danish kroner. It seemed strange, so much money sitting unprotected on the table, no security guard, no weapon in sight. But then he was an awfully big man, the money changer.

The place I remember most was the local bakery. Most of the time, it looked only like wooden scaffolding abandoned in an empty lot, but then several times each day the bakers would assemble. They'd fire the enormous vertical clay tandoor oven with juniper, the local abundant wood, making the neighborhood smell heavenly.

Then two or three of them would start shaping long rippled snowshoe-shaped nan, and the head baker would slap them onto the hot oven walls, his right arm reaching deep into the fiercely hot tandoor. Others stood by the oven selling the breads. Stacks and stacks of naan disappeared almost instantaneously out into the neighborhood, carried by women and children, carried by the armload. And then the baking would finish, and the bakers would disappear.

The bread was some of the best I've ever eaten, flavored by the smoke of the juniper and made with freshly ground wheat flour. And when I think back to the hitchhiker from Austria, the chapatti maker headed for India, I still wonder how a person so in love with bread ever got past Afghanistan.

Flatbreads cooling on a rack, Fez, Morocco

semolina crackers

Makes about 7 dozen very thin, pale yellow semolina crackers of varying size but averaging 1½ inches by 2½ inches

There is something about making crackers that we especially like. We make a large unleavened dough and let it rest for thirty minutes, then get our kitchen ready for "production." We assemble five or six baking sheets, a pizza cutter, a water sprayer, and a big bowl to hold the finished crackers, and we turn the oven on as high as it will go. Then we're rolling, literally, rolling and rolling and rolling. One sheet of crackers goes into the oven, then roll again. Then check, and pull out the crackers, then roll. Check and roll, check, pull out, and roll. As crackers come out of the oven, they get tossed into the large bowl, and soon the level of the crackers grows and grows.

This recipe for semolina crackers makes approximately seven dozen crackers, but it depends upon how large or small you cut them. When we're making crackers, we most often double or triple this recipe, because once we have our production going, it's fun just to keep going. The crackers are crisp, and they keep a long time, but they never last as long as we'd like. When we have crackers around, we eat them. And when they're gone, it's time to make more. Rolling out takes a little patience and a little practice, but soon you'll find a rhythm and you'll be turning out sheets and sheets of crackers.

2 cups coarse semolina (not fine semolina flour; see Glossary), plus extra for dusting

¾ teaspoon salt

About ¾ cup warm water

1 tablespoon olive oil

Fine sea salt for topping

Place the semolina and salt in a food processor and process for 10 seconds to mix thoroughly. With the processor on, begin adding water through the feed tube in a steady stream. When you've added about half the water, add the oil. Add the remaining water, processing until the dough comes together into a ball, then continue processing for 30 seconds.

Turn the dough out onto a surface lightly dusted with semolina. Knead the dough briefly, incorporating semolina from the surface as necessary to produce a smooth, elastic dough. Cover with plastic wrap and let rest for 30 minutes, or as long as 2 hours.

Place two racks above and below the center of the oven and preheat the oven to 500°F. Place several baking sheets or pizza pans by your work surface. Place a rack on the counter or on a table.

Divide the dough in half, then divide each half into 6 equal pieces. Leaving the other pieces covered, working on a surface lightly floured with semolina, flatten 2 pieces with your palms, then begin rolling one out, into either a rectangle or a circle, depending on whether you are using baking sheets or pizza pans. Roll from the center of the dough outward, with light, firm strokes. If the dough sticks to your rolling pin, dust the pin lightly with flour. Turn the dough a quarter turn or less after each stroke of the pin. Once it's fairly thin, let it rest while you begin rolling the other out to the same thinness. Then go back to the first dough and roll it even thinner: The short pause will have given it time to stretch and rest, so that it can be rolled thinner, to a rectangle about 14 inches by 8 inches, or a 14-inch circle. Don't worry if there are small tears or unevenness; it will still make great crackers.

When the dough is as thin as it can be, gently lift it from your work surface and place it on a baking sheet or pizza pan. Sprinkle it with sea salt. Using a knife or pizza cutter, cut parallel lines down the dough and then across it to make rectangular crackers about 1½ by 2½ inches. You can also just cut the dough lengthwise into strips to make long crackers; they look very attractive when presented standing up in a deep bowl or even a vase (see the photograph on page 298). Don't worry if your crackers are not all exactly the same

Tunisian baker outside his pastry shop, Marché Aligre, Paris

size; irregularities are part of the beauty of these crackers. Spritz lightly with water and place the baking sheet or pan on one of the oven racks. Note the time; the crackers will be starting to turn brown in about 3 minutes. Finish rolling out the other sheet of dough and place it in the oven on the other rack.

Keep an eye on the crackers already baking as you begin rolling out the next batch. The crackers will brown from underneath. Check on them 2½ minutes after they go in. The thinnest patches of dough should already have started to brown (noticeable from the top). If so, take them out; if not, check again in 30 seconds. It is better to take crackers out a little early than too late, when they may have burned. You will soon get a feel for

timing and degree of doneness: The exact heat of your oven and how thin you managed to roll out your dough will both affect timing. When they come out of the oven, some of the crackers will be crisp, while others will need a little time to crisp up.

Empty the crackers onto the rack, breaking up any that are incompletely separated. Continue to roll out the remaining dough until all the dough has been shaped and baked. Let the crackers cool completely and crisp up, then transfer to a tightly sealed cookie tin or a heavy plastic bag. Store at room temperature.

FOLLOWING PAGES: *Pushkar camel fair, Rajasthan, India. Plowing a field, Haryana, India.*

sweet anise and sugar crispbeads

Makes 8 crisp, 12-inch-long oval flatbreads, topped with a crunchy layer of anise-flavored sugar

At an artisanal bakery in Barcelona called Pa Artesia Fleca Balmes some years ago, I came across some whole wheat crispbreads topped with anise seeds and sugar. They were thick, a little crisp, not at all tough. This is our version of those breads: A simple yeasted dough is rolled out into long ovals and topped with anise and sugar. The breads are large, about twelve inches long and five to six inches wide. Right after baking, they are tender, but left out overnight, they dry into crackers. The intense blend of anise and sugar is a great taste hit, nothing shy about it.

2 cups lukewarm water

½ teaspoon active dry yeast

2 cups whole wheat flour

1½ teaspoons salt

2 tablespoons olive oil

2 to 2½ cups all-purpose flour

TOPPING

About 4 teaspoons anise seeds

About ¾ cup sugar

Place the water in a bowl, add the yeast, and stir to dissolve well. Stir in the whole wheat flour, a cup at a time, to make a smooth thick batter. If you have the time, let stand, covered with plastic wrap, for an hour or two.

Sprinkle on the salt and stir in, then add the olive oil and stir. Stir in 1 cup of the all-purpose flour, then add another cup and turn and fold the dough to incorporate it. Turn out onto a lightly floured surface and knead until very smooth and firm but not dry, about 5 minutes; incorporate flour only as you have to.

Place the dough on a floured spot on the counter, cover well with plastic, and let stand for about 1½ hours (or for 2 hours or more if you didn't let the batter proof earlier). Place a baking stone or unglazed quarry tiles, if you have them, on a rack in the middle of the oven and preheat the oven to 450°F. Line two baking sheets with parchment paper or lightly oil them. Fill a sprayer full of water.

Cut the dough in half. Set one half aside, well covered. Cut the remaining dough into 4 equal pieces.

Press both sides of each piece in flour and flatten gently under your palm. Cover 2 pieces with plastic and set aside. Start rolling out the other 2 pieces, rolling firmly but with a light touch, from the center outward. Gradually roll each piece into an oval about 12 inches long and 5 to 6 inches wide at the widest point; the dough will pull back as you roll, so alternate the pieces to give the gluten time to relax.

Place the breads side by side on a prepared sheet. Spritz generously with water. Sprinkle about ½ teaspoon anise seeds over each of them, then sprinkle about 1½ tablespoons sugar on each and then spread it more evenly with the palm of your hand. Prick the dough all over with a fork, about 20 times on each bread. Bake for about 10 minutes. When done, the breads will be just starting to turn golden at the edges. Transfer to a rack to cool and firm up.

Meanwhile, roll out a second pair of breads, place on the second sheet, and flavor and prick them. Bake once the first breads are out. Repeat with the remaining dough (or see the variations that follow). Let the breads cool on a rack. Once they are completely cool, store the breads in plastic bags.

VARIATIONS If you want to make only 4 sweet crackers, using half the dough, the remaining dough can be used to make savory crackers or to make slightly unorthodox kouignaman, the layered butter- and sugar-rich cake from Brittany (see page 363).

SAVORY WHOLE WHEAT CRACKERS Divide the second piece of dough into 4 pieces. One at a time, roll out 2 pieces very thin, into baking sheet–sized sheets. Place each on a prepared baking sheet. Spritz, and sprinkle on salt and other savory flavorings, such as grated Parmesan or cumin seeds, if you wish. Cut into crackers—long strips or squares, or diamonds, as you wish—using a pizza cutter or a sharp knife. Bake on two racks until starting to brown, about 6 to 8 minutes, depending on how thin they are. Repeat with the remaining 2 pieces.

WHOLE WHEAT KOUIGNAMAN Using half the dough, follow the instructions on page 363 for shaping kouig-naman, using the amounts of butter and sugar specified there, and the folding and shaping and slashing techniques. Place the shaped cake on a baking sheet, and let it proof for a good hour. Sprinkle on a little extra sugar just before baking. Bake in a preheated 450°F oven for 20 to 25 minutes, until richly brown. Place on a rack to cool for 20 minutes or more before serving in wedges. The combination of whole wheat and sugar and butter with a caramelized top is delightful.

Views of Barcelona

remnant rye-butter crackers

Makes just under 1 pound medium-thin all-rye crackers (a large wooden bowlful)

In Sweden, there are all kinds of crackers for sale—beautifully packaged, crisp, and tasting of grain. Some of them have long been exported to North America—rye crisps and knackebrod, *distinctive rippled dry raised crackers.*

When we were in Sweden, we ate a wide range of these "boughten" crackers and wanted to try making them at home. But after we had rolled out a yeasted rye flour dough into flour-dusted rounds to make knackebrod, we rolled the dough remnants into thin crackers. The crackers were a big success, but try as we might, we couldn't get the knackebrod to come out properly. So here are the remnant crackers, a pleasure both to make and to eat.

1 teaspoon active dry yeast

1 cup lukewarm water

1 teaspoon sugar

About 4 cups light rye flour

8 tablespoons (1 stick) unsalted butter,
at cool room temperature

½ teaspoon salt

Coarse salt for topping (optional)

Dissolve the yeast in the water, and stir in the sugar.

By hand: Place 3 cups of the flour in a bowl. Cut the butter into small chunks, then cut it into the flour with a pastry cutter or your fingertips, until well blended. Stir in the yeast mixture, add the salt, and stir to mix.

Using a food processor: Place 3 cups of the flour in the processor bowl. Cut the butter into several large chunks, add to the flour, and process to the texture of a coarse meal. Stir the yeast mixture. With the processor running, add the yeast, then the salt, and process for 30 seconds.

Turn the heavy, wet mass of dough out into a clean bowl, cover, and set aside to rest for 30 minutes.

When ready to proceed, dust a work surface with about ¼ cup flour and turn the dough out. Knead, incorporating flour as necessary, sprinkling more flour on your work surface when you need to in order to prevent sticking, and using a dough scraper to keep the surface clean, for about 4 minutes. (Because of the butter, the dough will be smooth and very kneadable, if a little sticky.) Set aside, covered with plastic, for a few minutes.

Put out two 18-by-12-inch nonstick baking sheets or lightly butter two regular sheets. Divide the dough into 4 equal pieces. Set 3 aside, covered. On a lightly floured surface, flatten the remaining piece into an oval disk, flouring both sides. Use a lightly floured rolling pin to roll it out to a rectangle about the size of your baking sheets, working with light strokes and rolling from the center outward. Don't turn the dough over once you start rolling: Use a dough scraper to separate it from the surface if it starts to stick, and reflour the work surface lightly as needed. Carefully transfer the thin dough to a baking sheet. Don't worry if it tears a little; you can mend the tear, and you'll be cutting it into crackers anyway. Cover loosely with plastic and repeat with another piece. Let the crackers rest for 30 minutes. If you have four baking sheets, you can roll out all the dough at once; if not, do the second pair after the first ones bake.

Meanwhile, place two racks in your oven, just above and just below the center. Preheat the oven to 450°F. Fill a sprayer with water. Use a pizza cutter or sharp knife to cut the dough into rectangles or diamonds, and spritz lightly with water. Sprinkle on a little coarse salt, if you wish. Place a sheet on each rack and bake until just starting to brown at the edges, about 8 minutes, switching the pans after 5 minutes. Break apart any crackers that have not separated and let cool completely on a rack. Repeat with the remaining dough. Store in a well-sealed container in a cool place.

second time around

An assortment of uses for leftover bread

Flatbreads, like loaf breads, often have a first life, a second life, even a third life. When dried out, or left over, they can be seasoned (or not) and crisped into crackers. As chips or crackers, they can be oven-baked (twice-cooked) or fried. They can be made into croutons, or ground into bread crumbs. We like saving several different ends of flatbreads and loaf breads, then using them together for making crisps or crumbs. The diversity of tastes is fun.

Oven-Baked Chips

Cut wheat flour tortillas or rotis into wedges. If they will split into two layers, open the wedges out and break apart to make triangles. Place on a baking sheet and bake at 450°F until crisp. If you wish, you can brush them with a little olive oil and sprinkle on some salt before baking. They make great snacks.

Fried Crackers

Leftover Mountain Women's Roti, dried out overnight or longer, makes great fried crackers. They're delectable, with good bite, and beautiful. You can also fry tortillas or other leftover thin flatbreads in the same manner.

Mountain Women's Roti (page 272) or tortillas, dried out overnight
Peanut oil for deep-frying
Sea Salt

Tear or cut the bread into pieces about 2 inches across.

Place a pair of tongs or a slotted spoon and a paper towel–lined platter by your work surface. Heat about 2 inches of oil in a stable pot over high heat. Test the temperature by dropping in a piece of flatbread: It should sink and then immediately rise to the surface,

without burning. Carefully slide several pieces of bread into the hot oil; as it sizzles up, slide in several more pieces. You will see the bread pieces turn golden within 30 seconds to a minute. Use the tongs or slotted spoon to lift them out of the oil, holding them over the hot oil for a moment to drain off excess oil, and place on the paper towels to blot them, then place them in a bowl, on their edges. Sprinkle on sea salt. Let crisp up. Repeat with the remaining flatbread.

Bread Crumbs

In Germany and Austria, village bakeries sell fresh bread crumbs in two sizes. The larger ones are for making knudeln, "fresh dumplings," and the finer ones are what the French call chapelure, *for coating schnitzel or for using to coat a strudel dough.*

Bread crumbs are easy to make at home. For fresh crumbs, just grate a loaf on the coarse side of a box grater. For crumbs from a stale loaf, cut off the crusts, then cut the bread into chunks and process in a food processor until fine. Crumbs are used, plain or lightly fried, in the filling for strudel or as a topping for piecrust (see Cherry Strudel, page 62, and Treacle Tart, page 19, for example), or as an ingredient in cakes (see Three-Layer Walnut Torte with Whipped Cream, page 370).

FOUR | CAKES AND COOKIES

Everyday Cakes and a Few Fancy Ones Too

All-Around-the World Cookies

THE IMPULSE TO ADD SUGAR TO FLOUR, and then to bake something sweet, seems almost universal. The cakes and cookies collected here come from all around the world, from Brazil to the Ukraine, from France to Uzbekistan. Wherever they are from, they are special, foods caringly given as gifts, foods that bring pleasure and express affection.

Cakes and cookies have changed with the times. From a home baker's point of view, working in a farmhouse kitchen a hundred years ago, a cake was just a little sweeter and richer than a festive bread. Since then, cakes have become sweeter, richer, more intensely flavored, more "cakey," and often more tender, as we've gained access to a wider range of ingredients and to good mixers.

Before the advent of baking soda and baking powder in the nineteenth century, cake was made either from a yeasted risen dough or from a batter raised by the beating of eggs (the air beaten into the eggs lightened the cake). Yeasted cakes were made from a piece of bread dough enriched with sugar, butter, and sometimes an egg. These additions weakened the gluten in the dough, making it softer and more tender. The "egg-raised" cakes were either dense-crumbed, clean-slicing rich cakes such as pound cake, or airier, drier sponge cakes.

Most of the cakes we've included in this section are easy everyday cakes, easy to remember or to improvise, such as Four-Minute Cake Valerie (page 343), New Year's Pear Cake (page 342), and Semolina 1-2-3 Cake (page 358). They're raised with baking powder and are very quick and flexible. We've also included some cakes from the older yeasted cake tradition; we love them because they're a bonus from bread making and need no exact recipe to be successful. Whenever we make bread, we can take a piece of the risen bread dough, incorporate butter and sugar, and have cake, treats like Breton Butter Cake (page 363) with its caramelized crust, or Fruit-Topped Country Cake (page 366). Even the more elaborate cakes included here are still easy, but they do take a little attention to measurement and timing: Three-Layer Walnut Torte with Whipped Cream (page 370) or Lemon Jelly Roll (page 355).

Cookies (the word is from the Dutch *koekje*; in England they're known as biscuits) have always been more straightforward than cakes. Most are as fun to make as they are fun to have around. Cookies use an amazing variety of doughs, flavorings, and shaping techniques. Some are made like pastry, rich with butter or egg, while others are made from a yeasted dough, then sweetened and shaped. Some are raised with baking soda or baking powder, some contain no wheat flour at all. What cookies have in common is that they often contain special ingredients, from nuts to spices to dried fruits, from butter and eggs to lard and coconut milk.

The other thing that cookies have in common is that they all fit happily into cookie jars!

On Butter

Butter is so often an important part of cakes and cookies that it deserves its own space here. What is butter? More specifically, what is good butter? Is it important to use good butter, even if it's going to be mixed into a cake batter or cookie dough?

Butter, historically, has been a great way to use up lots of milk, a way of storing the cream. It can be made from any animal's milk by separating out the cream (the milk is allowed to stand until the cream rises to the top and can be skimmed off) and then churning or shaking it until the butterfat separates from the milk and becomes a solid mass. On family farms in northern Europe and North America, churns were used; on the central Asian steppes, the cream went into a bag that was shaken until the butter separated out. Now most butter in Europe and North America is made in dairies, from small places to large factories.

What is in butter? The answer is short: butterfat and milk solids, and, sometimes, salt, especially in country butter. Why salt? To help preserve the butter and prevent it from going rancid. Most sweet baking recipes these days call for "sweet," or unsalted butter, but in rural places most farm butter is salted for longer keeping. (You'll notice that the recipe for Breton Butter Cake, page 363, calls for salted butter, a reminder of the cake's rural origins.) But if a recipe calls for unsalted butter, salted can be substituted, with an adjustment in the salt called for in the recipe.

Butter sold in North America usually comes in half-pound or one-pound packages and may be labeled salted or unsalted, sweet cream butter, or cultured butter; it may contain coloring, especially in winter. Those lucky enough to live near a creamery or cheese store may be able to buy their butter in bulk. We like buying cultured butter and then storing it in the freezer in half-pound packages, tightly wrapped. It's there to be grated onto a bread dough to transform it into cake, or to be warmed and softened for a cookie dough.

So what makes good butter, and what are the rules? In France, butter must be at least 82 percent butterfat (80 percent if salted butter), whereas in the United States it must be only 80 percent butterfat. Some specialty makers produce a higher-fat (higher-cost) butter, as much as 86 percent butterfat. If the cows are grass-fed and the butter is cultured and made by a small dairy, it will have more flavor—and you'll be able to tell the difference.

Butter may be used melted as a liquid in recipes, or grated or cut into flour to give a flaky texture, or used softened to blend with other ingredients such as sugar or flour. In the recipes, **cold butter** means butter just out of the refrigerator; **softened butter** means butter at or near room temperature, not melted.

Tools to Have on Hand

Over time we've accumulated **cake pans** of various shapes and sizes. They now take up half a drawer in the kitchen, but you don't really need a lot of cake pans, just a few reliables.

We use our **13-by-9-inch baking pan** a lot, for making double recipes of New Year's Pear Cake (page 342) or Semolina 1-2-3 Cake (page 358), especially when we have a crowd to feed. The other most useful pans are **8-inch round cake pans** and the **small square cake pans** Naomi inherited from her mother, one 7 inches across and the other 8 inches. They're great for gingerbread or small yeasted cakes. We like to use a **cake ring,** an expandable 9-inch one, placed on a baking sheet, for Breton Butter Cake (page 363), but it's not essential. Cake rings take up little space and are very handy for tarts too. A **tube pan** is useful for cakes that are dense or large, such as Brazilian Bolo (page 352) or Buttermilk Fruit Cake (page 347), because it ensures more even baking: With the hollow center, the middle of the cake is baked before the outside is overdone. Finally, as you'd expect from a household of bread makers, we also use **bread pans** (9-by-5-inch and 8-by-4-inch) to bake cakes, not just the easy sweet loaves in the Festive Breads chapter, but also the Ukrainian Honey Cake (page 345) and Lemon Pound Cake (page 348) included here.

You'll want several **wire racks** for cooling both cakes and cookies. **Fine-mesh racks** work best, for they support a cake more evenly and cookies are less likely to fall through them.

There's no special equipment needed to bake most cookies, other than several **baking sheets**. The heavier the baking sheet the more even the temperature, so look for heavy ones. If you're making bar cookies, which are baked as shallow cakes and then cut into cookies, you'll want the 13-by-9-inch cake pan or two of the square 8-inch pans mentioned above. Some cookies are easier to make if you have a **stand mixer,** but only one recipe here, Meringue Choices (page 381), requires a mixer. At the flea markets, garage sales, and rural auctions that we haunt, we always keep an eye out for old or interesting **cookie cutters,** and there's a small collection of them now in our baking drawer. You can use a **fine-edged glass** to cut out cookies; just dust the edge lightly with flour or sugar to keep it from sticking to a moist dough. Other cookies can be cut into diamonds or squares just before baking, just as crackers often are, using a **pizza cutter** or a sharp knife.

The thing that makes cookies appealing to cook and eater alike is how easy they are to keep and have on hand. Once the cook has made a batch, they can be stored in a tin and brought out at short notice. There's a feeling of wealth if you have cookies in the cookie jar. They really are food for "a rainy day," or the "something put by" of folk wisdom. For best keeping, all cookies, once completely cooled after baking, should be kept in a cool place in a tightly sealed container, crisp cookies with crisp, soft with soft.

EVERYDAY CAKES AND A FEW FANCY ONES TOO

new year's pear cake

Makes an 8-inch square cake with a golden top and pear chunks throughout; serves 6 to 8

One September day, our friend Kathy called to ask us all to dinner for the first night of Rosh Hashanah, the Jewish New Year. Traditionally it's a time for sweet things, to start the year on a happy note. We used some overripe pears, sweet and juicy, to flavor this simple square cake, the chunks of fruit suspended in a rich, dense crumb.

Since that first experiment, we've made the cake a lot. We've used plums and apples, and both are very successful (see Plum or Apple Cake below for details). And the recipe doubles easily, so it's a good one for parties. Serve the cake warm or at room temperature, on its own or topped with a scoop of ice cream or a drizzle of cream. It is also excellent the next day, at room temperature.

About 1 pound sweet ripe pears (about 2 cups chopped)

3 tablespoons freshly squeezed lemon juice

1½ cups all-purpose flour

1½ teaspoons baking powder

⅛ teaspoon salt

½ cup sugar, plus (optional) extra for sprinkling

2 extra-large eggs

6 tablespoons unsalted butter, melted,
  plus extra for brushing

1 to 2 tablespoons milk as needed

GLAZE (OPTIONAL)

2 to 3 tablespoons fruit syrup (from candying or
  poaching fruit), or 2 tablespoons honey

1 to 2 tablespoons hot water, if needed

Place a baking stone or unglazed quarry tiles, if you have them, (or a heavy baking sheet) on a rack in the lower third of the oven and preheat the oven to 350°F. Brush an 8-inch square cake pan with melted butter. Line with parchment or wax paper and brush paper with melted butter.

Cut the pears into quarters; peel, core, and place them in a medium bowl. Immediately pour the lemon juice over, turning the pears gently to coat. Set aside.

In a large bowl, combine the dry ingredients and mix well. Add the eggs and 6 tablespoons melted butter and beat to make a very stiff batter. Fold the chopped pears and juice into the batter. Add milk, as necessary, to moisten completely.

Turn the batter into the prepared cake pan and smooth the top with a wet spatula. Sprinkle on a little extra sugar, if you wish, and bake until golden brown on top, about 50 minutes to 1 hour. A skewer inserted into the middle of the cake should come out clean. Remove from the oven and turn out onto a plate.

To give the cake an attractive sheen, prepare the optional glaze: If your syrup or honey is stiff, dilute it with a little hot water, stirring well. Brush over the top of the cake. Let sit for at least 15 minutes to cool and firm up.

NOTE This recipe doubles easily. Use a well-buttered 13-by-9-inch cake pan. Bake at 400°F for 10 minutes, then at 350°F for another 40 minutes, or until the edges have pulled away and a skewer inserted into the center comes out clean. The cake will be a warm golden brown color.

PLUM OR APPLE CAKE If you have plums or apples, you can use them instead of pears. For apples, use a scant 1 pound, peeled, cored, and coarsely chopped. Toss them in several tablespoons of lemon juice, then sprinkle on about ¼ cup sugar (less if your apples are very sweet) and a little cinnamon, if you wish. For plums, pit and coarsely chop them, and sprinkle on several tablespoons sugar, up to ¼ cup, or more if using tart sour plums such as damsons. You don't need lemon juice, so unless the plums are very juicy, you will need to add one or two tablespoons of water to moisten the batter when you fold in the fruit.

four-minute cake valerie

Makes 1 golden brown loaf cake, dotted with dried cranberries and golden raisins

I have no idea where "Valerie" comes in. I've been making this cake for more than twenty years, and each time I make it I consult a three-by-five-inch note card that I copied the recipe onto when I was living on the southwest coast of Ireland (see Ventry, Just Outside Dingle, page 135). The recipe was given to me by the landlady of the house that I rented for the winter, and because her recipe was called Four-Minute Cake Valerie, so too is ours. Come to think of it, I have no idea what "four-minute" refers to. The cake is an easy, dependable, not particularly sweet, large loaf cake with a pale yellow crumb, and while it's relatively quick to make, it does take a little longer than four minutes to assemble.

Oh, well, recipe titles. We gotta love 'em.

12 tablespoons (1½ sticks) unsalted butter

¾ cup sugar

Scant 2¾ cups all-purpose flour

1 tablespoon baking powder

1 teaspoon salt

2½ cups dried fruit: roughly half and half golden raisins (sultanas) and dried cranberries

2 extra-large eggs

About ½ cup whole or reduced-fat milk

Place a rack in the center of the oven and preheat the oven to 350°F. Line a 9-by-5-inch bread pan with parchment paper or wax paper, or butter it generously and dust with flour.

In a heavy saucepan, melt the butter over low heat. Stir in the sugar and set aside.

Mix the flour, baking powder, and salt together in a medium bowl. Add the dried fruits and toss to break up clumps and coat with flour.

Break the eggs into a 2-cup measuring cup and add enough milk to make 1 cup total.

Stir the melted butter mixture into the dry ingredients, mixing well until coarse crumbs form. Whisk the eggs and milk together briefly, then add to the bowl and turn and stir to moisten all flour. The texture will be thick and gloppy.

Spoon the batter into the prepared pan and smooth the top. Bake for 1 hour and 10 minutes, or until the cake is golden brown and a skewer inserted into the center comes out clean.

Let cool in the pan on a rack for 30 minutes, then turn out of the pan and let cool completely on the rack, 2 or 3 hours. Or, better still, let stand overnight, to give the crumb a chance to firm up before slicing. The cake is delicious before that, but it will be slightly crumbly until cooled and set. It keeps very well.

ukrainian honey cake

Makes 1 loaf-shaped cake, dark brown and with a moist golden crumb, flavored with coffee, honey, and cinnamon

This classic eastern European cake is darkened in both color and taste with espresso coffee, and sweetened with honey. Honey cakes are often made fancy with nuts or raisins or complex spicing; we like the clean clear taste of this simple version, a close cousin of English–style gingerbread (see page 353). The cake bakes to a dark rich brown on top, with an invitingly tacky surface. It slices beautifully.

2 large eggs, separated, at room temperature

½ cup sugar

½ cup honey

4 tablespoons unsalted butter, melted

1½ cups all-purpose flour

1 teaspoon baking powder

½ teaspoon baking soda

⅛ teaspoon cinnamon

Pinch of salt

½ cup strong brewed coffee, cooled to lukewarm

Set a rack in the middle of the oven and preheat the oven to 350°F. Butter an 9-by-5-inch bread pan, then dust it with flour.

Using a mixer, or working by hand, beat the egg yolks and sugar until pale and smooth. Add the honey and melted butter and mix until blended and smooth.

Sift the dry ingredients into a bowl. Add half the dry ingredients to the egg mixture and stir in. Stir in the coffee, then stir in the remaining dry ingredients.

Beat the egg whites until soft peaks form. Fold them into the batter, then stir gently several times. The batter will be quite wet.

Pour the batter into the prepared pan and bake for 1 hour, or until a skewer inserted into the center comes out clean. Let cool for 10 minutes, then remove from the pan and place on a rack to cool completely before slicing. Eat plain or buttered, with hot tea or coffee.

Samarkand market, Uzbekistan

polish-jewish cheesecake

Makes one 8-inch square, firm European-style cheesecake, lightly flavored with lemon zest

The simplest cheesecake we know. There's no crust, no extra topping—just a light-textured baked custard cake made of classic eastern European pressed cottage cheese (see Cheeses in the Glossary), slightly sweetened and flavored. While the cake is still warm, the texture is light and soft; as it cools to room temperature, it compacts a little, becoming firmer. Either way, the cake invites you to take second and third helpings. Lemon zest is a traditional addition to cheesecake, from Corsica to Poland. The lemon tastes stronger right after baking, then gets milder by the next day. Eastern European Jewish cooks often use raisins instead of, or in addition to, the zest.

4 large eggs, separated, at room temperature

1 tablespoon unsalted butter, softened, or sour cream

$\frac{1}{2}$ cup vanilla sugar (see Sugars in the Glossary) or granulated sugar

2 tablespoons potato starch or cornstarch

Minced zest of 1 lemon ($1\frac{1}{2}$ to 2 teaspoons), or to taste

1 pound pressed cottage cheese, at room temperature

Place a rack in the upper third of the oven and preheat the oven to 325°F.

Set aside the egg whites in a medium bowl. Whisk the yolks in a large bowl. Stir in the butter or sour cream, then the sugar, starch, and zest. Add the cheese and stir thoroughly to blend well, about 1 minute.

Beat the egg whites until soft peaks form. Add about one-quarter of the beaten whites to the cheese mixture and stir in thoroughly. Fold in the remaining whites completely.

Pour the mixture into an 8-inch square cake pan and smooth the top. Bake until firm at the edges and almost set in the center, 30 to 40 minutes. Remove and let cool to room temperature. The texture will firm up and the center of the cheesecake will sink slightly as it cools.

NOTE Some cooks like to line the bottom of the cake pan with butter cookies or with crumbs for a contrast in texture and another layer of flavor.

buttermilk fruit cake

Makes 1 moist, date-and-raisin-laden 9-inch tube cake with a pale brown top

PHOTOGRAPH ON PAGE 356 *This soft-textured easy cake started life as a standard from my mother's kitchen. It came into the house when I was in primary school and then evolved, as family recipes do. It's made with no eggs and very little leavening, and it is aromatic with allspice, nutmeg, and cinnamon. Each mouthful is a satisfying blend of cake and dried fruit: dates, dark and golden raisins, and currants.*

1½ cups all-purpose flour

½ cup packed honey dates or pitted Medjouls
 (see Dates in the Glossary)

⅔ cup sugar

½ teaspoon salt

1 teaspoon allspice

1 teaspoon grated nutmeg

1 teaspoon cinnamon

1 teaspoon baking soda

1 cup buttermilk, heated until lukewarm, or 1 cup whole or
 reduced-fat milk with 1 tablespoon fresh lemon juice
 stirred in

8 tablespoons (1 stick) unsalted butter, melted

Packed ½ cup currants

½ cup dark raisins

½ cup golden raisins (sultanas)

Place a rack in the center of the oven and preheat the oven to 325°F. Butter a two-piece 10-inch tube pan (or a 9-by-5-inch bread pan) and dust lightly with flour. Place on a baking sheet.

Place ½ cup of the flour on your cutting board. Put the dates on the flour and coarsely chop (the flour prevents the dates from disintegrating or turning into a mush). Scrape the mixture into a bowl and set aside.

Place the remaining 1 cup flour in a large bowl, add the sugar, salt, spices, and baking soda, and stir to blend. Place the buttermilk in a bowl and stir in the melted butter, then pour the mixture into the dry ingredients. Add the flour and date mixture and the remaining fruit and stir to blend well. Immediately pour into the prepared pan. Smooth the top with a wet spatula.

Place the pan and baking sheet in the center of the oven and bake for about 50 minutes, or until the cake is golden and pulling away a little from the sides of the pan. A skewer inserted into the center of the cake should come out clean. Lift the tube out of the rim to remove the cake and place the cake on a rack to cool for 20 minutes or more before serving. Serve in thick slices.

NOTE We always leave this cake on the tube, storing it that way for the day or so it takes to get eaten. You can also remove it from the tube and place it on a plate: Run a knife between the cake and the tube to separate them, then tip the cake onto a plate.

lemon pound cake

Makes 1 large loaf cake, firm-textured and long keeping, with a lightly lemony taste and a smooth pale yellow crumb

The trick with pound cakes is good ingredients and long beating. It used to be such hard work to make them, but now with mixers, all you need is a little patience. This cake is an attractive golden brown on top, with the classic pound cake crack down the center. It keeps well for a week, getting better each day, it seems to us.

½ pound (2 sticks) unsalted butter, softened

About 2 cups sugar

4 large eggs, at room temperature

1 egg yolk, at room temperature

Grated zest of 2 (preferably organic) lemons

3 tablespoons freshly squeezed lemon juice

2 tablespoons cognac or other brandy

1½ cups all-purpose flour

1 teaspoon baking powder

Place a rack in the upper third of the oven and preheat the oven to 350°F. Butter a 9-by-5-inch bread pan and dust lightly with flour.

Work with a stand mixer fitted with the paddle attachment: Cream the butter well, then add the sugar and beat for 2 minutes at medium speed, until very smooth. Add the eggs, 1 at a time, beating for 30 seconds or more after each one, then beat in the egg yolk. Beat for 10 minutes.

Remove the bowl from the mixer. Stir in the lemon zest, juice, and cognac. Place a sieve over the bowl, add the flour and baking powder, and sift onto the egg mixture. Stir and fold in just until mixed.

Pour the batter into the prepared pan, using a spatula to smooth the top. Bake for about 1 hour and 10 minutes. The loaf will have a mounded top, with a crack down the center; a skewer inserted into the center of the cake should come out clean.

Let the cake cool in the pan for about 20 minutes then turn it out onto a wire rack to cool completely. Serve in thin slices cooled, or, even better, the next day. Store, once completely cooled, well sealed in plastic wrap, at room temperature for up to a week. Or, for longer storage, freeze, sealed in a double layer of plastic and foil, for up to 2 months.

naomi's any-day skillet cake

Makes 1 round low cake, about 9 inches in diameter and 1½ to 2 inches tall, with a tender crumb and a golden crust, topped with fruit if you wish

Make this quick cake plain, or toss on some fruit just before baking. It's a great cake to make when you're in a rush, with a moist light texture, and it slices beautifully once cooled. All you need is a heavy cast-iron or other ovenproof skillet, two bowls, a spoon, and a rubber scraper. The flavoring is up to you: You can substitute several tablespoons of rum or liqueur for the vanilla.

8 tablespoons (1 stick) unsalted butter, very soft,
    plus 2 tablespoons for buttering the pan

1 cup sugar

2 large eggs

1 cup plain full- or reduced-fat yogurt

1 teaspoon pure vanilla extract, or to taste

2 cups cake or pastry flour, or 1¾ cups all-purpose flour

1 teaspoon baking powder

½ teaspoon baking soda

½ teaspoon salt

1 teaspoon cinnamon

⅛ teaspoon ground cloves (optional)

TOPPING (OPTIONAL)

About 1 cup finely chopped fruit, such as plums, pears,
    apples, or peaches, or whole blueberries or raspberries

About 2 tablespoons sugar

Place a rack in the lower third of the oven and preheat the oven to 400°F.

Use a spoon or mixer to beat the butter and sugar together in a medium bowl. Add the eggs, yogurt, and vanilla and beat with a wooden spoon or with a mixer for about 1 minute. Set aside.

Place a 9- or 10-inch cast-iron or other heavy ovenproof skillet over low heat. Add about 2 tablespoons butter and melt it, then use a rubber spatula to spread the butter all over the inside surface of the skillet. Leave the skillet on low heat.

Meanwhile, combine the flour, baking powder, baking soda, salt, and spices in a large bowl and stir to blend. Add the yogurt mixture and fold in to blend well. Working fairly quickly, use a rubber scraper to scrape the batter into the warm skillet and smooth the top. Quickly arrange the fruit, if using, over the top, leaving a border, roughly 1 inch, around the edges. Sprinkle on the sugar.

Place the skillet in the oven, lower the temperature to 375°F, and bake until a skewer inserted into the center of the cake comes out clean, 30 to 35 minutes, depending on whether or not you used fruit. The top crust will be a rich golden brown. Let stand for 5 minutes.

Loosen the cake all around the edges with a knife, place a large plate over the skillet, and flip over to turn the cake out. (You can also serve it from the skillet.) Serve it fruit side down (this upside-down version gives you a nice smooth top surface if you're inspired to make a frosting), or use another plate and flip it back right side up again. Let cool for 30 minutes before serving. Refrigerate if keeping for longer than 24 hours.

Cacao, cloves, and cinnamon I found a taxi driver, Paolo, a young guy with an open face, to take me out looking for cacao trees. A friend of his named Rosa came along for the ride. Paolo slipped a cassette into the tape player, and as we drove along small roads that wound through the rolling Bahian countryside, the latest in Afro-bloco music pulsated from the car's speakers.

We pulled up to a tin-roofed house built into the side of a hill, hoping to get directions. There was a man next to the house digging in the hard red soil with a mattock. He straightened up and came over to meet us, shaking our hands with a steady gaze. His hand was big and work-roughened. He was living as the workers had a hundred years ago at the time of the cacao boom (just as I had read in Jorge Amado's famous novel *Gabriela, Cloves, and Cinnamon*), in one room with no electricity or running water.

He and Paolo talked for a bit, then Paolo pointed out several clove trees growing on the slope above the house. I climbed up to look at them more closely. They were spindly; the seed pods with their precious cargo were just small blobs at the ends of the branches, yet the air around the trees was aromatic with their sharp scent. Beyond was a graceful-looking cinnamon tree, with reddish-brown bark and a trunk no more than six inches across. Cinnamon sticks, or "quills," come from the bark, which is peeled off and rolled up. (The cinnamon we get in North America is more often cassia, a darker-colored, less subtle-tasting cousin of cinnamon.) The tree had slice marks on its trunk, and lots of dried-out leaves were lying around it. I picked some up, put them in my pockets, then realized I'd perfumed my hand with cinnamon.

A short while later, following the directions we'd been given, we drove down a small dirt lane and entered a cacao grove. The trees were as tall as big apple trees, and their thick, wide leaves made the light a watery green on the damp earth. The cacao fruits were large and hard, pale green to ivory. I'd been told that at the time of the boom, cacao was known as white gold, so great were the profits from growing it. The name hadn't made sense to me until then, since I'd thought of cacao as brown like chocolate. The fruits were shaped like small honeydew melons, with pointed ends. They grew not at the ends of branches, but out of the bark on the trunk of the trees, like foreign growths.

Paolo and Rosa showed me how to eat the fruit: "You start by breaking it in half, like this." Inside the thick peel was the flesh, gleaming white, with large dark brown seeds embedded in it. Following their example, I picked up a clump of the flesh, popped the whole thing in my mouth, and then sucked and

Bahian market vendor, Salvador, Bahia, Brazil

worked with my tongue and teeth to get all the pulp off the seeds. The fruit tasted wonderful, sweet and

perfumed like rambutan or a very intense lychee. The three of us stood in the grove eating fruit, happily

sucking and spitting.

I was embarrassed when I realized how little I knew about cacao fruit, the source of all the chocolate we

consume. The chocolate is in the seeds. If you bite into them, the seeds taste terrible, very bitter—kind of

like eating an olive straight off the tree, another bad taste experience. They have to be dried and processed

to produce cocoa solids and cocoa butter, then blended and sweetened to make chocolate. You wonder

how the ancients figured out the complicated process of making olives and cacao edible, let alone the way

to transform them into delicious foods.

There's another thing about cacao: The trees give off a subtle, enticing aroma of chocolate, like a hint

of the treasures that are hidden in the fruit.

brazilian bolo

Makes 1 tall ring-shaped or tube cake with a firm, moist crumb, lightly dusted with sugar

Mame, a longtime student of the art and culture of Bahia, in Brazil, passed on instructions for this simple cake with the following note: "Ana Christina Picky is from Salvador, Bahia, and she says this cake tastes just like the one her mother makes. When I served it to Brazilian and Argentinian visitors, they really liked it and called it bolo auténtico *("authentic cake")!!" It is leavened with beaten eggs and baking powder, but it contains no butter or other dairy—just coconut milk.*

2 cups all-purpose flour

½ cup cornstarch

2 teaspoons baking powder

5 large eggs, separated

1¾ cups sugar

1 cup coconut milk (well stirred before measuring)

2 teaspoons to 2 tablespoons confectioners' sugar for dusting (see Note)

Place a rack in the center of the oven and preheat the oven to 350°F. Grease a 10-inch Bundt pan or a tube pan, and dust lightly with flour.

Sift the flour, cornstarch, and baking powder together into a bowl. Set aside.

In a large bowl, beat the egg whites with an electric mixer (or a whisk) until stiff but not dry; set aside.

In a medium bowl, stir the egg yolks and sugar together to blend. Gradually add the yolk mixture to the egg whites, beating at medium speed (or whisking) until incorporated. Add about ¾ cup of the dry ingredients, mixing on low speed (or stirring in with a wooden spoon), then add about ⅓ cup of the coconut milk, and mix well. Repeat, alternating the dry ingredients and coconut milk and mixing completely.

Pour the batter into the pan. Bake until a wooden skewer inserted in the center of the cake comes out clean, about 40 minutes. Cool for 10 minutes, then invert onto a rack. Sprinkle on a dusting of sifted confectioners' sugar (about 2 teaspoons, or more if you wish). Let cool completely before slicing (see Note).

NOTE As the cake stands, the confectioners' sugar will melt and give it an attractive sheen. If you prefer the look of a white dusting of confectioners' sugar, just before serving dust the cake again with 2 to 3 teaspoons confectioners' sugar.

CITRUS BOLO We like to amend this simple cake by adding orange or lemon zest. Grated or minced zest from 1 (preferably organic) fruit gives the cake a great flavor. Add the zest to the sifted dry ingredients.

childhood gingerbread with molasses

Makes one 8-inch square cake with a shiny, dark surface and a tender, aromatic crumb

Working on this book has taken us new places, and also back to explore taste memories from the past and from travel. Sometimes we've stumbled on childhood tastes, and sometimes we've gone looking for them.

This dark gingerbread is from scribbled notes I found in an old cookbook of my mother's. I don't know where she got the recipe, but I do know that she made it regularly, especially in winter, when its rich, warm scent would draw us into the kitchen at dinnertime. Serve it as a snack or for dessert.

2 cups all-purpose flour

2 teaspoons baking powder

1 teaspoon cinnamon

1 teaspoon powdered ginger, or up to 2 teaspoons for a stronger ginger bite

½ teaspoon allspice

1 cup blackstrap molasses or dark molasses

1 cup boiling water

½ cup packed light brown sugar (see Note)

8 tablespoons (1 stick) salted butter (if using unsalted butter, add ¼ teaspoon salt to the dry ingredients), cut into small chunks, softened

2 large or extra-large eggs, at room temperature

Place a rack in the upper third of the oven and preheat the oven to around 365°F (set the dial halfway between 350° and 375°F). Generously grease an 8-inch square cake pan.

Combine the flour, baking powder, and powdered spices in a medium bowl and mix well; set aside. Pour the molasses into a 2-cup (or more) measuring cup, add the boiling water, and stir to dissolve thoroughly. Set aside.

Place the brown sugar and butter chunks in a large bowl and cream together with a wooden spoon, or a mixer. Briefly beat the eggs in another bowl, then stir them into the butter-sugar mixture. Add about ½ cup of the flour mixture and stir or beat in on low speed, then add about the same amount of warm molasses-water and stir. Continue to add the flour and liquid alternately, stirring or beating briefly each time. After the final addition, beat briefly (the batter will be quite liquid), then pour into the prepared pan.

Bake for 25 minutes, then lower the heat to 350°F and bake until done, for 15 to 20 minutes longer, until a skewer inserted into the center comes out clean.

Let cool in the pan for 20 minutes or more (to allow the crumb to set) before serving. Serve from the pan.

NOTE If your brown sugar has lumps, grind or pound to a powder in a mortar or food processor.

pain aux pruneaux

Makes one 9-inch round, low-rise moist cake, spiced with black pepper and dotted with cognac-soaked prunes

This low-rise cake tastes of rural France long ago. It's made of an all-buckwheat batter enriched with eggs and sweetened with a little honey. The recipe is an adaptation of one we found in a book of old "great-grandmother" recipes while we were staying in a small gîte in Normandy, not far from Mont-Saint-Michel. Unusual and delicious.

1 cup pitted prunes

½ cup cognac or Armagnac

1 tablespoon honey, heated until runny

2 large eggs

1¼ cups light buckwheat flour
   (see Buckwheat in the Glossary)

½ teaspoon salt

¼ teaspoon freshly ground black pepper

1 cup whole milk

Chop the prunes into 2 or 3 pieces each. Soak them in the cognac for 8 to 24 hours.

Place a baking stone or unglazed quarry tiles, if you have them, (or a heavy baking sheet) on a rack in the lower third of the oven and preheat the oven to 375°F. Butter a 9-inch cast-iron or other heavy ovenproof skillet.

Whisk the honey and eggs together in a medium bowl until tripled in volume. In a small bowl, mix together the flour, salt, and pepper. Stir ⅓ cup of the flour into the egg mixture, then stir in ⅓ cup of the milk. Repeat, alternating until all the flour and milk have been stirred in. Fold in the prunes and any remaining cognac.

Pour the batter into the skillet. Bake for 20 minutes, or until a faint line of brown forms around the edges of the cake and the cake is starting to pull away from the sides of the skillet. There will be small bubbles or holes on the surface.

Remove from the oven and let cool for 10 or more minutes before serving. The top surface of the cake will be tacky, but the crumb will be firm and spongy. Serve from the skillet, or flip onto a plate.

lemon jelly roll

Makes 1 sugar-coated moist jelly roll, lightly flavored with lemon and filled with prune paste or jam; 15 to 18 slices

PHOTOGRAPH ON PAGE 357 *My mother made jelly rolls once in a while. Her jelly rolls were pale yellow sponge cakes spread with a little jam, usually raspberry, then rolled up. The granulated sugar—coated outside gave them a pleasing crunch.*

We fill our jelly roll with prune paste, or jam, or lemon curd, even sweetened cream cheese. (The filling must be thick yet easy to spread—warm and soften it as necessary.) This recipe makes one long jelly roll—roulade, if you prefer the fancier name.

1¼ cups Prune Paste (page 37), or a scant 1¼ cups
    thick jam or lemon curd

¾ cup sugar, plus about ½ cup for coating the cake

½ cup water

5 large eggs

Minced zest of 1 lemon, or ½ teaspoon lemon oil
    (see Glossary)

2 tablespoons freshly squeezed lemon juice

Scant ¾ cup all-purpose flour

Place a rack in the center of the oven and preheat the oven to 375°F. Line an 18-by-12-inch baking sheet with parchment or wax paper; lightly butter the paper or brush with oil.

The filling should be smooth and very spreadable. If using prune paste or jam that is very lumpy, heat it gently, add a little butter or water to extend it and smooth it, and stir well until smooth; set aside.

Combine the ¾ cup sugar and the water in a saucepan and stir to dissolve the sugar over low heat, then bring to a boil, and boil for about 5 minutes.

Meanwhile, using a stand mixer fitted with the whisk attachment, whip the eggs until foamy, 1 to 2 minutes. Remove the sugar syrup from the heat, immediately turn the mixer on high speed, and slowly pour the hot syrup down the side of the bowl as you whip the eggs. (The syrup must be poured slowly down the side of the bowl—avoiding the whisk—so as not to spatter.) The eggs will turn runny and loose, then will whiten and lighten. Continue whisking on high speed until completely cool,

about 5 minutes. The eggs will more than triple in volume and turn pale.

Remove the bowl from the mixer. Add the zest or oil, and juice, then fold in the flour, ¼ cup at a time.

Pour the batter onto the prepared baking sheet and smooth with a spatula. Bake for 10 minutes, or until the cake is pale with touches of brown at the edges and is pulling away from the edges of the pan. Remove from the oven and set aside for a moment.

Rinse a cotton cloth or tea towel in cool water, then wring it out thoroughly. Lay the cloth flat on the counter, with a long side facing you, and sprinkle on about ½ cup sugar in a rectangular area the size of the cake. Carefully flip the cake out onto the sugared towel, with a long side toward you and the underside of the cake facing up. (It may feel a little scary the first time you do it, but in fact it just drops easily out of the pan and onto the sugar.) Peel off the baking paper. (The surface of the cake that is on the sugar will eventually be the outside of the roll.)

Spread the filling in a thin layer all over the cake, leaving a ½-inch border along the far side.

Grasp the towel under the front edge and use it to start rolling the cake away from you. Once you get the first edge turned, roll carefully, then pull the towel tightly around the outside of the cake and tuck in to hold the roll in its shape. Let stand for 3 minutes.

Unwrap the roll and place seam side down on a long platter. Let cool for 30 minutes before slicing.

semolina 1-2-3 cake

Makes 1 square golden cake, soaked in flower-scented honey syrup; about 16 servings

A traditional home-style cake from Lebanon called monmoura, *this useful cake is flavored with lemon, then doused in aromatic syrup the moment it comes out of the oven. It's as easy as 1-2-3. There are no eggs in it, just yogurt and semolina (the coarser grind,* semola *in Italian). It is traditionally served cut into squares and eaten as a snack with tea or coffee. Because of the honey syrup, the cake is very moist and keeps well.*

2 tablespoons unsalted butter, softened

½ cup sugar

1½ cups plain full- or reduced-fat yogurt

Minced zest of 2 lemons

½ teaspoon lemon oil (see Glossary),

    or 2 tablespoons freshly squeezed lemon juice

2 cups coarse semolina (not fine semolina flour; see Glossary)

¼ teaspoon salt

¼ teaspoon baking soda

SYRUP

1 cup sugar

½ cup water

½ teaspoon orange flower water

    (see Scented Waters in the Glossary)

½ teaspoon rose water

2 teaspoons freshly squeezed lemon juice

4 tablespoons unsalted butter, cut into small chunks

Place a rack in the center of the oven and preheat the oven to 350°F. Lightly butter an 8-inch square cake pan.

Beat the butter and sugar together in a small bowl, then beat in the yogurt. Stir in the lemon zest and oil or juice; set aside.

In a medium bowl, combine the semolina, salt, and baking soda. Stir in the yogurt mixture, mixing well.

Pour the batter into the greased pan and smooth the top with a wet spatula. Bake until the cake is touched with gold and pulling away from the sides of the pan, about 25 minutes.

Meanwhile, make the syrup: In a medium saucepan, combine the sugar and water and bring to a boil over medium-high heat, stirring to dissolve the sugar. Add the flower waters and lemon juice. Remove from the heat and add the butter, stirring until it melts. Set aside the syrup to cool to room temperature.

Pour the syrup over the hot cake as soon as it comes out of the oven; use just some or all of the syrup, as you please. Let the cake stand for an hour or longer so the syrup has time to penetrate the cake and infuse it with flavor. Serve from the pan.

PRECEDING PAGES: BUTTERMILK FRUIT CAKE *(page 347)*. LEMON JELLY ROLL *(page 355) filled with jam.*

simple frosting

Makes about 1 cup frosting

If you're making frosting for a building–block cake (see page 360), make plenty, then divide it into smaller containers so it can be tinted different colors with food coloring. When they were small, our children liked pink frosting on the castle or tower, and then blue for the moat, green for grass, etc.

Here are the basic proportions for a simple icing that we find very reliable.

8 tablespoons (1 stick) unsalted butter, melted
1½ cups confectioners' sugar
Up to 2 tablespoons milk or cream
2 drops pure vanilla extract (optional)

Pour the melted butter into a bowl. Sift on the sugar, then stir in, using a wooden spoon. Stir in a little milk or cream to thin it to a spreadable consistency. Stir in the vanilla, if desired. Cover and place in the refrigerator for 30 minutes to firm up a little before using.

To tint the frosting, add food coloring, a drop at a time (it takes very few drops of red to get a good pink color, for example), and do not mix more than two colors (say, a drop of red in a yellow-dyed batch to get a peach color, or a little blue into yellow to tint it green).

Building-block cake We've come to rely on a nontraditional version of *monmoura* (Semolina 1-2-3 Cake, page 358), without the syrup, to make our "building-block cake," which can be cut and stacked to make interesting frosted birthday cake structures. When they were smaller, our children liked the castle motif, and this cake makes a great four-layer fortified tower.

Make a double recipe of the semolina cake and bake it in a 13-by-9-inch baking pan. It will take about 10 minutes longer to bake through. Let the cake cool completely. Meanwhile, make about 2 cups of Simple Frosting, page 359.

To make a tower, cut the cake into quarters. Stack the squares on top of one another, using frosting between the layers to help hold them together. Cover the tower with frosting, then, using a knife or chopstick, draw brick patterns in it. Top with candies, if you wish, or with triangles of Toblerone chocolate bars to make "crenellations"—or whatever imagination suggests to you. You can also set the tower on a foil-wrapped tray and then tint another batch of frosting different colors to make a moat or grass or whatever else you can think up. Our children and their friends used to decorate the castle "lawn" with "flowers" (candies of various kinds).

Harborside, Manila, Philippines

uzbek layered walnut confection

Makes a multilayered chewy sweetmeat, thin flatbreads stacked with a sweetened walnut filling and drenched in butter-honey syrup

More like a "sweetmeat" than our North American idea of cake, this is ideal for serving the way we've had it in central Asia—when guests are visiting to celebrate an occasion. In Uzbek it's called paklama, *and it's like a very hearty baklava, but instead of phyllo, the layers are made of egg-rich flatbreads, rolled into thin rounds and layered with crushed walnuts and sugar. A thick butter-and-honey syrup seeps into the stack as it bakes, sweetening and enriching it.*

DOUGH

5 extra-large eggs

½ cup milk

¼ teaspoon salt

About 3¼ cups all-purpose flour

FILLING

2 cups coarsely chopped walnuts, lightly toasted
(see Nuts in the Glossary)

1¼ cups sugar

1 egg yolk, beaten with a scant tablespoon of water,
for egg wash

6 tablespoons unsalted butter, melted

½ cup honey, heated until lukewarm and runny

Break the eggs into a bowl, add the milk, and whisk until frothy, about 1 minute. Sprinkle on the salt, then add 2½ cups of the flour, and stir until smooth. Add ½ cup more flour and fold to combine it, then turn dough out onto a lightly floured surface and knead for 3 to 5 minutes. It should be soft rather than stiff, and very smooth. Cover with plastic and let rest for 1 hour.

Meanwhile, place a rack in the center of the oven and preheat the oven to 350°F. Lightly butter a baking sheet.

Mix the walnuts with the sugar in a bowl, and set aside.

On a lightly floured surface, roll the dough under your palms into a cylinder about 16 inches long. Cut it into 8 pieces. Roll each piece under your palm into a ball, then set aside, covered, to rest for 5 minutes.

Work with 2 balls at a time on a lightly floured surface, keeping the rest covered. Roll 1, then switch to the other to give the first ball time to relax, then roll it out more. Continue until each is a thin 8-inch circle.

Place one dough circle on the buttered baking sheet. Sprinkle on a generous ¼ cup of the walnut mixture and top with another dough circle. Repeat with the remaining filling and dough until all the dough is rolled out and stacked, ending with a dough circle. Brush the top of the stack with the egg wash.

Make 2-inch cuts about 1½ inches apart around the outside edge of the stack, as if marking it into wedges. Then make more cuts vertically through all the layers about 2 inches from the center, to make a dashed line that suggests a circle. Slowly pour the melted butter over the cake, so it can soak in through the cuts.

Bake for 10 minutes, remove from the oven, and then slowly pour on the honey so it penetrates the cuts. Bake for another 30 minutes, or until golden, basting with sweet drippings several times.

Transfer to a cake plate, and let cool completely before slicing.

NOTE In the fascinating collection called *A Taste of Thyme* (see Bibliography), there's an article by Charles Perry called "Layered Breads Among Nomadic Turks," in which he looks for the origins of baklava and finds them among the Turkic people of central Asia. He connects Turkmen *gatlama* with baklava and views layered flatbread confections like this as the "missing link" between the two.

breton butter cake

Makes 1 round golden cake with a caramelized top and bottom crust and a layered buttery crumb; serves 8 to 10

Kouignaman is the Breton name of this very traditional cake, made of yeasted bread dough enriched with butter and sugar. The butter is salted, as farm butter traditionally is for longer keeping, rather than the unsalted butter of most baking recipes. The dough is folded over the butter and sugar. This makes a layered crumb like a very simple puff pastry or croissant. The cake is so good, and so easy, that we find ourselves using the technique often with an end of risen bread dough. You can use a pound of any mostly white bread dough, homemade or store-bought, including pizza dough, or a quarter of the Standby Dough, or even a whole wheat dough (see the variation on page 331). The baked cake is a low golden dome with caramelized sugar on top and bottom.

1 to 1½ pounds risen yeasted mostly white bread dough or Standby Dough (page 367), at room temperature

¼ to ⅓ pound ice-cold butter, preferably salted butter (see headnote)

¼ teaspoon salt (if using unsalted butter)

About ¾ cup sugar

About 2 tablespoons salted butter, melted

On a lightly floured surface, flatten the dough out to a rectangle at least 12 inches long and 5 to 6 inches wide. Thinly slice the butter and divide it into 3 equal portions. Place 1 portion, in pieces, over two-thirds of the length of the dough. Sprinkle over about ¼ cup sugar. Fold the bare third of the dough over the butter, then fold the other flap over that, like folding a letter. Flatten the dough out again to a rectangle and repeat with butter and sugar. Flatten once more, then repeat with butter only. The dough will feel soft and the butter may be breaking though a little. Don't worry.

Lightly grease a baking sheet. Place the dough on the baking sheet and flatten it once more, pressing it out with your fingertips to form a round about 9 inches across. (If you want a very even round, place it inside a 9-inch cake ring.) Cut 6 or 7 cuts right through the dough, each about 2 inches long, in a starburst pattern radiating out from near the center. Cover with plastic and let rise for 45 minutes to an hour.

Meanwhile, place a rack in the lower third of the oven and place a baking stone or unglazed quarry tiles, if you have them, (or a baking sheet) on it. Preheat the oven to 450°F.

Just before baking, brush the melted butter over the cake and sprinkle on sugar generously, about 3 tablespoons. Bake for 20 to 25 minutes, until very golden brown. Both the top and bottom of the cake will have a caramelized surface—remove it from the pan, decide whether you want top or bottom side up, and place on a rack accordingly to cool for at least 30 minutes. Serve cut into wedges.

FOLLOWING PAGES: THREE-LAYER WALNUT TORTE WITH WHIPPED CREAM (*page 370*). EVA'S CHOCOLATE-FLAVORED CAKE (*page 368*) with CHOCOLATE ICING (*page 369*).

fruit-topped country cake

Makes 1 tender round or square cake, topped with sliced pear or apple; serves 8

This cake is adapted from a recipe for a cake from Burgundy in Mireille Johnston's evocative cookbook The Cuisine of the Rose. *It probably has its origins in the country habit of using the end of a yeasted bread dough to make a cake. In this case, the dough is enriched with a little butter, then topped with fruit and sugar before its second rise. Easy as pie . . . easier than pie! Serve it warm, like a baked dessert, or let it cool and serve it cut into slices like a cake.*

This recipe makes a dough from scratch. You can also begin with ¾ pound yeasted white flour bread dough instead (see the Note).

DOUGH

1 tablespoon sugar

¼ cup warm water

2 teaspoons active dry yeast

1 large egg

¼ teaspoon salt

1 tablespoon unsalted butter, softened

1½ cups all-purpose flour

TOPPING

1 large or 2 small pears or apples

About ¼ cup sugar

1 to 1½ teaspoons cinnamon

About 2 teaspoons unsalted butter, cut into small chunks

To make the dough, stir the sugar into the warm water, then stir in the yeast. Beat the egg in a medium bowl. Stir in the salt and butter, then ½ cup of the flour. Stir briefly, then add the yeast mixture and stir in. Add ¾ cup more flour and stir in, then turn the dough out onto a floured surface and knead until firm and smooth, about 4 minutes.

Place the dough in a clean bowl and cover well with plastic wrap. Let rise until doubled in volume, about 1½ hours.

When ready to bake, place a rack in the upper third of the oven and preheat the oven to 400°F.

Butter a 9-inch square or 10-inch round shallow cake pan or 10-inch tart pan. Prepare the fruit: Peel, core, and thinly slice; then set aside.

Flatten the dough out in the prepared pan. Sprinkle with half the sugar and half the cinnamon, then arrange the fruit slices decoratively on top, to cover the whole surface. Sprinkle on the remaining sugar and cinnamon and then dot with the small pieces of butter. Let stand, covered, for 10 minutes.

Bake for about 20 minutes, until golden. Serve hot or at room temperature.

NOTE You can also begin with about ¾ pound risen bread dough, such as the Standby Dough (page 367). Once the dough has had its first rise, knead 1 beaten egg into it, 1 tablespoon softened unsalted butter, and about ¾ cup flour (enough to absorb the liquid from the egg and make the dough less sticky). Let the dough rest, covered, for 15 minutes, then assemble and bake the cake as directed.

standby dough

Makes just more than 3 pounds tender dough

Make this dough, then divide it up and freeze it. You'll be pleased to have a dough on hand that you can use for yeasted cakes and tarts such as Breton Butter Cake, (page 363), Bread Baker's Fruit Tart (page 34), and Chocolate Bread Batons (page 256).

POOLISH

1 cup lukewarm water

Scant ¼ teaspoon active dry yeast

1 cup all-purpose flour

DOUGH

2 cups lukewarm water

1 teaspoon active dry yeast

2 cups pastry or cake flour

2 teaspoons salt

4 to 5 cups all-purpose flour

Make the poolish 10 to 36 hours before you wish to bake: Place the water in a bowl and stir in the yeast. Let stand briefly to make sure it dissolves. Stir in the flour and stir well until you have a smooth batter. Cover and let ferment for 6 to 24 hours.

When ready to proceed, place the poolish in a large bowl and stir in the water and yeast. Let stand for a moment to give the yeast time to dissolve. Stir in the pastry or cake flour until smooth, then sprinkle on salt and stir in. Add 3½ cups of the all-purpose flour, a cup at a time, stirring to incorporate the flour. Turn the dough out onto a generously floured surface and knead, incorporating flour as necessary, until smooth and still soft, but no longer sticky.

Place the dough in a clean bowl, cover with plastic wrap, and set aside to rise for 3 to 4 hours, until more than doubled in volume.

Use right away (or divide in pieces), seal well in plastic, and refrigerate for up to 2 days or freeze. Divide it in three (1 pound each), in four (¾ pound each), or in half (1½ pounds each). Bring back to room temperature before using.

eva's chocolate-flavored cake

Makes one 8-inch round two-layer cake, flavored with chocolate and nuts and topped with a chocolate icing

PHOTOGRAPH ON PAGE 365 *My great-aunt Eva lived well into her nineties, and as far back as I can remember, she lived in the same house at the corner of 17th and Custer in Laramie, Wyoming. A pretty white picket fence enclosed her yard and garden.*

Eva, who was my godmother as well as my great-aunt, had a beautiful warm smile and sparkling eyes, and every time I would go to visit, from the time I was a small child, she would put out tea and cookies.

When I was eighteen and just starting to be keen about cooking, she invited me over for an afternoon, sat me down (with tea and cookies), and brought out fifteen or twenty of her favorite recipe cards. She took me carefully through each one. There was a baked spaghetti, a chicken casserole, a meat loaf. All were good, all, like Eva, warm and welcoming.

Every year on my birthday Eva baked a cake, and every year she would ask me ahead of time what kind of cake I would like. I always asked for this one, my favorite. I liked the cake so much that as I grew older I would ask my mother not to bring the cake out when other people were around; that way there would be more for me (it was my birthday, after all). When the cake was down to half, I would freeze the rest, and for weeks thereafter I would reach into the freezer, take out the foil-wrapped rock-hard cake, and cut off a sliver with a sharp chef's knife. Even in the tiniest of slices, it was the best.

Years after Eva died, our friend Dina used Eva's recipe to bake the cake for me on a special occasion. "It's barely chocolate!" Dina cried out, tasting a first bite. "All these years you've been going on about this chocolate cake, and it's barely chocolate." I had to admit that she was right. It wasn't particularly chocolatey, and not particularly sweet.

"Who cares?" I said to Dina. "This is the cake I like."

Eva's cake is an older style of chocolate cake; it uses chocolate as a restrained kind of flavoring and has only a mild chocolate taste. The frosting is very chocolatey though, and that's how I like it, the frosting a contrast to the cake. If you want more chocolate taste in the cake itself, you can substitute 1 tablespoon cocoa powder for 1 tablespoon of the flour.

2 cups packed light brown sugar

1 cup vegetable shortening, or ½ pound (2 sticks)
    unsalted butter, softened

2 ounces unsweetened chocolate, melted and cooled
    to lukewarm

4 extra-large eggs, separated

Pinch of salt (omit if using salted butter)

2 cups sifted all-purpose flour

1 cup milk

½ cup chopped sliced almonds or chopped walnuts

Chocolate Icing (recipe follows) or confectioners' sugar
    for dusting

Place a rack in the center of the oven and preheat the oven to 350°F. Lightly grease two 8-inch round cake pans.

Use a mixer fitted with the paddle attachment to cream the sugar and shortening or butter together until pale and smooth. Add the cooled chocolate and beat until incorporated. Add the yolks and salt and beat until smooth. Remove the bowl from the mixer.

Add ½ cup flour to the butter mixture and stir it with a wooden spoon; stir in a third of the milk. Go on alternating until all the flour and milk have been added. Stir in the nuts.

Use a mixer or a whisk to beat the whites to soft but sturdy peaks. Scoop about a quarter of the beaten whites onto the batter and mix in well with a wooden spoon. Add the remaining whites and fold in.

Pour the batter into the prepared pans. Smooth the tops with a wet spatula. Bake for about 25 minutes. A skewer inserted into the center of each cake should come out clean. Turn the layers out onto a fine-meshed wire rack to cool and firm up. You can serve each cake just dusted with confectioners' sugar, but we prefer to make a stacked cake with chocolate frosting.

Place one layer on a plate upside down and spread a layer of icing on top, using a rubber spatula. Place the other layer on top, again upside down, and frost the top. If you wish to coat the sides of the cake as well, spread the frosting from the top downward, smoothing it with the spatula.

chocolate icing
Makes about ½ cup firm, smooth dark chocolate frosting
(enough to fill and frost an 8-inch round two-layer cake)

This is the simplest frosting we know: two ingredients, imprecise proportions, a smooth texture for spreading, and a good taste. James Beard attributed it to his friend Helen Evans Brown, author of The West Coast Cookbook. *Use whatever dark chocolate or semisweet chocolate you like the taste of. Do not use milk chocolate.*

This makes enough to fill the layers, as well as frost the top and sides of the cake. If you'd rather leave the sides unfrosted (the British way), use only 3 ounces chocolate (or 3 ounces chocolate chips) and 3 tablespoons sour cream.

4 ounces bittersweet or semisweet chocolate,
    chopped, or bittersweet chocolate chips
About ¼ cup sour cream (full-fat)

In a small heavy saucepan, heat the chocolate over medium-low heat until just melted. Set aside to cool to room temperature.

Use a wooden spoon to stir the sour cream into the chocolate, 1 tablespoon at a time, until it reaches a thickened spreadable texture. Use the icing immediately.

three-layer walnut torte with whipped cream

Makes one 7-inch pale brown, airy torte, flavored with walnuts and layered with whipped cream

PHOTOGRAPH ON PAGE 364 *The fine baking traditions of the Austro-Hungarian Empire have traveled far and wide, from the Viennese contribution to Danishes and French* viennoiseries *(enriched white breads and rolls) to the strudels and croissants made in bakeries from Berlin to Boston. Home bakers, too, carry their traditions with them when they emigrate, so it's not all that strange—though it's still wonderful—to come across a recipe dated 1943 for a traditional homemade walnut torte in the* Bryn Mawr Cookbook. *(The small spiral binder was passed on to us by a friend.) The contributor says it comes from her family's housekeeper, who had emigrated from Hungary.*

The cake is made of ground walnuts and fresh bread crumbs, all held up and made airy by well-beaten eggs. The walnuts disappear into the cake, giving it flavor and a little bite. The three layers that make up the torte are shallow round cakes that can be made ahead and assembled in a stack at the last minute, with a little whipped cream between them. The torte looks like the special-occasion confection it is, a great party cake, meant to be demolished by a hungry crowd.

This is an adaptation of the bare-bones recipe (instructions were spare, assuming a familiarity with cakes and baking; the filling was left to the cook's imagination). We use a mixer—the recipe, while very simple, requires much beating of eggs. In earlier times, of course, all that whisking would have been done with muscle power. With a machine to help, the whole cake takes just minutes, and no sweat, to make.

10 extra-large or 12 large eggs, separated,
**   at room temperature**

1 cup sugar

¾ cup fairly packed fresh white bread crumbs (see Notes)

2½ cups ground walnuts (see Notes)

1 teaspoon ground cloves

FILLING

Scant 1 cup heavy (whipping) cream

About 3 tablespoons sugar or vanilla sugar
**   (see Sugars in the Glossary)**

2 to 3 drops pure vanilla extract (optional)

Place a rack in the center of the oven and preheat the oven to 400°F. Lightly grease three 7-inch round cake pans (even if they are nonstick), using an oiled cloth or a spray. Dust them very lightly with flour.

Using a stand mixer fitted with the whisk, start beating the egg yolks, then gradually add the sugar as you continue to whisk. Whisk for 4 to 5 minutes to get a thick, smooth mixture. Transfer to a large clean bowl. Stir in the bread crumbs, walnuts, and cloves to make a thick heavy batter and set aside, loosely covered.

With a clean whisk, in a clean mixer bowl, whisk the egg whites at high speed until you have stiff peaks. Add about one-quarter of the whites to the batter and stir them in, then use a rubber spatula to fold in the rest. You'll feel awkward perhaps, because there is such a large amount of whites and the batter is heavy—just turn and fold gently, without worrying too much. Some further blending will also happen as you pour the batter out into the cake pans.

Divide the batter equally among the cake pans and gently smooth the top of each with a spatula. Bake for about 20 minutes. A skewer inserted into the centers will come out clean, and the cakes will look quite brown and a little bumpy on top; don't worry. Let the cakes cool in their pans for 15 or 20 minutes.

Put out several fine-wire mesh racks. Ease a knife around the rim of each cake layer to detach sticking places and turn them out onto the wire racks to cool completely. Once they are completely cooled, cover loosely to prevent them drying out while they wait.

Just before you wish to serve the cake, whip the cream with the sugar and flavoring, if using, until stiff. Place one cake layer on a plate upside down. Spread about ¼ cup whipped cream on top of it to just short of the edge all around, then repeat with the next layer. Place the third cake on top, again with the smooth bottom side up. Leave the top of the torte plain, or spread a little whipped cream on it. Serve a small dollop of the remaining whipped cream with each slice, if you wish.

Use a finely serrated knife to cut into slices. Serve immediately.

NOTES Cut slices from a large loaf of good white bread and trim off the crusts. Break the slices into several pieces and place in a food processor. Process briefly to get crumbs. (See also page 333.)

Walnuts must be very fresh to be good. Taste your walnuts before you begin, to be sure they are fresh. We like to begin with walnut pieces (less expensive than whole walnuts) and use the food processor to grind them. Be sure to process briefly, only until they are small crumbs; if you go on too long, they'll turn into a paste. Store walnuts well sealed in two layers of plastic in the freezer for no longer than 2 months.

Walnut seller in the main market, Tbilisi, Georgia

ALL-AROUND-THE-WORLD COOKIES

vietnamese peanut cookies

Makes 22 to 24 rich, small round cookies, each topped with a peanut half

Of all the cookies we've made, these rank among the top for universal approval among tasters young and old. They're small, flattened, tender rounds, sweet but not cloying.

This recipe makes a small amount. For a bigger batch, double all the ingredients, but make the doubled sugar a scant measure. You can substitute butter or shortening for the lard, if you wish.

½ cup skinned unsalted peanuts, lightly toasted
   (see Nuts in the Glossary)
1 large hard-boiled egg yolk
½ cup packed chopped palm sugar, or ¼ cup each
   packed light brown sugar and chopped maple sugar
   (see Sugars in the Glossary)
2 tablespoons lard, vegetable shortening, or unsalted butter
½ cup unbleached pastry flour, or a scant ½ cup
   all-purpose flour
About 2 tablespoons confectioners' sugar

Position a rack in the center of the oven and preheat the oven to 325°F. Line a baking sheet with parchment paper or lightly grease it.

Split 12 peanuts into their 2 halves and set aside.

Place the egg yolk, sugar, and the remaining peanuts in a food processor and process until crumbly but not pasty. Add the lard (or shortening or butter) and flour and process just until combined, less than 1 minute.

Place the confectioners' sugar in a shallow bowl near your work surface. Scoop up a heaping teaspoon of dough, roll between your palms into a ball, roll it lightly in the confectioners' sugar, and place on the prepared baking sheet. Top with one of the reserved peanut halves, pressing it in gently to flatten the cookie slightly; if the cookie cracks, just smooth the edges. Repeat with the remaining dough, leaving about 1 inch between the cookies.

Bake for 6 to 8 minutes, or until flattened and just beginning to turn golden. Let cool slightly on the pan, then transfer to a wire rack to cool completely before serving.

coriander cookies

Makes 2 baking sheets' worth (2 dozen large rectangles) of pale medium-thin cookies, flavored with coriander seed and sugar

PHOTOGRAPH ON PAGE 397 *This is our take on a cookie recipe dated 1805 in André Simon's* Cyclopedia of Gastronomy. *It's a great find, simple and very good. The cookies keep well, so they're a perfect cookie jar item. They're a little sweet, and make a pleasing semicrisp snack with tea or coffee.*

1 cup sugar, plus (optional) sugar for sprinkling

½ cup water

3¼ to 3½ cups all-purpose flour

4 tablespoons cool unsalted butter, cut into small pieces

Scant ½ teaspoon baking soda

1 tablespoon coriander seeds, lightly toasted and ground

¼ teaspoon salt

**1 large egg, beaten with about 1 tablespoon milk,
   for egg wash (optional)**

Position a rack in the center of the oven and preheat the oven to 325°F. Lightly butter two baking sheets.

In a small saucepan, dissolve the sugar in the water and place over medium heat. Bring just to a boil, without stirring so it stays smooth. Set aside to cool to lukewarm.

In a large bowl or a food processor, combine 3¼ cups flour and the butter, cutting in the butter with a pastry cutter or your fingertips, or pulsing to mix. Add the baking soda, ground coriander, and salt, and mix. Add the sugar syrup and mix until a firm dough forms, tossing a little extra flour if necessary to get a firm dough.

Turn the dough out onto a lightly floured surface and cut into 2 equal pieces. Cover 1 well to prevent it from drying out while you work with the other. (You can also seal it in plastic wrap and refrigerate it, a good idea if your kitchen is warm or if you don't have time to bake the second batch now. Bake it within 2 days.) Roll out the dough about ⅛ inch thick. Cut out cookies—into 1-by-2-inch rectangles or 2-inch rounds—using a cookie cutter, a sharp knife, or the rim of a fine glass. Transfer the cookies to one of the greased baking sheets, leaving about ¼ inch between them. Roll out any scraps one more time to eke out a few more cookies. (This dough can be rolled out only twice, or it will get tough, so any scraps left after the second rolling out should be discarded, or baked as is.)

Brush the tops with egg wash, if you want a slight sheen on your cookies, and then sprinkle on a little sugar, if you like. Bake for 15 minutes, or until the cookies puff slightly; they won't brown. Transfer to a rack to cool. Shape and bake the rest of the dough.

Once the cookies have cooled completely, store in a cookie tin. They keep well for several weeks, though usually they're eaten long before that.

independent brownies

Makes 22 to 24 round brownies, 2 inches across, with a thick rich bite

PHOTOGRAPH ON PAGE 378 *It all began with the brownies that our friend Trisha produced one day, fresh from a grocery store—bought package. They were small and round, not squares, and they had a chewy quality that pleased everyone, especially our children.*

How to make brownies like this at home? The secret ingredient is corn syrup, we realized, which gives them a firm chewiness. We bake them in regular muffin cups; that way, each brownie is large and independent, not sliced from the herd.

12 ounces bittersweet chocolate, coarsely chopped

2/3 pound (2¾ sticks) unsalted butter

4 large eggs

1½ cups light corn syrup

1½ teaspoons pure vanilla extract

1 cup all-purpose flour

½ teaspoon salt

Position a rack in the center of the oven and preheat the oven to 350°F. Lightly grease 24 regular muffin cups (or, if necessary, grease 12 cups—bake the first batch, then regrease and bake the second batch).

Place the chocolate and butter in a heavy saucepan and melt over low heat, stirring occasionally until blended and smooth. Remove from the heat and set aside to cool for 5 minutes.

Whisk the eggs in a small bowl, then add the corn syrup and vanilla and whisk until combined. In another small bowl, combine the flour and salt. Stir the egg mixture into the chocolate-butter mixture until smooth. Fold in the flour mixture, using a rubber spatula to stir only enough to combine.

Pour the batter into the muffin cups, filling them only two-thirds full. Bake for 20 to 25 minutes. Test several with a knife; the center should be cooked but still moist (the knife should come out clean but not dry).

Let stand in the pans for 10 minutes to firm up, then turn out onto a rack to cool completely.

traveler's date cookies

Makes 2 dozen rich cookies, either round mounds or high decorated ovals, filled with aromatic date paste

PHOTOGRAPH ON PAGE 397 *Like shortbread in Scotland, these cookies, called* mamoul, *are found everywhere in Lebanon and Syria. They're rich semolina cookies shaped around a date paste perfumed with orange flower water and rose water (see Scented Waters in the Glossary). They're a beautiful pale yellow, easy to bite into.*

½ teaspoon active dry yeast

¼ cup lukewarm water

1 tablespoon orange flower water

1 large egg

8 tablespoons (1 stick) unsalted butter,
    melted and cooled to lukewarm

1½ cups coarse semolina
    (not fine semolina flour; see Glossary)

2 tablespoons sugar

¼ teaspoon salt

1 cup all-purpose flour

Milk for brushing

FILLING

¾ cup honey dates (see Glossary)

3 tablespoons sugar

1½ teaspoons orange flower water

1½ teaspoons rose water

In a large bowl, dissolve the yeast in the water. Stir in the orange flower water, egg, and melted butter. Add the semolina and stir in, then sprinkle on the sugar and salt and stir. Add the flour and stir and turn to combine until crumbly but holds together when squeezed. Cover with plastic wrap and let rest for 1 hour.

Meanwhile, prepare the filling: Place all the ingredients in a food processor and process to a paste. Transfer to a bowl and set aside, covered.

Place a rack in the center of the oven and preheat the oven to 350°F. Set out an 18-by-12-inch baking sheet near your work surface.

To shape the mamoul (see Note), use a tablespoon to scoop up a full level tablespoon of dough. Place it in the palm of one hand and use the thumb and fingers of the other hand to flatten it into a nearly 3-inch-diameter round. Scoop up 1½ teaspoons of the filling and place it on the center of the round. Pull the edges up to cover the filling, then roll the cookie lightly between your palms to make a ball. Place seam side down on the baking sheet. Repeat with the remaining dough and filling, placing the cookies about ½ inch apart. Prick each cookie decoratively with a fork. Brush the tops with a little milk.

Bake until touched at the edges with golden brown, 20 to 25 minutes. Transfer immediately to a wire rack to cool.

NOTE We give instructions here for round mamoul decorated only by pricking with a fork. In Syria and Lebanon, and in some specialty grocery stores in North America, you can find elaborately carved mamoul molds. If you have a mold, oil it with olive oil and then oil again lightly every 3 or 4 mamoul. Fill the mold almost full of dough and use your thumb to press down in the center. This will make a hollow in the center and will also give you thin walls of dough around the edges. You may need less filling, say 1 teaspoon each. Place the filling in the center, then fold the thin walls over and pinch off any excess dough. Pull the shaped mamoul up gently from the mold and transfer to the baking sheet, decorative side up. Repeat with the remaining dough and filling.

high-altitude chocolate chip cookies

Makes nearly 3 dozen airy raised cookies, dotted with chocolate chips and chopped nuts

One day, my father came home from work and handed me a cookbook written by two friends who worked with him at the University of Wyoming. It was called Baking at High Altitude, *and it was published by the Agricultural Experiment Station at the university. It provided forty-three recipes for home bakers, all adapted from everyday standards to adjust for high altitude, where the boiling point is lower than at sea level, and there is less air pressure. The standard adaptation requires decreasing sugar in a recipe by 1 to 2 tablespoons per cup, and sometimes increasing the liquid. This compensates for the increased evaporation at high elevation. Less sugar also helps lower the temperature at which a batter will set (compensating for the lower boiling point).*

The first recipe my mother and I tried was the one that follows. The cookies turned out perfectly, and they kept their loft. We liked them so much that we made them every week or so for the next few years. Unfortunately, we never got around to making any other recipes from the book.

Make these cookies if you're baking at elevations between five thousand and seventy-five hundred feet.

½ cup vegetable shortening

¼ cup plus 2 tablespoons granulated sugar

¼ cup plus 1 tablespoon packed light brown sugar

½ teaspoon pure vanilla extract

¼ teaspoon water

1 large egg

1¼ cups sifted all-purpose flour

½ teaspoon baking soda

½ teaspoon salt

1 cup chocolate chips

½ cup chopped walnuts or pecans

Place a rack in the center of the oven and preheat the oven to 375°F. Lightly butter two large baking sheets or line with the parchment paper.

Place the shortening in the bowl of a stand mixer fitted with the paddle attachment and cream until smooth. Add the sugars and cream until light and fluffy, about 5 minutes on low speed, then several minutes on high. Add the vanilla extract, water, and egg and beat well.

In a medium bowl, combine the flour, baking soda, and salt and mix well. Stop the mixer, add the dry ingredients, and mix on low speed until just combined. Scrape down the sides of the bowl as necessary to incorporate all the dry ingredients. Remove the bowl from the mixer, add the chocolate chips and nuts, and turn gently with a wooden spoon to mix in.

Use two spoons to shape the cookies: Scoop up a generous teaspoonful of dough with a spoon, then use a second spoon to scoop it onto the sheet. Drop the batter at even intervals, leaving 2 inches between cookies, in three or four rows of 3 cookies each. The cookies will spread out while baking.

Bake for 8 to 10 minutes, or until the cookies are golden brown. Remove from the oven and let stand for 5 minutes to firm up, then use a spatula to transfer the cookies to a wire rack to cool completely. Meanwhile, repeat the shaping and baking with the remaining dough.

NOTE A key to good chocolate chip cookies is, of course, good-quality chocolate chips.

PRECEDING PAGES: INDEPENDENT BROWNIES *(page 376). Homemade butter cookies, Tioute oasis, Sousse valley, southern Morocco.*

meringue choices

Makes 3 cups Italian meringue, enough for about 7 dozen small meringue cookies, flavored with almonds, rum, vanilla, or other choices to your liking

We have a taste for Italian meringue—the soft version of meringue, like marshmallow Fluff—because of our love for Thai Tuiles (page 296) with their blend of sweet meringue filling and pungently savory toppings. If you're going to make a batch of Italian meringue to fill the tuiles, it might as well be a big batch. This recipe makes 3 cups; even if you use 1 cup for the tuiles, you'll still have enough for about 5 dozen baked meringue cookies, which you can flavor in various ways.

All the meringues are baked the same way. The choice of flavorings is up to you: a little extract or liquor, or ground almonds or hazelnuts. (If you use ground nuts, the meringues will be a little weighed down, pleasingly chewy in the center.)

¾ cup granulated sugar

3 tablespoons water

2 large egg whites

2 tablespoons confectioners' sugar

FLAVORINGS (FOR EACH CUP MERINGUE)

1 teaspoon rum or cognac, ½ teaspoon pure vanilla or
   almond extract, or 1½ tablespoons ground almonds or
   ground hazelnuts

Preheat the oven to 250°F. Line one or two baking sheets with parchment paper.

Place the sugar and water in a small heavy saucepan and stir briefly to dissolve. Bring to a boil, *without stirring,* over high heat. Boil to the hard ball stage, about 8 minutes (to test, drop a little syrup into a glass of cold water; if a hard ball, as opposed to a soft syrupy ball, forms, the syrup is ready).

Meanwhile, use a stand mixer to whip the egg whites until stiff. (Shut off the mixer if the whites are ready before the syrup is, leaving the whites in the bowl.) When the syrup is ready, turn the mixer to high and slowly pour the hot syrup down one side of the bowl (to minimize splatter). Continue to whip the meringue until cool. Turn off the mixer, sprinkle on the confectioners' sugar, and fold in. (The meringue can be stored in a covered container in the refrigerator for up to 3 days.)

If using a variety of flavorings, transfer the meringue, in 1-cup batches, to separate bowls and gently fold in the flavorings you've chosen.

Pipe (using a large plain tip) or drop (from a spoon) heaping teaspoons of meringue onto the parchment-lined sheet(s), leaving an inch between blobs. Place the sheet in the center of the oven, prop the oven door ajar to let moisture escape, and bake for 20 minutes or so until dry to the touch; they should not brown. (If you have two baking sheets' worth of meringues, bake both at once, just above and just below the middle of the oven; switch the sheets after 10 or 15 minutes.)

Leave the meringues on the parchment paper for 20 minutes to firm up, then gently lift them off the paper and place on a wire rack to cool completely. Store in an airtight container once absolutely cool. Meringue cookies without nuts keep very well; with nuts, store in a cool place for no more than 2 weeks.

sablés

Makes about 25 round 1-inch cookies, or 20 larger 1½-inch rounds, with a sandy and slightly fragile texture

Sablés are like fine shortbread cookies. Some version or other can be found all over Europe. In the port of Honfleur in Normandy, in a small boulangerie that made very good bread, we came across simple sablés, roughly shaped by hand. We've modeled this recipe on those cookies, which were rolled out thin and flattened gently on one side with two fingertips to give then subtle undulations.

Sablé means "sandy" in French, an apt description of the pleasing texture of these cookies on the tongue, just before they melt in your mouth. They're made with a dough that can also be used to make tarts (see page 27). If you use pastry flour, the cookies will be softer; with all-purpose flour, they'll have a slightly biscuit-crisp edge.

1¼ cups all-purpose flour, or 1⅔ cups pastry flour

⅓ cup sugar

Pinch of salt

8 tablespoons (1 stick) unsalted butter, cut into chunks, softened

3 large egg yolks

TOPPING

Granulated or light brown sugar

Cinnamon (optional)

Sift the flour into a bowl or onto a work surface. Add the sugar and salt, then add the butter and blend together with your fingertips. Make a well in the center and add the egg yolks. Use your fingers to gradually incorporate the yolks into the flour mixture.

Once they're somewhat mixed, if using a bowl, turn the dough out onto a cool work surface. Pull a bit of moistened dough away from the mass and rub it firmly along the counter under the heel of your hand to smooth it. Lift it off the work surface with a dough scraper, then repeat with another section of the dough. Gradually the whole dough will be smooth and blended. Pull the pastry together into a mass. Cut into 2 equal pieces. Place each in a plastic bag, flatten into a disc, and seal the bags well. (You will have just under 1 pound dough.)

Refrigerate for at least 30 minutes, or for as long as 24 hours. (You can also freeze it for up to 1 month;

bring back to refrigerator temperature before using.)

Place a baking stone or unglazed quarry tiles, if you have them, on a rack in the lower third of the oven and preheat the oven to 400°F. Do not bake until at least 15 minutes after the oven reaches temperature. Lightly butter a baking sheet and set aside.

Gently flatten one piece of pastry with the palm of your hand into a larger disk. Place between two sheets of wax paper and roll out until thin, rolling from the center outward. Sprinkle your work surface generously with sugar or a blend of sugar and cinnamon. Remove the top sheet of wax paper and flip over the pastry onto the sugared surface. Peel off the second sheet of wax paper.

Cut out cookies, using a cookie cutter or the rim of a fine glass, 1 to 1½ inches in diameter. Transfer the cookies sugared side up onto the buttered baking sheet, leaving ½ inch between cookies. Piece together the dough remnants, flatten with a rolling pin, and cut out more cookies. If you wish, press two fingertips lightly on one side of each cookie to make a rippled mark.

Place the baking sheet on the baking stone or tiles and bake for about 10 minutes, or until the edges of the cookies are just starting to brown. (The cookies will bake unevenly; remove those that brown first and leave the others for another minute or two.) Use a spatula to transfer the cookies to a rack to cool; handle them carefully, because they're brittle and break easily. Repeat with the remaining dough.

Bakery in Locronan, Brittany, France

Coffee time, chai shops *Habit* is not quite the right word. I like coffee—I mean, I love coffee—and for sure I have a habit of drinking it, at least one large cup every morning and maybe another midafternoon. But coffee is so much more than a habit. It's coffee shops, conversations, and cookies to eat along with my coffee; it's that little break in time when all I have to do is to sit and relax.

I'm not a coffee connoisseur. Even instant is fine with me, especially when I'm traveling and it's the only thing available. China's terrible for coffee drinkers, but great if you carry your own instant, because there is boiled water kept hot in thermoses everywhere, even in the cheapest hotels.

I can go without coffee and drink tea. In India, tea, *chai,* is usually served with milk, and the milk is especially tasty when it's buffalo milk, which is richer in fat. Chai shops are as good as it gets when it comes to atmosphere, steamy in the early morning hours and lively come late afternoon. In South India, milk tea is made incredibly frothy by pouring it from one large cup to another, more than three feet up in the air, an arc of beautiful brown chai flying from one cup to another.

One of my favorite pleasures in North India are the sweets shops that cook huge quantities of milk in large woks all day long so it gets thick and thicker. (The milk solids, called *khoya,* are used to make sweets.) I like going late in the day, or at night in the winter, to get hot milk, often flavored with cardamom, poured into my own cup. Then I pull out my little bag of powdered coffee and stir in a heaping teaspoonful. And then, of course, I have to have a sweet!

A lot of people I know drink coffee black. If there is no milk around, I will drink coffee black, but it's not the same for me, especially when I'm traveling. And when I'm traveling, when and if I can get my hands on one, I also love reading a North American sports page. For me the sports page is just like coffee. It's familiar and it makes me feel good. I gaze across the page with all the numbers, the standings, results, transactions. For a moment, I'm happily suspended in time.

Recently, I found a coffee shop close to home, in the Spadina-Kensington Market area of Toronto. I take my laptop, plug it in under the table, and start writing away. They play good music, and behind a glass counter there are plates of cookies, brownies, and sweet buns to choose from. And, of course, the coffee's good. So I've started a little routine of breaking up my day by walking over and having a cup of coffee. There's a Starbuck's just around the corner from where we live, and it's fine, but I prefer this place in the market. Coffee shops should all be different, don't you think? The coffee is the familiar part, but the coffee shop should be different. It's like traveling in my own town.

Pouring and making chai, India

greek biscotti with wine and spices

Makes about 3 dozen biscottilike cookies, ½ to ¾ inch thick, flavored with cinnamon, cloves, and white wine

In Crete, paximadia are everywhere, taking up one of five aisles in the local grocery store, crumbled into salads, eaten as a snack. Paximadia are rusks—twice-cooked breads—either savory or sweet. They're baked first in a long loaf, then cut or broken off into slices and slow-baked. Sweet ones like these resemble Italian biscotti or Moroccan feqqas *(see page 388).*

This recipe makes a rich dough, heavy and crumbly with olive oil, that is shaped into four loaves for the first baking. Then the loaves are broken into pieces that slow-bake to a light rusk texture. As they bake, they have an enticing aroma of clove and cinnamon blended with olive oil. Paximadia keep almost forever, satisfying everyday snacks with or without tea or coffee to dunk them in.

1 cup olive oil, preferably Greek

⅔ cup sugar

¼ cup white wine

2 tablespoons freshly squeezed orange juice

½ teaspoon baking powder

½ teaspoon baking soda

1 scant teaspoon ground cloves

1 scant teaspoon cinnamon

3 cups all-purpose flour

Position a rack in the center of the oven and preheat the oven to 350°F. Set out a large baking sheet (or two).

Place the olive oil and sugar in a bowl, then add the remaining ingredients in order and stir to make a dough. It will be stiff and oily and breakable. Knead for several minutes in the bowl, folding and turning.

Turn the dough out onto a lightly floured surface. Cut it into 4 equal pieces, and shape each into a low mound about 8 inches long, 3 inches wide, and 1 inch high. Use a sharp knife or dough scraper to make parallel crosswise cuts halfway through the dough mounds at ¾-inch intervals.

Place the loaves on the baking sheet. Bake until golden and baked through (a skewer inserted into the center should be clean and dry), about 45 minutes. Remove from the oven, and lower the oven temperature to 225°F.

Break each loaf apart along the cut lines. Lay the cookies on one or two baking sheets and bake for 45 minutes to an hour. They should be dried and crisp right through, but not tough to the bite. Let cool completely on racks before sealing in an airtight container.

mandel-melbas

Makes about 4½ dozen very thin, crisp, golden yellow rectangular cookies, dotted with almonds

PHOTOGRAPH ON PAGE 391 *Mandel-melbas are slightly sweet melba-toastlike cookies, airy and crisp, thin and golden, and dotted with large almonds (*mandeln *in German and Yiddish). They're a classic from the Jewish communities of Poland and Russia, made with eggs and no butter. This recipe is very simple and makes a large batch of very attractive cookies, ideal for a glass cookie jar.*

When I went to Australia, I found that mandel-melbas seem to have been adopted by Australians as their own. You can find them for sale in the big cities, beautifully packaged, far from their origins in the shtetls of Eastern Europe.

4 large or extra-large eggs

¾ cup sugar

1½ cups all-purpose flour

½ teaspoon pure almond extract (optional)

1 cup whole almonds, toasted (see Nuts in the Glossary)

Place a rack in the center of the oven and preheat the oven to 350°F. Grease a 9-by-5-inch bread pan and dust it with flour.

In a medium bowl, beat the eggs and sugar together with a spoon until blended. Stir in the flour until you have a smooth batter. Add the extract, if using, and the almonds and stir in. The batter will be sticky to pourable. Pour or spoon it into the prepared pan, smoothing the top surface lightly with a spatula.

Bake for 40 minutes, or until lightly browned and pulling away from the sides of the pan; a skewer inserted into the center should come out clean. It will look like a failed pound cake. Let stand for 10 minutes, then remove from the pan and cool on a rack for an hour, or as long as overnight.

Place the loaf in the freezer, sealed in plastic, for 40 minutes to firm up.

Meanwhile, preheat the oven to 300°F.

Slice the chilled loaf as thin as you can—6 to 8 slices to the inch. Place the slices on their sides on two baking sheets and bake for 10 to 15 minutes. Watch! Take out when just browning.

Let stand overnight or for at least 12 hours on a rack to cool and crisp up. This also gives the flavors time to settle. Store in a well-sealed jar or other container.

moroccan biscotti

Makes 7 to 8 dozen oval biscotti, lightly golden, dotted with raisins and rich with ground almonds

Hospitality, tradition, dry air, aromatics—these words all add up to a wide repertoire of sweets that are offered to guests and eaten with tea, at any hour, in Morocco. Moroccan biscotti are called feqqas. *We love these cookies, flavored with ground almonds and a little orange flower water, and studded with raisins.*

As with mandel-melbas and paximadia, the dough is first baked in low mounds, then cooled and sliced. After a long slow second bake, the feqqas are ready, pale gold, firm, and crunchy. They're best left for another day, to completely dry out and crisp up.

1¾ cups whole almonds

1 cup sugar

3 large eggs

4 tablespoons unsalted butter, melted

¼ cup peanut oil or vegetable oil

1½ cups dark raisins

2 teaspoons baking powder

1 tablespoon orange flower water (see Scented Waters in the Glossary) (optional)

½ teaspoon cinnamon

3 to 3½ cups all-purpose flour

Place two racks just above and below the center of the oven and preheat the oven to 350°F. Line two baking sheets with parchment, or lightly grease them.

Bring about 4 cups of water to a vigorous boil in a medium pot. Toss in the almonds and blanch for 1 minute. Drain, and slip the almonds out of their skins; discard the skins.

Place the almonds on a separate unlined baking sheet and toast lightly in the oven for about 15 minutes, shaking the pan after about 10 minutes to ensure that none are burning. Transfer the almonds to a food processor and pulse several times until coarsely chopped. Set aside.

Place the sugar in a medium bowl. Break in the eggs, and beat with a whisk or an electric mixer until thickened and smooth, about 5 minutes with a whisk, less with a mixer. Add the melted butter and oil and beat until smooth, about 1 minute more. Stir in the ground almonds, raisins, and baking powder. Stir in the orange flower water, if using, and cinnamon. Sift in 3 cups flour, turn and stir, until the dough is smooth, not sticky, yet pliable (add a little more flour if necessary to prevent stickiness).

Lightly flour a work surface, then turn the dough out. Cut it into 8 equal pieces. Work with 1 at a time, keeping the others lightly covered. Shape the dough into a mounded baton shape, about 6 to 8 inches long, 2 inches wide, and ¾ inch high. Transfer to a baking sheet. Repeat with the remaining dough, leaving ½ inch space between the batons.

Bake for about 30 minutes; the loaves should be fairly firm but not browned. Remove from the oven and set aside on a rack to cool and firm up for 6 to 8 hours, or overnight.

When ready to proceed, preheat the oven to 325°F. Slice each loaf into ¼- to ½-inch-thick slices. (A few of the slices will break and crumble; set these aside to be eaten as cookies.) Lay the whole slices on their sides on two ungreased baking sheets.

Bake for 15 minutes, then turn over and bake for another 10 minutes, or until lightly golden brown on both sides. Transfer to a rack to cool and crisp up, preferably overnight. Once dried out, store in a well-sealed cookie tin.

lime zest macaroons

Makes about 30 pale green coconut cookies, flavored with sugar and fresh lime

The extra—egg whites problem has been around for a long time, and so it's no surprise that macaroons have a long history. The Penguin Companion to Food *tells us that they're found in cookbooks from the late 1600s, made of finely chopped almonds mixed with sugar and beaten egg whites. They were served with wines or liqueurs and were also used, crumbled, to add texture to desserts or cakes. Incidentally, the word* macaroon *is also the name of the finest grade of grated coconut.*

For those who like coconut, these pretty pale green cookies are as good as it gets: fresh with a hit of lime, sweet but not cloyingly so.

2 large egg whites

½ cup sugar

1¼ cups dried shredded unsweetened coconut
(see Glossary)

2 tablespoons pastry or cake flour

¼ teaspoon salt

1 teaspoon pure vanilla extract

Grated zest of 2 limes

Place a rack in the center of the oven and preheat the oven to 300°F. Line a baking sheet with parchment paper.

In a large heavy saucepan, combine the egg whites, sugar, coconut, and flour. Cook over medium-low heat, stirring constantly, until the mixture comes away from the sides of the pan, about 10 minutes. Remove from the heat and stir in the salt, vanilla, and zest.

Immediately begin shaping the cookies: Scoop up a heaping teaspoon of the mixture and drop onto the prepared baking sheet. Repeat until the mixture is used, leaving nearly 1½ inches between the cookies.

Bake for 10 to 12 minutes, until the coconut shreds have turned opaque and the cookies are very lightly browned on the bottom.

Lift the cookies, still on the parchment, onto a rack to cool and firm, then peel them off the paper and let them cool completely, so they crisp up a little. Store, once cooled, in a well-sealed container. These cookies keep beautifully.

FOLLOWING PAGES: MARTHA'S MOTHER'S COOKIES *(page 392).* MANDEL-MELBAS *(page 387).*

martha's mother's cookies

Makes about 30 puffed finely layered, sugar-topped 1½-inch round cookies, or about 4 dozen smaller round or square cookies

PHOTOGRAPH ON PAGE 390 *A friend was given this recipe by her friend Martha, whose mother used to make these delicate, sophisticated cookies. They were known in Martha's house simply as "The Cookies." The original recipe called for a little orange or lemon zest, but we like the simplicity of doing without extra flavoring. The cookies are made from a processor-mixed dough of classic cream cheese pastry proportions—equal weights of butter, cream cheese, and flour. The dough is rolled out and folded several times like a simple puff pastry (see page 19), then cut into rounds.*

½ pound (2 sticks) unsalted butter, softened

8 ounces (1 cup) cream cheese, softened

Scant 2 cups all-purpose flour

Pinch of salt

1 large egg, separated

A 1-inch strip of orange or lemon zest (optional)

Sugar for coating

In a food processor, combine the butter, cream cheese, flour, salt, egg yolk, and zest, if using. Process until smooth. Transfer to a heavy plastic bag and flatten with the palms of your hands into a square about 6 inches across. Seal the bag well, and chill for 1 to 3 hours, or as long as 2 days. (Refrigerate the reserved egg white in a sealed container until ready to bake the cookies.)

Turn the dough out onto a very lightly floured surface. Rolling from the center outward, and without rolling over the edges of the dough, roll out to a rectangle about 12 inches by 8 inches. Fold in thirds, like a business letter. Lightly dust your rolling pin with flour, and then roll out again, to about 16 inches by 8 inches. Fold again in thirds, using a dough scraper if necessary to detach the dough from your work surface. Repeat rolling out and folding one more time, then roll out to a rectangle 16 or 17 inches by about 10 inches and about ⅛ inch thick.

Drape the dough over your rolling pin and transfer it to a baking sheet. Place the sheet in a plastic bag and seal well, or cover with plastic wrap, and refrigerate for 30 minutes to 2 hours, whatever is most convenient.

Meanwhile, place two racks just above and below the center of the oven and preheat the oven to 350°F. Line two baking sheets with parchment paper or wax paper.

When ready to proceed, place the egg white in a bowl and beat with a fork until frothy. Place about ¼ cup sugar in a shallow bowl. Remove the dough from the refrigerator and, leaving it on the baking sheet, cut out 1½-inch round cookies using a cookie cutter or a fine-rimmed glass—you want a good clean cut. Brush the rounds with the egg white. Pick up one round and place face down on the sugar, then transfer to a prepared baking sheet coated side up. Repeat with the remaining rounds, leaving a ¼-inch space between cookies. (You can also simply sprinkle the rounds with sugar, but we like the thick crust of sugar we get with this method.)

Bake until shiny and risen, 18 to 20 minutes; after the first 10 minutes, rotate the sheets. When the cookies are done, wait about 2 minutes, then gently transfer them to fine-meshed wire racks to cool. (The dough scraps can be pulled together, rolled out, and cut into squares. Brush them with egg white, sprinkle on sugar, and bake as above.)

PUFFED SQUARES Instead of cutting out rounds, which leaves you with dough scraps, you can cut the chilled dough with a pizza cutter or a sharp knife into small squares or rectangles. After cutting, brush the squares with egg white and sprinkle sugar generously over. Use a spatula to transfer the squares to the prepared baking sheets, leaving a ¼-inch space between squares. Bake as above.

Bohemian farmhouse, Czech Republic

light as air spirals

Makes 40 small, pale dry-textured cookies with an attractive coiled-spiral shape

These delicate cookies from Central America are made with cornstarch, not flour. As a result, they're light and a little dry, best washed down with tea or coffee or a sweet wine. In Spanish, their name, sospiros, *means "sighs"—light like an exhaled breath, perhaps. The cookies keep well in a sealed jar or tin, and they're ideal for people with an allergy to gluten as well as for those who prefer dry textures to moist.*

8 tablespoons (1 stick) unsalted butter, softened

½ cup sugar

1 large egg, lightly beaten

2 teaspoons rum

2 cups cornstarch, plus extra for dusting

¼ teaspoon cinnamon

¼ teaspoon salt

TOPPING

Scant 1 tablespoon sugar

¼ teaspoon cinnamon

Line one baking sheet or two small sheets with parchment paper.

In a medium bowl, cream together the butter and sugar, using an electric mixer or a wooden spoon. Add the egg and rum and beat or stir in. In another bowl, combine the cornstarch, cinnamon, and salt. Add the dry ingredients to the butter mixture and mix until just combined.

Turn the dough out onto a work surface lightly dusted with cornstarch. Divide into 4 pieces and then divide each piece into 10 pieces (½ ounce each).

Dust your palms with cornstarch, then roll 1 piece of dough out under your palms to a 9-inch-long rope about the thickness of a pencil. Anchor one end on the work surface and coil the rope around itself in a flat spiral to make a round about 1¼ inches across. Pinch the end lightly against the side of the coil to secure it, then transfer the cookie to the prepared baking sheet. Repeat with the remaining pieces, leaving ½ inch between cookies, and redusting your palms and work surface with cornstarch as necessary. Refrigerate for 1 hour, loosely covered.

Meanwhile, place a rack in the center of the oven and preheat the oven to 300°F. Mix the sugar and cinnamon in a bowl.

Sprinkle the cookies with the cinnamon sugar and bake for about 7 minutes, until puffed and firming up. (They will start to puff up after 4 to 5 minutes.)

Let cool slightly on the pan to firm up, then transfer to a rack to cool completely. Store in a well-sealed container (on their own or only with other dry cookies).

oatcakes

Makes 4 baking sheets' worth (about 5 dozen) very thin square or round cookies, tender with butter and flavored with oats and brown sugar

PHOTOGRAPH ON PAGE 396 *I was so pleased to find a recipe for oatcakes among my mother's papers. It was carefully written out in my grandmother's clear, round hand. She and my mother and my aunt Wendy all made them: thin, mildly sweet cookies that my English-born grandmother called oatmeal biscuits. They mixed the dough by hand, rolled it out into thin sheets, then cut the sheets with a sharp knife like crackers into squares or diamonds. We mix our dough in the processor and often use a glass to cut rounds instead.*

2 cups rolled oats

1 cup whole wheat flour

1 cup all-purpose flour

1 cup packed light brown sugar

¼ teaspoon salt

½ pound (2 sticks) cold unsalted butter, chopped

1 teaspoon baking soda

1 cup hot water

Place the oats in a processor bowl and process for 20 seconds or so to chop to a finer texture. Add the flours, sugar, and salt and process briefly to mix. Add the butter and pulse until you have the texture of fine meal. You may have to stop to scrape down the sides of the bowl with a spatula. Stir the baking soda into the hot water, then, with the processor running, pour into the flour mixture. Stop processing as soon as it comes together into a mass.

Transfer the dough to a bowl, cover with plastic wrap, and refrigerate for 30 minutes, or as long as 4 hours.

When ready to proceed, place two racks just above and below the center of the oven and preheat the oven to 325°F. Lightly butter two baking sheets.

Remove the dough from the refrigerator and cut into 4 equal pieces. Set 3 aside, covered with plastic wrap.

Place the remaining piece of dough on a lightly floured work surface. Flatten gently with the palm of your hand, then use a rolling pin to roll it out to an approximately 18-by-12-inch rectangle, using light strokes of the pin and moving the dough a little between strokes to ensure that it is not sticking.

To make classic oatcakes, transfer the rolled-out dough to one of the baking sheets (this is most easily done by draping it over the rolling pin). Use a pizza cutter or a sharp knife to cut the dough into squares or diamonds. *To make round oatcakes,* use a 2- or 2½-inch round cookie cutter or fine-rimmed glass to cut out the oatcakes. Lightly combine the scraps and roll out to give you a few more. (Each piece of dough will yield 15 to 18 oatcakes.) Place on a baking sheet, leaving ⅛ inch between them.

Place the baking sheet in the oven and bake the oatcakes for 10 to 15 minutes, until touched with light golden patches. Use a spatula to transfer the oatcakes to a fine-mesh rack. Repeat with the second piece of dough, placing the filled sheet on the other rack in the oven.

Repeat with the remaining dough. Leave the oatcakes out on the rack overnight to cool and crisp up. Store in an airtight tin, once crisp.

FOLLOWING PAGES: OATCAKES. (LEFT TO RIGHT) CORIANDER COOKIES *(page 375)*; TRAVELER'S DATE COOKIES *(page 377)*.

Last Easter at the bakery George Stephanopolis makes me smile. His smile makes me smile. Forty-five years a baker, thirty-five years beside the same wood-fired oven on Selinou Street in Chaniá, the second city of Crete, he stokes the fire every day with olive wood, loads and unloads his breads, and talks with customers. From before dawn until after dark, he stands by the oven and bakes bread. While he works, he keeps a straight, workmanlike face, but under his long gray mustache, there's a smile, an about-to-smile smile, an infectious look.

But this Easter bake will be George's last. He's sixty-seven years old; he's going to turn the bakery over to his daughters, Anna and Helena. A sign's already been made—Anna and Helena's Bakery—but it's not yet up; it's still lying against the wall outside. For now, this is still George's bakery, and it's Easter, a special time of year.

For one week before the holiday, George's oven becomes a community oven. From all around the neighborhood people first bring in large black baking sheets packed with *tsoureki,* buttery yellow fingerlike Easter cookies. Some people prefer to bake their tsoureki at home, but most bring them to George. "It's the smell of the wood fire, the taste from the olive wood," the older folks say. "And we like it here, seeing everyone. It's our tradition."

People bring in so much tsoureki that the baking sheets get piled high in stacks, waiting for oven space, waiting for George. On each, Anna places a slip of paper with the family name; otherwise it would be impossible to know which is which. Each sheet has at least fifty tsoureki, and there are many stacks of sheets, ten to twelve a stack. There are thousands of tsoureki here. But people help if they can, and there is much good humor.

George readying to bake

And sometimes not. An older woman comes in, dressed in black, low to the ground and sturdy. "Are mine finished yet?" she demands.

"No," replies George calmly, looking out across the bakery overrun with baking sheets. "Look how many I have to bake."

"But I brought mine in before these others," she retorts.

It's not true. I've been taking pictures the whole time, a fly on the wall, and I know that her sheets aren't even close to going into the oven. And George knows too. "If you want them done quickly, do them at home in your electric oven," he replies. "If you want a wood fire . . ." He turns and gets back to work. She leaves in a huff.

But when he puts the next batch in, he pulls her sheets out of the stack and in they go, out of order—the "squeaky wheel" getting special treatment, jumping the queue. George looks over at me and smiles. It's Eastertime.

After dark on my first day, I pack up and return to my hotel, but there are still thousands of tsoureki to be baked. George and Anna will be up all night, as they will be for many nights to come. When I return the next morning, there are even more tsoureki, and there is even more commotion. In and around the tsoureki, George is baking the regular bakery bread, ninety loaves at a time. He loads them skillfully into the 500°F oven with a long wooden peel. When they're ready to come out, he uses a different peel, pulling out three or four at a time. The breads are hot and crusty, and from the peel they fall off onto a large wooden table more than half the size of the bakery.

As the breads cool and crack, they get grabbed up. A customer picks a bread up, then puts it down and picks up another. The breads are almost identical, but not to the discerning buyer. One bread is a little browner, a little softer, a little irregular in shape. Some are sprinkled lightly with white sesame seeds, some with black. Some people want the bread hot from the oven, others just the opposite. And all the while there is chat, Easter chat. The bakery could be a village well.

The olive wood burns hot, the smell of the bread penetrates into the neighborhood. Do they all know how lucky they are to have George and Anna and the bakery? Yes, I think they do, even Squeaky Wheel.

greek easter cookies

Makes 18 large or 24 smaller buttery cookies, flavored with cognac and vanilla and shaped into flattened rectangles or curved finger-width cylinders

This version of tsoureki *(see Last Easter at the Bakery, page 399) is rich with butter and has a slightly crumbly texture. The dough can be shaped in several different ways. We like making flattened rectangles with ridges marked down their length, but you can also form the dough into fingerwide cylinders and coil them or bend them into shapes. Both options are set out below. Traditionally, tsoureki are quite large, but we've come to prefer a slightly smaller cookie. Baking time will vary a little with the shape you make.*

12 tablespoons (1½ sticks) unsalted butter, softened

¾ cup sugar

¼ cup whole milk

2 large egg yolks

1 teaspoon pure vanilla extract

1 tablespoon cognac

1 tablespoon freshly squeezed lemon juice

½ teaspoon baking soda

¼ teaspoon salt

3½ to 4 cups all-purpose flour

Place a rack in the center of the oven and preheat the oven to 350°F. Lightly butter a large baking sheet.

In a large bowl, cream the butter and sugar together with a mixer or by hand. Add the milk and egg yolks and beat until smooth. Add the vanilla, cognac, and lemon juice and stir, then sprinkle on the baking soda and salt and stir in. Add the flour, a cup at a time, mixing well until you have a stiff dough.

Divide the dough in half and set one half aside, covered. Divide the other half into 9 pieces for larger cookies, or 12 pieces for smaller cookies (see headnote): For 9 cookies, divide the dough in 3 and then each piece in 3; for 12, divide it in half, then half again, then each piece into 3. Flatten each piece into a rectangle. The larger cookies will be about 3 inches long and an inch wide, the smaller ones 2 inches by 1¾ inches. Use a knife blade or dough scraper to make several indentations down the length. Alternatively, roll each piece into a cylinder the thickness of your middle finger and coil or bend in half or into an S-shape, as you wish.

Place the cookies on the baking sheet about 1 inch apart, then repeat with the other half of the dough.

Bake for 25 to 30 minutes, until the tops are lightly touched with golden brown and the bottoms brown. Let cool on a rack.

NOTE Aglaia Kremezi, cookbook author and journalist from Greece, tells us that in Corfu, tsoureki are flavored with orange peel. To make this version, stir in 1 teaspoon minced candied citrus peel (see page 60), or finely minced orange zest, just before you add the flour.

mennonite oatmeal cookies

Makes about 3 dozen large golden cookies, somewhere between crispy and chewy

In her book Cookies and Squares with Schmecks Appeal, *one of a series of books based on the cooking traditions of the Mennonite community of southern Ontario, Edna Staebler gives a recipe for oatmeal cookies made with rendered chicken fat, schmaltz. The Mennonites settled in Ontario about a century ago to farm and to build a self-sufficient community. Some now use farm machinery, while others still shun modernity.*

It's unusual to find rendered chicken fat in a cookie. We find the schmaltz too strong tasting when used alone, but used in a blend with butter, it produces great cookies. This recipe is adapted from the original to get the rich good flavor but mute the schmaltz. If you do use straight chicken fat, set the cookies aside for a day before serving them, for after twenty-four hours, the schmaltz flavor blends in and becomes less forward.

12 tablespoons (1½ sticks) unsalted butter, melted,
   or ¾ cup melted chicken fat (see **Fat** in the **Glossary**)
   or a half-and-half blend of butter and chicken fat
1 cup packed light brown sugar
1 tablespoon pure vanilla extract
2 cups rolled oats (not instant)
1¾ cups pastry flour, or 1½ cups all-purpose flour
1 scant teaspoon baking soda
¼ teaspoon salt

Place two racks just above and below the center of the oven and preheat the oven to 350°F. Line two baking sheets with parchment paper, or generously butter them.

Mix the melted butter and/or fat with the brown sugar and vanilla in a medium bowl and set aside. In a large bowl, mix together the oats, flour, baking soda, and salt. Add the butter mixture and stir to mix well.

Scoop out a heaping tablespoon or so of dough and roll briefly between your wet palms to form a ball. Flatten the ball on a cookie sheet with wet fingertips until as thin as possible. Repeat with the remaining dough, leaving a 1-inch space between the cookies.

Bake for 6 to 7 minutes. The cookies will spread a little as they bake, puff up, and then flatten. When baked, they will be a beautiful deep gold color. Let the cookies cool and firm up on the baking sheet, then transfer to a tin to keep crisp.

chewy pecan bar cookies

Makes one 13-by-9-inch pan of golden brown nut-rich cookies, to be cut into squares or bars, chewy and delectable straight out of the oven, moist and tender when cooled

What is it about kids who don't like nuts in their cookies, cakes, and breads? Jeffrey remembers not liking nuts in baking as a kid, but now as an adult he loves them. We first made these pecan bar cookies thinking that our kids could take them in their lunch boxes instead of granola bars, but the kids would have nothing to do with them. "We don't like nuts or raisins in cookies," they both told us. Oh, well, that meant more pecan cookies for the two of us.

Bar cookies are easy for the cook, for they're baked in a pan, then cut into bars or squares after they cool.

12 tablespoons (1½ sticks) unsalted butter, melted

3 cups packed light brown sugar

¾ teaspoon salt

2 teaspoons pure vanilla extract

3 large eggs

1¼ cups all-purpose flour

1 teaspoon baking powder

2 cups pecans, coarsely chopped

Place a rack in the center of the oven and preheat the oven to 325°F. Lightly butter a 13-by-9-inch baking pan.

Combine the butter, brown sugar, salt, and vanilla in a large bowl. Stir in the eggs. In a medium bowl, combine the flour and baking powder. Stir the dry ingredients into the wet, then stir in the chopped nuts.

Pour the batter into the buttered pan. Bake for 25 to 30 minutes, until golden brown on top and a wooden skewer inserted in the center comes out clean (the cookies will brown before they are cooked, so you'll have to bake them a little longer than you might think).

Let them cool completely in the pan on a rack before cutting them into squares or rectangles, as you wish.

ukrainian hazelnut roll-ups

Makes 4 dozen hazelnut-filled rolled-up cookies

Rohalyky is the name for these Ukrainian cookies, filled and rolled up, a little like rugelach in shape (see page 36). These days, they're more likely to be made of a baking powder–raised dough, but traditionally they're made of a tender yeasted dough, the version we prefer.

This recipe makes a large batch, a great contribution to a party or potluck dinner. The rich dough rises in a bath of lukewarm water, a method probably dating back to the days before central heating, when special measures were needed to keep yeasted doughs warm. The risen dough is rolled out, cut into wedges, and filled with a sweet, chewy hazelnut mixture bound with egg whites.

Store the cookies, once completely cooled, in a well-sealed container in a cool place for up to ten days. Or put them in the freezer for up to a month—they freeze beautifully.

DOUGH

1 tablespoon active dry yeast

1 teaspoon sugar

½ cup lukewarm water

4 to 4½ cups all-purpose flour

½ pound (2 sticks) unsalted butter, cut into small cubes

4 large eggs, beaten

1 teaspoon salt

About ½ cup sugar for rolling out

FILLING

½ cup rolled oats (not instant)

6 ounces hazelnuts (about 1⅓ cups), toasted and skinned (see Glossary)

3 large egg whites

¾ cup sugar

½ teaspoon cinnamon

1 teaspoon pure vanilla extract

TOPPING

1 egg yolk, beaten with 1 tablespoon water, for egg wash

About 2 tablespoons sugar

Dissolve the yeast and sugar in the water and set aside for 5 minutes.

Place the flour in a large bowl or the bowl of a stand mixer. Add the butter and rub it in with your fingertips or mix at medium speed, to a coarse meal. Add the eggs and salt, then add the yeast mixture. Use a wooden spoon or a mixer fitted with the dough hook to mix together to a soft dough. If the dough is very sticky, knead in a little extra flour.

Place the dough in a heavy plastic bag and tie tightly, leaving room in the bag for the dough to expand. Place in a second bag and tie tightly. Fill a large bowl or pot three-quarters full of lukewarm water and place the dough in the water. Let stand until the dough rises to the surface, about 1¼ hours.

Meanwhile, prepare the filling: Place the oats in a food processor and process to a slightly finer texture. Add the hazelnuts and finely chop.

Beat the egg whites in a large bowl until stiff, but not dry. Fold in the oats mixture, then add the remaining ingredients and fold in to make a coarse paste. Set aside.

Place two racks just above and below the center of the oven and preheat the oven to 375°F. Line two baking sheets with parchment, or lightly grease them.

Turn the dough out onto a well-floured surface and knead briefly. Cut into 6 equal pieces. Sprinkle about 2 tablespoons sugar onto an unfloured part of the work surface. Work with one piece of dough at a time, leaving the others loosely covered with plastic: Flatten the dough on the sugared surface with the palm of your hand, then roll out to a circle about 6 inches across and just less than ¼-inch thick. Cut into 8 wedges. Place 1½ teaspoons filling across the widest part of each wedge, then roll each up toward the point. Place on a prepared baking sheet point side down, leaving an inch between them. Repeat to shape the remaining cookies, sprinkling a little sugar (1 or 2 tablespoons) on your work surface each time before rolling out the dough. Let the cookies rise, loosely covered, for 15 minutes.

Brush the cookies with the egg wash and sprinkle with a little sugar. Bake for 12 minutes, or until lightly golden. Let cool on fine-mesh racks before serving.

Wooden cabin, Gotland, Sweden

Grandmum When my grandmother was old—and she was old for a long time (she died just short of her one hundred seventh birthday), I think the thing she enjoyed most was the freedom not to have to cook.

She'd come to British Columbia from England after the First World War to marry my grandfather. They'd met in England during the war, when he was in the Royal Air Force and she was working in a hospital. My grandad was a very eccentric guy, a hardhead and a confirmed antimodernist. He was born in Alsace and educated in England, then studied agriculture in Canada. He was the only one of his siblings to survive the Great War, and he hated war, and motors, and electricity.

A year after Grandmum came out to marry him, they moved to a one-room log cabin on a "quarter section"—160 acres of land—far north in British Columbia. Behind their land stretched thickly forested, unmapped open range. Over time, they added to the log cabin, cleared more land, built barns and other outbuildings out of logs, and eked out a subsistence living, just as farmers have been doing for centuries. The house was full of books, but they never had electricity or running water, and they never had a telephone. Grandad wouldn't.

All this meant that Grandmum spent a lot of time *slaving* (her word) over the hot woodstove, especially in summer and fall. She cooked three huge meals a day for the haying crew during harvest season; she boiled up pots of fruit to make jams and jellies. She put up fruit; she put up the moose Grandad shot every fall to help extend their food supply. In between all these seasonal cooking chores, she made bread and cakes and easy cookies and simple tarts; she churned butter; and she cooked three meals a day for the family (three kids plus extras).

My grandparents' life was a pretty closed system, a form of self-sufficiency that depended on good health and determination. And then, when they were well into their sixties, my grandfather inherited some money unexpectedly. He'd never had a bank account, never bought a big-ticket item. They decided to buy a propane refrigerator and a car, despite his aversion to machines. Grandad built a carefully chinked log garage to house the car, and Grandmum, at the age of sixty-five, learned to drive.

But still she did all the cooking, all the washing up and laundry, and Grandad still cut and hauled firewood in winter, then split and stacked it. And they still carried all their water up from the creek.

Only with true old age, in her mid-eighties, was my grandmother freed from cooking: My grandfather died, their extraordinary log house burned down (a fire caused by the propane refrigerator), and eventually she moved south to a village on Vancouver Island. There she lived in her own small house for many years, eating toast and prunes for breakfast and avoiding the stove as much as possible.

pfeffernusse

Makes approximately 7 dozen small, round spicy cookies, crisp, aromatic, and shiny golden brown

In German their name means "peppernuts," and these cookies do, in fact, pack a powerful flavor of blended spices and black pepper into a small walnut-sized shape. They're traditional Christmas fare in Germany and wherever else in the world there's an established German community. Spices are now so easily available to us, but whenever we bite into a crisp nuggetlike pfeffernusse, we like to imagine earlier times, when spices were a luxury in northern Europe, a luxury that came from faraway places on sailing ships. How special these cookies must have tasted then.

Pfeffernusse can be small round balls or flattened disks, whichever you prefer. After shaping, the cookies are set aside to dry for 8 to 12 hours before being baked.

2 large eggs

½ cup packed light brown sugar

1 tablespoon brewed strong coffee

1¼ cups all-purpose flour

½ cup whole wheat pastry flour, sifted

⅛ teaspoon baking powder

⅛ teaspoon salt

¼ teaspoon allspice

¼ teaspoon mace

¼ teaspoon ground cloves

¼ teaspoon cardamom

¼ teaspoon freshly ground black pepper

½ cup ground almonds

2 tablespoons candied citrus peel, homemade (page 60)
  or store-bought, finely chopped

2 teaspoons minced lemon zest

In a large bowl, using a mixer, whip the eggs with the sugar until doubled in volume. Add the coffee.

In another bowl, combine the flours, baking powder, salt, and spices. Fold the flour mixture into the eggs. Add the almonds, citrus peel, and zest and turn gently to stir in. Cover and refrigerate for 2 hours.

Line two baking sheets with parchment paper or wax paper. Shape the dough into round balls or flattened disks: Pull or cut off about 1½ teaspoons dough and shape it between your palms into a ball, or flatten it into a small ¼-inch-thick disk. Place on one of the baking sheets, leaving ½ inch space between cookies. Repeat with the remaining dough.

Leave the cookies out to dry for at least 8 hours, or overnight, lightly covered with a cotton cloth. Position two oven racks just above and below the center of the oven. Preheat the oven to 300°F. Fill a sprayer with water.

Spritz the cookies with water, and bake for 20 minutes, or until a beautiful golden brown color and shiny. Switch the positions of the baking sheets and rotate them halfway through baking. Transfer to wire racks to cool completely and crisp up before storing alone or with other crisp cookies in a cookie tin.

muhn cookies

Makes about 4 baking sheets' worth (about five dozen 3-inch rounds; more if cookies are cut smaller) of crisp, pale gold cookies, flecked with poppy seeds

We've made many versions of muhn cookies, a traditional eastern European poppy seed cookie (muhn means "poppy seed" in German and in Yiddish). Some are very sweet and heavily coated with poppy seeds; others are less sweet and rolled thin. The fact is that anyone whose mother made muhn cookies when he or she was growing up will have a favorite version, and the possibilities vary widely.

This recipe uses oil rather than butter in the dough. The cookies are crisp and medium-sweet, a beautiful, palest cream color and speckled with tiny black poppy seeds. They keep well in a sealed cookie jar.

1¾ cups all-purpose flour

¼ teaspoon salt

2 large eggs

¾ cup sugar

⅓ cup safflower or other neutral-tasting vegetable oil, or melted unsalted butter

1 teaspoon pure vanilla extract

¼ cup poppy seeds

In a medium bowl, combine the flour and salt; set aside.

In another bowl, whisk together the eggs, sugar, and oil, then stir in the vanilla and poppy seeds.

Make a well in the dry ingredients and pour in the wet ingredients. Stir to blend well; the dough will be stiff, so you may want to use your hands to briefly mix the ingredients thoroughly. Seal the dough in a plastic bag and refrigerate for 1 hour. (The dough can be made up to 24 hours ahead.)

When ready to proceed, place two racks just above and below the center of the oven. Preheat the oven to 350°F. Line two (or more) baking sheets with parchment paper or wax paper.

Place the dough on a lightly floured surface and cut into 4 equal pieces. Roll out 1 piece as thin as possible to an even thickness (less than ⅛ inch). Use a cookie cutter or a fine-rimmed glass to cut out large (up to 3 inches) or small rounds, or crescents, rectangles, or any other shape you wish. Transfer the cookies to one of the baking sheets.

Bake for 7 to 10 minutes, until the cookies are pale gold with a tinge of brown at the edges; rotate the sheets after 5 minutes to ensure even baking. Use a spatula to transfer the cookies to a fine-mesh wire rack to cool completely. Roll out, cut, and bake the remaining cookies.

LEMON-FLAVORED POPPY SEED COOKIES Substitute 1 teaspoon freshly squeezed lemon juice for the vanilla extract—it gives the cookies a fresh flavor. Brush the cookies with a little milk and sprinkle on some granulated sugar just before baking.

FOLLOWING PAGES: *Woman, Yerevan, Armenia. Young girls, near Lhasa, Tibet.*

russian rye cookies

Makes 1 baking sheet's worth (about three dozen 2-inch cookies) of all-rye cookies, firm and crisp and slightly sweet

These very plain cookies make a great mid-morning snack, like an alternative version of an English digestive biscuit. I like them dunked into coffee; Jeffrey prefers his crisp. They have an agreeable grain taste and are only a little sweet. They're best after they've had time to cool for a few hours, or overnight. Store them in a tightly sealed jar and they'll keep a long time.

3 tablespoons sugar, plus (optional) sugar for sprinkling

2 tablespoons unsalted butter, melted

2 large eggs

2 tablespoons sour cream (full-fat)

½ teaspoon baking soda

About 2 cups light rye flour

1 egg yolk, beaten with 1 tablespoon warm water, for egg wash

Place a rack in the center of the oven and preheat the oven to 425°F. Generously butter a baking sheet.

In a large bowl, using a wooden spoon or an electric mixer, beat the sugar into the melted butter. Beat in the eggs, then add the sour cream and blend well. In another bowl, mix the baking soda with ½ cup of the rye flour. Add the mixture to the wet ingredients and stir well or beat on low speed, then add the remaining flour and mix until smooth.

Turn the dough out onto a lightly floured surface and knead very briefly, then roll it out to a rectangle about 16 to 18 inches by 8 inches. Brush all over with the egg wash, then score with a fork in long decorative undulating lines. For sweeter cookies, sprinkle several tablespoons of sugar evenly over the dough.

Use a round or other cookie cutter or a fine-rimmed glass to cut out cookies. Place on a baking sheet.

Bake until just turning golden on the underside, 15 to 20 minutes. Cool on a rack.

These are best if allowed to sit out overnight to firm up. Store in a well-sealed container.

SWEET RYE CRACKERS If you wish, roll out the dough scraps and make one or two larger thin crackers to bake on another sheet or directly on a hot baking stone or unglazed quarry tiles, if you have them. The baking time will depend on how thin you roll the crackers; start checking them after 5 minutes of baking if thinly rolled.

minipancake street food cookies

Makes about 7 dozen tender little pancakes, each about 1 inch in diameter

Our favorite hotel in Bangkok is the Opera Hotel, in a section of town called Pratunam. It dates from the Vietnam War era. An air-conditioned double room with cable TV costs fifteen to twenty dollars, and the hotel has a great old swimming pool. Flying into Bangkok from North America after twenty-four hours of airports and planes, we love arriving at the Opera, swimming in the pool, taking it easy. Close by is a lively food market with great prepared foods.

These cookielike minipancakes are but one of our favorite treats to be had at the market. They're only about an inch across, and light in the mouth. We serve them like cookies, with tea or coffee, or to accompany a dessert of ice cream, sorbet, or stewed fruit. They'll keep in a well-sealed container for several days.

¾ cup glutinous rice flour (see Glossary)

**½ cup unsweetened shredded fresh, frozen,
   or dried coconut, toasted (see Glossary)**

⅛ teaspoon salt

**3 tablespoons grated palm sugar (see Sugars in the Glossary)
   or light brown sugar**

¼ cup coconut milk

1 large egg

Place the flour, coconut, and salt in a bowl and stir.

Place the sugar in another bowl and add the coconut milk, stirring until the sugar is completely dissolved. Add the egg and whisk for several minutes. Add the flour mixture and beat with a spoon until well blended. Let stand, loosely covered, for 10 to 15 minutes.

Set out two spoons and a bowl of water. Place a medium or large heavy skillet over high heat. Oil a paper towel or a cloth and rub it over the cooking surface of the skillet. Lower the heat to medium. Begin by making just one pancake, so you can understand how it works: With one spoon scoop up a teaspoon of batter. Dip the other spoon in the water to wet it, and use it to flip the batter off the first spoon onto the skillet, then use the back of the wet spoon to gently pat the batter into a round about 1 inch across. Cook for 40 to 50 seconds on the first side, then use a wide spatula to flip it over. It will immediately rise up. Cook for only 30 to 40 seconds on the second side, then transfer to a fine-mesh wire rack or to a platter.

Once you have made 1 pancake, you will be able to cook 3 or 4 at a time, quickly scooping batter and dropping it onto the skillet. Rub the skillet with the oiled paper or cloth after every two or three batches. Serve warm or at room temperature.

raisin drop cookies

Makes 4 dozen small, lumpy, raisin-studded drop cookies, sweet and chewy

There were always handfuls of these simple drop cookies for scavenging hungry after-school fingers to find in our family cookie jar. They look like small raisin-studded rocks, but they're actually soft and very easy to eat in quantity. Each cookie is a small morsel, two or maybe three bites at most.

2 cups all-purpose flour

2 teaspoons baking powder

¾ teaspoon salt

1 cup packed light brown sugar

12 tablespoons (1½ sticks) unsalted butter, softened

1 large egg

¼ cup milk

½ teaspoon pure vanilla extract

1 cup dark raisins

Place a rack in the center of the oven and preheat the oven to 375°F. Lightly butter two baking sheets.

Sift together the flour, baking powder, and salt into a large bowl. Add the brown sugar, butter, egg, milk, and vanilla. Mix to blend the ingredients and beat with a spoon or a mixer for about 1 minute. Add the raisins and mix thoroughly.

Drop the batter by heaping teaspoonfuls onto the greased baking sheets, leaving about ½ inch between them. (Do not flatten; the cookies hold their shape and stay lumpy as they bake.)

Bake one sheet at a time for 10 to 12 minutes, until just starting to be touched with color on top and golden on the bottom. Transfer to a rack to cool completely.

The cookies are best a day or more after they're baked. They keep well in a sealed cookie tin.

OATMEAL-RAISIN COOKIES For a little more texture, substitute ¼ cup rolled oats for ¼ cup flour. Add to the flour mixture before mixing with wet ingredients.

persian cardamom cookies

Makes about 3 dozen small, round, pale, cardamom-flavored butter cookies, decorated with chopped pistachios

We keep trying to go to Iran, but we haven't figured out how to get a visa to travel there independently. We've met several other people who have recently visited, but they all seem to have a particular connection that enabled them to get a visa. We've also met people who got in by going directly to the Iranian border with Turkey and applying for a visa at the border, hoping for luck. I've never been to Iran. Jeffrey has, long ago, but it was when he was traveling overland from Europe to India and more focused on keeping moving, on getting through Iran, than on stopping and exploring. We know that we will get there sooner or later, if only to eat the breads and the cookies. From all the Persian baking we have tasted made by Iranians living outside the country, such as these delicate cardamom cookies made entirely from rice flour, we know that what we'd find in Iran would be truly dazzling.

½ **pound (2 sticks) unsalted butter, melted**

1 cup confectioners' sugar

1 large egg yolk

1 teaspoon freshly ground cardamom (seeds from about
 5 green cardamom pods)

2 cups rice flour (see Rice in the Glossary), plus a little extra
 for kneading

Pinch of salt

About 2 tablespoons chopped pistachios

In the bowl of a stand mixer fitted with paddles, beat together the butter and sugar until pale. Add the egg yolk and cardamom and mix in. Mix together the flour and salt, then add 1½ cups flour, ½ cup at a time, and mix in. Add the remaining ½ cup flour. The dough will be a little stiff for the mixer, so turn it out onto a lightly floured surface and knead for several minutes, until well blended, smooth, and soft.

Wrap the dough in plastic and refrigerate for at least 2 hours, or as long as 12 hours.

Place two racks just above and below the center of the oven and preheat the oven to 350°F. Line two baking sheets with parchment paper or wax paper.

Knead the chilled dough briefly, then divide it into 4 equal pieces. Cover and refrigerate 3 pieces while you work with the remaining piece. Cut off a generous teaspoon of dough and roll it under your palm to make a ball, then place on one of the prepared sheets and flatten it slightly. Repeat with the remaining dough, leaving about 1 inch between cookies. Use a thimble or a fork to press a pattern onto the top of each cookie, and sprinkle some chopped pistachio on each.

Bake for 15 to 18 minutes, or until the cookies are slightly brown on the bottom; switch the positions of the baking sheets and rotate them after 10 minutes. Like all shortbread-style cookies, these are fragile right after baking; use a wide spatula to transfer them carefully to a wire rack to cool. Once cooled, store in an airtight tin.

glossary of ingredients and techniques

ALLSPICE This reddish-brown round seed is not a spice blend but a single spice that is grown mostly in Jamaica. It has a complex taste, like a mix of cloves and black pepper with other aromas blended in, hence its name. It is used in sweet baking and also in some savory preparations, especially marinades. It is available in any supermarket; if necessary, substitute a blend of black pepper and cloves.

ALMONDS Almonds are the nuts of a tree that is related to the peach, plum, and cherry. They may be bitter or sweet; until recently, bitter almonds were not available in North America, but they are widely used in Europe for baking, since their flavor is more penetrating. Almonds are used in baking whole, sliced, chopped, or ground. They are also made into a paste with sugar to produce marzipan. They are rich in oil, and almond oil is very prized. Taste almonds before using to make sure they are fresh, and store well sealed in the refrigerator or freezer. **Whole almonds,** sometimes called natural almonds, have a medium-brown thin, edible skin. They can be used raw or lightly roasted in a hot skillet until aromatic (see Nuts). Almonds can be purchased blanched, or skinned. Blanch whole almonds by dropping them briefly into boiling water, to soften the skins so they can easily be peeled off; this also softens the nuts, making them less crunchy. **Sliced almonds** are sold unblanched or blanched; **slivered almonds** are always blanched. **Ground almonds** make a great thickener in custards and in cakes and are the essential ingredient in almond paste. **Almond extract,** or **essence,** is a concentrated flavoring, sold in dark glass bottles. Buy only pure, not artificially flavored, almond extract. Use sparingly to perfume cake batters and cookie doughs.

AMARANTH Amaranth is actually the name of a class of plants, some of which are eaten as cooked greens, and one of which yields a seed that is sometimes known as Inca grain. It is tiny, light beige, and hard. Wash in several rinses of warm water to soften slightly before adding it to doughs. Small quantities of amaranth seeds or flour can be added to wheat flour doughs as an extra flavoring (see Country Baguettes, page 184, for example).

ARROWROOT Also called **arrowroot flour** or **arrowroot powder,** arrowroot is a fine, powdery starch made from the ground roots of any of several varieties of a tropical plant. Arrowroot is very digestible (hence arrowroot biscuits for babies). It is used as a thickener, like cornstarch and potato starch, and also, like cornstarch or rice flour, used as a gluten-free filler in combination with wheat flour to make baked goods more tender.

ATTA FLOUR *See* Durum Wheat.

BAKING POWDER, BAKING SODA Baking powder and baking soda are both leavening agents. **Baking soda** is a base, an alkali, that gives off carbon dioxide when combined with an acid: cream of tartar or an acidic ingredient such as buttermilk, yogurt, sour cream, or lemon juice. Because the carbon dioxide is released quickly (unlike the slower longer-term release of carbon dioxide by yeasts in a yeast-leavened dough), doughs and batters leavened with baking soda should generally be baked as soon as they've been stirred together. **Baking powder** combines a base (baking soda) and an acid (traditionally cream of tartar or tartaric acid) in a powder that, when combined with liquid, gives off carbon dioxide. Modern versions of baking powder, usually labeled "double-acting baking powder" also include a slower-acting acid that reacts with the base only when it is heated; this gives more rise to baked goods once they're in the oven.

BAKING STONES, UNGLAZED QUARRY TILES Both baking stones and quarry tiles can be placed on a rack in the oven to provide an unglazed clay surface for baking hearth breads and flatbreads. As the oven preheats, the stone or tiles heat up too. The hot stone or tiles help hold in the oven's heat and give the bottom crust of breads baked directly on it a traditional firm crispness, like that obtained when breads are baked in a baker's hearth oven or in a tandoor.

Baking stones are rectangular, with an unglazed clay top surface. They are sold in cookware stores; buy the largest one that will fit on a rack in your oven leaving a small space (an inch or so) all around for air to circulate. **Pizza stones** are round baking stones and less practical because of their smaller size. **Unglazed quarry tiles** are square or rectangular and come in many sizes; they are sold in tile stores. Buy the thickest ones you can find and get enough to line a rack in your oven, leaving a space all around for air to circulate between the oven walls and the tile surface. Fitting them is easier if you get smaller tiles, about 3 by 5 inches. Buy a few extras in case of breakage. Wash them before using them for the first time, scrubbing them if necessary, but do not soak them, for the absorbent clay will take up a lot of water and will then take a long time to dry out.

We leave our baking stone on a rack in our oven for all baking, placing baking sheets of cookies and pie plates right on it. We find it evens out the oven's heat. Whenever you are using a baking stone or tiles, allow them to continue to preheat for at least 15 minutes after the oven has come to temperature.

BANNETON A French bakery word for the baskets used to hold shaped bread doughs as they rise. They may be long or round. We substitute a wooden bowl lined with a flour-dusted cotton cloth. The shaped boule or other loaf is placed upside down in the bowl to proof.

BARLEY Barley grows in places where wheat cannot survive, at high elevations in Tibet and in cold or very dry climates. **Barley flour** is milled from pearl barley (barley grains that have had the germ removed). It is very low in gluten and gives breads a darker color than whole wheat flour, a nutty taste, and a moister texture. Barley flour is often parched (dry-roasted) to bring out its flavor before being used for baked goods.

BEANS, DRIED Dried beans of many kinds are widely available in grocery stores. Stored in a well-sealed container away from direct sunlight, they keep well. **White beans** or **navy beans** are round to oval and gray-white in color; they are very hard and take quite a while to cook. Never add salt to the cooking beans until they have softened or they will take much longer to cook (and may not soften completely); and always cook beans in plenty of water. *To make about 3 cups cooked beans,* combine 1 cup dried beans in a heavy pot with 4 cups water. Bring to a boil and boil vigorously for 10 minutes, then reduce the heat to medium, to keep at a rolling boil, and cook half-covered until tender, about 2 hours (timing will depend on size and age of the beans). Once the beans are tender, add salt (allow 1 teaspoon salt per cup of dried beans, and adjust to taste once the beans are cooked) and simmer for another 5 minutes. Beans can be flavored with fresh herbs. They can also be processed to a puree or turned into soup. Store, once cooled, in a sealed container in the refrigerator, or freeze for up to 2 months, a great staple to have on hand. *See also* Dal.

BERRIES The whole grains of wheat, rye, and other grains are often called berries, as in **wheat berries** or **rye berries**. They are sold in natural foods stores and need long soaking or cooking to soften. *See also* Barley; Oats; Rye; Wheat.

BICARBONATE OF SODA *See* Baking Soda.

BIGA The Italian name for a kind of starter dough. For more information, see page 111.

BOULE *Boule* is a French word for "ball"; it is also used to mean a round bread. Boules may be small, less than 8 inches in diameter, or as large as 15 inches across and domed on top. *To shape a boule,* pick up the slightly flattened dough at one edge and pull it into the center. Repeat all around the edge of the dough, pinching it together at the center. Turn the dough over and cup it in your hands, pulling downward a little to tighten the surface of the dough over the top of the mound. If the dough is very firm, the boule can be left to rise on the counter, covered with plastic; but most doughs, to keep the shape of the boule, need to proof, upside down, in a flour-dusted basket or bowl (see Banneton and page 114 for the technique).

BRAN Bran is the outer layer of a grain, a protective coat over the endosperm. Both **wheat bran** and **oat bran** are widely used in specialty baking, and they can be found in health food stores and many large grocery stores. Most other types of bran (rice bran, for example) are used for animal feed or other purposes. The wheat bran is left in whole wheat flour and sifted out of white flour; oat flour usually has the bran removed. Bran contains mostly fiber and minerals. Oat bran is believed to have a role in lowering blood cholesterol. Wheat and oat brans are not interchangeable by volume, since oat bran weighs only half as the same amount of wheat bran.

BREAD PANS Made of coated aluminum and other metals, bread pans come in standard sizes, though a visit to a flea market may also yield some older odd-sized pans. The ones we use most frequently are 9-by-5-inch pans; 8-by-4-inch pans are also handy. Cookware stores and some hardware stores stock standard pans. See page 117 for a detailed description of bread-baking equipment.

BUCKWHEAT Buckwheat is the hard brown triangular seed of a grass, not a cereal. It grows in cold climates and in rough ground. It is a staple in parts of Russia, in Normandy and Brittany, and in parts of Quebec. It may be coarsely ground into **buckwheat groats** and then roasted to make **kasha,** or instead finely ground into **buckwheat flour** for making pancakes and crepes. The lighter the flour, the less of the bran is included.

BUTTER, BUTTERMILK Butter is made from cream that is beaten until the fat in the liquid separates out from the liquid. Butter can be made from cow's milk, buffalo's milk, goat's milk, sheep's milk, or yak's milk. Traditionally, milk was left standing until the cream rose to the top and it was skimmed off. The cream was then churned—placed in a tall cylinder and stirred vigorously with wooden paddles or poles—using a method that is common from Tibet and Nepal to the farmhouses of Europe and North America. The products of churning are butter and a watery liquid, **buttermilk.** These days, commercial buttermilk is made from low-fat milk and a souring agent, and it usually contains very little fat (see also page 424).

CARDAMOM Cardamom is an aromatic spice that is native to Sri Lanka and southern India. It is sold whole or ground. The whole spice, the dried fruit of the plant, is a fine oval shell containing many brown to black seeds. The shell may be pale green or bleached white. (Two other kinds of cardamom, brown and black, are not used in this book.) Buy whole green cardamom if possible, for a fresher taste. Whole cardamom pods are used to flavor pilafs and other dishes, especially in India; ground cardamom seeds are used to flavor baked goods and other sweets. For freshly ground cardamom, crack open the pods, tip out the seeds, and grind them to a powder in a spice grinder or coffee grinder or using a mortar with a pestle.

CASSIA Much of the "cinnamon" sold in North America is actually cassia. The two are closely related, both being the bark of trees that are members of the laurel family. Various varieties of cassia are grown in Vietnam, China, and Indonesia. Cassia has a more forceful punchy flavor and is a darker red brown in color than the warm tan of cinnamon. Like cinnamon, cassia is sold in quills, rolled-up pieces of bark, as well as in ground form. Cassia bark is tougher than cinnamon bark, harder to grind, and coarser in texture.

CHEESES, FRESH **Cottage cheese** was traditionally made by keeping fresh milk in a warm place to separate into curds and whey, a process known as clabbering. The liquid whey was drained away and some cream was stirred or beaten in to the large, soft curds. When cottage cheese is drained, it becomes a little drier and firmer, like crumbled white curds. **Pot cheese** is a medium-dry cottage cheese, also known as **pressed cottage cheese**. If drained until dry and crumbly, it becomes **farmer's cheese**. Both pot cheese and farmer's cheese can be found in eastern European grocery stores and cheese shops; many supermarkets also stock farmer's cheese.

Cream cheese is also a fresh cheese, smooth and white, sometimes stiff and thickened with gum arabic. The best cream cheeses are a little softer, especially if artisanally made, because they contain no thickeners. If using a very soft, moist cream cheese, let it drain briefly in a sieve lined with cheesecloth or a wet tea towel before using. Cream cheese combined with butter makes a very smooth pastry dough.

In the eastern Mediterranean (Greece, Turkey, Lebanon, and Syria) there are a number of fresh cheeses that are now becoming more available in North America. These include **kanefa** and **haloumi,** available in specialty stores and great for stuffing sweet pancakes (see Sweet Ramadan Half-Moons, page 295). **Ricotta,** another fresh cheese, is now widely made in North America, although some of the best is still imported from Italy. It has a smooth texture and mild sweet taste. **Ricotta salata** is like feta,

however, and is made from fresh ricotta that has been salted and dried. It is available in supermarkets. *See also* Milk; Butter.

CHICKPEAS Also known as garbanzo beans, chickpeas are a warm pale tan in color, round, with a curved indented line circling the round. They are usually sold dried and they take a long time to soften and cook. In India, they are cooked and eaten as dried beans and they are also ground into flour that is used to make flatbreads and to coat deep-fried vegetables (*pakoras*). **Chickpea flour** (widely known by its Hindi name, **besan)** is made of finely ground chickpeas, which are called **channa** or **Bengal gram** in India—hence its other common name, **gram flour.**

CHOCOLATE Chocolate comes from the beans of the cacao tree. It varies greatly in quality, depending on the variety of tree, where it is grown, and how it is processed. There are many kinds of processed chocolate, from cocoa powder to unsweetened, bittersweet, semisweet, and milk chocolate. **Chocolate** is made from cacao beans that have been dried, processed, and ground. The fat contained in the cacao bean is known as **cocoa butter;** the remainder, strongly chocolate tasting and very bitter, is called **cocoa liquor** or **cocoa solids.** In processing, the cocoa butter is separated from the solids or liquor. When other ingredients, primarily additional cocoa butter and sugar, are added to chocolate liquor, its intense bitter chocolate flavor is diluted and softened and the texture is made smoother and more palatable. If only cocoa butter is added, with no sugar or flavoring, the result is **unsweetened chocolate.** In baking, you often want an intense chocolate taste that can still be punchy even when combined with other ingredients and baked. That is why so many recipes call for unsweetened chocolate. If a certain amount of sugar is added to the mix, then it becomes **bittersweet chocolate.** (The most intense bittersweet chocolate we have found is by Lindt and is 85 percent cocoa liquor; one with 70 percent is also very intense; 65 percent chocolate is milder still, and very good as a plain eating chocolate.) If more sugar is added, the result is standard bittersweet or **semisweet chocolate.** The best chocolate contains only cocoa liquor, cocoa butter, sugar, and vanilla. If other fats are substituted for cocoa butter (to make a less expensive product), then the chocolate will have a waxier texture when you bite into it (cocoa butter melts at body temperature, but other, cheaper fats melt at a higher temperature). It will also have a more muted chocolate taste. Some of the fats in mild-tasting **milk chocolate** are milk solids, so the chocolate melts less smoothly in the mouth and has a less forceful taste.

For the home baker, making North American standards such as brownies and simple chocolate cake, Baker's or Ghirardelli, both widely available brands, are excellent. If you are using shards or whole pieces of bittersweet chocolate in baked goods (rather than melting them as a flavoring), then a higher-quality chocolate with a higher-percentage cocoa liquor (60 to 70 percent, such as those made by Lindt) may be more satisfactory. Note that higher-percentage chocolate *cannot* usually be substituted in baking recipes that use melted chocolate as a flavoring.

CINNAMON A close relative of cassia (they are both members of the laurel family), cinnamon is native to Sri Lanka. The spice comes from the dried bark of the tree, which is rolled into "quills," also known as cinnamon sticks, smooth and quite brittle. Cinnamon is a warm tan color, paler than cassia, and with a milder flavor. Most of the "cinnamon" sold in North America is actually cassia. *See also* Cassia.

CITRON A lumpy-looking citrus fruit that looks like a very large misshapen lemon, citron has a thick aromatic peel and dryish pulp. It is mostly used to make candied peel. Citrons are grown in the Mediterranean, in Italy, Greece, Israel, Morocco, and Corsica, but unfortunately, they can be hard to find in North America; look for them in specialty markets.

CLOVES Cloves are dark red brown in color and shaped like nails or screws. They grow on trees (they are actually flower buds) and are cultivated in Indonesia, Malaysia, Zanzibar, Madagascar, and Brazil. They have an intense smell and taste. Like other spices, cloves have the most intense flavor if they are bought whole and then ground just before using, but ground cloves are certainly easier to use and still quite pungent.

COCONUT Fresh coconuts are now shipped from the tropics to the rest of the world, but most bakers in more temperate climates rely on packaged processed coconut products. *To grate fresh coconut,* crack open the coconut and pour off the liquid inside: Place the pointed end of a screwdriver on one of the "eyes" of the coconut and bang hard with a hammer to pierce, then pour off the liquid. Pierce another eye, then bang hard on the coconut; it should crack open. Use a coconut scraper, if you have one, to grate the meat; otherwise, break off the hard thick shell, peel off the thin papery brown skin, then grate the meat on a box grater. It should smell sweet and be quite moist.

Dried shredded coconut may be sweetened or unsweetened, and comes in coarse flakes or in longer shreds; it is widely available. The supermarket type of shredded coconut is fairly moist and is usually sweetened; other more dessicated versions tend to come in finer flakes. Dry-roast it (see below) to bring out its flavor. **Frozen**

unsweetened shredded coconut is available in the freezer section of many Asian groceries. It is moister than the dried shredded coconut, and recipes often call for it to be dry-roasted to eliminate excess liquid and to bring out its flavor. *To dry-roast shredded coconut,* place the coconut in a heavy skillet over medium heat. If using fresh or moist coconut, or frozen coconut, stir and turn to break up any clumps, and wait until the moisture starts to bubble out of the coconut shreds before lowering the heat a little. Cook, stirring constantly, until dried and lightly golden, 10 to 15 minutes. If using dried coconut, lower the heat a little after the first minute and keep stirring and turning to prevent burning; the coconut will be pale golden in less than 5 minutes if it's very dry and 5 to 10 minutes if it is moister.

CONFECTIONERS' SUGAR *See* Sugars.

CORIANDER Coriander is an annual plant that grows in temperate and subtropical climates. **Coriander leaves,** also known as **cilantro,** are widely used as an herb, from Mexico to Southeast Asia. **Coriander seed** is pale tan and round. It's a spice used in curries, pastas, pickles, and in some sweet baking.

CORN Corn is a grain that is native to the Americas. At the time of the European conquest, corn was grown and used in very sophisticated ways in many parts of North, Central, and South America. It is now grown on six continents. Corn is milled into flour, yellow or white or blue, depending on the variety of corn it was milled from. It contains no gluten, so it can be safely eaten by celiacs. If it is finely ground, into a fine powder, the result is **corn flour.** Corn flour is available in some grocery stores and in specialty stores serving Italian and Portuguese communities. (Note that in Britain, "corn flour" means cornstarch.) Coarsely ground corn, with a more granular texture, is known as **cornmeal.** Cornmeal is used not only as an ingredient in breads and cakes, but also (like semolina) is dusted onto peels to prevent bread doughs from sticking. Corn kernels may also be parched and cracked. **Cracked corn** can be used, after soaking, to flavor bread (see Galician Hearth Bread with Whole Corn, page 204). Look for dried cracked yellow corn kernels in Portuguese groceries or in Mexican or Latin American stores. They're pale yellow and very hard; they keep well, sealed in plastic in the cupboard.

Cornstarch is a finely ground white powder, the starch from grains of corn. It is used as a thickener in sauces and fillings (see Jamaican Coconut Pie, page 56). It is also used to dust surfaces to prevent dough from sticking and is added to wheat flour to make finer-textured cake batters and cookie doughs.

Corn tortillas (and tamales too) are made from **masa,** or *nixtamal,* dough made from processed corn in a technique developed long before the conquest: Dried corn kernels are simmered in a water and calcium solution. (In Mexico and Central America, the calcium comes from slaked lime; in other places in the Americas, wood ash or lye—the Hopi use chamisa ash, for example—provides the calcium.) The processing makes the corn nutritionally more valuable, an understanding that scientists have only recently come to appreciate. The soaked corn is then drained and rinsed, and the skins are removed. The softened kernels, known as **hominy,** may be used to make corn dishes or ground to make masa.

Fresh masa has a distinctive corn taste and smell, and makes wonderful tortillas. Unfortunately, it doesn't keep well, so unless you make your own, or live right by a tortilla factory where you can buy it, you will have to use the next best thing, **masa harina,** literally "masa flour." Masa harina is made from fresh masa that has been dried and ground into a fine flourlike powder. The brand widely available, in Mexico and in the rest of North America, is Quaker. Reconstituted with water, masa harina can be used to make good home-style corn tortillas and pupusas (see Easy Cheese and Bean Rounds, page 84).

CORNSTARCH *See* Corn.

CORN SYRUP Corn syrup is a thick, viscous, pale yellow sweet syrup derived from cornstarch. The starch is converted to sugar by enzymes; the process was developed in the nineteenth century to provide an alternative to molasses.

COUCHE A French bakery word for the heavy flour-dusted cloths used to hold and shape breads as they are rising. The proofed loaves are then turned onto a flour- or cornmeal-dusted peel and placed in the oven.

CRACKLINGS If you render lard or lamb fat, the other product of that easy process is cracklings. Store, once cooled, in a plastic bag in the refrigerator or freezer. You can often find pork cracklings in Latin, Asian, and large grocery stores. Use a cleaver to chop them small for use in recipes such as Corn Bread with Cracklings (page 169). *See also* Fat.

CREAM CHEESE *See* Cheeses, Fresh.

DAL *Dal* is the term used in much of South Asia for split beans and peas and for lentils. There are many kinds of dal, but here we use only two: **split moong dal,** often simply called **mung dal,** is the name for mung beans that have been split in half and skinned. Whole mung beans are khaki green in color, small, round, and hard. When they are split and hulled, they are small golden yellow disks that cook much more quickly than the whole beans. Mung dal is available in well-stocked supermarkets and in Southeast Asian and Indian grocery stores, as well as in many natural food stores. **Urad dal** is a small, dried split bean with a black skin and gray-white interior; sometimes the skin has been cleaned off. Urad dal is sold in South Asian grocery stores.

DATES Dates grow in hot, dry places, from North Africa to California's Death Valley. They are mostly available dried. They should be dark and moist and very sweet. The best dates are **Medjool dates,** from North Africa. They are very sweet, with an intense flavor; they are tender but hold their shape during baking. **Honey dates** are available in supermarkets, usually sold in plastic containers, whole or pitted. They are also very sweet, but without the fruity complex flavor of Medjools. They disintegrate into a sticky goo when chopped, so it's best to toss them in flour before chopping.

DOUGH HOOK *See* Stand Mixer.

DOUGH SCRAPER Dough scrapers are flat strong blades, nearly square, with a handle along one side. The best have a stiff, flat metal blade 3 or 4 inches wide and 4 to 6 inches long, with a wooden or metal handle. Available in cookware stores, they are one of the most useful tools in the kitchen. They are great for scraping surfaces clean, for cutting doughs into pieces, and for carrying chopped ingredients from one surface to another; we use a dough scraper to lift the edges of a very wet or sticky dough when we first turn it out to knead it. You can also find firm **plastic scrapers,** which are fine for cleaning surfaces but cannot be used for cutting doughs, since their edge is too flexible.

DRIED FRUIT Drying fruit is an age-old way of preserving it, intensifying its flavor and sweetness in the process. In order to prevent spoilage, much dried fruit is treated with sulfur; look for fruit labeled "unsulfured." Store dried fruit away from light in well-sealed containers. To rehydrate most dried fruits, immerse in warm water or another liquid, such as black tea.

Currants are dried black Zante grapes, smaller than other raisins. The name is derived from their origins; the grapes are native to Corinth. **Dried apples** come in sliced rings or long strips. They should be rehydrated by briefly soaking or simmering in water (or other liquid). **Dried apricots** may be orange or dark orange-brown, depending on the drying method used. Bright orange **dried**

papaya is usually sold in large strips or chunks (look for it in natural foods stores and large grocery stores). **Dried plums,** still more commonly known as **prunes,** come pitted or whole. They should be fairly plump and smooth, not dried out and very wrinkled. Dried plums are used in purees (see Prune Paste, page 37) and whole in baking (see Pain aux Pruneaux, page 354, for example). **Dark raisins** are dark brown to blue-black. **Golden raisins,** also known as **sultanas,** are golden yellow.

DRIED ORANGE PEEL Dried orange peel looks dark and unpromising in the small cellophane packages it usually comes in. Look for it in specialty stores and in Middle Eastern grocery stores. It must be boiled in hot water to remove excess bitterness. Once well softened by boiling, it can be easily minced and added to doughs or other dishes (it's used in some Persian savory stews, for example), where it gives a distinctive tart orange flavor.

DURUM WHEAT Durum is a variety of wheat, *Triticum durum,* that is known for its hardness. It is used to make atta flour and semolina. A very finely milled flour made from durum wheat, **atta flour** is pale yellow. It is a high-extraction (whole wheat) flour, very high in protein, and thus makes doughs that are strong enough to be rolled out very thin. It is the traditional flour for making roti and chapattis in India and Pakistan. **Semolina** (*semola* in Italian), a coarse grind of durum wheat with small, irregular yellow granules, is used to make pasta. Like coarse cornmeal, it can be dusted onto a peel or other surface to prevent an uncooked dough from sticking. It is also used as bread flour in Puglia, and in Tunisia and Morocco. Semolina is the core of couscous as well: The granules are moistened and hand- or machine-rolled in fine durum flour to make round, even balls of couscous. **Semolina flour,** also known as **durum flour,** is finely ground. It is very high in gluten. It can, like semolina, be used to make bread, but because it is so high in gluten, the bread dough will be stiff and the bread fairly tough.

EGGS In this book, recipes call for large or extra-large eggs. If you need to substitute different-sized eggs, these proportions should help with the calculation: To get 1 cup eggs, you need 4 extra-large, 5 large, or 6 medium eggs. **Large eggs** are about 3 tablespoons liquid (a little more than 2 tablespoons white and 1 tablespoon yolk); they weigh about 2 ounces (60 grams); **extra-large eggs** are about ¼ cup liquid and weigh nearly 3 ounces (85 grams). If you need to measure out ½ large egg, whisk the white and yolk together and then measure out 1 tablespoon plus 2 teaspoons.

To separate eggs, have three bowls on your work surface. Wash the eggs and dry them (see below). Eggs are easier to separate when they are cold, straight from the refrigerator. Break an egg against the side of one bowl, then hold half of the shell in each hand, over the bowl, and let the yolk slide from one half of the shell into the other, while the white falls into the bowl. Pour the yolk into the second bowl. Transfer the white to the third bowl. Repeat, accumulating the whites in the third bowl and the yolks in the second; this way, if you break a yolk as you're separating an egg, you don't get yolk into all your whites. Refrigerate yolks or whites, tightly covered, for no longer than one day.

Egg yolks contain fats and protein; they add richness to doughs and pastries and custard fillings and can also give them strength and loft. They also emulsify oils very well. **Egg whites** are mostly protein, the protein albumen, and give loft and strength to doughs. They cannot emulsify fats, and contain no fats themselves, so if used on their own, they result in drier, tougher baked goods. When beaten, both egg whites and egg yolks incorporate air; before the invention of baking powders and baking soda, beaten eggs were the primary leaveners for unyeasted cake batters. When beaten with sugar, egg yolks turn pale and develop small air bubbles that will lighten a cake. Whites may be beaten until they form soft peaks, or until they form stiff glossy peaks, then folded into a cake batter. (Note that if there is any fat at all in the whites, a little yolk, say, the whites will be weighed down and cannot be whisked as high.) With electric mixers, the labor has been taken out of what used to be a demanding kitchen task; egg whites beaten by mixer have a little less loft than those whisked by hand, but they tend to be a little more stable and easy to work with. *To fold whites into a batter,* gently fold in a quarter of the whites at a time, incorporating them completely. When used as an **egg wash** on baked goods, beaten whole eggs or egg whites give a gleam or gloss to the baked surface.

Store eggs in the refrigerator, in their box (that way, you can see the sell-by date). In general, use eggs as fresh as possible; extremely fresh eggs (less than three days old), however, will have stiff whites that will not whisk as high. Washing whole eggs before use is necessary to clean bacteria off the shell that may contaminate the egg as you crack it, but the freshness of an egg depends on the shell being nearly airtight. Washing cleans off the natural coating on a shell and allows air to penetrate the egg and age it. Do not wash eggs until just before you use them.

FAT, CRACKLINGS To get ¼ cup rendered lamb fat to use in Silk Road Non (page 302), you will need about 4 ounces lamb fat. Ask your butcher for the fat trimmings from a leg of lamb, and store in the refrigerator or freezer until ready to use. Trim off any meat, then coarsely chop the fat. Place in a heavy skillet and set over medium heat. Use a wooden spoon to press the pieces against the heated surface occasionally; the fat will take about 20 minutes to melt. Strain it through a sieve; the rendered fat will be pale and almost clear when liquid, becoming pale white as it cools. It has a very mild smell and taste. The pieces remaining in the sieve are lamb **cracklings,** delicious as a topping or accompaniment to bread.

Of course you can buy **lard** (rendered pork fat), but it's very easy to make your own, and then you have the cracklings to use in breads or to snack on. One day when we needed lard, we defrosted a slab of pork skin and fat that we'd cut off a piece of fresh pork belly and frozen. We chopped it into thin strips, the strips went into a medium-hot wok, and soon the fat was melting off the skin; you can also use a large skillet. Cook the sliced or chopped pork fat over medium heat, stirring and moving the pieces around to prevent scorching, until the cracklings are crisp and free of their fat. Lift out the cracklings with a slotted spoon and blot them on paper towels, then place in a bowl and sprinkle on a little salt. (You can also freeze them, once they've cooled completely, in a well-sealed plastic bag). Pour the liquid lard through a sieve into a bowl and set aside to cool; it will turn opaque white and softly solid. Store in a well-sealed container in the freezer, and use in recipes for pastry or breads.

When we skim the **fat** off **chicken** broth, we store it in the freezer for later use in cooking and baking.

FLAXSEED Also known as **linseed** (*leinsamen* in German), flaxseed is an oil-rich black seed. Small, slender, and ricelike in shape, it is also rich in Omega-3 (linoleic) acids, now viewed as an important element in fighting cardiovascular diseases and cancer. Flaxseed may be added whole to bread doughs (see Country Baguettes, page 184). The flax plant is grown for its long fibers, which are used to make linen; flaxseed is also the source of **flaxseed oil.**

FLOUR *See* specific grains (Wheat, Rye, etc.).

FOOD PROCESSOR Food processors are useful for blending and chopping nuts and cold butter, as well as for quickly mixing up unyeasted doughs. We always use the steel chopping blade, rather than the plastic dough blade.

GINGER Ginger is a flavoring that comes from the rhizome of the ginger plant. Fresh ginger may be young, with tender pale skin, or older, with a thicker tan-colored skin. It is widely used in Southeast Asian and Chinese cooking. **Powdered ginger** is ginger that has been dried and ground. It has a hotter, more concentrated flavor than fresh ginger and is used as a spice in sweet baking.

GOLDEN SYRUP This product of sugar refining is pale yellow, less thick than corn syrup, and very smooth. Developed in England in the nineteenth century by Thomas Lyle and Son, it is still sold as **Lyle's Golden Syrup.** It is available in specialty stores and some supermarkets. Corn syrup cannot usually be substituted; use maple syrup instead. *See also* Corn Syrup; Maple Syrup.

HAZELNUTS Hazelnuts, known as **noisettes** in French, are sometimes called **filberts** in the United States. They grow wild and are cultivated in much of Europe and North America and are an important crop in Turkey. Shelled hazelnuts still have their papery thin brown skins. The easiest way to remove the skins is to lightly roast the nuts and then rub them between your hands or in a towel. *See* Nuts for dry-roasting and storing information.

HONEY Some of our recipes call for honey as a sweetener. It's easiest to use liquid honey; if your honey has crystallized, just warm it slightly to make it liquid. **Buckwheat honey** is a dark strong-tasting honey made by bees that have fed on nectar from buckwheat. It's common in Quebec and also in some parts of rural France. Its flavor is so distinctive that it should not be substituted for regular clover or other mild-tasting honey in baking recipes.

KAMUT Kamut is another form of wheat, *Triticum polonicum*. Like spelt, it is often marketed as an "ancient" grain. Kamut flour is slightly yellow in color, like durum flour, and relatively high in protein. It can be substituted for some of the wheat flour called for in bread recipes, to give a slightly different color and taste.

KNEADING Although kneading can be done by machine (using a stand mixer fitted with the dough hook), home bakers have traditionally kneaded by hand. It's a very relaxing, pleasurable activity once you are used to it and can let your reflexes take over. In kneading, the dough is folded over on itelf, then flattened, then again folded, and so on. Kneading transforms a wet, loose dough into a slightly firmer, elastic dough that has good structure. A well-kneaded dough has a texture like a sponge, with lots of small holes created by the repeated folding of the dough. As the yeasts in the dough give off carbon dioxide (during fermentation as the dough is proofing or rising), the holes expand, causing the dough to "rise" (expand). During baking, the carbon dioxide expands in the heat, making the bread rise even more (a process known as oven spring).

LAMB CRACKLINGS *See* Fat.

LARD *See* Fat.

LEAVENINGS *See* Baking Powder, Baking Soda; Yeast.

LEMON OIL OR ESSENCE This intense citrus oil is a specialty baking product sold in small glass jars in gourmet markets and baking supply shops. It is a useful, and very easy, substitute for lemon zest. If you're not going to heat it, use ½ teaspoon oil to replace the grated zest of 1 lemon; if you'll be heating it, then use 1 to 1½ teaspoons oil. It adds a good clean lemon flavor.

LEMON ZEST *See* Zest.

MACE The lacy outer covering of the nutmeg seed, mace is also a spice. It is usually sold ground, but is also available in pieces. It has an aroma and taste similar to nutmeg but is less assertive. *See also* Nutmeg.

MALT SYRUP Malt is a grain product that is added to bread dough to condition it, giving it a good rise and a more complex, slightly sweet taste. Both **barley malt syrup** and **wheat malt syrup** may be used in bread baking. They help convert the starches in the dough into sugars. Malt is produced industrially, and it is most easily available as a syrup; bakeries often use it in powdered form. To make malt, the whole grains (the berries) of barley or wheat are warmed and moistened so they germinate, then heated to arrest the germination, milled, and dissolved in water: This is the syrup. At germination, the sugars in the grain are at their most concentrated, so the syrup is a form of sweetener with no added sugar. Barley malt syrup and wheat malt syrup are sold in jars in specialty stores and can be used interchangeably in the recipes in this book (Vietnamese Minibaguettes, page 226, and Baker's Sign Pretzels, page 230). Store them in the refrigerator.

MAPLE SYRUP Made from the concentrated sap of sugar maple trees, maple syrup comes in several grades: Grades AA, A, and B are the most commonly available. Grade AA is lightest in color and least intense in flavor. Grade B has a more robust flavor and is darkest colored. Store, once opened, in the refrigerator. **Maple sugar** is made from cooled-down, more concentrated maple syrup. *See also* Sugars.

MASA HARINA *See* Corn.

MASTIC Mastic is a resin, like the gum from pine trees, that is harvested from bushes or small trees. The bark is slashed and then the resin slowly oozes out. It can be chewed, like chewing gum, and is also used as a flavoring in sweets (see Greek Easter Cookies, page 401). It adds a sweet-heavy fruity taste; it should be used sparingly. Most commercially available mastic comes from the Greek island of Chios.

MEASURING To measure flour or another dry ingredient, scoop it out with a measuring cup, then level by sweeping off the extra from the top with a knife. Because flours vary in their ability to absorb moisture, many of our recipes, especially the bread recipes, give a range for the flour measurement and describe the texture of the finished dough, so you can determine just how much flour you need.

MILK, CREAM, YOGURT Milk is an important ingredient in baking; we imagine that baking originally was a good way of making use of excess milk and milk products such as buttermilk and sour milk. When used in breads, rolls, or scones, milk or milk products help keep the dough moist, as well as adding to its nutritional value. Cow's milk contains between 3.5 and 4 percent butterfat and nearly 5 percent sugar (most of it lactose), as well as proteins, vitamins, and enzymes; the rest is water. **Whole milk** still contains most or all of the cream. If the milk is **homogenized,** as commercial milk is, the cream will not rise to the top but will remain blended with the rest. Milk with some of the butterfat removed is known as **reduced-fat milk,** or **2% milk** in some places; it contains between 1.8 and 2 percent butterfat. In many places 1% **milk** is also available. **Nonfat milk,** or **skim milk,** has almost all the fat removed; it is thinner and a bluish white in color.

In North America, all commercially available milk is pasteurized; that is, it has been heated to about 150°F. This kills most bacteria, so the milk keeps longer. Older recipes often call for milk to be *scalded* (heated until nearly boiling, then cooled) before using it in yeasted doughs. The purpose was to kill off bacteria in the milk that might thrive during fermentation (rising of the dough) and give the bread a bad taste. With pasteurized milk, there seems to be no need to scald the milk before using it in bread dough.

Sour milk, which results from the action of naturally occurring lactic acid–producing bacteria in milk, cannot be made from pasteurized milk; when pasteurized milk spoils, it is not "sour milk" but just bad-tasting and must be discarded (or fed to animals). To get an equivalent acid milk product using pasteurized milk, add a little lemon juice or vinegar to warmed milk. This will cause the milk to curdle and separate in a way similar to that brought about by natural souring. Sour milk is a common ingredient in traditional soda-raised breads and cakes.

Cream is categorized according to the amount of butterfat, from **light cream,** or **coffee cream,** which has 10 percent butterfat, to **whipping cream,** or **heavy cream,** at 35 percent butterfat. In some places, there are other categories; in France and England, for example, it is possible to buy a heavy cream that is 50 percent butterfat. **Sour cream** is made from processed cream that has been soured. This results in a thicker texture and an agreeable slightly sour taste.

Try to avoid ultrapasteurized cream (and milk); it has been treated with very high temperatures, which alters the taste.

Yogurt is made from milk that is soured or fermented with acidopholus bacteria. It too is categorized by richness, from full-fat (about 3.5 percent milk fat) to reduced-fat to nonfat. We call for either full-fat or reduced-fat yogurt, since nonfat yogurts are thickened with gums and other agents and behave differently from yogurt containing only milk fat and milk solids. *See also* Butter, Buttermilk; Cheeses, Fresh.

MILLET Hulled millet seeds are small and yellow. They can be used to add texture and flavor to loaf breads. They are sold in some gourmet shops and health food stores.

MOLASSES Molasses is a by-product of the sugarcane refining process. The darkest, least sweet molasses is **blackstrap** (from the Dutch word for "black syrup"). Table molasses is less dark (medium brown rather than black in color), milder, less acid tasting, and sweeter. Molasses is used as a flavoring and as a sweetener. Try to find unsulfured molasses.

MUFFIN TINS Muffin tins or pans have six or twelve cups. In this book, we call for regular muffin pans, with cups that are 2 inches wide at the bottom, tapering out to 2½ inches wide at the top, and about 1¼ inches deep. We use them to bake deep (such as Teresa's Coconut Custard Tarts, page 53) and shallow tartlets (such as Mince Tarts, page 58, or Butter Tarts, page 28), as well as various muffins and the odd cookie (see Independent Brownies, page 376).

MUSTARD POWDER Strong and hot, dried mustard powder is a staple in English spice cupboards. It's moistened with water to make a paste and served as a condiment for beef or other meat. The most common brand is Colmans. Look for it in small and large tins, in supermarkets and gourmet shops.

NIGELLA SEED These small black teardrop-shaped seeds have an oniony flavor, hence their common name, **onion seed.** They are the seeds of the nigella flower, a garden plant related to baby's breath, carrots, and Queen Anne's lace. In India, they are known as **kalaunji** and are used in spice blends, especially in Bengal. Nigella seeds are often sprinkled on top of flatbreads in central Asia and in northern India and Pakistan. They're now widely available in stores specializing in spices, as well as in South Asian groceries.

NUTMEG The spice we call nutmeg is the seed of the fruit of the nutmeg tree. It grows with a brittle netlike covering that is sold as a separate spice, mace. Nutmeg looks like a hard, medium brown nut. It is sold whole or ground. For best flavor, buy it whole and grate it just before using. *See also* Mace.

NUTS, NUT OILS Nuts contain oils, which can easily turn rancid. Nuts in the shell keep best, but shelling can be an onerous job, so buying shelled whole nuts is often more practical. Store nuts in a well-sealed jar or container in the freezer. Chop or grind just before using. To bring out the flavor of nuts and make them a little more crunchy, dry-roast them on a baking sheet in the oven or in a heavy cast-iron skillet on the stove top until aromatic or starting to be touched with brown. Store **nut oils** (such as almond or walnut) in the refrigerator. *See also* specific nuts.

OATS Oats are a staple of the traditional Scottish kitchen. They are rich in fats; oats are generally heat-treated, to help stabilize the fats. **Oat bran** is the ground-up outer coating of oats. It is finer and lighter than wheat bran and has been credited with helping lower cholesterol by slowing the absorption of fats in the digestive tract. Oats may be ground ("steel-cut") into oatmeal or rolled and flattened into rolled oats. **Oatmeal,** or steel-cut oats, comes in coarse, medium, and fine consistencies and has a chopped texture. It is traditionally used for making porridge in Britain and Ireland, and fine-cut oatmeal is also used for making oatcakes. **Rolled oats,** which are more widely available in North America than oatmeal, are flattened grains. They are used to make the cookies known as oatmeal cookies but can be substituted for oatmeal in recipes for oatcakes only if finely chopped (in a food processor).

ORANGE FLOWER WATER *See* Scented Waters.

PARCHMENT PAPER Parchment paper comes in large sheets and in rolls and is sold in gourmet shops, cookware stores, and some larger grocery stores. Parchment paper is very useful, for it can be used to line baking sheets to prevent cookies from sticking and it does not burn during baking; it can also be reused several times. **Wax paper** can be substituted, but it is more likely to burn a little in the oven, it is not as strong, and it comes in narrower rolls.

PEANUTS Peanuts are actually legumes, not nuts. They grow in shells underground, hence their other name, groundnuts. Native to Peru, peanuts have become one of the world's most important crops; they are grown in China and India and throughout Southeast Asia, as well as in West Africa and in North America from Florida to Ontario. **Peanut oil** has a very high smoke point and so is ideal for high-temperature cooking, such as deep-frying and wok cooking. Store in a dark container in a cool place.

Peanuts that are not fresh may have a mold on them that is highly carcinogenic. Also, some people are allergic to peanuts and have severe and sometimes fatal reactions to peanuts even if eaten in the smallest quantity. Such people must avoid peanut oil and all peanut products. *See* Nuts for general information on dry-roasting and storing.

PECANS A variety of hickory nut, pecans are native to the southern United States. The ovals shells are smooth and red-brown. *See* Nuts for general information on dry-roasting and storing.

PEEL A baker's peel (from the French word for shovel, *pele*) is a flat surface (usually wood, sometimes metal) with a long handle that is used to place breads on an oven hearth or baking stone. The risen shaped bread is placed on a flour-dusted peel; the baker then thrusts it into the oven and pulls it out sharply from under the bread, leaving the bread on the hot baking surface. Professional baker's peels often have very long handles so the baker can reach into the back of a large oven. For a home kitchen, a peel need only have a short handle. The back of a baking sheet, dusted with semolina or cornmeal, can be substituted.

PINE NUTS Pine nuts are the fruit of many types of pine tree, from the piñon of the American Southwest to the stone pine of the Mediterranean. Pine nuts from a nut pine grown in China tend to be larger and blander tasting than pine nuts from the Mediterranean or from the Southwest, which are more expensive because they are labor-intensive both to grow and to harvest. Like other nuts, pine nuts are rich in oils and thus can turn rancid quickly. And, as with other nuts, they are more flavorful if lightly dry-roasted. *See* Nuts for general instructions on dry-roasting and storing.

PISTACHIOS Pistachios are the kernel of the fruit of a tree that is native to western Asia but now grown also in California and Australia. They are generally sold in their shells, which may be pale tan to reddish or dyed a strong pink; the nuts are green unless they've been dyed. The fine shells have often been cracked open at the seam to make removing the nuts easy. Pistachios are related to the trees that produce mastic. *See* Mastic.

POOLISH A poolish is a quickly mixed lightly yeasted batter that is allowed to ferment before being added into a dough. It is a way of giving yeasted doughs more flavor and improving their texture. For more information, see page 111.

POTATOES Potatoes are a tuber native to the Americas, but they are now a staple in many parts of the world, from villages high in the Nepal Himalaya to Ireland to Siberia. There are many varieties of potato, though only a small range finds its way into grocery stores. Generally potatoes are divided, according to their cooked texture, into **waxy** or **floury.** Use floury potatoes, often called **baking potatoes,** when you want to cook and mash them to mix with flour to make a dough (for Country Apple Pie in a Potato Crust, page 32, for example), for they will crumble nicely into a fine texture and blend easily with the flour. If using potatoes as a topping, in slices or cubes (see Potato Pletzel, page 74, for example), choose waxy firmer potatoes (sometimes labeled "for boiling") that will keep their shape when cooked. **Potato starch,** also called **potato flour,** is a fine white powder; it is washed out of potatoes and then dried. Like cornstarch, it is used as a thickener for sauces and fillings. *See also* Sweet Potatoes.

POWDERED GINGER *See* Ginger.

PUMPKIN SEEDS Pumpkin seeds are flat ovals with pointed tips and are a beautiful pale green in color. They make an attractive topping for breads or rolls, and are also used, ground, in Mexican *moles*. Pumpkin seeds are often known by their Spanish name, **pepitas.** Store in the refrigerator or freezer, as you would any nut or seed.

QUINCE Quinces originated in the Caucasus but spread to the eastern Mediterranean and southeastern Europe at least two millennia ago. The quince tree is a relative of both the apple and the pear, and the fruits have a similar core, containing small seeds. Unlike apples and pears, quinces are sour and astringent, and they must be cooked to be palatable. They look like large, lumpy, pale yellow pears the size of a canteloupe, with a well-defined indented bottom. Even uncooked, they are very aromatic. When cooked, the flesh turns pink and sweetens. Quinces can be baked or simmered; in medieval times, they were used widely to make quince paste, which is still very popular in Spain and Portugal. Quinces are available from September until December in specialty fruit markets and in some large grocery stores (see Provençal Quince Loaf, page 128).

RICE Most rice is eaten as a whole grain. It can also be ground into flour. A fine-textured white powder, **rice flour,** also known as **rice starch,** contains no gluten. It is used as a thickener and to soften wheat flour (it's often blended with wheat flour in shortbread recipes, to make them crisper and less tough). Rice flour is also used on its own to make baked sweets (see Rice Flour Muffin-Cakes, page 241, and Persian Cardamom Cookies, page 415). **Glutinous rice flour** is made from rice that has a stickier texture (hence its name) than other rices, because of the balance of starches in the grain: It contains more amylopectin and less amylose than other rices. (Like regular rice flour, it contains no gluten.) Glutinous rice flour makes softer and stickier doughs, very different from those made with regular rice flour; the two are *not* interchangeable. Both are sold in Southeast Asian groceries and in some large grocery stores.

ROSE WATER *See* Scented Waters.

RYE Rye is a grain that originated in western Asia and is now widely grown in Germany and in northern and eastern Europe; some rye is also grown in North America. Rye tolerates cold and can be cultivated in areas where wheat does not flourish. It can be used as a whole grain but is more commonly ground into **rye flour.** It may be used on its own or in combination with wheat flour to make bread. In England, a blend of rye and wheat flours used for bread was traditionally known as **maslin;** the term has largely fallen into disuse.

The lighter the rye flour, the less of the rye bran is included in the flour, but even the lightest rye is pale brown, not white. Doughs made with only or mostly rye flour are sticky, moist, and dense. Rye contains only the gluten-forming protein gliadin, not glutenin. Consequently, a straight rye flour dough is not as strong as a wheat flour dough and thus rye breads tend to have a closer, denser texture than wheat breads. Rye flour absorbs more water than wheat and retains moisture well after baking, so rye loaves keep well. Rye sours quickly due to naturally occurring bacteria in the grain; a rye and water starter will develop flavor very quickly and will become oversour much sooner than a wheat flour starter will.

RYE SOUR A rye sour is a kind of fermented batter that adds flavor to bread doughs. For more information, see page 116.

SAJJ Sometimes spelled saj or saaj, a sajj is a domed metal surface that is placed over a fire. A metal wok can be substituted. It is primarily used for cooking very thin flatbreads, by the Bedouin in the Sinai and nomadic peoples from Turkey to southern Iran (see Lebanese Sajj Bread, page 271).

SALT Although you can use table salt in these recipes, we prefer the clean taste of **kosher salt** (rock salt extracted from the ground, with nothing added; traditionally used for koshering meat) or the more complex taste of **sea salt** (extracted from seawater by evaporation). Ordinary **table salt** has a dusty back taste that we don't like. We keep a wooden box with three kinds of salt on our counter, coarse and fine sea salt and kosher salt. Fine sea salt dissolves more quickly and so is preferable if you are adding it to a sponge or dough.

SCENTED WATERS **Orange flower water** and **rose water** are clear liquids infused with aroma. Used sparingly, they add a wonderful perfumy taste to baked goods. They are available in Middle Eastern grocery stores and in specialty shops. They keep well if well sealed in dark glass bottles, losing potency gradually over time.

SEMOLINA *See* Durum Wheat.

SESAME SEEDS Sesame seeds are sold both hulled and whole. We call only for hulled sesame seeds in this book. Because they are rich in oil, sesame seeds can quickly go rancid, so store them in the refrigerator (well sealed), and taste for freshness before you use them.

SICHUAN PEPPER Also known as **fagara,** Sichuan pepper is a spice, the husk of the seed of a variety of prickly ash. It has been used in regional Chinese cooking for several millennia and is closely related to the Japanese spice **sansho.** It is aromatic with a slightly resinous taste and it leaves a warming-to-hot feel on the tongue and throat. Sichuan pepper is available in Chinese grocery stores, specialty shops, and some grocery stores. As with any spice, it is preferable to buy it whole and grind it to a powder just before using. Store in a well-sealed container.

SPELT Spelt is a variety of wheat, *Triticum speltum,* which can be grown in less fertile soils than other wheats. It has become a specialty wheat widely used in artisanal bread baking in Germany and North America. It is often marketed as an "ancient" or "traditional" grain. **Spelt flour** behaves very like regular wheat flours, and it is usually fairly high in gluten-forming proteins, around 12 percent. Look for finely ground spelt flour. Use it to make crackers, or as a substitute for some of the wheat flour in bread recipes. **Whole wheat spelt flour** behaves like regular whole wheat flour; it is usually 100 percent extraction (see Wheat Flours), but often with very coarse bran. Sift out the coarsest bran before adding to a bread dough.

SPONGE A sponge is an early stage of a dough, in which some of the flour has been stirred into yeasted liquid and then allowed to stand for a while to ferment. For more information, see page 111.

SPRITZING We often call for the breads or rolls to be spritzed, given a quick spray, with water after they go into the oven. We use a small plastic sprayer for this job. Spritzing softens the top of the loaf so it can expand when it first goes into the oven with less chance of cracking or splitting (not a tragedy, but it's better not to) and, more important, helps create a crisper crust. It's a home baker's way of mimicking the steam-injected baking of some professional bakery ovens.

STAND MIXER For years, we made bread entirely by hand, and we still make large doughs by hand. But some years back, a KitchenAid stand mixer arrived in our kitchen, and we've come to rely on it for mixing and kneading many bread doughs, especially really sticky ones. The *dough hook* attachment kneads dough very well. Use it on low speed, so as not to tear the dough. Fitted with other attachments (a paddle or a whisk), the mixer is also a big help for sweet baking tasks such as whisking egg whites and whipping cream. Get the largest stand mixer you can afford and have room for; for the larger the mixer, the bigger the bread dough it can handle. It's helpful to have a spare bowl or two, especially for sweet baking.

SUGARS When we call for sugar in this book, we mean **granulated sugar,** refined from sugarcane or sugar beets. During sugar refining, the dark thick molasses that is a by-product is set aside. **Light** and **dark brown sugars** are made by mixing some of the molasses, or crude sugar, back into refined sugar. The darker the brown sugar, the deeper the taste. Brown sugar hardens easily, so store it in a well-sealed container (we add a prune to keep the sugar from hardening). **Confectioners' sugar,** also known as **powdered sugar** (or **icing sugar** in Canada and Britain), is often used as decoration to dust the top of cakes or cookies. It is also the main ingredient in frosting. It is finely ground sugar with a little cornstarch added to prevent clumping. Before using, it should be sifted to eliminate lumps.

Demerara sugar is a granular dark brown sugar that smells and tastes of molasses and has a distinctive, sometimes overwhelming, flavor. **Maple sugar** is cooked-down maple syrup. It is a rich golden brown and is sold in small blocks in specialty stores and at regional markets in the regions where it is produced: much of New England, as well as Quebec and Ontario. **Palm sugar,** known in India as **jaggery,** is made by boiling the sap of the sugar palm. It is sold in disk-shaped or square blocks, and it may be pale tan or dark brown.

The darker the color, the deeper and more smoky the taste. To use, slice off thin pieces, then finely chop.

Pearl sugar has large round granules that keep their shape when baked. It is used as a decorative topping for baked goods, especially in northern Europe. Pale yellow shiny chunks of **rock sugar** are sold in cardboard boxes in Chinese and other Asian grocery stores. Rock sugar is made from processed sugarcane.

Vanilla sugar is granulated sugar that has been perfumed with vanilla. It's handy to have a supply of vanilla sugar for flavoring cakes and cookies without darkening them with extract. *To make vanilla sugar,* place a vanilla bean in a jar of sugar and seal well. After a week, the sugar will be perfumed with the aroma of vanilla. When you use the sugar, top up the jar; the vanilla bean will stay strong for months. *See also* Vanilla.

SUNFLOWER SEEDS In Robin's Bread (page 150) we call for hulled unsalted sunflower seeds. Sunflower seeds are rich in oil and should be stored, well sealed, in the refrigerator. Taste them before using them to make sure they are still fresh.

SWEET POTATOES Native to the Americas, like potatoes, sweet potatoes are the tubers of an unrelated plant in the morning glory family. They may be white or orange or even red skinned, with white or yellow or orange flesh.

TAHINI This pale beige paste is made of ground sesame seeds and sold in jars or cans in Middle Eastern stores, health food stores, and large grocery stores. It has a texture like that of peanut butter, but is drier on the tongue. The oil tends to separate out; stir back in before using.

TAMARIND Tamarind gives a tart fruity taste to savory dishes. It is widely used in the Caucasus and in Iranian cooking, as well as in India and Southeast Asia. The flavoring comes from the pulp that surrounds the seeds of the tamarind tree, which appear in long pods. In North America, tamarind is sold as **pulp** (in cellophane-wrapped square blocks) or as **paste** (in jars). The pulp produces a better flavor. To use, dilute a measured amount of pulp with an approximately equal amount of boiling water. Let soak for a few minutes, then stir and press to dissolve the pulp off the seeds into the water. Pour through a fine-meshed sieve, and discard the seeds and fibers. Use the resulting dark brown liquid as directed.

TAPIOCA Extracted from the root of the cassava plant, a native of South America, tapioca grows in poor ground in tropical and subtropical areas; it is known as *manioc* in many places. It is a staple food in Brazil, used in savory dishes and in sweet baking. **Tapioca flour,** also called **tapioca starch,** gives elasticity to doughs made of rice flour. **Tapioca pearls** are used to make sweet desserts.

TEMPERATURES *See* Note on Baker's Temperatures, page 117.

TUILES The word *tuile* means "roof tile" in French. In baking, the name refers to thin cookies that have a curve or bend in them, like curved roof tiles (see Thai Tuiles, page 296).

VANILLA Vanilla beans are long, narrow dark brown pods, the dried seed pods of the vanilla vine. They are very aromatic, and the seeds inside are dark brown and oily. Vanilla beans are picked unripe, then dried and processed. The best-quality beans are about 6 inches long, tapered, dark brown, and supple, with a light dusting of white crystals on them; lower-quality beans are lighter brown in color. Vanilla beans can be used and reused whole many times to flavor milk (rinse off and wipe dry between uses) or sugar. Vanilla originated in Mexico, where the Aztecs used it to flavor chocolate. These days good vanilla comes from Mexico, Madagascar, Réunion, Indonesia, and Tahiti. Store the beans in a well-sealed container. Try storing a bean in a jar of sugar to perfume it. **Vanilla extract** is made by soaking vanilla beans in alcohol. It is sold in small bottles, as is artificial vanilla extract. Real vanilla extract is more expensive than artificial vanilla, with a more subtle aromatic vanilla taste. *See also* Sugars: Vanilla sugar.

WALNUTS Walnuts are widely used in European baking, and also in savory dishes in Turkey and the Caucasus. They grow on trees in temperate climates and are members of the same family as pecans, hickory nuts, and black walnuts. The nut is inside a hard, round, pale brown shell, generally about an inch in diameter. The nut is in two symmetrical curving halves, separated by a hard bitter membrane. Walnuts are sold in the shell or shelled, either whole or in pieces (which are less expensive). They are rich in oil and they do not keep well. Always refrigerate after opening and taste before using them to make sure they are still fresh. (*See* Nuts for general dry-roasting and storing instructions.) **Walnut oil** is a clear oil that is available in specialty stores and is widely used in France and northern Italy in salads; it is quite expensive and rather perishable.

WATER We use springwater rather than chlorinated tap water for baking, but that's mostly personal preference. Only when you are trying to develop a natural starter, from naturally occurring yeasts (in Salt-Raised Bread, page 196, for example, or Chickpea Spice Breads, page 198) is it really important that your water be free of any

disinfectant (such as chlorine) that could interfere with the development of the useful bacteria in the starter.

WHEAT FLOURS The most common flour for baking in North America is **wheat flour,** milled from standard wheat, *Triticum aestivum.* Wheat flour is categorized in several ways, according to how it is milled and how it behaves when baked (its protein content). **Whole wheat kernels,** also called **wheat berries,** have a bran coating and contain the germ, or embryo; if the seeds were planted, they would germinate. When the kernels are milled, **whole wheat flour** is produced; it may also be known as "100% extraction flour" (meaning the whole wheat berry is included in the flour). Some flours labeled whole wheat are 100 percent extraction, but most have some of the bran sifted out and are more like 90 percent extraction. Those used in bread doughs are usually about 12 percent protein. Whole wheat flour may be a pale brown in color or nearly white, depending on the variety of wheat used; some "white wheats" have a very pale bran. If some or all of the bran and germ are sifted out, then a lower-extraction flour is produced. **White flour** (all-purpose, pastry, cake, or bread) is usually about 70 percent extraction.

Wheat flour contains the gluten-producing proteins glutenin and gliadin. As a batter or dough is mixed, gluten strands develop; during kneading, they are folded over and over and make a structure that supports the bread and gives it strength. The ideal flour for bread making depends on the type of bread, but it will generally be between 10 and 13 percent protein. If a flour is very soft, it will have relatively little gluten-forming protein and will make a tender soft dough or batter that is better for cake. If a flour is very strong (high in protein), it will make well-risen bread loaves but will produce tough cake or pastry. (In Britain, bread flour is known as **strong flour.**)

All-purpose flour is a blend of wheat flours designed for general baking; it is usually about 12 percent protein (slightly more in Canada; less, down to 10 percent, in parts of the United States). It makes good bread and can also be used for pastry and cakes. It may be bleached or unbleached; we prefer unbleached for its creamy color and better flavor. **Bread flour,** available in large grocery stores and specialty shops, is usually unbleached and has a protein content of 12 to 14 percent. We prefer to use unbleached all-purpose because it makes a less tough crumb.

Like pastry flour, **cake flour** is made from a blend of softer wheats, for a protein content of 8 to 9 percent. Cake flour is bleached with chlorine, which means it produces a very pale crumb. The chlorination also means that the bubbles created by leavening agents (baking soda or baking powder) will be distributed more evenly in a cake batter, because the bubbles are able to move more easily through the flour. Cake flour produces a more tender, even crumb than all-purpose flour. Lower in gluten-forming proteins than all-purpose flour, and thus not as strong, **pastry flour** is usually very finely milled and powdery in texture. It has about 9 percent protein. When blended with all-purpose flour, it can be used as a substitute for French-style bread flours, which are softer. Because it is fine-textured, it may clump, so it should be sifted before using. Try to find unbleached pastry flour. **Whole wheat pastry flour** is a whole wheat flour made of softer wheat, and it is usually more finely ground than regular whole wheat flour; again, sift before using. **Cake-and-pastry flour** is a combination flour that is like an "all-purpose" for cakes and pastries, softer than all-purpose, with a protein content of about 9 percent. It is sold in some grocery stores.

WORCESTERSHIRE SAUCE This bottled flavoring, a thin, nearly black liquid, is a seasoning from Britain, tasting of vinegar and spices. It is available in large supermarkets and keeps well at room temperature.

YEAST We call for **active dry yeast** in the recipes in this book because we find it the most practical kind to use. It has a long shelf life and keeps well in the refrigerator. The alternative is **baker's yeast,** also known as compressed **fresh yeast,** which is sold in fresh moist blocks and has a shorter shelf life. Baker's yeast must be kept refrigerated. To convert dry yeast amounts to baker's yeast, double the amounts (if the recipe calls for 2 teaspoons active dry yeast, use 4 teaspoons compressed yeast).

Yeast is an organism that is dormant in cold temperatures, and dry yeast is stable until it is moistened. With moisture and warmth, the yeast starts metabolic activity, feeding on starches and sugars (in flour or sugar, for example). As it feeds, it multiplies and gives off carbon dioxide and water. Temperatures above 115°F kill yeast, so well before a bread has finished baking, the yeast in the bread is no longer active.

YOGURT *See* Milk.

ZEST The zest is the fine colored part of the peel of a citrus fruit. It has flavor and scent and essential oils. *To zest a lemon, lime, or orange,* rub the fruit with a fine grater or a citrus zester, or use a potato peeler to carefully scrape long fine pieces from the top surface of the peel, keeping clear of the bitter white pith below. If possible, use organic citrus for zest.

conversions and pan sizes

measurement conversions (rounded off for easy remembering)

WEIGHTS (ALSO KNOWN AS DRY MEASURES)

1 ounce = scant 30 grams

¼ pound = 4 ounces = 115 grams

½ pound = 8 ounces = 225 grams

1 pound = 16 ounces = 450 grams

2 pounds = 32 ounces = 900 grams

100 grams = scant ¼ pound = 3½ ounces

500 grams = 1.1 pounds = nearly 18 ounces

1 kilogram = 2.2 pounds = about 35 ounces

VOLUMES

1 teaspoon = about 5 ml (if liquid, weighs about 5 grams)

1 tablespoon = 3 teaspoons = ½ fluid ounce measure = 15 ml
(if liquid, weighs 15 grams)

¼ cup = 4 tablespoons = 2 fluid ounces = about 60 milliliters

½ cup = 8 tablespoons = 4 ounces = just under 125 milliliters

1 cup = 16 tablespoons = 8 ounces = about 250 milliliters

2 cups = 16 ounces = 1 pint (American)

2½ cups = 20 ounces = nearly 1 Imperial pint

100 milliliters = 10 deciliters = ½ cup

125 milliliters = just over ½ cup

250 milliliters = 1⅛ cups

500 milliliters = 2¼ cups = just over 1 pint (American)

1 liter = 4.5 cups = just over 1 quart (American)

WEIGHT TO VOLUME/VOLUME TO WEIGHT

½ pound (8 ounces/225 grams) butter = 1 cup =
16 tablespoons (2 sticks) = 250 milliliters

1 pound (16 ounces/450 grams) butter = 2 cups =
450 milliliters

½ pound (8 ounces/225 grams) sugar = nearly 1¼ cups =
250 milliliters

1 pound (16 ounces/450 grams) unsifted all-purpose flour =
about 3½ cups = 450 milliliters

1 cup (16 tablespoons) unsifted all-purpose flour =
4½ to 5 ounces = 125 to 140 grams

LENGTHS

1 inch = 2.5 centimeters

10 inches = 25 centimeters

12 inches = 30 centimeters

1 yard = 90 centimeters

1 centimeter = 0.4 inches

5 centimeters = 2 inches

10 centimeters = 4 inches

50 centimeters = 20 inches

pan sizes

We had a very interesting time describing pan sizes for this book. We work with a small selection of ordinary loaf pans, cake pans, muffin tins, and pie plates that we've accumulated over the years. When we measured them so we could give pan sizes in inches in the recipes, we discovered that pans are measured in different, inconsistent ways and that they are manufactured in slightly varying "standard sizes." As a result, all the inch measures set out below should be read as approximate. Small variations in pan size are unimportant in the world of home baking, so don't worry if your pans aren't exactly the size described.

This is a list of all the pans called for in the book. It should be a useful shopping list for those who did not inherit old pans from an aunt or a grandmother and need to go looking for them. You can buy standard pans and tins at most cookware stores and some department and hardware stores. Or you can go hunting for what you need at flea markets and tag sales (garage sales). Sometimes they can yield baking equipment treasures. (If you're buying used pans, you may need to scrub off a little rust or dirt with steel wool, then wash the pan in very hot soapy water and dry thoroughly.)

Generally, pans are measured across the top.

BREAD PANS (LOAF PANS)

All are about 2¾ inches deep, with slightly sloping sides; top measures given below:

standard: just over 9 by 5 inches

medium: about 8 by 4 inches

long: 13 by 4 or 4½ inches

PIE PLATES, TART PANS

We use just one size of pie plate, an 8-inch plate; it measures about 8 inches straight across the top, 7 inches across the bottom, and has sloping sides. We also use a 9-inch fluted tart pan with a removable bottom.

CAKE PANS

All are about 1½ or 2 inches deep:

standard rectangular pan: 13 by 9 inches

round cake pan: 9 inches across

square cake pan: 8 inches on a side

round cake pan: 8 inches across

10-INCH TUBE PAN

All are about 4 inches deep; top, outside rim to rim, 10 inches; bottom, 8 inches across.

MUFFIN TINS

The cups of "regular" muffin tins are just over 2½ inches across the top, 2 inches across the bottom, and 1¼ inches deep.

EQUIVALENTS

An 8-inch round pan has about the same volume as a 7-inch square pan.

A long bread pan (about 13 by 4 inches) has almost the same volume as two 8-by-4-inch loaf pans.

bibliography

Alford, Jeffrey, and Naomi Duguid. *Flatbreads and Flavors: A Baker's Atlas.* New York: Morrow, 1995.

Babbar, Purobi. *Rotis & Naans of India.* Bombay: Vakils, Feffer, and Simons, 1987.

Baggett, Nancy. *The International Cookie Cookbook.* New York: Stewart, Tabori & Chang, 1988.

Baker, Jenny. *Kettle Broth to Gooseberry Fool: A Celebration of Simple English Cooking.* London: Faber & Faber, 1996.

Barboff, Mouette. *Terra mae a terra pao.* Camara Municipal do Seixal/Ecomuseu, 1997.

Batmanglij, Najmieh. *Food of Life.* Washington, DC: Mage, 1990.

Beard, James. *Beard on Bread.* New York: Knopf, 1973.

Beltran, Lourdes. *La cocina Jarocha.* Mexico D.F.: Pax Mexico, 1991.

Benghiat, Norma. *Traditional Jamaican Cookery.* London: Penguin, 1985.

Benkirane, Fettouma. *Secrets of Moroccan Cookery.* Paris: Taillandier-Sochepress, 1985.

Benoit, Jehane. *The Encyclopedia of Canadian Cooking.* Winnipeg: Greywood, 1970.

———. *Madame Benoit Cooks at Home.* Toronto: McGraw-Hill, 1978.

Beranbaum, Rose Levy. *Rose's Christmas Cookies.* New York: Morrow, 1990.

Berger, Pamela. *The Goddess Obscured: Transformation of the Grain Protectress from Goddess to Saint.* London: Robert Hale, 1988.

Boehringer Ingelheim Backmittel GmbH. "Tracking Down the Right Flour." Bingen am Rhein, n.d.

Borghese, Anita. *The International Cookie Jar.* New York: Scribner's, 1975.

Boutet, Gérard. *Nos grands-mères aux Fourneaux.* Paris: Seld/France Loisirs, 1993.

Bremzen, Anya von, and John Welchman. *Please to the Table.* New York: Workman, 1990.

Brobeck, Florence, and Monika Kjellberg, *Smorgasbord and Scandinavian Cookery.* New York: Grosset and Dunlap, 1948.

Brown, Helen. *Helen Brown's West Coast Cook Book.* Rev. ed. New York: Knopf, 1991.

Bryn Mawr Alumnae. *The Bryn Mawr Cookbook.* Crockett, TX: Publications Development, 1985.

Campbell, Georgina. *The Best of Irish Breads and Baking.* Dublin: Wolfhound, 1996.

Child, Julia, Louisette Bertholle, and Simone Beck. *Mastering the Art of French Cooking.* Vol 1. New York: Knopf, 1967.

Clement, Jean-Louis. *Les pains et viennoiseries de l'Ecole Lenôtre.* Paris: Jerome Villette, 1995.

Cookbook Committee St. Gregory Catholic Church, Sitka, Alaska. *Favorite Recipes.* Collierville, AK: Fundcraft, n.d.

Corey, Helen. *The Art of Syrian Cookery.* New York: Hippocrene, 1962, 1992.

Cost, Bruce. *Foods from the Far East.* London: Century, 1990.

Cowan, Cathal, and Regina Sexton. *Ireland's Traditional Foods.* Dublin: Teagasc, 1997.

Dabdoub-Nasser, Christiane. *Classic Palestinian Cookery.* London: Saqi, 2001.

David, Elizabeth. *English Bread and Yeast Cookery.* London: Penguin, 1977, 1987.

Davidson, Alan. *The Penguin Companion to Food.* London: Penguin, 2002.

De Gale, Laurice. *Down to Earth Jamaican Cooking.* Toronto: Sister Vision, 1996.

de Pomiane, Edouard. *Cooking with Pomiane.* New York: Modern Library, 2001 (1976).

Elges, Annette. *Dr. Oetker Brot backen.* Stuttgart: Unipart, 1987, 1996.

Farelli, Maria Helena, and Nilza Paes Da Silva. *Comida de Santo (tambem cozinha baiana).* Rio de Janeiro: Pallas, 1980, 1997.

Field, Carol. *The Italian Baker.* New York: Harper & Row, 1985.

Fitzgibbon, Theodora. *A Taste of Ireland.* London: Pan, 1970.

———. *A Taste of Scotland.* London: Pan, 1971.

Flandrin, Jean-Louis. *Chronique de Platine: Pour une gastronomie historique*. Paris: Odile Jacob, 1992.

Fussell, Betty. *The Story of Corn*. New York: Knopf, 1992.

Gajdostikova, Hana; Jana Jennings, trans. *Czech National Cookbook*. Prague: Kanzelsberger, 1998.

Ghanoonparvar, M. R. *Persian Cuisine Book One: Traditional Foods*. Costa Mesa, CA: Mazda, 1982.

———. *Persian Cuisine Book Two: Regional and Modern Foods*. Costa Mesa, CA: Mazda, 1984.

Gollan, Anne. *The Tradition of Australian Cooking*. Canberra: Australian National University Press, 1978.

Good, Phyllis Pellman, and Rachel Thomas Pellman. *Breads from Amish and Mennonite Kitchens*. Lancaster, PA: Good Books, 1983.

Graham, Peter. *Mourjou: The Life and Food of an Auvergne Village*. London: Penguin, 1999.

Grant, Rosamund. *Caribbean & African Cookery*. London: Virago, 1989.

Gray, Patience. *Honey from a Weed*. London: Prospect, 1986.

Greenspan, Dorie. *Baking with Julia*. New York: Morrow, 1996.

Grigson, Jane. *Jane Grigson's Fruit Book*. New York: Atheneum, 1982.

Guinaudeau, Z. *Fez: Traditional Moroccan Cooking*. Rabat and Paris: n.p., 1976.

Hamady, Mary Laird. *Lebanese Mountain Cookery*. Boston: Godine, 1987.

Harmon Jenkins, Nancy. *Flavors of Puglia*. New York: Broadway, 1996.

———. *Flavors of Tuscany*. New York: Broadway, 1998.

Harney, Bill. *Bill Harney's Cook Book*. Melbourne: Lansdowne, 1960.

Hartley, Dorothy. *Food in England*. London: Macdonald and Jane's, 1954, 1975.

Heatter, Maida. *Maida Heatter's Cookies*. New York: Cader, 1997.

———. *Pies & Tarts*. New York: Cader, 1997.

Hekmat, Forough. *The Art of Persian Cooking*. New York: Hippocrene, 1961, 1994.

Helias, Pierre Jakez. *Le cheval d'Orgueil*. Paris: Plon, 1975, 1999.

Hess, O., and A. Hess; Carla Schlesinger, trans. *Viennese Cooking*. New York: Crown, 1952.

Iny, Daisy. *The Best of Baghdad Cooking, with Treats from Teheran*. New York: Saturday Review Press, 1976.

Johnston, Mireille. *Cuisine of the Rose*. New York: Random House, 1982.

Jones, Bridget, ed. *Mrs. Beeton's Complete Book of Cakes and Biscuits*. London: Ward Lock, 1989.

Jones, Judith, and Evan Jones. *The Book of Bread*. New York: Harper & Row, 1986.

Kapoor, Sibyl. *Simply British*. London: Penguin, 1999.

Karslake, Pamela, ed. *Friends' Favourite Foods*. N.p.: Surrey Association of Youth Clubs, n.d.

Kennedy, Diana. *The Essential Cuisines of Mexico*. New York: Clarkson Potter, 2000.

King, Caroline B. *Victorian Cakes*. Berkeley: Aris, 1941, 1969.

Kouki, Mohamed. *Cuisine et pâtisserie tunisiennes*. Tunis: n.p., 1991.

Krasheninnikova, A. *Russian Cooking*. Moscow: Mir, 1978.

Krauss, Irene. *Chronik bildschoner Backwerke*. Stuttgart: Matthaes Verlag, 1999.

Kuster, H., U. Nefzger et. al. *Korn: Kulturgeschichte des Getreides*. Salzburg: Pustet, 1999.

Leader, Daniel, and Judith Blahnik. *Bread Alone*. New York: Morrow, 1993.

Leonard, Thom. *The Bread Book*. Brookline, MA: East-West, 1991.

Luard, Elisabeth. *The Old World Kitchen*. New York: Bantam, 1987.

McGee, Harold. *On Food and Cooking: The Science and Lore of the Kitchen*. New York: Collier, 1984.

———. *The Curious Cook*. San Francisco: North Point Press, 1990.

Majpuria, Indra, and Diki Lobsang. *Tibetan Cooking*. Rev. ed. Lalipur Colony: S. Devi, 1994.

Malgieri, Nick. *How to Bake*. New York: HarperCollins, 1995.

Mathiot, Ginette, and Lionel Poilane. *Pain: cuisine et gourmandises.* Paris: Albin Michel, 1985.

Medrich, Alice. *Cookies and Brownies.* New York: Warner, 1999.

Mehta, Jeroo. *Enjoyable Parsi Cooking.* Bombay: Vakils, 1992.

Meyer, Romelia C. A. *Arte caseira de Fazer Paes.* São Paulo: Global, 1985.

Michelson, Patricia. *The Cheese Room.* London: Michael Joseph, 2001.

Middione, Carlo. *The Food of Southern Italy.* New York: Morrow, 1987.

Mintz, Sidney. *Sweetness and Power.* New York: Viking, 1985.

Morand, Simone. *Crêpes et galettes en Bretagne.* Châteaulin: Jos Le Doare, 1998.

Norman, Jill. *The Complete Book of Spices.* London: Dorling Kindersley, 1990.

Ojakangas, Beatrice. *The Great Scandinavian Baking Book.* Boston: Little, Brown, 1988.

Oetker, A. *German Baking Today.* Bielefeld: Ceres-Verlag, 1987.

Oliver, Raymond; Nika Standen Hazelton, trans., with Jack Van Bibber. *La Cuisine: Secrets of Modern French Cooking.* New York: Tudor, 1969.

O'Sullivan, Donal J. *The Story of Corn and Flour Milling in Ireland* (booklet). Co. Kerry: n.p. 1995.

Pasley, Virginia. *The Christmas Cookie Book.* Boston: Little, Brown, 1950.

Peck, Paula. *The Art of Fine Baking.* New York: Simon & Schuster, 1961.

Powers, JoMarie. "Ukrainian-Canadian Breads: Shape, Symbolism and Spirituality," in *Look and Feel: Studies in Texture, Appearance and Incidental Characteristics of Food* (Proceedings of the Oxford Symposium on Food and Cookery, 1993). Harlan Walker, ed. London: Prospect, 1994.

Price, Sandy. *Exploring the Flea Markets of France.* New York: Crown, 1999.

Psilakis, Maria, and N. Psilakis. *Cretan Cooking.* Heraklion: Karmanor, n.d.

Radojkovic, Jon. *Barns of the Queen's Bush.* Port Elgin, Ontario: Brucedale, 2001.

Rambali, Paul, and Maria Rudman. *Boulangerie.* New York: Macmillan, 1994.

Reejhsinghani, Aroona. *Vegetarian Wonders from Gujarat.* Bombay: Jaico, 1972.

Robertson, Laurel, with Carol Flinders and Bronwen Godfrey. *The Laurel's Kitchen Bread Book.* New York: Random House, 1984.

Roden, Claudia. *The Book of Jewish Food.* New York: Knopf, 1996.

——. Foreword in Maxime Rodinson, A. F. Arberry, and Charles Perry. *Medieval Arab Cookery.* London: Prospect, 2001.

Rogers, Rick. *Kaffeehaus: Exquisite Desserts from the Classic Cafés of Vienna, Budapest, and Prague.* New York: Clarkson Potter, 2002.

Salikhov, Sh. G. *Blyuda: uzbekskoi kuchny* [Uzbek Cookery]. Tashkent, Uzbekistan: n.p., 1991.

Sanchez, Irene Barraza, and Gloria Sanchez Yund. *Comida Sabrosa: Home-Style Southwestern Cooking.* Albuquerque: University of New Mexico Press, 1982.

Santos, Aldaci (Dada) dos. *Tempero da Dada.* Salvador, El Salvador: Corrupio, 1998.

Sax, Richard. *Classic Home Desserts.* Shelburne, VT: Chapters, 1995.

Schunemann, Claus, and Gunter Treu. *Baking: The Art and Science.* Calgary: Baker Tech, 1988.

Shaida, Margaret. *The Legendary Cuisine of Persia.* London: Penguin, 1992, 1994.

Simon, André L. *A Concise Encyclopedia of Gastronomy.* New York: Overlook, 1952, 1981.

Snacks of Thailand. Bangkok: The Color Books, n.d.

Son, Ly Van. *Vietnamese Cookery Book.* Bien Hoa: Dongnai, 1995.

Spivey, Diane M. *The Peppers, Cracklings, and Kinds of Wool Cookbook.* New York: SUNY Press, 2000.

Staebler, Edna. *Cookies and Squares with Schmecks Appeal.* Toronto: McGraw-Hill Ryerson, 1990.

——. *Muffins and Quick Breads with Schmecks Appeal.* Toronto: McGraw-Hill Ryerson, 1990.

Stavroulakis, Nicholas. *The Cookbook of the Jews of Greece*. Northvale, NJ: Aronson, 1986, 1996.

Tannahill, Reay. *Food in History*. 2d ed. New York: Crown, 1988.

Tavares, Maria Helena. *Cozinha regional da Beira Alta*. Lisbon: Europa-America, 1996.

——. *Cozinha regional do Minho*. Lisbon: Europa-America, 1995.

Taylor, John Martin. *Hoppin' John's Lowcountry Cooking*. New York: Bantam, 1992.

Toomre, Joyce, trans. and ed. *Classic Russian Cooking: Edna Molokhovets' A Gift to Young Housewives*. Bloomington: Indiana University Press, 1992, 1998.

Tropp, Barbara. *The Modern Art of Chinese Cooking*. New York: Morrow, 1982.

Tujibi, Ibn Razin. *Les delices de la table et les meilleurs genres des mets*. Translated from the Arabic by M. Mezzine and L. Benkirane. Fez: Association Fes-Sais, 1997. (Original between 1238 and 1266).

Ukrainian Women's Association of Canada, Daughters of Ukraine Branch. *Ukrainian Daughters' Cookbook*. Regina, Saskatchewan: Centax, 1984.

Uvezian, Sonia. *The Cuisine of Armenia*. New York: Hippocrene, 1974, 1996.

Visser, Margaret. *Much Depends on Dinner*. Toronto: McLelland and Stewart, 1987.

Visson, Lynn. *The Art of Uzbek Cooking*. New York: Hippocrene, 1999.

Weinrich, Moira. *The Tea Lover's Handbook*. Vancouver: Intermedia, 1980.

Wolfert, Paula. *Mediterranean Grains and Greens*. New York: Harper-Collins, 1998.

Women of Saint Paul's Greek Orthodox Church. *The Art of Greek Cookery*. New York: Doubleday, 1963.

Women's Service League of St. Paul's Church. *Out of Vermont Kitchens*. Rev. ed. Burlington, VT: George Little, 1951.

Zubaida, Sami, and Richard Tapper, eds. and comps. *A Taste of Thyme: Culinary Cultures of the Middle East*. London: Tauris Parker, 2001.

acknowledgments

Our thanks go out in a great many directions, to our family and friends, and to people we've encountered along the way over the years, for contributions both obvious and subtle that have merged into what is our understanding of home baking.

First, love and thanks to Dominic and Tashi for their company on our travels and their good-humored acceptance of endless recipe testing. You help us remember what is most important in life.

In Sweden, thanks to Tina and Henryk, and Tina's grandparents Anna and Sune Hogberg, for introducing us to the world of Gotland and showing us how to make *slagbrot*. In Crete, warm thanks to George Stephanopoulos and his daughter Ana for good-humored tolerance of a stranger with a camera in the bakery during the busiest weeks of the year. In Portugal, thanks to Teresa, the baker in Soajo, for giving generous access to the back of the bakery and for introducing us to Galician baking traditions; and to Margarida and the other women of the village oven in Sabugueiro who were patient and welcoming to a curious stranger. In Hungary, thanks to Peter in Abda, to George near Pésc, and to the staff at the bakery in Köszeg. Thanks to the baker and his wife in eastern Austria. Thanks also to Yvette in Normandy, to Senora Abbondanza and the head baker in Specchia Minervina in Puglia, and to Carol Field and Nancy Harmon Jenkins for help in talking with them.

In Brazil, thanks to Nelson Gomes and to Zete in Cachoeira; to Guaraci and Pina in Valença; to Ilma of San Antonio in Salvador for an afternoon of shopping and cooking; and to Barbara Cervenka and Mame Jackson, and their friend Neto, for generously sharing insights and information.

In Australia, thanks to John Downes, of McLaren Vale, South Australia, for a memorable day of baking and conversation; to Cherry Ripe for generous hospitality in Sydney and helpful introductions; to John Newton for introductions; to Gay Bilson, Maggie Beer; and Ronnie.

In the United States, thanks to Ed and Kathleen Weber and their son Aaron Weber of Della Fattoria in Petaluma, California; to Chad the baker in Point Reyes; and to Jonathan Stevens in Massachusetts for being welcoming and patient with us as we photographed them and their breads. Thanks to Holly Briwa for help finding California bakeries; to Robert Jorin and Dietmar Eilbacher for conversations about rye breads and artisanal baking; to Rohit Singh, chef-owner of Breads of India in Berkeley, California, for fun with the tandoor; and to Dachman the baker for conversations about berber breads in Algeria. Thanks to Terry and Michael McNally of London Grill in Philadelphia. We also thank Charles Perry for conversations about food traditions in the Arab world and central Asia.

Closer to home, we thank Jon Radojkovic, Lillian Burgess, and Philly Marcowitz for helping us to open our eyes to Grey County, Ontario; Ethan Poskanzer; Trisha Jackson; Cassandra Kobayashi; Mary Kainer; Kathy Wazana; Allyson Taché; Hillary Buttrick; Lianne Mack Dwyer; Paul Holroyd for the grain mill; Martha Fieltsch for passing on her mother's elegant cookie recipe; and Maureen Davidson for conversation at Keady market about the merits of lard versus shortening in pie crust.

While a big part of our research involved travel and talking to people, another important part involved reading old cookbooks (traveling, as we imagined it, through time). Books we found especially enlightening include Dorothy Hartley's *Food in England; Ukrainian Daughters' Cookbook;* André Simon's *A Concise Cyclopedia of Gastronomy;* Carol Field's *The Italian Baker;* Elizabeth David's *English Bread and Yeast Cookery;* Elisabeth Luard's *The Old World Kitchen;* and Gérard Boutet's *Nos Grands-mères aux Fourneaux.* If you want to look at these or any of the other books we refer to (all listed in the Bibliography), many can be found easily, while others might be difficult. If you are hunting for a hard-to-find cookbook and having no success, we recommend that you contact Kitchen Arts and Letters in New York City.

Two names appear frequently in the book, Dina and Dawn, our friends Dina Fayerman and Dawn Woodward (also known as Dawnthebaker), who both played big roles in making the book what it is. Huge thanks to Dina for generous suggestions and research, for tasting and discussing everything, and also for family recipes: Simplest Apple Pie, Mandel-Melbas, Polish-Jewish Cheesecake. Many thanks to Dawn for lots of good-humored time in the kitchen with us, recipe testing and problem solving, and also for her Lime Zest Macaroons, Mamoul (Traveler's Date Cookies), Lobiano (Hearty White Bean Pie), and Chewy Pecan Bar Cookies, as well as her grandmother's Cathead Biscuits.

We feel very lucky that Richard Jung is the studio photographer on this book, as he was on *Hot Sour Salty Sweet*. He's given each photograph life and strength, this time with the help of stylists Suzy Theodorou and Bette Blau and of Dawn Woodward. Thank you, all. And we are delighted to again have a book in the sure hands of the gifted design team at Level, Cliff Morgan and David Hughes. They care so much, and are wonderfully attentive to content as well as to design.

We appreciate enormously the thoughtful support of Ann Collins and Sharon Klein at Random House Canada, and of Sarah Davies.

Thanks as always to Liv Blumer, our agent, for insights and encouragement, and for always being so present.

Here we are at the end of another project, the fourth cookbook we have worked on with our fabulous editor, Ann Bramson. Ever since our first book, *Flatbreads and Flavors,* she has imagined us making a book about baking, and here it is, finally. It's been a big project, and humbling. We deeply appreciate Ann's patience and guidance, and her good judgment, as well as her commitment to great design. Two other people have also worked on all our books: Debbie Weiss Geline, editor and painstaking reader, and Judith Sutton, copyeditor. We're very grateful for all their care and attentiveness. Thanks also the the rest of Artisan's talented team: Nancy Murray, Vivian Ghazarian, Amy Corley, Pamela Cannon, Joy Gotthardt, Judit Bodnar, and Barbara Peragine.

index